The Social (Re)Production of Architecture

The Social (Re)Production of Architecture brings the debates of the 'right to the city' into today's context of ecological, economic and social crises. Building on the 1970s' discussions about the 'production of space', which French sociologist Henri Lefebvre considered a civic right, the authors question who has the right to make space, and explore the kinds of relations that are produced in the process. In the emerging post-capitalist era, this book addresses urgent social and ecological imperatives for change and opens up questions around architecture's engagement with new forms of organization and practice. The book asks what (new) kinds of 'social' can architecture (re)produce, and what kinds of politics, values and actions are needed.

The book features 24 interdisciplinary essays written by leading theorists and practitioners including social thinkers, economic theorists, architects, educators, urban curators, feminists, artists and activists from different generations and global contexts. The essays discuss the diverse, global locations with work taking different and specific forms in these different contexts.

A cutting-edge, critical text which rethinks both practice and theory in the light of recent crises, making it key reading for students, academics and practitioners.

Doina Petrescu is Professor of Architecture and Design Activism at the University of Sheffield, UK.

Kim Trogal is lecturer at the Canterbury School of Architecture, University for the Creative Arts, UK.

GW00759777

THE SOCIAL (Re)PRODUCTION OF ARCHITECTURE

POLITICS, VALUES AND ACTIONS IN CONTEMPORARY PRACTICE

Edited by
Doina Petrescu and Kim Trogal

Routledge
Taylor & Francis Group

LONDON AND NEW YORK

First published 2017
by Routledge
2 Park Square, Milton Park, Abingdon, Oxon
OX14 4RN

and by Routledge
711 Third Avenue, New York, NY 10017

*Routledge is an imprint of the Taylor &
Francis Group, an informa business*

© 2017 selection and editorial matter, Doina
Petrescu and Kim Trogal; individual chapters,
the contributors

The right of Doina Petrescu and Kim Trogal
to be identified as the authors of the editorial
material, and of the authors for their individual
chapters, has been asserted in accordance
with sections 77 and 78 of the Copyright,
Designs and Patents Act 1988.

All rights reserved. No part of this book may
be reprinted or reproduced or utilized in any
form or by any electronic, mechanical, or other
means, now known or hereafter invented,
including photocopying and recording, or in any
information storage or retrieval system, without
permission in writing from the publishers.

Trademark notice: Product or corporate
names may be trademarks or registered
trademarks, and are used only for
identification and explanation without
intent to infringe.

Publisher's Note
This book has been prepared from camera-
ready copy provided by the editors.

British Library Cataloguing-in-Publication Data
A catalogue record for this book is available
from the British Library

*Library of Congress Cataloging-in-
Publication Data*
Names: Petrescu, Doina, editor. |
Trogal, Kim, editor.
Title: The social (re)production of architecture :
politics, values and actions in contemporary
practice / [edited by] Doina Petrescu and
Kim Trogal.
Description: New York : Routledge, 2017. |
Includes bibliographical references and index.
Identifiers: LCCN 2016004290 |
ISBN 9781138859487 (hb : alk. paper)
ISBN 9781138859494 (pb : alk. paper)
ISBN 9781315717180 (ebook)
Subjects: LCSH: Architecture and society. |
Architecture—Political aspects. | Lefebvre,
Henri, 1901-1991.
Classification: LCC NA2543.S6 S615 2016 |
DDC 720.1/03—dc23
LC record available at
http://lccn.loc.gov/2016004290

ISBN: 978-1-138-85948-7 (hbk)
ISBN: 978-1-138-85949-4 (pbk)
ISBN: 978-1-315-71718-0 (ebk)

Book design by Brave New Alps.
Typeset in Grotesque MT (cover)
and Akzidenz Grotesk (inner pages).

Printed and bound by CPI Group (UK) Ltd, Croydon, CR0 4YY

CONTENTS

FIGURES   VIII

TABLES   XI

NOTES ON CONTRIBUTORS   XII

1. **The social (re)production of architecture in 'crisis-riddled' times**   1
Doina Petrescu and Kim Trogal

PART I – POLITICS

2. **Notes on social production. A brief commentary**   21
Tatjana Schneider

3. **Making places, building communities, empowering citizens: participatory slum upgrading in Thailand**   29
Supreeya Wungpatcharapon

4. **Out in prison: taking the case of spatial rights to a prison court(yard)**   45
Gabu Heindl

5. **Tea or coffee? Politics and bingo on the pavements**   59
Peter Mutschler and Ruth Morrow

6. **Decolonizing architectural education: towards an affective pedagogy**   77
Pelin Tan

7. **Neighbourhood claims for the future: feminist solidarity urbanism in Vancouver's Downtown Eastside**   93
Elke Krasny

8. Is "tactical urbanism" an alternative to 113
neoliberal urbanism? Reflections on an
exhibition at the MoMA
Neil Brenner

9. Software and spatial practice: the social 129
(co)production of software or software for
social (co)production?
Phil Langley

PART II — VALUES

10. Diverse economies, space and architecture: an 147
interview with Katherine Gibson
Katherine Gibson, with Doina Petrescu and
Kim Trogal

11. Caring: making commons, making connections 159
Kim Trogal

12. Trade as architecture: public realming through 175
tangible economies
Kathrin Böhm

13. Metropolitan commons: spatial commoning in 191
Berlin's Großer Tiergarten and Tempelhofer Feld
Sandra Bartoli and Mathias Heyden

14. Social property and the need for a new urban 211
practice
Gabriela Rendón and Miguel Robles-Durán

15. Affordable housing in your lifetime? 225
Ana Džokić, Marc Neelen and Ana Vilenica

16. Popular Brazilian architecture in the making — 239
or the power of productive consumption
Rainer Hehl

PART III − ACTIONS

17. **Tent cities, people's kitchens, free universities:**   257
    the global villages of occupation movements
    Peter Mörtenböck and Helge Mooshammer

18. **Tactical practices of creative dissent**   271
    Ana Betancour

19. **In action: searching for the in-between city**   285
    Alex Axinte and Cristi Borcan (studioBASAR)

20. **Ways to be public**   299
    Rory Hyde

21. **Cultivating spatial possibilities in Palestine:**   311
    searching for sub/urban bridges in Beit Iksa,
    Jerusalem
    Nasser Golzari and Yara Sharif

22. **Old news from a contact zone:**   329
    Action Archive in Tensta
    Meike Schalk

23. **The Hustadt story − so far**   347
    Apolonija Šušteršič

24. **A bakery as a site of resistance**   361
    Jeanne van Heeswijk

INDEX   377

FIGURES

3.1   Participatory mapping and modelling of houses used as a tool for dialogue among groups of households and the architect
3.2   The Bang-Bua community network, comprised of 12 communities informally built along the Bang-Bua canal
3.3   Extensive development of the networks of the Bang-Bua through the participatory process
3.4   The CAN exhibition in ASA'2014 Expo, Bangkok, showing projects from the network and the students' workshop for the participatory design of a community centre and a playground
4.1   The prison yard, before the *Out in Prison* project
4.2   Dimensioned plan of Krem's prison courtyard
4.3   Twisting the sports field into the narrow prison yard
4.4   Prison yard with folded up sports field, indicating the lack of space
4.5   Outside in the prison yard (anonymity of users protected)
4.6   Fold in the lawn, usable as a bench
5.1   Protest camp, Twaddell Avenue, North Belfast, 2013
5.2   Village fair, Ballykinler village green, 2011
5.3   Rhyzom workshop, Ballykinler, village green, 2010
5.4   UP-Down project: bicycle-limousine workshop, Ballykinler, 2011
6.1   *Campus in Camps*, Edward Said Library, March 2015
6.2   Square, Al Fawar Camp, Director of Women Center, Ayat Al Thursan
6.3   Gezi Park Library, Drawing of Ad Hoc Design Structure.
6.4   Gezi Park Speaker's Point, Drawing of Ad Hoc Design Structure.
7.1   *Mapping the Everyday: Neighbourhood Claims for the Future* installation view, Audain Gallery, Vancouver, 2011–2012
7.2   *Mapping the Everyday: Neighbourhood Claims for the Future* installation view, Audain Gallery, Vancouver, 2011–2012
7.3   *Mapping the Everyday: Neighbourhood Claims for the Future* installation view, Audain Gallery, Vancouver, 2011–2012
7.4   *Mapping the Everyday: Neighbourhood Claims for the Future* sketch showing the alliances and collaborations
7.5   Collective Futures in the Downtown Eastside: forum and discussion
8.1   MoMA *Uneven Growth* exhibition
8.2   KiTO neighborhood strategy, by *aaa*

8.3   KiTO posters for actions, by *aaa*
9.1   Photos by workshop participants
9.2   Design 'hacks' by workshop participants
9.3   Maps created by @simulationBot and Phil Langley
11.1   'If you can read this thank a teacher' poster displayed in the window of a canal boat.
11.2   Dolores Hayden's Book, *The Grand Domestic Revolution*.
11.3   *Eco Nomadic School* visit to the Odaie, in the mountains outside of Brezoi, Romania
12.1   2016 Company Drinks Range (group photo)
12.2   Rural Women's Economies Workshop (group photo), Eco Nomadic School, Frensdorf, 2013
12.3   Village Produce (group photo), International Village Shop, TENT, Rotterdam, 2011
13.1   Tiergarten, *Fanmeile* during World Championship
13.2   Tiergarten, picnic in the forest
13.3   Tempelhofer Feld, landing strip
13.4   Tempelhofer Feld, community garden project 'Allmende-Kontor'
14.1   Cooperative Housing Trust: a hybrid tenure framework for New York City
14.2   Rethinking housing as a site of production
15.1   Working table, drafting statute of a 'smarter' housing cooperative
15.2   Establishing the price point for affordable housing
15.3   Expedition to possible construction sites, city centre
15.4   'Land for sale', expedition to possible construction sites, periphery
16.1   Informal commerce added to the generic model of Brazilian mass housing. Parauapebas, Brazil, 2010
16.2   The table-stands (cavaletes) used by street vendors in Rio can be dismantled spontaneously as soon as the police arrives. Rio de Janeiro, 2012
16.3   Low-income settlement established by the Brazilian social housing program, Minha Casa, Minha Vida, Parauapebas, Brazil, 2010
16.4   Guard securing the exhibition 'A.P.B.' at Studio-X during the protest. Rio de Janeiro, 2013
17.1   Occupy Central, Hong Kong, 2011
17.2   Occupy Finsbury Square, London, 2012
17.3   Occupy Finsbury Square, London, 2012
17.4   Occupy Frankfurt, 2012

18.1 Genova Libera/Free Genoa, demonstration against the G8 meeting in Genoa, Italy, July 2001

18.2 Sentada, V de vivienda/sit-in, in the campaign V de Vivienda, Barcelona, 2006

18.3 Retratos fotográficos contra los desahucios de Calatunya Caixa/Portraits against the evictions by Caixa Catalunya, by *TAF!*

19.1 The Palace of Parliament (formerly the House of the People) seen from Union Boulevard (formerly the Victory of Socialism Boulevard), Bucharest, 2012

19.2 The Public Bath – temporary installation, Arthur Verona Street, Bucharest, 2012

19.3 The Letter Bench' – public furniture, Arthur Verona Street, Bucharest, 2009

19.4 'Spaces of Representation' – student workshop, Timişoara, 2013

19.5 'My Place Behind the Blocks' – community action, Sinaia, 2013

20.1 Sina's Café, Skegoneill, Belfast

20.2 Sabarmati Waterfront, Ahmedabad, Gujarat

20.3 Sabarmati Waterfront, Ahmedabad, Gujarat

20.4 Painting by Now Office, architects of the *Kulttuurisauna*

21.1 Surface, air and underground: cutting and breathing

21.2 The concept of the Memory Belt as a tool to stitch the village to its surrounding context

21.3 Zooming into Her Space: moments from the Eco Kitchen and the children's Eco Play along with the bird folly

21.4 Construction in progress: the Eco Kitchen

22.1 The mobile archive at the opening of the show, *Tensta Museum: Reports from New Sweden,* at Tensta konsthall (Tensta Art Centre)

22.2 International Housing Renewal Conference in Tensta, 1989

22.3 Witness seminar at Tensta konsthall (Tensta Art Centre)

22.4 Guided tour by architect Ylva Larsson of the participatory renewal project, Glömminge (1989–1995)

23.1 *Hustadt Project*, Actions, 2008–2011, Bochum, Germany

23.2 Brunnenplatz, *Hustadt Project*, Actions, 2008–2011, Bochum, Germany

23.3 Temporary pavilion in progress, *Hustadt Project*, Actions, 2008–2011, Bochum, Germany

23.4 Community Pavilion in progress, *Hustadt Project*, Actions, 2008–2011, Bochum, Germany

24.1 'As the dough rises, we rise' by Fred Brown, Anfield Liverpool, 2011
24.2 Housing market renewal, put on hold, Anfield, Liverpool, 2010
24.3 *Homebaked*, Brick by Brick, Loaf by Loaf we build ourselves, project block of houses and former Mitchells Bakery, Anfield, Liverpool, 2011
24.4 Design workshop remodelling the bakery block, Anfield, Liverpool, 2012
24.5 Baking workshops, Anfield, Liverpool, 2014
24.6 Sue's House, Anfield Home Tour, Anfield, Liverpool, 2012
24.7 *Homebaked* still in the clearance zone, Anfield, Liverpool, 2012

TABLES

7.1 List of initiatives: All my relations
8.1 Five types of relations between tactical and neoliberal urbanisms

NOTES ON CONTRIBUTORS

Sandra Bartoli is Visiting Professor at the Department of Architecture and Urban Studies at the Akademie der Bildenden Künste in Nürnberg, Germany. She was research associate (2009–2015) at the Technische Universität Berlin. Her office, Büros für Konstruktivismus, founded with Silvan Linden, is a practice of architecture and research. She is the author of the book *Tiergarten* (60 pages, 2014) and is co-publisher and editor of *Architektur in Gebrauch* (Architecture in Use), an architectural magazine which explores the value of use in the production conditions of architecture. She co-authored the book *La Zona – Index* (ngbk, 2012). She conceived and co-organized the international symposium 'Tiergarten, Landscape of Transgression' (TU Berlin) at the Haus der Kulturen der Welt in Berlin in 2015; the book, co-edited with Jörg Stollmann, is forthcoming.

Ana Betancour is an architect and Rector of the UMA School of Architecture, Umeå, Sweden, where she is also a Professor in Architecture and Urban Design. She was previously Professor in Urban Design at Chalmers University of Technology and Director of the Master's programme Architecture and Urban Design. She founded A + URL/Architecture + Urban Research Laboratory, and ran the architectural practice Urban + Architecture Agency, whose work includes numerous projects that range from architectural and urban design, academic research, multidisciplinary cultural and new media projects. Her work investigates alternative strategies and ways to operate and catalyse change within the global transformations affecting cities today. She is widely published, exhibited, and is a member of various international reference groups, networks and organizations, nationally and internationally.

Kathrin Böhm is an artist and founding member of the London-based art and architecture collective public works, and the pan-European artist initiative Myvillages, whose work is collaborative and focused towards an expansive and productive public realm. Current projects include 'Company: Movement, Deals and Drinks' in east London (2014, ongoing), the 'International Village Show' at the Museum of Contemporary Art in Leipzig (2015–2016) and the ongoing 'Haystacks' series.

Neil Brenner is Professor of Urban Theory at the Harvard Graduate School of Design, Cambridge, MA. His most recent books are *Critique of Urbanization* (Birkhäuser, 2016) and *Implosions/Explosions:*

Towards a Study of Planetary Urbanization (Jovis, 2013). He directs the Urban Theory Lab at the Harvard GSD (urbantheorylab.net), a research team that uses the tools of critical urban theory, historical geopolitical economy and radical cartography to decipher emergent patterns of urbanization. He is currently completing several books, including *New Urban Spaces: Urban Theory and the Scale Question* (Oxford University Press) and *Is the World Urban? Towards a Critique of Geospatial Ideology* (with Nikos Katsikis; Actar).

Ana Džokić and **Marc Neelen** (Belgrade/Rotterdam) are architects, who have been working since 2000 under the name **STEALTH.unlimited**. Their practice operates between the fields of urban research, spatial interventions and cultural activism, pointing to the responsibilities and capacities of architecture in contemporary societies and opening up space for citizens' involvement in urban development. They are members of the Smarter Building initiative, Belgrade.

Katherine Gibson is an economic geographer with an international reputation for innovative research on economic transformation, and over 30 years' experience of working with communities to build resilient economies. As J.K. Gibson-Graham, the collective authorial presence she shares with the late Julie Graham (Professor of Geography, University of Massachusetts Amherst), her books include *The End of Capitalism (As We Knew It): A Feminist Critique of Political Economy* (Blackwell, 1996) and *A Postcapitalist Politics* (University of Minnesota Press, 2006). Her most recent books are *Take Back the Economy: An Ethical Guide for Transforming Our Communities*, co-authored with Jenny Cameron and Stephen Healy (University of Minnesota Press, 2013), *Making Other Worlds Possible: Performing Diverse Economies*, co-edited with Gerda Roelvink and Kevin St Martin (University of Minnesota Press, 2015) and *Manifesto for Living in the Anthropocene*, co-edited with Deborah Bird Rose and Ruth Fincher (Punctum Press, 2015).

Nasser Golzari and **Yara Sharif** are practising architects and academics. Both teach at Oxford Brookes University as well as the University of Westminster, London. Having lived and worked in conflict zones, they developed a special interest in the subject of cultural identity, politics and responsive architecture. They mainly look at design as a means to facilitate and empower communities. Combining practice with research, they co-founded the Palestinian Regeneration Team (PART), which aims to explore creative and responsive spatial practices that can heal the fractured landscape of Palestine. Their work, with both their architecture practice NG Architects and with PART, has been published widely, Sharif has been granted the 2013 commendation award – RIBA's President Award for Research for Outstanding PhD Thesis. Their collaborative work with Riwaq on the historic centre of Birzeit won the 2013 Aga Khan Award for Architecture, while the revitalization of the historic centre of Beit Iksa won the 2014 Holcim Award for Sustainable Construction.

Rainer Hehl is an architect/urban planner and is currently Professor for the Architecture and Urban Design Innovation Program at the Technische Universität Berlin. He directed the Master of Advanced Studies in Urban Design programme at the ETH Zurich, conducting research and design projects on urban developments in emerging territories, with a focus on informal settlements and mass housing in Brazil. In addition to having lectured widely on urban informality, popular architecture, and hybrid urbanities, he is founder of the Bureau for Architecture Urban Design and Collaborative Action (BAUCO). Rainer holds a PhD from the ETH Zurich, on urbanization strategies for informal settlements, focusing on case studies in Rio de Janeiro.

Gabu Heindl is an architect and urban researcher in Vienna. She is the director of GABU Heindl Architektur, a practice specializing in public interventions, cultural and social buildings, and urban research/planning. She is the curator of exhibitions, lectures and symposia on issues of politics in architecture and urban planning. Gabu currently teaches at the Academy of Fine Arts in Vienna, having studied in Vienna, Tokyo and Princeton. She is the author of several publications in books and architectural journals (*JAE, Umbau, GAM, dérive* a.o.), editor of *Just Architecture* (ERA21, 2012), *Arbeit Zeit Raum: Bilder und Bauten der Arbeit im Postfordismus* (turia+kant, 2008) and co-editor of *position alltag – Architecture in the Context of Everyday Life* (HDA Verlag, 2009). Since 2013, she has been Chairwoman of the Austrian Society for Architecture (www.gabuheindl.at).

Mathias Heyden is the co-founder of the Berlin community project, K 77, where he is engaged as a political activist and cultural worker, inhabitant and builder, craftsman and designer. With his office ISPARA, he co-produced, among other works, the event and book, *Under Construction: Strategies of Participative Architecture and Spatial Appropriation*, the exhibition and pamphlets, 'An architektur 19–21: community design. involvement and architecture in the US since 1963', and the visual research project, 'Where if not us? Participatory design and its radical approaches'. Parallel to lecturing in Europe and the USA, he was guest professor at Akademie der Bildenden Künste in Nürnberg, and is research assistant at the Technische Universität Berlin.

Rory Hyde is the Curator of Contemporary Architecture and Urbanism at the V&A Museum, London, Adjunct Senior Research Fellow at the University of Melbourne, and author of *Future Practice: Conversations from the Edge of Architecture* (Routledge, 2012).

Elke Krasny is a curator, cultural theorist, urban researcher and writer. She is a professor at the Academy of Fine Arts Vienna, Austria. Elke's theoretical and curatorial work is firmly rooted in socially engaged art and spatial practices, urban epistemology, post-colonial theory and feminist historiography. In her conceptually driven and research-based curatorial practice she works along the intersections of art, architecture, education, feminism, landscape, spatial politics and urbanism. Recent curatorial works include *The Force Is in the Mind: The Making of Architecture,* including a publication of the same name (Birkhauser, 2008). *Women and the City: A Different Topography of Vienna* (2008), *Penser Tout Haut: Faire l'Architecture* (2010), *Hong Kong City Telling*, Hong Kong Community Museum Project, (2011); *Hands-on Urbanism 1850–2012.* Her *Hands-On Urbanism 1850–2012: The Right to Green* was invited to the 2012 Venice Biennale. She has edited and authored a number of books on architecture, urbanism and feminist historiography, and her writing has been published widely in edited volumes, exhibition catalogues and magazines.

Phil Langley is an architect and computational designer, based in London, and is also a PhD candidate at the School of Architecture at the University of Sheffield. Phil has worked in practice for over ten years and specializes in the design of digital tools and hacks to modify and disrupt the existing, proprietary software platforms currently used in the industry. His research further explores other ways of engaging with digital technology for spatial design practice, with a particular focus on open source approaches to software and coding. He is also a founding member of OPENkhana, a collaborative group that works between architectural, computational and artistic practice.

Helge Mooshammer is the director of the international research projects, Relational Architecture and Other Markets (www.othermarkets.org) at the School of Architecture and Urban Planning, Vienna University of Technology, Austria. He is currently a Research Fellow in the Department of Visual Cultures at Goldsmiths College, University of London. His research is concerned with changing forms of urban sociality arising from the processes of transnationalization, capital movements, informal economies, and newly emerging regimes of governance.

Peter Mörtenböck is Professor of Visual Culture at the Vienna University of Technology, and visiting researcher at Goldsmiths College, University of London, where he has initiated the Networked Cultures project (www.networkedcultures.org), a platform for global research on collaborative art and architecture practices. His current work explores the interaction of such practices with resource politics, global economies and urban transformation.

Mörtenböck and **Mooshammer** have published numerous articles on contemporary art, bottom-up urbanism and collaborative forms of spatial production, including in *Grey Room*, *Architectural Research Quarterly* and *Third Text*. Their recent books include *Visual Cultures as Opportunity* (2016), *Informal Market Worlds: The Architecture of Economic Pressure* (2015), *Space (Re)Solutions: Intervention and Research in Visual Culture* (2011), and *Networked Cultures: Parallel Architectures and the Politics of Space* (2008) (www.thinkarchitecture.net).

Ruth Morrow is the curatorial advisor to PS² and Professor of Architecture at Queen's University Belfast. Ruth has a long-standing interest in people and place and believes that fundamentally architectural practice is pedagogical: the focus of her next project.

Peter Mutschler is an artist, curator and director of PS², Belfast. His curatorial focus is on projects which are artistically and socially relevant with the aim of re-connecting art with society. Besides the rotating programme in PS², he works on two long-term projects with artists and communities in the small village of Ballykinler and at an interface site in North Belfast.

PS² is a voluntary artist collective with studio space in the centre of Belfast. A project space is used for an experimental, fast-revolving series of art projects and cultural activities. Alongside the 'indoor' programme, PS² curates long-term 'outdoor' projects at 'critical' locations. The focus of these neighbourhood-centred projects is urban intervention and social interaction by artists, cultural practitioners, architects and multidisciplinary groups and theorists. Ongoing outdoor sites are in the village of Ballykinler and an interface area in North Belfast. The projects are initiated and organized by **Peter Mutschler**, PS² Director with **Ruth Morrow** (www.pssquared.org; www.temporaryplaces.org; www.villageworks.org.uk).

Doina Petrescu is Professor of Architecture and Design Activism at the University of Sheffield. She is co-founder, together with Constantin Petcou, of **atelier d'architecture autogérée (*aaa*)**, a collective platform which conducts explorations, actions and research concerning participative architecture, resilience and cities co-produced transformation. Recent projects include Ecobox and Passage 56 in Paris and R-Urban, a participative strategy for local resilience in the Parisian Region. These projects have received international recognition and numerous awards across the years including the Zumtobel Award (2012), the Curry Stone Prize (2011) and the European Public Space Prize (2010). Her publications include *R-Urban Act: A Participative Strategy of Urban Resilience* (2015), *Agency: Working with Uncertain Architectures* (2009), *Trans-Local Act: Cultural Politics Within and Beyond* (2009), *Altering Practices: Feminist Politics and Poetics of Space* (2007), *Urban/ACT: A Handbook for Alternative Practice* (2007) and *Architecture and Participation* (2005).

Gabriela Rendón is an architect, urban planner and co-founder of Cohabitation Strategies, a not-for-profit cooperative for socio-spatial research, design and development based in Rotterdam, The Netherlands, and New York City, USA. Her research areas of interest and expertise include neighbourhood decline and restructuring processes, as well as collective and non-speculative housing models providing affordable housing and equitable development. Rendón is an Assistant Professor of Urban Planning at The New School, in New York City. She has also taught graduate urban studies at Delft University of Technology in the Netherlands, where she received a Masters in Urbanism and is currently following doctoral studies at the Chair of Spatial Planning and Strategy.

Miguel Robles-Durán is an urbanist, Assistant Professor of Urbanism at The New School/Parsons the New School for Design in New York City, and co-founder of the not-for-profit Cohabitation Strategies, a cooperative for socio-spatial research, design and development based in Rotterdam, The Netherlands and New York City, USA. His main research is centred on the strategic definition/ coordination of trans-disciplinary urban projects, as well as on the development of tactical design strategies and civic engagement platforms that confront the contradictions of neoliberal urbanization, such as homelessness, housing crises, gentrification, the effects of financialization in the real-estate industry, inter-urban competition and urban social movements.

Meike Schalk is an architect based in Stockholm and in Berlin. She is Chair of the cross-disciplinary MSc programme, Sustainable Urban Planning and Design, at KTH School of Architecture and the Built Environment, in Stockholm. Her research on architecture and urban questions combines critical inquiry into issues of sustainability and resilience, critical-creative participation in urban development processes, and practice-led research. Schalk is co-founder of the feminist architecture teaching and research group *FATALE* and an editor of *SITE* magazine. Since 2013, she has run the not-for-profit association Action Archive (Aktion Arkiv) together with Helena Mattsson and Sara Brolund de Carvalho.

Tatjana Schneider is a researcher, writer and educator based at the School of Architecture in Sheffield, UK. She is also co-founder of research group 'Agency' and was a founder member of the workers' cooperative G.L.A.S. (Glasgow Letters on Architecture and Space), which aimed to construct both a theoretical and practical critique of the capitalist production and use of the built environment. Her current work focuses on the changing role of architects and architecture in contemporary society, (architectural) pedagogy and spatial agency. She has an interest in employing and implementing theoretical, methodological and practical approaches that expand the scope of contemporary architectural debates and discourses by integrating political and economic frameworks that question normative ways of thinking, producing and consuming space. She is the co-author of *Spatial Agency: Other Ways of Doing Architecture* (2011), *Flexible Housing* (2007), *A Right to Build* (2011), and co-editor of *Agency: Working with Uncertain Architectures* (2009) and the journal *glaspaper* (2001–2007).

studioBASAR was established in 2006 by **Alex Axinte** and **Cristi Borcan**, both as an architectural studio and as a team of urban observation and intervention. Preoccupied in the last few years with the dynamics of local urban culture and the disappearing importance of public spaces in transitional Bucharest, studioBASAR's projects range from public space interventions, art installations, urban research, educational workshops to competitions and different typologies of residential and public buildings. In 2010, studioBASAR published the book *Evicting the Ghost: Architectures of Survival*, which was awarded 'Best Book' at the Bucharest Architectural Annual. In 2014, the project Public Bath was a finalist in the European Prize for Urban Public Space.

Apolonija Šušteršič is an architect and visual artist. Her work is interested in the critical analysis of space; usually focused on the processes and relationships between institutions, cultural politics, urban planning and architecture. Her broad-ranging interests start with a phenomenological study of space and continue their investigation into the social and political nature of our living environment. She usually undertakes extensive research into specific situations found on location, which she uses as a starting point of her projects. Apolonija has a PhD from the University of Lund, Malmö Art Academy, Sweden; and runs her own art/architecture studio practice in Lund, Sweden, and in Ljubljana, Slovenia. Recently she was appointed Professor in Visual Art at Oslo National Academy for the Arts, to build up the MA studies under the title 'Art & Public Space'.

Pelin Tan, sociologist and art historian, is an Associate Professor in the Department of Architecture at Mardin Artuklu University and Research Professor at Hong Kong Polytechnic, Design Strategies (Spring, 2016). She completed her PhD on locality in urban art projects at ITU, and her postdoctoral study on artistic research methodology at MIT, Cambridge, MA. Her publications on architecture, urbanism and art include 'Transversal Materialism' featured in *2000+: Urgencies of Architectural Theories* (GSAPP, 2015), chapters in *Becoming Istanbul: An Encyclopedia* (2008); *When Things Cast No Shadow* (5th Berlin Biennale, 2008); *Megastructure Reloaded* (2008); *Contemporary Art in Turkey: 1986–2006* (2007) and *With/Without Spatial Politics in the Middle East* (2007), *Recht-auf-Stadt* (2011) edited with A. Çavdar, *Istanbul'un Neoliberal Kentsel Dönü ümü* (Neoliberal Urban Transformation of Istanbul, Sel Pub. 2013). Tan is a lead author of the International Panel on Social

Progress (IPSP), and contributed a chapter in *Towards an Urban Society*, edited by Saskia Sassen and Edgar Pieterse (2015–2017). Tan is a principal researcher of the 'Spatio-Social Analysis of Refugee Camps in Southeast Turkey' project (2015–2016, MAU).

Kim Trogal is a lecturer at the Canterbury School of Architecture, University for the Creative Arts, and Postdoctoral Researcher at Central Saint Martins, University of the Arts London (2014–2016). She completed her architectural studies at the University of Sheffield, including a PhD in Architecture (2012) for which she was awarded the RIBA LKE Ozolins Studentship. Kim was research assistant for the Building Local Resilience platform at the Sheffield School of Architecture (2012–2015), exploring issues of local social and ecological resilience. Kim's research examines the intersections of ethics and economies in spatial practice from feminist perspectives.

Jeanne van Heeswijk is a visual artist who facilitates the creation of dynamic and diversified public spaces in order to 'radicalize the local'. Van Heeswijk embeds herself as an active citizen in communities, often working there for years at a time. These long-term projects, which have occurred in many different countries, transcend the traditional boundaries of art in duration, space and media, and question art's autonomy by combining performative actions, meetings, discussions, seminars and other forms of organizing and pedagogy. Inspired by a particular current event, cultural context or intractable social problem, she dynamically involves community members in the planning and realization of a given project. As an 'urban curator', van Heeswijk's work often unravels invisible legislation, governmental codes and social institutions, in order to enable communities to take control over their own futures. Her work has also been featured in numerous books and publications worldwide, as well as in internationally renowned biennials such as those of Liverpool, Busan, Taipei, Shanghai and Venice. She was Keith Haring Fellow (2014–2015) in Art and Activism at Bard College and has received the 2012 Curry Stone Prize for Social Design Pioneers, and in 2011, the Leonore Annenberg Prize for Art and Social Change.

Ana Vilenica is a researcher, theoretician and activist, based in Serbia. She holds a PhD in Theory of Art and Media from the University of Art in Belgrade. She is co-editor of the book, *On the Ruins of the Creative City*, and editor of the journal for art, theory, politics and activism *uz)bu))na)))*. She is a member of the Smarter Building initiative, Belgrade.

Supreeya Wungpatcharapon is a full-time lecturer in the Faculty of Architecture, Kasetsart University in Bangkok, Thailand. Her main research interests are participatory approaches in building and urban design, low-income housing, empowerment, and sustainable community development. She has also been involved in the development of the Community Architects Network (CAN), in association with the Asian Coalition for Housing Rights (ACHR), to support community-driven projects in Asia and Thailand.

1 – INTRODUCTION: THE SOCIAL (RE)PRODUCTION OF ARCHITECTURE IN 'CRISIS-RIDDLED' TIMES

Doina Petrescu and Kim Trogal

(RE)PRODUCTION IN THE EMERGING AGE OF POST-CAPITALISM

This book was written during the rise of a new political moment in global capitalist society. It is a 'crisis-riddled time' and, in the field of economics on different sides of the political spectrum, some thinkers have concluded that, whether we like it or not, we are moving into a different era, beyond neoliberal capitalism.[1] The claims that any crisis is 'different' might be easy to dismiss, since capitalism is remarkably versatile and adaptive. But many agree that today's crisis, and the climate crisis in particular, are different. What marks this era as different from the others is that it is *a crisis of reproduction* not only of production, as the very basis on which things and life are produced is under threat. In times of austerity politics and the loss of waged work globally, in times of unprecedented migration flows and resources wars, it is reproduction, namely, how we sustain ourselves and our world that has become a 'political battleground'.[2] As various national states withdraw their support for welfare, it is housing, health, education, childcare, care, the environment, wildlife, low-carbon technologies, the civic sector and culture, to name only a few, which are all targets. This is a time of transition, but what the transition is to is uncertain and some scenarios are grim.[3] However, a number of thinkers argue that co-produced lives are possible but they need to

---

1   See for example Paul Mason's *PostCapitalism* (2015) or Jeremy Rifkin's *The End of Work* (2000).

2   The cultural theorist Marina Vishmidt writes, 'In times of crisis, when the ration of waged to unwaged starts to tilt negatively, reproduction becomes the political battleground' (2011, n.p.).

3   At the beginning of his recent book, *PostCapitalism*, Paul Mason cites economists who argued that 'for neoliberalism to survive, democracy must fade'. He suggests that the current prospect is widening inequality as austerity is continued to be used as the means 'to hold globalisation together'. Alternatively, when ordinary people refuse to pay, as in Greece, globalization falls apart with rising conflicts, as nations try to impose the costs on each other (Mason, 2015: x–xx).

be made and struggled over in the here and now, at many scales and at many levels.[4]

There is an imperative to change, to find new forms of organizing and means to sustain ourselves in the world. This demands new forms of collective politics, values and actions, in which space and architecture must play a role. This is already happening through a grassroots proliferation of new forms of (re)production, from community-supported agriculture, aquaculture, community actions on energy, water and environmental concerns, new kinds of collective practices of lending and sharing, new currencies, peer-to-peer production as well as new legal forms of ownership, rights and responsibilities 'in common'. It is 'a new way of living in the process of formation' (Mason, 2015: xv).

Among the diversity of initiatives that are building new possibilities, some have started to work with the reproductive capacities of architecture. This engagement with (re)production is in the context of crisis and transition and, as such, it is different from the modernist project of architecture that took place under the welfare state.

Architecture needs to reinvent itself, it needs to revise its value systems, its means and definitions, its vocabulary of practice. The project of the future is very much one of 're-' … The '(re)' of the book's title, whose brackets serve both as a critical elision and a reminder of the taken-for-granted status of reproduction, follows feminist work over the past 40 years to affirm that *we can no longer speak about production without speaking about reproduction at the same time.*[5] Following feminist work, we must read beyond Marxist notions of production and beyond binary oppositions of production/reproduction, production/ consumption. In the context of a built environment that is overproduced and overproduces in its turn, our 're' also refers to other ecological 're's, all with reproductive dimensions: reparation, recycling, reuse, resilience and the reconstruction of other spatial relations. In this trajectory and specifically in this book, we find spaces that are concerned with both production and reproduction (such as commons, community land trusts, cooperative housing), activities (such as consumption also considered as a form of production), and a concern with plural, diverse others (slum dwellers, prisoners, informal street sellers).

---

4   For two different examples, see J.K. Gibson-Graham's *A Postcapitalist Politics* (1996b) and J.K. Gibson-Graham and Jenny Cameron's *Take Back the Economy* (2013) or Massimo De Angelis's *The Beginning of History: Value Struggles and Global Capital* (2007).

5   See especially works by Silvia Federici (2004), Maria Mies (1986), Nancy Folbre (2003), Leopoldina Fortunati (2007), Mariarosa Dalla Costa and Selma James (1975), and Kathi Weeks (2011).

In opening up broad questions of (re)production in contemporary architecture, the book addresses three main concerns: (1) *politics*: what kinds of politics of (re)production do we need? How do we think through 'the political' in the social (re)production of architecture?; (2) *values*: in both the economic and ethical sense of the term, where and how is value (re)produced in and through architecture, and what constitutes that value?; and (3) *actions*: we suggest that architecture, art and design can bring specific (re)productive actions as a means to be active in, and change, places and contexts. These three main concerns are reflected in the three Parts: Part I, 'politics'; Part II, 'values'; and Part III, 'actions'.

THE RIGHT TO THE CITY/THE RIGHT TO ARCHITECTURE

When speaking about the politics of (re)production in architecture, one important reference is, of course, Lefebvre's (1991) famous work on the 'social production of space'. According to Lefebvre, space, and we can also infer architecture, shape society and are shaped by it. Space and architecture are (re)productive, and citizens of any society, he wrote, have a right to shape that society in and through its spaces (Lefebvre, 1968). Later, after the 1968 upheaval, he claimed a 'right to the city' as one of the fundamental rights of all citizens. In the context of a society regulated by global capital, David Harvey analysed these reproductive capacities from the perspective of political economy, emphasizing how capitalist economies and relations are specifically produced through space and urban development. He showed how planning and development reproduce capitalist relations, and therefore argued that the production of injustice, through space, is systemic (1973, 2008).

With concerns regarding the reproductive aspects of architecture, our aim in this book is to explore *what (new) kinds of 'social' architecture can reproduce*. The notion that all citizens have the right to shape their societies in and through its spaces, suggests, of course, participation, but contemporary conditions demand that we go beyond participatory or 'socially engaged' approaches to work with more radical forms of politics and values. Drawing on recent debates on the 'right to the city', we argue that a 'right to architecture' not only concerns 'having a say' in development, but rather concerns real material rights (such as the right to housing, to public space, the rights to space) as well as the more elusive, psychological rights that Lefebvre evoked, such as the rights of imagination, or the right to play.[6] These rights are seen 'more as an emancipatory project, emphasizing the need to freely project alternative possibilities' (Crawford, 2011: 34). Keeping in mind Lefebvre's immaterial rights and a 'multiplicity of representations and interventions', we also try to work with Harvey's assertion, that the 'right to the city' (and architecture) necessitates collective, global dimensions. As Harvey asserts, the right to the city is a common right, it has to be claimed mutually and collectively. The social (re)production of architecture, for us, is part of an 'emancipatory project', material and immaterial, individual and collective. The right to the city and a right to architecture involve not any architecture, but a *just*, ecological, creative, imaginative architecture, that we claim as users, managers, citizens and architects.

The social (re)production of architecture suggests that we have a different kind and quality of relationship with architecture as both practitioners and citizens. In the social (re)production of architecture, the aspects of architecture that become important are not the ones of form, surface, style or even structure, but rather demand working upon the ecological, economic, collaborative and processual aspects of making space. This book thus aims also to open up what architecture is in dealing with the challenges of our times, particularly when the conditions of reproduction have been radically altered in the last few decades. In the post-capitalist era, the social (re)production of architecture takes place under new conditions.

A DIVERSITY OF SCALES, LOCATIONS AND (RE)PRODUCTIVE APPROACHES

This book has a global span, with chapters discussing Australia, Austria, Brazil, Canada, Germany, Netherlands/Serbia, Sweden, Palestine, Romania, Spain, Thailand, Turkey/Kurdistan, the UK and the USA to contextualize the (re)production of architecture and the architectures of (re)production. This takes different specific forms in these different global contexts: in Brazil, it is 'popular' (Hehl); in Kurdistan, on the front line of a war zone, it is 'forensic' (Tan); in the Mediterranean, it is 'tactical' (Betancour); in occupied Palestine, it is poetic and 'speculative' (Golzari and Sharif); and in Thai slum upgrading, it is networked and empowering (Wungpatcharapon).

---

6   Lefebvre wrote of both the 'right to participate' (the right to produce the city, as 'Œuvre') and the 'right to appropriate', which is not only about accessing spaces but also the freedom to create new spaces, through use and imagination, and 'a multiplicity of representations and interventions' (Crawford, 2011: 34).

The (re)production documented in this book takes place in specific 'local' contexts: in prisons, villages, metropolitan neighbourhoods, in suburbs, abandoned buildings, large parks and public squares. It makes use of different means, from pedagogy, curating, art, activism, installations, community fairs, networks, as well as buildings. The inclusion of diverse forms is for us deliberate, with diversity constituting part of a political project, following an approach taken by many feminist thinkers and activists.[7] Such diversity also questions 'Architecture', and what we call architecture both as a discipline and profession. The architecture in this book includes architecture without architects, architecture which is relational and not solely physical (not least because reproductive work is always relational[8]). It includes different scales of architecture, from objects to regions and geopolitical areas that all have architectural agency. As such, the social (re)production of architecture can be considered to involve particular, relational processes, such as participatory ones (Mutschler and Morrow; Šušteršič; or van Heeswijk) and transversal, decolonizing ones (Tan; Krasny).

ARCHITECTURE FOR RADICAL, FEMINIST AND 'AGONISTIC' POLITICS

As thinkers have noted, neoliberal capitalism contradicts democracy and particularly so in contemporary development.[9] Yet the democratic models we operate with are in crisis, they need to be reclaimed and transformed, and an important question in this volume is *how, through architecture, can we enable a more democratic spatial production within critical conditions?* Authors here directly confront issues of control and rights in spatial (re)production following Marxist approaches, yet are also developing 'agonistic' (Mouffe, 2013), radical, feminist and post-human approaches (Haraway, 2003, 2008; Braidotti, 2013).

---

7 Diversity was privileged by Lefebvre, see Margaret Crawford's (2011) writings, and for diversity as a feminist approach in architecture, see Petrescu (2007).

8 For instance, taking care labour as an example of 'reproductive work', care is always relational as it is always for someone or something. It has affective, emotional qualities, to care about someone, and, as an activity, care creates and sustains relationships.

9 See, for example, Erik Swyngedouw's work on post-politics (2013) and work on regulatory capitalism in urban geography, such as by Mike Raco (2014).

Authors, such as Tatjana Schneider and Supreeya Wung-patcharapon, highlight the importance of taking control over the social production of space. In Chapter 2, Schneider suggests we need to find ways of 'acting otherwise', taking control of spatial production collectively through mutual knowledge and action. We find a concrete example of this in Wungpatcharapon's Chapter 3 concerning the spatial rights and justice of slum dwellers in Thailand. Her case study of a marginalized population struggling to defend their presence in society shows how they have taken control of their own development. This involves not only the architectural development of buildings and spaces (primarily housing) but also the development of a range of associated tools such as networks, welfare schemes, saving schemes, income generation and the establishment of mutual rules. It is a good example of what Neil Brenner calls 'institutional re-design' in Chapter 8. He advocates practices that actively interrupt 'rule-regimes associated with market-oriented, growth-first urban development' (p. 116) to (re)design the systems 'that govern the production, use, occupation and appropriation of space' (p. 119). He argues that together with tactical approaches, *we still need architectural strategies if we are to counter politics of neoliberal urbanism at scale.*

A number of the claims to spatial rights in this volume are taking place in extreme or exceptional conditions, which can increasingly be seen as paradigmatic of our times. In a prison, a war zone or refugee camp when criticality is difficult, what kind of politics will guide us? A number of authors here bring in Chantal Mouffe's concept of 'agonistic politics'. In agonistic politics, difference can and should emerge. It demands the creation of democratic spaces in which conflict and divergence may appear, and their work helps raise questions around the limits of who or what is excluded.

In Chapter 4, Gabu Heindl presents the dilemmas of working with a prison and considers prisoners' 'rights to space' in such conditions. She asks how to intervene in a situation of spatial injustice in a way that is not purely commentary, nor simply making a 'wrong' situation acceptable? With Pelin Tan, in Chapter 6, we learn from the limiting condition of the front lines of war. We see how, through pedagogical processes, staff and students at the Faculty of Architecture at Mardin Artuklu University are creating critical and transformative connections to the conditions they are in. Through different methodologies (affective, transversal, forensic), she suggests that 'architectural research that transverses and functions in both institutions *and* societies directly, can play a role in transforming knowledge and public "truth"' (p. 77). Those things that are cast 'outside' of architecture come (back) in, expanding the field as a tool for democratic practice and justice.

In the context of Northern Ireland, in Chapter 5, Peter Mutschler and Ruth Morrow acknowledge the potential of small and transitory moments of injustice resulting from complex post-conflict situations, to generate radical politics and new spatialities involving unexpected relations. They advocate slow engaged actions, sometimes modest with little or no resources, but involving a broad and heterogeneous diversity of actors, such as pensioners, families, children, teenagers and artists.

Elsewhere in the volume we find other forms of democratic space-making in the limiting conditions of Palestine (Golzari and Sharif), or the precariousness of sustaining protest movements (Mörtenböck and Mooshamer). In these chapters we learn that under extreme conditions architecture might expand its remit, as in all these practices the usual tools we use for democratic spatial production, such as participation, are questioned. The politics become more nuanced in achieving a sensitivity to the contexts in which they operate.

The chapters also present feminist and radical political approaches. This is a politics of working with and across differences and beyond binaries, constituted in power relations. Tan talks specifically about education as a reproductive activity, reproducing the norms, habits, practices and values of the society. Intervening in this (re)production, she argues for the necessity of 'decolonizing' architectural education from the values and norms it inherits from the current profession and the injustices it reproduces within society. Like Tan, Elke Krasny, in Chapter 7, brings the concept of transversality as one tool to work across difference. Krasny asks how to build solidarity across difference in the context of a gentrifying Vancouver neighbourhood. She asks what kind of relations are possible between unequal and sometimes opposing neighbours? Here she acknowledges invisible reproductive work in architecture through a feminist and situated approach to curating. The curatorial processes involved women's groups, together with universities and art galleries, and made the women's role in (re)producing and shaping the neighbourhood visible.

For Phil Langley, in Chapter 9, a radical approach to post-human politics (Haraway, 2003) in architecture can help us to re-situate ourselves as co-producers with technology. Software, he suggests, could be considered 'companion species' with which we co-evolve in complex ways. He brings 'queer technologies' (Blas, 2006) to challenge normative binaries oppositions, and states that the social (re)production of architecture could be enriched by the relations we have with software, which should be seen as a site of creativity and collective activity.

The politics of the (re)production of architecture suggests we need nuanced and sensitive approaches. In these 'crisis-riddled times', we need to learn how to become paradoxical and contradictory: how to act quickly and at the same time to slow down, to be engaged and generous, yet remain vigilant and critical, to (re)produce more and to consume less, to allow the contestation of the many voiceless, and to find ways to construct positively in conflicts.

ARCHITECTURE WHICH (RE)PRODUCES 'OTHER VALUES'

Architecture (re)produces values, a word we use here to invoke the co-implicated senses of financial value, value as meaning and values as ethics (Graeber, 2001). The values that architecture can produce occur in a number of ways, but specifically here we are concerned with what political economist Massimo De Angelis has called 'value practices'.[10] By this, he means that 'actions and processes, as well as correspondent web of relations, … that are both *predicated on a given value system and in turn (re)produce it'* (De Angelis, 2007: 24). The 'other values' we refer to (borrowing De Angelis's term) are 'other' to the dominance of market rationality and neoliberalism. They are the values of commoning: specifically, interdependence, care and 'being-in-common' (Gibson; Bartoli and Heyden), of sharing and making the public (Böhm), of the popular (Hehl), and of collective, self-determination (Džokić, Neelen and Vilenica; van Heeswijk; Šušteršič). These are the values of co-produced lives, the values of mutuality and cooperation.

In considering space and architecture as tools to perform and enact 'other values', in Chapter 10, Katherine Gibson gives us the concept of 'diverse economies', a re-framing of 'the economy' less as a machine external to our lives but rather seen as a range and diversity of practices and relationships that we participate in. In questioning how 'diverse economies' might be enabled through architecture, we

---

10   The use of the term practice is used here in a broad, social sense rather than in a conventional architectural sense. It is understood as recursive and 'routinized kind of behaviour' which is cultural rather than individual. These are 'blocks' or 'patterns' of action, which the individual participates in, and through which values are both performed and reaffirmed through their repetition. For an introduction to different theories of social practice, see Shove, Pantzar and Watson's book, *The Dynamics of Social Practice* (2012: 4–8).

find with Gibson that every moment is latent with possibility. Moments in the process, of specification, choices of materials, of inhabitation, of the design of spatial arrangements, all are moments to enact care in acknowledging our interdependence with others.

'Care' as both value and form of action is taken up in Trogal's Chapter 11, which suggests that 'care' can be a form of spatial (re)production. Following feminist work, she looks at different spatialities, such as 'commons' that are produced by care labour. Considering activities of direct reproduction and subsistence, the chapter suggests not only are there spaces, such as commons, that have a community of care attached to them but, as Kathrin Böhm states in her Chapter 12, objects and products can also be a locus for collective activities and (re)production of other values.

Kathrin Böhm's work has, over a number of years, been con- cerned with the ways that products are both a means for collective activities though their making, as well as means for their narration and sharing with others in public. The (re)production is also a question of time(s). Böhm speaks about practices of resilience restructuring urban citizenship, such as the collective 'hopping', involving diverse suburban residents travelling to the countryside and working together on harvesting their food: a practice that took place historically, in other times of crises, such as after the war. She suggests that such practices can be reproduced now, in new times of crises, with new meanings, values and enhanced significations: ecology, climate change, carbon reduction and so on. From her, we learn that (re)production also means learning from the past, in order to better understand the future. It concerns the reconstruction of the memory of a community.

Returning to the question of diversities of 'scales', we are interested in both smaller initiatives, whose values lie in the personal significance of intimate encounters and enabling participation, as well as an interest in the 'strategic alliances' required in order to become more powerful and to make those values travel. In Part II, we find three different responses to the diversity of scales. One is making the 'trans-local' operative (Gibson; Trogal; Böhm); the second is through 'scaling-up' the commons, such as the Metropolitan Commons of Berlin (Bartoli and Heyden); the third is through establishing hybrid entities and structures such as Land Trusts, Cooperative Housing, Credit Unions, that can make alliances across levels (Rendón and Robles-Durán).

In trying to privilege diversity, it is not only a question of who or what is included, but how those people and things are included and acknowledged. We find, through architecture, the invention and implementation of different mechanisms to recognize, re-distribute, protect, and support the processes and the participants in them (see chapters by van Heeswijk; Rendón and Robles-Durán; Džokić, Neelen and Vilenica; and Wungpatcharapon).

In Chapter 15, Džokić, Neelen and Vilenica, for example, address the pressing needs of housing, where affordable housing is no longer part of societal, welfare provision. They suggest taking the matter 'into your own hands' and intervene in the normal value practices of the market. In their project *Smarter Building*, a collective 'dissect house pricing, explore forms of direct democratic decision-making' (p. 230). They work with the cooperative as a known model, whose *smarter* aspects include the mechanisms that allow for the reproduction of different values, such as rules to protect prices from rising, and keeping housing both non-profit and accessible for others outside the group in the future.

Rainer Hehl, in his Chapter 16 on the popular tactics of informal urbanism in Brazil, draws attention to the specifically Brazilian tactics of 'Tropicalia', an open, yet tactical, 'process of cultural creation'. He suggests this introduces a different kind of value by providing another vision of cultural identity, one that incorporates 'creative counter-cultural practice within the predominant conditions of an emerging mass culture' (p. 244).

However, as Džokić, Neelen and Vilenica point out, reclaiming (re)production from the terrain of the market damages the market and is perceived as a threat by those who benefit from it. While Hehl's examples of how urban informality introduces new value chains, he also highlights the difficulties when regulatory spaces of formal order and corporate interests are imposed, and spatial strategies are used to suppress the appropriation of urban space through everyday practices. It is for this reason, that (re)production and its values need, therefore, politics *and* actions.

ARCHITECTURE IN ACTION

In this volume we present an architecture that is *in* action, which means an architecture that is *in and among* the actions of living, of activism, of social practice and therefore also includes 'architecture' without architects. It is an architecture that is engaged with the politics of the place in which one lives, an architecture that questions the rules of current architectural and urban practices to promote new ways of working. These ways are not service-led, nor client-oriented, but involve new roles and new kinds of actions, as well as familiar ones. These practices act *with* others (rather than on their behalf) and empower them to become agents themselves, to take collective responsibility in the process of (re)production.

With architecture *in* action, authors draw attention to the role of spatial and built structures in political actions, specifically here the Occupy movement. In Chapter 17, Mörtenböck and Mooshammer suggest that the spatial and architectural elements of the movement were key to the social (re)production of that movement. Ana Betancour, on the other hand, in Chapter 18, looks at how political actions and mobilizations are an essential part of the (re)production of the city, particularly as a means to contest neoliberal urbanism. She argues that mobilizations, such as *15M* and *V de Vivienda* have equally 'fuelled a re-imagining of both the production and distribution of culture' (p. 271), where we now see new forms of working in artistic and spatial practices.

With the expression 'architecture in action', we also suggest that architecture can be found in the actions and relational practices of everyday life. In Šušteršič's Chapter 23, her project involves political actions, which are not the actions of protest, but operate with everyday activities. Engaged to work as an artist in the regeneration programme of the suburb of Hustadt, Germany, Šušteršič moved to the area to create a new role for herself as inhabitant. Through this double role of artist-inhabitant she co-initiated 'low threshold' actions, such as walking, reading and gardening, to create a platform with local residents and activists, through which they could both develop their own actions, and contest and (re)shape the dominant planning processes taking place. In Chapter 22, Meike Schalk also works with 'low threshold actions' such as 'walking, showing, telling and drawing in groups' in the participatory project, *Action Archive*. In this critical history project, new kinds of actions are also introduced into archi-tecture, such as the 'witness seminars', which are used to create new collective spaces for, in this case, the rewriting of urban histories.

In architecture *in* action, there is a diversity of temporalities and duration, with some actions, such as those in Hustadt taking place over a year or longer, and others much more fleeting, lasting only a few hours or days. Yet both forms can be a way to test new forms of sociality in shared and public spaces. StudioBASAR in Bucharest (Chapter 19), for instance, works with urban tactics, individual user actions and prototypes of micro-urbanism in the contested context of post-totalitarian public space. These kinds of actions are public tests, conceived and performed in close observation with their individual contexts.

Being *in* action thus involves different strategies and scales for (re)producing the 'social'. Rory Hyde emphasizes the importance of a diversity of actions with examples at different scales and temporalities, ranging from the socio-spatial relations of a café, a sauna, to a large-scale waterfront development and to the use of architectural representation as a tool for justice at a national level.

The chapters suggest that architecture in action is *located*. The contributions highlight that the importance of action is not only the changes they enable, but also entails the showing and performing of possibilities in places with the inhabitants of those places. Actions open up the imaginary, a quality that is particularly important in places of limiting conditions, such as those of occupation (Golzari and Sharif) and protest (Mörtenböck and Mooshammer; Betancour). In occupied Palestine, we find different spatial components being developed to meet both imaginary and material needs. We find prototypes that are both spatial, social and ecological: kitchens, bus stops and bird follies are all important interventions that (re)claim space, (re)build networks and foster participation.

In building spaces of possibility, Golzari and Sharif assert the importance of memory and, as Schalk argues in Chapter 22, heritage and history are processes that reproduce normative practices and values. Schalk suggests that repressed historical material can question 'hegemonic positions in urban development', and, like Golzari and Sharif, she argues this can 'attempt to make openings for new spatial and political imaginaries' (p. 329).

One of the defining features of architecture in action, irrespective of duration, is the importance of provisionality (Mutschler and Morrow; Golzari and Sharif; Šušteršič; van Heeswijk). In the case of the Occupy camp, Mörtenböck and Mooshammer argue the 'camp' is a radical form of spatial praxis. It is *both* community and action 'whose determinant feature is its indeterminacy', namely, its openness to remaking by those who participate. In Chapter 24, Jeanne van

Heeswijk remarks that the significant feature of the *Homebaked* project was its constant evolution and improvisation. Spaces and structures need to be able to evolve and be open enough in order that people may develop them themselves. In enabling one of the first Community Land Trusts in the UK, *Homebaked* is an inspiring example of how actions with others can be both a form of protest and resistance to neoliberal planning and development and *at the same time* an 'attempt to demonstrate that residents can do things for themselves' (p. 373).

What interests us is not only what these actions do, but how we (as architects, artists, researchers, in creative spatial practices) can begin to develop different modes of engagement for ourselves. To borrow Rory Hyde's words in Chapter 20, the examples of actions here offer 'an alternative trajectory for architecture's production of the social' (p. 308), in which new roles are being created in order to perform those actions: as invisible architects (Golzari and Sharif), as co-developer (van Heeswijk), as artist-as-inhabitant (Šušteršič), who test the very limits of what is permissible, possible and useful within that role of the '(re)productive specialist', either architect, artist, curator, theorist or economist.

This is perhaps one of the main messages of this book: that we have a role to play in these crisis-riddled times, which will start with re-evaluating our own professional agency through radical politics, value systems and actions. We need to increase our own reproductive capacity as specialists and citizens, who look into our uncertain future with hope.

NOTE

This book originated in a series of lectures on the subject of the Social Production of Architecture under the aegis of the School Forum at Sheffield School of Architecture, January–April 2012.

REFERENCES

Blas, Zach (2006) *What Is Queer Technology?* Available at: www.zachblas.info/publications_materials/whatisqueertechnology_zachblas_2006.pdf

Braidotti, Rosi (2013) *The Posthuman*, Cambridge: Polity Press.

Crawford, Margaret (2011) 'Rethinking "rights", rethinking "cities": a response to David Harvey's "The Right to the City"', in Zany Begg and Leo Stickells (eds) *The Right to The City*, Sydney: The Sheds Gallery.

Dalla Costa, Mariarosa and James, Selma (1975) *The Power of Women and the Subversion of the Community*, 3rd rev. edn, Bristol: Falling Wall Press Ltd.

De Angelis, Massimo (2007) *The Beginning of History: Value Struggles and Global Capital*, London: Pluto Press.

Federici, Silvia (2004) *Caliban and the Witch: Women, the Body and Primitive Accumulation*, New York: Autonomedia.

Folbre, Nancy (2003) 'Caring labor', *Republic Art*. Available at: www.republicart.net/disc/aeas/folbre01_en.htm (accessed 11 October 2011).

Fortunati, Leopoldina (2007) 'Immaterial labor and its machinization', *Ephemera: Theory and Politics in Organization* 7(1): 139–157.

Gibson-Graham, J.K. (1996) *A Postcapitalist Politics*, Minneapolis, MN: University of Minnesota Press.

Gibson-Graham, J.K. and Cameron, Jenny (2013) *Take Back the Economy: An Ethical Guide for Transforming Our Communities*, Minneapolis, MN: University of Minnesota Press.

Graeber, David (2001) *Toward an Anthropological Theory of Value: The False Coin of Our Own Dreams*, New York: Palgrave.

Haraway, Donna J. (2003) *The Companion Species Manifesto: Dogs, People and Significant Otherness*, Chicago: Prickly Paradigm Press.
(2008) *When Species Meet*, Minneapolis, MN: University of Minnesota Press.

Harvey, David (1973) *Social Justice and the City*, London: Edward Arnold.
(2008) 'The right to the city', *New Left Review* 53: 23–40.

Lefebvre, Henri (1968) *Le droit à la ville*, Paris: Anthropos.

(1991) *The Production of Space*, Oxford: Blackwell (1st edn in French, 1974).

Mason, Paul (2015) *PostCapitalism: A Guide to Our Future*, London: Allen Lane.

Mies, Maria (1986) *Patriarchy and Accumulation on a World Scale: Women in the International Division of Labour*, London: Zed Books.

Mouffe, Chantal (2013) *Agonistics: Thinking the World Politically*, London: Verso.

Petrescu, Doina (ed.) (2007) *Altering Practices: Feminist Politics and Poetics of Space*, London: Routledge.

Raco, Mike (2014) 'Delivering flagship projects in an era of regulatory capitalism: state-led privatization and the London Olympics 2012', *International Journal of Urban and Regional Research* 38(1): 176–197.

Rifkin, Jeremy (2000) *The End of Work: The Decline of the Global Work-Force and the Dawn of the Post-Market Era*, London: Penguin.

Shove, Elizabeth, Pantzar, Mika and Watson, Matt (2012) *The Dynamics of Social Practice: Everyday Life and How It Changes*, London: Sage.

Swyngedouw, Erik (2013) *Designing the Post-Political City and the Insurgent Polis*, Civic City Cahier 5, ed. Jesko Fezer and Matthias Görlich, London: Bedford Press.

Vishmidt, Marina (2011) 'Human capital or toxic asset: after the wage', *Mute* 10, January. Available at: www.metamute.org/community/your-posts/human-capital-or-toxic-asset-after-wage (accessed 14 August 2015).

Weeks, Kathi (2011) *The Problem with Work: Feminism, Marxism, Antiwork Politics, and Postwork Imaginaries*, Durham, NC: Duke University Press.

ds at the Women's Centre (2005)

妇女的动力 (2010)   In Our Own Voices (2

Housing Now (2010)   N

Pow Wow (2005)

o Racism (19   askí   nited We Stand

989)   our Ground (1990)   Always Pl

Winter (1990)

sis in the   985)

for the Fam   pport One

2 – NOTES ON SOCIAL PRODUCTION: A BRIEF COMMENTARY

Tatjana Schneider

In recent times, particularly since the economic crisis in 2008/9, the notion of social production has gained much prominence, and was proposed by the Palo Alto-based Institute for the Future, an independent non-profit research group, as one of the key themes over the next ten years. Social production, the Institute proclaims, is beginning to define a form of production that 'draws on contributions from large networks of people, enabled by social technologies, to create new kinds of wealth' (Davies, 2011). It is argued that things that are socially produced are not only made by many, but also benefit many. In doing so, it sometimes explicitly, sometimes implicitly, challenges unequal distributions of power and often sits in opposition to hierarchical forms of organisations or capitalist forms of production.

It is not just think tanks, organisations, such as the one cited above, and academic writers that keep coming back to this term, more and more practices with backgrounds ranging from art, architecture and urban planning to human geography are working on projects that focus on common making, the fostering of cultural and social networks, the creation of new kinds of public spaces, and the implementation of frameworks and strategies that allow for more equitable access to resources. The predominant economic model and associated modes of making, which focus on the accumulation of capital rather than the welfare of the wider society, are regarded as inflexible, unjust, and therefore unable to deliver responses to urgent societal issues such as affordable housing, ecological approaches to building or, indeed, social justice. A new way of making (one that is focused on notions of communality, cooperation, making things together, and is located outside of the fixed structures of bureaucracy, policy and an economy focused on benefiting the few rather than the many) is emerging and is seen as a remedy that will take back the city from the grip of neoliberalism. To use the term 'social production' has become, if not necessarily a call for change, then at least an acknowledgement of the perceived necessity of moving away from current predominant modes of production and exchange, towards *something else* which takes account of – in very broad terms – 'society' or 'the social'.

There is a tendency, however, not only to use it uncritically but also to romanticise the term. Against this tendency, this chapter calls for a closer reading of the term 'social production' and argues that its current application, in particular with regards to architecture, needs to take into account not only how one produces but also how the resulting products – things, buildings or spaces – are then distributed and consumed.[1] It introduces Marxist definitions of social production, through the work of German-born political theorist, Friedrich Engels, and the writings of the French philosopher, social theorist and activist, Henri Lefebvre, to explore this field in relation to the production of space, or, more specifically, architecture.

ENGELS: FROM SOCIAL PRODUCTION TO THE SOCIAL APPROPRIATION OF PRODUCTION

Friedrich Engels was a German-born political theorist and collaborator with Karl Marx who published extensively on the production of the political economy and the conditions of the working classes. In the late 1870s, he wrote a series of papers entitled *Socialism: Utopian and Scientific* (translated into English in 1892), in which he outlined the changes occurring in modes of production during the Industrial Revolution in England. He describes how, during this period, which marks the beginning of modern capitalism, the mode of production changed from one that was based on individual production by individual workers to social production. Engels uses the term 'social production', however, in a particular way. Social for him refers to a form of production that is 'only workable by a collectivity of men' (Engels, 1892: 308). He writes:

> *The spinning wheel, the handloom, the blacksmith's hammer, were replaced by the spinning-machine, the power-loom, the steam-hammer; the individual workshop, by the factory implying the co-operation of hundreds and thousands of workmen. In like manner, production itself changed from a series of individual into a series of social acts, and the production from individual to social products. The yarn, the cloth, the metal articles that now come out of the factory were the joint product of many workers, through whose hands they had successively to pass before they were ready.* (Ibid.: 308)

---

1   This chapter draws on ideas that developed from the collaborative research project, Alternative Architectural Praxis/Spatial Agency, which involved a large number of groups and practices that were and are practising 'otherwise' – taking into account not only production, but also use. In attempting to construct an alternative history of modes of operating, the project also aimed to valorise them, as collective and ethical forms of production.

What was new in this form of production, which developed from the middle of the eighteenth century onwards, was that factory goods could be made and sold more cheaply than individually produced goods. In principle, this system, whereby goods are produced collectively, was 'introduced as a means of increasing and developing the production of commodities' (ibid.: 309). On the one hand, capitalists increasingly controlled the means of production (the factories) as well as the produced commodities. On the other hand, however, the labourer or worker was reduced to a mere wageworker and therefore completely disassociated from the product or part of the product they helped to produce. In this process, the producers lose, as Engels writes, 'control over their own social inter-relations'. For Engels, this disassociation is the key problematic in the capitalistic appropriation of production. Seeking solutions to the workers' loss of control over the produced commodities, he calls for the 'practical recognition of the social nature of the modern forces of production, and therefore in the harmonising of the modes of production, appropriation, and exchange with the socialised character of the means of production' (ibid.: 319). While some of his contemporaries see these capitalist forces if not countered, then at least balanced, by the transformation of the forces of production into other forms of organisations, such as trusts or joint-stock companies, for Engels, this does not present a resolution to the fundamentally changed relationships between the producer and the product. Instead, Engels calls for a much more radical approach. He argues that social forces need to be mastered and production socially regulated 'upon a definite plan, according to the needs of the community and of each individual' (ibid.: 309). Instead of a capitalistic appropriation of production, Engels demands its social appropriation, whereby the socialised means of production are transformed into public property. This, in turn, does away with production being dominated by capital accumulation and instead focuses on the 'public' good – an act, which Engels calls 'universal emancipation' (ibid.: 325).

LEFEBVRE: THE SPACE OF THE ARCHITECT VERSUS THE SOCIAL PRODUCTION OF SPACE

Henri Lefebvre, French Marxist sociologist, philosopher and activist, revolutionised not only understandings of 'production' but more importantly of 'space'. His seminal book *The Production of Space*, first published in French in 1974 is, as Adrian Forty argues, the 'most comprehensive and radical critique of "space" [that] calls into question almost everything about space within architecture' (Forty,

2000: 256). Lefebvre's work has been extremely popular in recent architectural discourse and this particular book, though written and published more than 40 years ago, has become a seemingly unavoidable reference for those interested in something that has been called socially aware architecture.

This socially aware way of practising is often portrayed as in opposition to that of a range of architects whose work is more interested in formal and tectonic gestures rather than the consequences of a spatial intervention, or indeed their potential to address the urgent challenges of our time. Despite increasingly scathing criticisms, form is still the single most celebrated feature of the architectural discipline (Buchanan, 2015). Lefebvre provides, if not the earliest, then at least one of the most dismissive attacks on the figure and space of the architect. He writes:

> As for the eye of the architect, it is no more innocent than the lot he is given to build on or the blank sheet of paper on which he makes his first sketch. His 'subjective' space is freighted with all-too-objective meanings. It is a visual space, a space reduced to blueprints, to mere images – to that 'world of the image' which is the enemy of the imagination … The tendency to make reductions of this kind – reductions to parcels, to images, to facades that are made to be seen and to be seen from (thus reinforcing 'pure' visual space) – is a tendency that degrades space. (Lefebvre, 1991: 361)

The production of forms as 'images' still tends to be an accepted focus in both the education of architects as much as in architectural practice itself. The reduction of the production of space to the production of images, however, is limiting in many ways. It is an abstraction that puts emphasis on the exchange value and thereby fails to take notice of the use value of spaces and buildings. And, yet, none of this happens accidentally. Lefebvre argues that there is always intent when it comes to the production of space. Space is never something that simply comes into being and then goes on to exist, but *it is produced and reproduced through human – or social – interaction*; and, further, whether it is large infrastructural projects such as airports, motorways or dams, or, indeed, small-scale buildings such as houses or pavilions, each project will privilege some activities and social relations and inhibit others. At the same time, he argues, that the interests of those who commission, inhabit or use these spaces and structures also shape them. The much-criticised landscape of buildings and spaces we find ourselves in, especially in the growing bulk of 'global cities', dominated by speculatively built office and housing blocks, is an expression of these forces which limit action and agency through an effective privatisation of urban space.

It is in *The Production of Space* where Lefebvre makes this much quoted, and memorable suggestion: '(social) space is a (social) product' (ibid.: 26), and with this, delivers the ammunition for a new generation of architects, designers and planners who are keen to stress the interrelationship between people and space. Or, in other words: buildings only begin to make sense when considered through, and in, 'use'. Placing emphasis on this, or, saying that architecture is not just about the object beautiful (or the object that carries exchange value) but about the broader (social) context within which it is produced suggests to this new breed of socially aware architects that there is hope, yet again, for *growing* spaces that not only are made socially, but continue to foster social relationships (which might then be reproduced and potentially multiplied). While this might seem almost too obvious a statement to make, under-standing buildings socially creates a powerful tool for analysis. It begins to question the access to and rights within spaces, and at the same time provides the base from which to analyse and critique existing constructions of space, as well as propose alternative interventions. Focusing on the social in the production of space moves attention away from the purely visual analysis of space and allows questions about ownership, management, governance and maintenance as well as politics.

SOCIAL PRODUCTION: A NEW MODEL OF SPATIAL PRODUCTION?

A note of caution at the end. I am not proposing to take Lefebvre's or Engels' writings as conceptions to be used to understand, describe or 'solve' the complexities of the production of space as it unfolds today. Although I use their words, I am all too conscious of their context: they were written in different historical, geographical and personal circumstances. Still, I use their work to push forward my own argument and, indeed, ideological position and I believe that within the limited scope of this commentary, some general observations can be made. These could be framed as sketchy pointers towards a more critical reading, not only of what it means to produce space socially, but how it can be intentionally produced as such.

One of the lessons from Lefebvre's work lies in the introduction, acknowledgement and valuing of the 'soft' aspects of a city which rejects the 'physicalist fallacy of architecture' (Gottdiener, 1985: xv): space is not just purely visual or abstract, but concerns the lives of people and is made and re made through their experiences. The social and the spatial are inextricably intermingled and cannot be separated. When most architects and planners believed and continue to believe in form as the main means of expression, the notion of social production suggests that both the spatial and the social need to be considered in tandem. Or, as Mark Gottdiener writes, 'Every intervention in the service of social liberation must produce its own space in order to succeed. Social relations that improve life must take on material form through the social production of space' (ibid.: xiv).

It is in this context that Engels' explanation of the origins of the notion of social production, as a description of the relationship between social relations and working method, provides suggestions as to a meaningful and transformative contemporary use of social production. If, as Lefebvre argues, spatial design has to be considered as one aspect of the productive forces of society (1991: 123–124), then this productive force of 'intervening' can be used for change. When it comes to the question of how to intervene, Engels' call for the necessity of social appropriation could and should play a crucial role, not least because it gives concrete suggestions as to how it can be conceptualised and realised. Further, social appropriation clearly also talks about the agency of (social) producers on a collective scale. And, arguably, *it is only the notion of social appropriation through its outlining of value systems which begins to define the space that is being made through social production*: namely, one that is about collective effort and cooperation, which at the same time leads to shared benefits. In this sense, social production begins to refer to a type of production in, or through which the producers of a product or space, govern both the product or space and the means of its production.

REFERENCES

Buchanan, Peter (2015) 'Empty gestures', *The Architectural Review* March: 30–35.

Davies, Anna (2011) 'Future now', Institute for the Future, 13 April. Available at: www.iftf. org/future-now/article-detail/ exploring-social-production-in-education/

Engels, Friedrich (1892) *Socialism: Utopian and Scientific*, London: Swan Sonnenschein & Co.

Forty, Adrian (2000) *Words and Buildings: A Vocabulary of Modern Architecture*, London: Thames & Hudson.

Gottdiener, Mark (1985) *The Social Production of Urban Space*, Austin, TX: University of Texas Press.

Lefebvre, Henri (1991) *The Production of Space*, Oxford: Blackwell.

3 – MAKING PLACES, BUILDING COMMUNITIES, EMPOWERING CITIZENS: PARTICIPATORY SLUM UPGRADING IN THAILAND

Supreeya Wungpatcharapon

For a long time, spatial production in Thailand has been dominated by the powerful: the Thai state is allied with the network of elites, technocrats, businesses and the military, who have played a major role in the development of the country.[1] Most ordinary people have had limited access to, or control over, political power and resources. The Thai state has long operated under hierarchical administrative structures and bureaucratic systems. The conventional top-down processes, driven by capitalist interests and dominated by their vision and prospects, have dramatically transformed urban spaces in recent decades. However, these processes make a profit for the few and tend to marginalise people, notably impoverished groups. The processes undervalue the 'lived spaces' of ordinary people, which are treated as a commodity potential to be realised.

Thailand's uneven development has also resulted in mass rural-to-urban migration and, consequently, the lack of affordable housing in urban areas has left many Thais living in congested settlements with poor services and insecure tenure. Those informal settlements have been struggling to defend their presence in society and claim their 'right to the city', as Henri Lefebvre put it (1996). For Lefebvre, the right to the city is a principal right for inhabitants, permitting them to make decisions about the production and design of urban space. Lefebvre maintains that the production of urban space should be restructured, by fundamentally shifting the control of decision-making to all urban inhabitants, and it should not be limited only to the state's decisions. He points out two principal rights for inhabitants, namely, the right to participation and the right to appropriation. The right to participation maintains that inhabitants should play a central role in any decision that contributes to the development

---

1   This chapter was written while Thailand was being ruled by the military junta, which toppled the elected government in a military coup d'état on 22 May 2014, and, as yet, there has been no sign of a democratic election.

of urban space in their city. The right to appropriation is not only the right of the inhabitants to access, occupy and use the urban space physically, but is also the right to produce urban space to meet their needs and desires. While Lefebvre insisted on the right of individuals to participate and appropriate the social space they occupy, David Harvey asserts that claiming the right to the making of cities should operate mutually and requires a democratic process. Harvey notes:

> *The question of what kind of city we want cannot be divorced from that of what kind of social ties, relationship to nature, lifestyles, technologies and aesthetic values we desire. The right to the city is far more than the individual liberty to access urban resources: it is a right to change ourselves by changing the city. It is, moreover, a common rather than an individual right since this transformation inevitably depends upon the exercise of a collective power to reshape the processes of urbanization.*
> (2008: 23)

It was estimated that approximately 11.5 per cent of the urban population in Thailand, or some 750,000 households, are under immediate threat of eviction (Boonyabancha, 2013). The Thai government has developed several strategies to cope with slums, such as providing medium-rise accommodation, relocating people to the urban fringes or, in the worst case, when negotiation fails, forcibly evicting the poor who illegally occupy the urban areas under insecure tenure. However, these programmes cannot deal with the increasing number of poor communities in the country, while the government cannot afford to cover all the costs and supply all the resources. More importantly, the poor have never exercised their right to participation, leading to the failure of these solutions.

This chapter, through a discussion of the Baan Mankong slum upgrading programme and the example of the Bang-Bua canal community network in Bangkok, therefore, argues that people's participation in the production of place is a social and political process. It has not only physically transformed the locale, but also has socially reproduced the 'community' and politically empowered the citizens to exercise their mutual 'right to the city'. The practices of this programme nationwide also are an influence on the Thai architectural discourse itself to be more socially relevant.

PARTICIPATORY SLUM UPGRADING PROGRAMME AS A SOCIAL PRODUCTION OF ARCHITECTURE

A recent slum upgrading programme, *Baan Mankong* (Secure Housing), implemented by the Community Organizations Development Institute (CODI), Thailand,[2] in 2003, differs from conventional approaches. It employs participation as a tool and uses local people as the main subject of change. The community organisations and their networks are the key actors who control funding and management. The government subsidises the infrastructure and gives housing loans to the community cooperative, while the people use their household savings as collateral to access loans collectively. Flexible finance is provided, allowing community organisations and local partnerships to plan, implement and directly manage the priorities and possibilities, tailored to suit each community's needs (Boonyabancha, 2005). Upgrading can take many forms, either minor improvements, the reconstruction of houses, or relocation to nearby land. The solution is based on the mutual agreement of everyone involved. According to CODI, in the past ten years of operation, the Baan Mankong programme has reached out to 1,637 communities, in 286 towns and cities, in 71 provinces, providing legal entitlement and secure housing to 93,100 households.

The participatory process of housing design and community planning is crucial to any Baan Mankong projects. The architects need to engage with local inhabitants in order to understand their needs, concerns, tacit knowledge and inherent capacities, since genuine participation demands two-way communication between the architect and the users. The instruments and means of communication with individuals, who are neither designers nor professionals, are designed by the architects in order to enable the inhabitants to play an active role. They visualise alternative possibilities and share the power of decision-making by facilitating dialogues, creating mutual interventions, and acting together during the process of design and planning for each community. Participatory tools and techniques, such as drawing and modelling a dream house by the people, co-mapping the existing community layout, GIS training, participatory community planning, or building 1:1 housing prototypes, were selectively employed,

---

2   The Community Organizations Development Institute (CODI), Thailand, is an independent public organisation developing more participatory models of support for low-income groups, through supporting community-based savings and credit groups, covering 30,000 rural and urban community organisations.

depending on what the architects deemed appropriate for the condition and the size of the community in which they were engaged, or the specific information they needed (Figure 3.1). Those techniques enhance the skills of the communities to become 'para-architects' and 'para-professionals', who can continue the design, planning and other technical work, such as surveying and mapping, by themselves when the architects are absent (Luansang *et al.*, 2012: 501).

Figure 3.1 Participatory mapping and modelling of houses were used as a tool for dialogue among groups of households and the architect during the process. Photos taken 2015.
Photos: Mek Sayasevi, taken at Sapan-Mai II community, a recent community joining the network of Bang-Bua canal

For the Bang-Bua community, participatory activities were found to be more effective when carried out in small groups of four or five households informally, formed according to the socio-spatial relations of the locals rather than organised via formal public events. The final design of the houses and the planning followed not only design principles or practicality, but also depended on how much every household could afford financially. The aesthetics and style of architecture are arguable and should not be romanticised, however. The architect cannot control everything and needs to let people make their own decisions. This participative process requires humility and can only succeed if based on systems of trust, and on people's ability to solve their own problems (Boonyabancha, 2011: 67).

Working in a participatory way with people is, however, unavoidably a conflictual process. In several of the Baan Mankong projects, tension and conflict between people arose due to the newly proposed spatial configurations, which might affect the environment in which people have been accustomed to living. They may be required to relinquish the plots they previously occupied to accommodate other houses, roads or communal spaces. At Bang-Bua, it took more than five years to complete the construction of two of the 12 communities, while others have not even started yet. The participatory process requires a huge investment in terms of time for negotiation at many levels and between several stakeholders. An understanding of the forces of conflict, and a shift towards more proactive, less conflictual models of engagement are necessary, as Miessen and Mouffe argue (2008: 179). The architect is thus unavoidably challenged, to change agonising conflicts into constructive possibilities.

FROM SOCIAL PRODUCTION TO SOCIAL TRANSFORMATION

Through the social process of designing houses and community planning with the Bang-Bua canal communities, various concerns were voiced by different groups of locals at their focus group meetings, including inadequate social welfare for the poor, household debts, and drugs. Those discussions revealed unseen agendas to everyone, including the architects, that were discussed mutually. A working group consisting of representatives from each household decided, therefore, to distribute their collective funds to support those marginalised groups as well as initiating working teams to organise activities for inhabitants of all ages. In each community, a *Baan-Klang* (central house), a welfare house accommodating the elders and disabled people, was also built with their collective savings. Additionally, various welfare schemes have been initiated by the locals, such as funds for births, marriages or funerals, and a scholarship for children. After the devastating mega-flood in Bangkok in 2011, the communities' network initiated the mutual disaster rehabilitation fund to support affected households. These types of social welfare are normally provided by the state, but fail to reach the poor due to their insecure tenure and illegal status in the city. This participatory slum upgrading programme has enabled the urban poor communities to improve their quality of life by themselves. Further, local initiatives for income generation have been launched in the Bang-Bua communities' network. Women's groups formed catering services, or sold handmade crafts. A group of local builders, who have relevant experience and skills, set up a collective enterprise called *Chang Chumchon* (community builders) as a community-based contractor that provides services to other poor communities to reduce the costs of reconstruction. Currently, a national network of *Chang Chumchon* has also been established. CODI consider these types of entrepreneurship to be a technical support mechanism for the upgrading process, as well as a job creation scheme in the form of collective enterprises.

Once the communities had successfully negotiated their secure tenures, the land and the newly constructed houses are then collectively owned and repaid over at least 15 years, according to the loans granted by CODI (Figure 3.2). A common rule is that, if anyone wants to sell their house, they must sell it to the community cooperative, not to outsiders. The condition of collective ownership and management has been shown to unite people. It has created social interactions and (re)invented the 'community' in which people negotiate their individual and mutual needs and values. They shared the risks and responsibilities due to their co-production of places. Those constant activities are crucial as they encourage people to embrace one another. If repeated performance is necessary to stabilise the effects of empowerment, as Kesby (2005) argues, then these incomplete activities of sharing matter. *Participatory practice aimed at genuinely empowering people needs a mechanism and condition that catalyses and encourages people to constantly share and act collectively so that empowerment can sustainably take effect.*

Figure 3.2 The Bang-Bua community network, comprised of 12 communities informally built along Bang-Bua canal. They joined the Baan Mankong upgrading programme in 2005 after coming under threat from a relocation plan. Since then, the old houses that previously encroached on the canal have been incrementally reconstructed with secure tenure. Photo taken 2015.
Photo: Supreeya Wungpatcharapon

BUILDING 'IMAGINING COMMUNITIES'

According to in-depth interviews with local members of the Bang-Bua community, previously, people had lived separately, *tang-kon-tang-yoo* (in Thai), and would only meet for traditional ceremonies or religious activities. The recent participatory projects, with their horizontal exchanges via various activities, have caused them to unite in order to think and act reciprocally, and become interdependent (*pueng-pa-ar-sai*). Their sense of 'community' has been strengthened through the social process of upgrading, not only within the community-bounded territory but also across administrative borders. The locals' attitudes have revealed their sympathetic consideration of the 'community' beyond their bounded lived spaces. They have begun searching for other urban poor communities located in their city, discussing their situation and concerns, and enabling them to access public services. These '(re)invented communities' are not bound to any particular type, or limited to a specific place, but are organised more like networks at various levels, through engagement in different activities at certain times. What the Bang-Bua community has shown is consistent with what Shigeharu Tanabe suggests; modern Thai communities, especially those that have struggled through particular crises, tend to reorganise themselves into networks, as 'a never unitary whole but rather the open-ended context of the community through which powers are not only constituted but also resisted and re-appropriated' (2008: 11). Further, they constitute power in what he calls 'imagining communities', 'a more active agency that imagines, creates, and reflects its own *sens pratique*, knowledge and desire, which in turn makes them more proactive than reactive, and become reflexive' (ibid.: 19).

NETWORKING AS A TOOL OF EMPOWERMENT

Although the poor can practise their collective power through forms of resistance, such as direct action and protests, these practices still focus on the 'power as things' perspective and eventually fail to shift the power relations and possibly avoid negotiating power. The people's participation in the Baan Mankong slum upgrading, in turn, has empowered them and restructured their power relations with others. The relationship between the actors gradually evolved through collective action at each step, resulting in an extensive formation of networks across various groups of actors at different levels.

Exchanges facilitated by visiting and hosting activities organised by the locals are another vital mechanism for gradually building networks. Being visited by groups from other places benefits both the visitors and the hosts alike. The visitors learnt by seeing and hearing, by sharing and exchanging their ideas, comments and experiences. They gained a comparative perspective of their own situation and, as Arjun Appadurai (2001) states, these activities, designed and organised by the poor, represent the locals' cosmopolitan links to public and local politicians, and act as a factor in increasing their credit in local political negotiations. The networks gave voices to, and empowered, ordinary people to negotiate with the governmental institutions in diverse aspects to claim their 'right to the city', for example, tackling the security of land tenures, building regulations revision, and infrastructure provision. As Knoke (1990) argues, the more the community can access other resourceful organisations through its multiple networks, the more it gains essential resources to achieve its political purpose. What is gained is not only the physical and social transformation of their locales, but more importantly, the political power of the people to determine their own lives and lived spaces. Their capacity and collective power are acknowledged by the government authorities. Further, once the people have proved their capability to manage themselves, they are legitimately entitled to access other support from the authorities, such as social welfare, job opportunities, and financial support from various organisations. These benefits demonstrate empowerment to the people, whereas in the past, the local people were patronised by the authorities. It is as Kesby states: 'Empowerment can never be delivered: outsiders can only facilitate insiders' struggle to "take" or "achieve" it for themselves' (2005: 2051).

It should also be noted that a relationship between the community and its networks had existed before the architect's intervention and could have been an obstacle to or enrichment of the participatory design, depending on how the architect approached it. The connections between the actors in these networks are, to some extent, powerful and can influence the process and the end results. In this mode of practice, the architects need to critically engage with others, and must mediate and operate tactically within the network of actors in order to uncover any possibilities beneficial to the interventions.

PARTICIPATORY SLUM UPGRADING AS A POLITICAL PRACTICE

In contrast to conventional spatial production in Thailand, which is inherently political and exercised by the powerful, participatory slum upgrading is considered a political practice by ordinary citizens at the local level. The actions taken by the locals, together with other actors, especially architects, NGOs and academics, have shown the transformative capacity of the people, as well as achieving their recognition and acceptance by the powerful. Oakley (1991) explains that an obstacle to participation is related to the social aspect, identified as 'a mentality of dependence' that has its roots in peoples' lives. It is relevant to the Thai social structure, whereby the poor have been dominated by the government, especially the bureaucrats, and dependent upon the powerful, such as local politicians, and their patronage, for generations. Satterthwaite and Mitlin (2014) criticised such clientelism, arguing that a patron–client network, linking the people to more powerful social groups, functions as an exchange of partial services for votes and other manifestations of political support, and actually maintains the powerlessness and disadvantages of the poor, who lack opportunities and experiences to initiate or manage projects by themselves. However, the interviews with the main local leaders have shown that participating in the nationwide programme of Baan Mankong has enabled them to become more political and self-determined. They have mutually exercised their right to participate in the making of their locales and have appropriated their living conditions. The people no longer want to be patronised by the local government or relevant institutions and demand to be seen by them as their main resources and partners, rather than their inferiors. As some locals put it:

> We need to engage people in making decisions and let them lead, not the local government. If every community works in this way, Thailand will be better.
>
> With other authorities, we need to act and prove that we can be self-managed. We are not going to be the recipient waiting for others to help us any more. We need to be active. Then we'll gain acceptance from others. The authorities should just support us, not work for us. It's important for the community to take the vital role. Waiting for help from the authorities wastes time and we would be obstructed by the rules and difficulties of the system.

These views are very different from the typical Thai belief in acceptance of the hierarchical social structure and continuing political silence. As Sattayanurak stresses:

> The traditional Thai concept of 'high social spaces' and 'low social spaces', indicates the hierarchical social structure as good and proper since it results in 'order', 'stability' and 'peace'. This also made Thais ignorant of social injustices that exist in almost every dimension of society ... Consequently, Thais typically remain 'politically silent' and ignore political movements that demand individual rights, community rights or ways to supervise the government.
> (2005: 61)

Being organised and engaging in a participatory process have progressively transformed those passive inhabitants into active citizens. That is because participation has brought about tangible changes for the inhabitants, while other methods, such as protests and direct action, only keep people hoping and waiting for decisions made by others to deliver services to them. Their perceptions reveal the decline of 'clientelist' political relations.

The social and political processes that triggered and promoted democratic values and actions are not only embedded at the local level, but have also built up other trans-local networks of coalitions (Figure 3.3). Through a decade of 'learning by doing', the poor communities' network founded a national alliance called NULICO (National Union of Low-Income Community Organisations) in 2006, to work towards improving the living conditions of the poor in Thailand and tackle urgent agendas related to land acquisition, housing improvement, accessing state welfare, facilitating community mobilisation and capacity building programmes. Recently, NULICO has successfully negotiated for the revision of building regulations of low-income housing. They also formed a collective financial mechanism called Community Development Funds (CDFs), by pooling together various smaller funds and savings groups from communities in each city. CDFs started at the city level and have expanded across the country, now covering 31 cities in Thailand (with 91,758 members from 1,500 saving groups), which have accumulated US$1,674,056 in savings (Archer, 2012). The CDFs allow lending and the giving of grants for different purposes. In some cases, CDFs act as a bridging fund, providing housing loans while waiting for larger-scale Baan Mankong funding from CODI. The city committee, comprised of representatives

from community networks, city officials and other partners, was established to manage and decide how to use these funds. According to
Archer (2012), CDFs, as financial networks, create multi-dimensional
links; horizontally ranging between savings groups in a city, between
different cities in a country or internationally; and vertically between
poor communities, local and national governments, as in the case
of the National Disaster Fund, which was established following the
devastating floods of 2011, Thai communities received contributions
from communities in Mongolia and Vietnam (Figure 3.3).

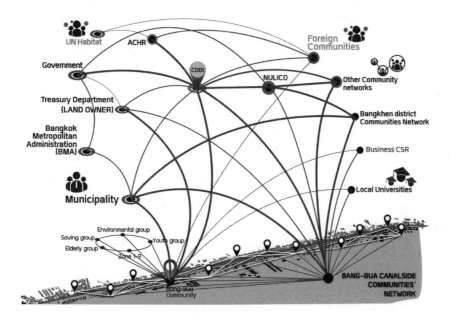

Figure 3.3 Extensive development of the networks of the Bang-Bua through the participatory process

These recent movements showing that people can act interde-
pendently across social networks and extend beyond their administrative boundaries and private lives are consistent with what the
political scientist, Iris Marion Young, has termed 'relational autonomy'.
She notes:

> In so far as their activities affect one another, peoples are in
> relationship and ought to negotiate the terms and effects of the re-
> lationship. When self-determining peoples understand themselves
> as constituted in relation to one another, they recognise that there
> are many respects in which they live and act together with others.
> (2000: 259)

Their efforts and achievement further constitute what Arjun Appadurai has defined as 'democracy without borders', attempts that value the increased capacity of the emerging networks of communities in partnership with powerful agencies. This enables them to perform more effectively as instruments of democracy in the local context. As Appadurai stresses: 'With internal critics and debate, horizontal exchange and learning, and vertical collaborations and partnerships with more powerful persons and organisations together form a mutual sustaining cycle of processes' (2001: 42–43).

EXPANDING ARCHITECTURAL PRACTICES IN THAILAND

Certain renowned professionals and scholars have pointed out that Thai architectural practice has long been attached to real estate development, which led to the crisis in the profession after the economic collapse of 1997 (Tipatas, 2010). They urge Thai architectural practice to redefine the knowledge of 'architecture', by expanding its definition and responsibility beyond the economic-oriented approach to become more socially relevant. According to these scholars, the roles and status quo of architects in Thai society should change so that the architectural profession will survive, despite the crises they may face. However, architects have rarely practised this recommendation. Some may have only tried on a voluntary basis or pro bono projects, not as a professional. The recent Baan Mankong slum upgrading programme, however, has significantly promoted socially engaged design approaches and simultaneously trained participatory designers through its nationwide projects. The initial stage of Baan Mankong needed architects to assist its process in terms of physical transformation and technical support. Since 2003, CODI, therefore, has collaborated with various schools of architecture and private architectural firms to work with local people, as the few CODI in-house architects could not cope with the demands of slum communities nationwide. Since then, participatory design with the local people has been practised through Baan Mankong's pilot projects and has attracted architects to partake in this socially engaged design approach. CODI currently houses 25 architects and engineers in its office.

A few architectural studios, especially young professionals who are interested in participatory design, have been founded. Community Architects for Shelter and Environment (CASE) studio was the pioneer in co-designing with informal communities. The other self-trained architects, through the participatory process of Baan Mankong projects, have recently widened their interest beyond low-income housing, but still are practising participation as the main strategy to enable people to co-produce their lived spaces and built environment. For example, *Kon-Jai-Baan*, a practice based in northern Thailand, has worked with local people and the municipality to develop a sustainable livelihood master plan for the *Mae-Tha* subdistrict in Chiang Mai Province, as a pilot project for the sustainable rural development programme in collaboration with CODI. Openspace studio and its recent practice *Tar-Saeng* Company, in Bangkok, have focused on 'differently-abled design', to co-produce and reappropriate lived spaces with disabled people in remote areas of Thailand. The *Arsomsilp* Institute, based in Bangkok, is the first private school running an undergraduate architectural programme and a graduate programme on participatory design and community development in Thailand, and supports various projects related to participatory heritage conservation by local people.

These practices, to name a few, are examples of professionals who acknowledge the role of architects beyond design. They are extending the practice of architecture to serve the 'majority others', who although they cannot afford the design fee, still deserve the right to appropriate their everyday lived spaces towards their own well-being. Though small in numbers, these emerging practices have collectively formed the Community Act Network (CAN),[3] a platform to promote socially engaged design practices and demonstrate that this approach can be a rewarding profession for architects, not as a pro bono service (Figure 3.4). The dissemination of participatory practices, skills, principles and values of this 'spatial agency'[4] to the wider public and especially to mainstream architectural practices and education, may incrementally enable the architectural practices in Thailand to become more inclusive, moving towards a more ethical and democratic production of space and architecture with the local people.

---

3   CAN, Thailand, was informally formed in 2010 as a part of the Community Architects Movement in Asia (more details at www.communityarchitectsnetwork.info). It is now integrated as a member of the Association of Siamese Architects (ASA) and works extensively to promote socially engaged design approach through activities, such as the annual exhibition and seminars, student workshops and actual projects in collaboration with diverse actors.

4   Spatial Agency is a term I borrow from Awan, Schneider and Till, who define the spatial agent as 'one who effects change through the empowerment of others, allowing them to engage in their spatial environments in ways previously unknown or unavailable to them, opening up new freedoms and potentials as a result of reconfigured social space' (2011: 32).

Figure 3.4 The CAN exhibition in ASA'2014 Expo, Bangkok, showing projects from the network and the students' workshop for the participatory design of a community centre and a playground, with Klong Takok Baan Mankong community in Central Thailand. Photos taken 2014.
Photos: Supreeya Wungpatcharapon

The participatory approach of the Baan Mankong programme significantly demonstrates that poor people's involvement in design and decision-making not only has changed their place, but also has transformed their social relations, by reinventing their sense of 'being in common', reshaping how they mutually live, manage their own affairs, and financially maintain their locales collectively. People who have been empowered to become self-determined citizens have, moreover, consistently built their political power across administrative borders. Working with multiple stakeholders, they are enabled to negotiate, mutually, their right to inhabit and appropriate their locales and city, with the democratic process being led from below.

REFERENCES

Appadurai, Arjun (2001) 'Deep democracy: urban governmentality and the horizon of politics', *Environment & Urbanization* 13(2): 23–44.

Archer, Diane (2012) 'Finance as the key to unlocking community potential: savings, funds and the ACCA programme', *Environment & Urbanization* 24(2): 423–440.

Awan, Nishat, Schneider, Tatjana and Till, Jeremy (2011) *Spatial Agency: Other Ways of Doing Architecture*, London: Routledge.

Boonyabancha, Somsook (2005) 'Baan Mankong: going to scale with "slum" and squatter upgrading in Thailand', *Environment & Urbanization* 17(1): 21–46.
　(2011) 'Trusting that people can do it', in Cynthia E. Smith *et al.* (eds) *Design with the Other 90%: Cities*, New York: Cooper-Hewitt, National Design Museum Smithsonian Institution, pp. 61–71.
　(2013) 'Housing inequity', in Aphiwat Ratanawaraha (ed.) *Inequity and Injustice in Accessing Resources and Basic Services in Thailand*, Bangkok: Chulalongkorn University, pp. 131–149.
Harvey, David (2008) 'The right to the city', *New Left Review* 53: 23–40.

Kesby, Mike (2005) 'Retheorizing empowerment-through-participation as a performance in space: beyond tyranny to transformation', *Signs: Journal of Women in Culture and Society*, 30(4): 2037–2067.

Knoke, David (1990) *Political Networks*, Cambridge: Cambridge University Press.

Lefebvre, Henry (1996) *Writings on Cities*, Oxford: Blackwell.

Luansang, Chawanad, Boonmahathanakorn, Supawut and Domingo-Price, Lourdes Maria (2012) 'The role of community architects in upgrading; reflecting on the experience in Asia', *Environment & Urbanization* 24(2): 497–512.

Miessen, Markus and Mouffe, Chantal (2008) 'Violating consensus', in ACTAR (ed.) *Verb Crisis*, Barcelona: ACTAR, pp. 168–180.

Oakley, Peter (1991) *Understanding Participation*, Geneva: ILO, pp. 1–24.

Sattayanurak, Saichon (2005) 'The construction of mainstream thought on "Thainess" and the "truth" constructed by "Thainess"', *Fah Deaw Kan*, 3(4): 40–67.

Satterthwaite, David and Mitlin, Diana (2014) *Reducing Urban Poverty in the Global South*, London: Routledge.

Tanabe, Shigeharu (ed.) (2008) *Imagining Communities in Thailand: Ethnographic Approaches*, Chiang Mai: Mekong Press.

Tipatas, Pusadee (ed.) (2010) *Architecture after 2540: Crisis and Alternative Approach for Thai Architects*, Bangkok: ASA Publishing.

Young, Iris Marion (2000) *Inclusion and Democracy*, Oxford: Oxford University Press.

4 – OUT IN PRISON: TAKING THE CASE OF SPATIAL RIGHTS TO A PRISON COURT(YARD)

Gabu Heindl

> *In the end everything in politics turns on the distribution of spaces. What are these places? How do they function? Why are they there? Who can occupy them? For me, political action always acts upon the social as the litigious distribution of places and roles. It is always a matter of knowing who is qualified to say what a particular place is and what is done to it.*
> (Rancière, 2003: 201)

SPATIAL RIGHTS

We could go along with Robert Gutman (1992) and say that architecture's 'natural market' is monuments, to serve the elite and powerful. But we could also claim a right to (another) architecture for everybody; architecture, understood as a social practice towards a more just distribution of spaces. With regard to Lefebvre's concept of the 'right to the city', as a right of those who suffer from how existing cities are organized and regulated, the right to architecture I have in mind here is not so much a right to just any kind of architecture, but to one that is not part of a repressive regulatory order. As a right for everybody, it is first and foremost the claim of those who suffer from architecture being in service to capitalist spatial production. With regard to the qualities of the city, such as centrality, anonymity or openness to chance, we should put forward the question about the qualities of architecture, not as a minimum but as a maximum to be achieved, or about a minimum of repression that architecture could aim for. This more just distribution of spaces is based on concepts of social justice, as found in the work of Harvey and of spatial justice, as in the work of Soja or Fainstein. I regard justice neither as 'foundation-al' nor as consensual, but as something to be disputed, an impulse for dissensus and as a strategic term to test decisions and contest injustices (for instance, to involve justice as a planning concern that responds to the current austerity politics). If dissensus or conflict is the basis for the production of democratic spaces, situations and subjectivities (Rancière, 1999), this also involves understanding one's own critical architectural practice to be without fixed foundations and thus as a matter of self-reflection and self-criticality.

The discipline of architecture is one agent in the production of social space (understood as being necessarily politicized): it is an active part of the process of the contested 'distribution of the sensible' (Rancière, 2004). This means that architecture can also become active for the sake of an increase in spatial justice. Yet, first of all, there is the general knowledge that not only architecture, but all art, is entangled with hegemonic powers, which, when it comes to architecture, are often quite visible. On the one hand, architecture is based on hegemonic power: after all, building activity is usually dependent on the accessibility (ownership) to the ground (site), on large budgets, on building rights, or when it comes to public buildings, on a public need. On the other hand, architecture also helps to 'build' hegemonic power by the creation of the everyday built environment to which people (must) get accustomed. The critique of the modernist understanding of architecture as a service to the engineering of society culminates with the understanding of how every 'humanitarian' improvement seems to serve the continuation of the (sometimes inhuman) condition it works on.

As a practising architect, I will use one of my own projects to analyse the complexity and conflictual dimensions and dilemmas of spatial interventions and try to make a claim for action as a kind of exercise in 'minimal politics' (Marchart, 2010: 289–301). By minimal politics, I understand a kind of politics that, while neither 'minoritarian' nor 'reformist' in its intention, acknowledges the potentials inherent in whatever small and transitory moments of contestation of an unjust order. I work with a 'minimal politics' rather than the 'maximalist' and purist claims that politics has to be an all-changing event or heroic act. Or, at least, I claim to act critically, as critically as possible, within architecture.

SPACE – MORE THAN A MINIMUM

The project is located in a prison, the kind of space, which, for Michel Foucault, was the paradigmatic space of disciplinary social power relations and acted as a model for other similarly structured public institutions, such as hospitals, schools or universities. Foucault's historic analysis of the prison showed it to be a model of disciplinary power and part of a larger 'carceral system' (1995: 293–308). The ongoing investigation, 'Million Dollar Blocks', by architect and university teacher Laura Kurgan and her students aims to identify and make visible the contemporary carceral system in the USA. The project maps the role of prisons in wealth (re)distribution: the (non)investment of public money in the infrastructure of specific neighbourhoods and overlays it with the number of inmates in the same neighbourhoods and, consequently, the public money invested in their imprisonment (Kurgan, 2013: 187–205). These maps make obvious how the site of the prison is chosen for the 'policing' of people, in the expanded, Foucault-derived sense of Rancière: attributing a specific place to specific people, often with racist and class-related motivations.

I want to further conceptualize the prison as maybe the most extreme public architecture in terms of its extreme form of seclusion. Everything is walled in, hidden away and yet everybody has an image of what a prison is, what it looks like, about the minimum amount of private space attributed to prisoners. As a 'public space', it is the object and the subject of conflict at the same time. It is central to a field of very different questions, ranging from whether there is a need for more and/or different prison space, to how to achieve a world in which it would be possible to tear down all prisons and live in a prison-free society.

What becomes clear here, is that when it comes to spatial production, the larger context and the temporal dimension of the process are not to be ignored. One of these neglected issues is the question of when and where the public conception of a prison begins. Prison buildings are part of the jurisdictional system and penal law.[1] Whenever it is public money being invested, the process of finding a plan/a planner has to relate to the respective regulations (in our case, European) on the award of contracts, which often means a process using an anonymous design competition. As with school construction, the brief for a new prison is usually written by the respective ministry together with the specific prison direction. In this brief, the spatial programme is described, such as the minimum spatial requirement of the prison cells. There is an interesting analogy to this cell size: it corresponds roughly to the size of the Frankfurt kitchen as defined by Margarete Schütte-Lihotzky in 1926 (Noever,1996). As is well known, Schütte-Lihotzky used scientific motion studies to investigate the pos-sibilities of an extreme reduction of the movements necessary to cook in the optimized Frankfurt kitchen, of around 7 square metres in size.

---

1   In Austria, prisons are run by the Justice Ministry and the prison buildings are owned and maintained by the state-owned company, Bundesimmobiliengesellschaft (BIG).

However, these motion diagrams turn into cynical tools, when, as a thought experiment, they are mapped onto the layout of a prison cell. The space that in the one case is deliberately reduced to a minimum to avoid unnecessary movement, would be the only place for private movement in the other case, in the prison's restricted environment. Prisoners' spatial rights are to be defined in a way quite different from the needs of cooks. Imprisonment per se does not have its essence in the reduction of space to an absolute minimum – rather, this reduction is due to the quest for efficient management of imprisonment, of attributing as little space as necessary, with 'minimum costs' for the public (supposedly).

The prison space thus brings to the foreground the very basic need of a certain amount of space for everybody, such as the question of the minimum of private space, in which the dignity of the inmates is preserved. The production of space also contributes to creating levels of privacy; what about the privacy rights for prisoners? Isn't it a perfidious irony, that finally even in kindergarten design, privacy for small children became an issue when recently a 'safety' regulation was dropped? This regulation ordered that the doors to the children's toilets had to be so low, that grown-ups could look over them in case the children needed help. While in today's kindergartens, the restoration of children's 'toilet privacy' is seen to be a worthwhile aim (winning out over security aspects motivating permanent observability), in a prison, guards can still peek into the prisoner's private cell at any time through the door viewer.

A CASE STUDY AND ITS VOICELESS SUBJECTS

My case study takes us to a specific prison, to a spatial intervention called 'Out in Prison' (2010–2011) in the courtyard of the Austrian, provincial short-term prison in Krems. With this case study I hope to be able to present some of the many dilemmas one faces when acting under such conditions. This is where my point of view as an architect is most directly and intensely intermingled with questions of political theory, mentioned above. I was not asked to design the actual prison extension to the existing prison, a task I would have declined. As an architect also working in the field of site-specific art, I was invited to enter a 'Kunst am Bau' (art in architecture)[2] competition, which

2   The 'Kunst am Bau' programme is a commitment by the state to dedicate roughly 1 per cent of the construction costs of a public building to the commission of an art project – comparable to the Percent-for-Art policy.

often accompanies public construction in Austria. The invitation was to propose an independent art project in the existing prison. As the prison was built in the 1930s, it is protected as a heritage building, which allows no changes to its protected structure. The fact that the prison is located in the centre of a small town and that the site cannot be enlarged, means that with the construction of an extension automatically comes a further shrinkage of the outdoor space. On my first visit, the lack of outdoor space was evident at once: a small courtyard with an asphalt floor and little direct sunlight was used as the men's only yard (Figures 4.1 and 4.2).[3] As with other projects, I asked if we could talk to the users of the space, who in this case were the inmates, rather than only to the personnel working in the prison. However, due to security and anonymity reasons, we were only allowed to speak to some of the guards, who were instructed to answer our questions. The fact that this was a prison for short-term imprisonment (up to a maximum of 18 months) was also mentioned as the reason why we should not consider the inmates to be relevant users. Thus, our questions about the space were answered by the prison guards, in some way acting as representatives for the prisoners or, on a more paternalistic note, by guards representing the state, 'taking care' of things and people.

Figure 4.1 The prison yard, before the *Out in Prison* project
Photo: Gabu Heindl

---

3   The size of this specific prison yard is 190 m², roughly 10 by 20 metres, see Figure 4.2.

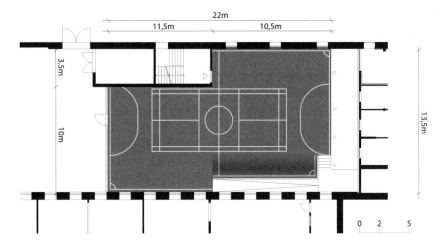

Figure 4.2 Dimensioned plan of the courtyard

When I asked where the inmates practise sports or play football, the guards told us that there is a general lack of interest in football; the prisoners would rather play with their PlayStations. After repeatedly asking, I found out that football was not allowed because people could get hurt too easily on the asphalt floor and the rough walls surrounding the courtyard; a situation difficult to handle within the safety procedures of a prison. The fact that nobody was playing because playing was forbidden was used as 'evidence' that there wasn't any interest in the first place. This occurrence became the basis for my proposal. What this instance further illustrates is the problem with context-sensitivity in architecture, especially when the respective context (let alone the larger context) is difficult to understand due to intimidating conditions or inaccessible information. Context-specific work can be awfully beside the point one wants to make. Does that mean one should ignore the context?

THE DILEMMAS OF 'CRITICAL' ACTION WITHIN A SPACE OF UNJUST PRECONDITIONS

To propose any art in architecture project 'freely' within this site was of course not free at all, as there were so many options that posed dilemmas where the stakes were very high (i.e. people's daily living conditions). To start with, the project could be a proposition connected to dignity, as mentioned above, a quasi-Rancièrian argument: to give autonomous art to those who are not expected to have any wish for it or understanding of it (Rancière, 1991). Why not bring to the prison an abstract painting, or something from within my own reference system as an artist/architect? Yet, wouldn't that lead us right into an aestheticist and elitist projection?

Shouldn't we rather look at needs in situ? Of which, of course, there is an endless number, if the place is compared to minimum standards of housing as defined in architecture, even when measured using the standards of low-cost housing or housing for the existential minimum.[4] Needless to say, it would be difficult to establish the needs of the prisoners. Would that not be a projection in the above sense, par excellence? As we know, choosing and assigning needs for somebody else, taking an elitist outside perspective is paternalistic (no matter if you decide that 'these people' require more high art or more simple entertainment). Of course, we could ask them, organize workshops and try to create good lines of communication, yet, at the same time, we would not have the means to turn the outcome of such a process into anything close to reality. That means that any 'participatory' approach would risk ending up a mockery, presenting inmates with all-too-meagre outcomes of a discussion project they were invited (or made) to engage in.

A 'simpler' approach, one of well-intended beautification of the existing spatial situation would, however, almost necessarily act as a mere cover-up of the spatial injustice of their everyday conditions. Helping to make the space more appealing would run into the well-known dilemma, in that it helps to justify its power regime. Just improving the everyday conditions only helps the system to work better.[5] Yet, wouldn't any intervention in the prison, which does not worsen the situation, logically do exactly that? How to escape pacification by design? And then, of course, most radically: Should artists or architects not refuse entirely to work in this context?

This might be the place to insert a short paragraph about another recent construction, one *not* by my office, namely a 'Schubhaftzentrum',[6] a new prison-like building type to hold in custody illegalized immigrants selected for immediate deportation out of the country.

---

4   Giancarlo de Carlo commented on how humanist modernists enthusiastically worked on the 'Housing for the Existenzmimimum', creatively supporting capital's suppression of the workforce (de Carlo, 2005 [1970]).

5   This of course is a widespread but rarely self-reflected-on, position of architects, who see themselves as providing a service for the tasks of society, providing a service to the state, which, when run by elected politicians, is to be made responsible for the ideologies behind the tasks. Architects like to see themselves as 'only' taking on the responsibility of doing their best for a good environment, and of humanizing, calming, and reducing harshness in the case of economic or political pressures.

6   In English, these are called 'Immigration Removal Centres' or 'Immigration Detention Centres'.

This project was greatly debated in architecture circles. It was not the Ministry of Justice, but the Ministry for Internal Affairs that organized an architectural competition for this 'Schubhaftzentrum' in the Styrian village of Vordernberg, requesting the design of a type of pre-deportation short-term prison. While this new building programme is being discussed in architectural circles for its achievements in architectural design (in narrow architectural terms) and with regard to its technical challenges (such as the fire escape routes if the prison-like building were to catch fire), it is hardly discussed with regard to the repressive modes of imprisonment used against people who are, and this has to be emphasized, not necessarily guilty of any crime (they are only guilty of not having a EU passport or entitlement of residence). This example is relevant, as one can see more and more prison space built and used outside of penal law, especially in migration politics (or rather, migration policing). The specific function of the 'Schubhaftzentrum' is to use imprisonment and punishment measures against asylum seekers.

The young group of architects, who won the competition, used specific well-meaning arguments in the public marketing campaign for their design, such as how they could increase a homely feeling of the space and reduce the prison-like elements, such as fenced windows, and install break-protected glass instead. Planners and sympathetic critics would call it 'social' architecture, and discuss it using the term the 'ethics' of architecture. Yet in this specific case, such humanism indirectly helps to imprison asylum seekers. With every press release and every award for the architecture office's 'human' design, they have contributed to reducing public resistance against the institution of the incarceration of migrants. Their counter-argument to such a critique would be that it would be much more of a problematic space without their engagement. While, in my view, and also in the view of activist groups supporting the 2012/13 Viennese refugee protests, every critical citizen and architect should radically oppose any such institution, hence should not work for it, but should critique it. On the other hand: can we really ignore the issue of improving a spatial situation for those who are already subject to such injustice? After all, it is the time of people's lives which is at stake. In this case, any such improvement has to be critically measured against its function within the routines and institutions of the EU's violent repressive measures against illegalized migration.

THE 'WRONG' SOLUTION

I return to *Out in Prison*: the art project in the prison mentioned above (a 'conventional' one, basing its use of force on penal law).[7] Confronted with all the dilemmas discussed above, I chose an approach with a double-face, a self-contradictory approach. Rather than only commenting on the spatial injustice by use of the intervention (which could be self-satisfying, but easily sarcastic or cynical), and rather than only 'improving' part of the spatial situation, I decided to combine the two: help *improve*, but also *expose*, or in other words: to describe the injustice by a critique turned into an aesthetic 'move', while at the same time increasing the usability and spatial quality of the courtyard by architectural means. In the end, I proposed to create the football field, which the prison administration had declared was both unnecessary and impossible to implement within the given spatial situation. The goal was to make the impossible happen, even though or precisely because there was indeed not enough space for it.

Within this paradoxical set-up, what *Out in Prison* tried to describe was not a right, but a 'wrong' solution, not a solution but rather a 'non-solution' (using the odd term from Siegfried Kracauer's theory of historical experience; Robnik, 2014). The non-solution is a solution that remains risky and highly debatable, and in this sense, rather than the modest renouncing of a solution, there really is one, but a solution that is at the same time not a solution, or one that remains visibly haunted and affected by its utter incompleteness or, what's more, an openness to being contested and disputed (see also Robnik, 2013).

Wittgenstein once asked if, when we measure the table with a ruler, do we not also measure the ruler?[8] In our case, the object as well as the ruler were measured. The courtyard was tested for its capacity to fit a football field, which turned out to be an impossibility. Not even the dimensions of the tiniest football field, which would be a 'Bambini' football field, would fit into the space, which is supposed to be *the* only outdoor space for up to fifteen people at the same time, in total for around one hundred prisoners during their imprisonment. The intervention measured the courtyard as much as the sports field, which defines the space as too small for football,

---

7   I want to clarify what I mean by the difference between a prison and an Immigration Detention Centre: Even though prisons are also filled with victims of racist or class injustice to a large extent, they are not exclusively designed for that purpose; in prison, we could, for example, also find the president of the Bayern Munich football club sentenced for tax evasion.

8   I am referring to Wittgenstein as quoted in Leitner, 2000.

but not too small for a prison courtyard. What are the criteria used by the decision-makers (including the architects) that determine the yard's size? The balancing, the calculation is done by expert opinion, as there is no norm or regulation for a minimum of so many square metres of outdoor space per person.

I needed to 'wrinkle' the standardized Bambini football field into the prison courtyard to expose rather than cover up the choices, which led to this explicit example of uneven spatial distribution (Figures 4.3–4.5). The drawing of the field on the wall and on the folded landscape can be read as a mapping of the missing space, as an inscription of the (missing) conflict between the value of the built volume versus the value of free space, an everyday struggle in planning generally, so conspicuous in this prison.[9] *Out in Prison* does not change the underlying value system (the ruler), but since the spatial non-relation is drawn on the wall, it is staged *as a wrong* and we can make use of the inscription, to point out that there is a wrong relation, that the ruler is as wrong as the space. As a public art-in-architecture project, the image of the courtyard can be made public, even though prison space is usually quite secretive. It can be used as a picture for the situation (also by the political right-wing, of course, for example, to display the nonsensical use of public money), or it could even be used by the prisoners, who live or have lived with it, for instance, to address the authorities in a dispute over the withholding of space that they must suffer. But, more humbly put, what has been built as art in architecture can also simply be used as a place to sit, play, hang out, lie in the sun (Figure 4.6), or play inventive football or other sports.

REACTIONS AND FAILURES

The repeated concern of the prison administration during the design process was that the football field would not be used, but rather would be vandalized immediately. In fact, a distanced 'let's see' position from the prison administration was the best I could get, and this was, at any rate, more valuable than resentful arguments against the project, often articulated in economic terms. One counter-argument was about spending too much public money for a football field for prisoners who would not value it, but would destroy it – or more

---

9   This struggle is less obvious when planning public buildings such as schools, social housing, old people's homes, for which the project brief dedicates just enough free space for that not to become a matter of conflict.

Figure 4.3 Twisting the sports field into the narrow prison yard
Figure 4.4 Prison yard with folded up sports field, indicating the lack of space
Figure 4.5 Outside in the prison yard (anonymity of users protected)
Figure 4.6 Fold in the lawn, usable as a bench
Photos: Gabu Heindl (4.3, 4.4 and 4.6) and Renate Höllwart (4.5)

resentfully, who were not really worth the investment. While people would have liked to see us use the cheapest lawn material, we used the best quality, with good endurance features and a pleasant feel. Some weeks after the courtyard was in use, I visited the site to see how it was working. Before I could even enter it, I was told that it looked vandalized and ugly: full of cigarette butts. When we entered the courtyard, I could see the floor was covered with cigarette butts, but I could also see that in my planning, I had forgotten a most crucial thing in this, the only outdoor space: not a single ashtray had been provided. Yet, the desire of some of the prison staff to prove their argument of vandalism was stronger than an acknowledgement that we had all forgotten the ashtray, or further, to blame the architect for that omission, which, in any other construction situation, would have been a foreseeable reaction. The butts and ashtray 'problem', however, could easily be solved. To date, every time when visiting the prison on a not-too-rainy day I have seen prisoners using the lawn in multiple ways, doing some sports on the field, which since the installation of the lawn is no longer forbidden.

While this may seem like a 'positive' outcome, another incident showed how the critical aspect of the project can easily be seen in quite the opposite way than the one intended. A journalist enthusiastically published the image of the folded lawn in the context of a story about the tearing down of the Berlin Wall, labelling it a way of 'overcoming' the wall in the prison. Yet, *Out in Prison* does not intend to miraculously effect or plainly make-believe that the wall in the prison yard is no longer an obstacle; it does not pretend that we have managed to do away with the wall. Surely this would be an ideologically ridiculous and pretentious claim. Instead of such a compromised humanism or delusions of grandeur, architecture should opt for and work to expand rooms of play for conflict oriented towards more – even if minimally more – democratic spatial production.

REFERENCES

De Carlo, Giancarlo (2005 [1970]) 'Architecture's public', in Peter Blundell Jones, Doina Petrescu and Jeremy Till (eds) *Architecture & Participation*, London: Spon Press.

Fanstein, Susan S. (2010) *The Just City*, Ithaca, NY: Cornell University Press.

Foucault, Michel (1995) *Discipline & Punish: The Birth of the Prison*, New York: Vintage Books.

Gutman, Robert (1992) 'Architects and power: the natural market for architecture', *Progressive Architecture* 73(12): 39–41.

Harvey, David (2009 [1973]) *Social Justice and the City*, Athens, GA: University of Georgia Press.

Kurgan, Laura (2013) *Close Up at a Distance: Mapping, Technology and Politics*, New York: Zone Books.

Leitner, Bernhard (2000) *Das Wittgenstein Haus*, Hamburg: Hatje Cantz.

Marchart, Oliver (2013) *Die politische Differenz: Zum Denken des Politischen bei Nancy, Lefort, Badiou, Laclau und Agamben*, Berlin: Suhrkamp Verlag.

Noever, Peter (ed.) (1996) *Margarete Schütte-Lihotzky, soziale Architektur: Zeitzeugin eines Jahrhunderts*, Böhlau.

Rancière, Jacques (1991) *The Nights of Labor: The Workers' Dream in Nineteenth-century France*, Philadelphia, PA: Temple University Press.

(1999) *Disagreement*, trans. Julie Rose. Minneapolis, MN: University of Minnesota Press.

(2003) 'Politics and aesthetics: an interview', *Angelaki: Journal of the Theoretical Humanities* 8(2): 191–211.

(2004) *The Politics of Aesthetics: The Distribution of the Sensible*, London: Continuum.

Robnik, Drehli (2013) 'Side by side als wirkliche Gegner: Zu politischen Einsätzen im Film-Denken von Kracauers *History*', in Drehli Robnik, Amàlia Kerekes and Katalin Teller (eds) *Film als Loch in der Wand. Kino und Geschichte bei Siegfried Kracauer*, Berlin: turia+kant: pp. 160–182.

(2014) 'Reading/reclaiming/recovering Siegfried Kracauer's film thinking of nonsolutions within postfoundationalist political theory', conference paper, available at: www.academia.edu/9816237

Soja, Edward W. (2010) *Seeking Spatial Justice*, Minneapolis: University of Minnesota Press.

5 – TEA OR COFFEE? POLITICS AND BINGO ON THE PAVEMENTS

Peter Mutschler and Ruth Morrow

TWADDELL AVENUE, NORTH BELFAST

August 2014: several years ago, shortly after the 12th of July annual parades in Northern Ireland, political campaigners set up a 'civil rights camp' at Twaddell Avenue, North Belfast.[1] Located on a small patch of derelict land next to a roundabout, the organizers, mostly men, use a caravan and container as operational centres. Decorated with all the insignia of pro-British imagery, it serves as shelter and meeting place. The surrounding fences are covered by British and Northern Irish flags, protest banners and messages of support: 'Respect our Culture', 'No Surrender', 'British and Proud' (Figure 5.1).

Figure 5.1 Protest camp, Twaddell Avenue, North Belfast, 2014
Photo: PS[2]

---

1   Twaddell Avenue is named after a Unionist politician, murdered by the IRA in 1922.

The reason for their ongoing protest is a stretch of road where the Orange Order, a Masonic-style organization and defenders of the Loyalist/Unionist/Protestant tradition, were and still are not allowed to parade upon.[2] The civic right they are campaigning for is to make the homeward march along a traditional route. This includes a short section of street through a Republican area: one of many interface zones in Belfast and Northern Ireland, where Protestant and Catholic communities border and are still entrenched in sectarian segregation and polarization. A walk of six minutes which was stopped by anti-parade protestors at the 12th of July parade in 2013, was followed by days of violent clashes with police and rioting on both sides of the community.[3]

Since then, every evening, the Twaddell protesters march with banners and flags towards the 'demarcation line' in an attempt to complete their parade. And every evening they are prevented from passing by a cordon of police, trying to avoid a reoccurrence of the clashes.[4] It is by now a well-choreographed daily routine; here the protesters, there the police; both sides framed by pro- and anti-march supporters and spectators. In the language of Northern Ireland's peace policy, the protest is part of a well-managed conflict repertoire.

There are many parades in cities and villages across Northern Ireland by the Orange Order during the summer season, especially for the 12th of July commemorations.[5] Most of the marches are peaceful,

---

2   The Orange Order with its origins in the seventeenth-century battle for supremacy between Protestantism and Catholicism, is the largest Protestant organization in Northern Ireland with at least 75,000 members, mostly male. 'The parading tradition which the Orange Order upholds is an honourable and historic tradition, which was the norm for other fraternities in the past. The parades of the Orange Order are the largest public Protestant witness of their kind anywhere in the world.' See: www.grandorangelodge.co.uk/parading#.VGkGs8IFu0N

3   The march moves between the home lodge and the city centre. They are allowed to march the full route early in the morning but are not allowed to make the return march in the evening.

4   Daily updates about the campaign are posted on Facebook: Proud to be Protestant www.facebook.com/pages/Proud-to-be-a-protestant-banter/436131339783285

5   According to the Parades Commission for Northern Ireland Annual Report and Financial Statements for the year ended 31 March 2014:

   The number of notified parades organised by the loyal orders and broad Unionist tradition at 2,766 represents 59% of the overall total (in 2012–13 the number of notified parades was 2,569). The number of notified parades by organised Nationalist groups at 119 was a slight decrease from the previous year but remains low at 3% of the overall total (in 2012–13, it was 175). The number of notified parades deemed to be sensitive increased significantly to 491 (in 2012–13, it was 215). The significant increase is largely due to the nightly and weekly parades at Woodvale/Twaddell areas of Belfast.

See: www.paradescommission.org/getmedia/c4e4de29-3a2f-4eed-b021-985706d4a8a6/NorthernIrelandParadesCommission.aspx

watched and celebrated by many people with an inclination or firm belief in Protestantism and the union between Northern Ireland and Britain. However, pro-Irish, Republican citizens (in the majority Catholics) see these marches as sectarian and expressions of triumphalism, more so, when the marching routes cross community lines (Komarova and McKnight, 2013).

This ethno-national categorization in Protestant/Catholic is of course a simplification of a conflict which mainly took and takes place in working-class areas of high deprivation on both 'sides' and which still reverberates, more than a decade after the peace agreement in 1998.[6] This binary simplification is partly due to the fact that even today more than half of the population of Belfast is living in wards that have a 90 per cent Catholic or Protestant background (Parades Commission for Northern Ireland Annual Report, 2013). The segregation is even higher in interface areas, with homogeneous communities in terms of national/religious identity. The 'cultural' division between the two communities finds its spatial and architectural expression in territorial demarcations: through 30.5 km of high fences, euphemistically named 'peace walls'; through flags on lampposts and painted curbstones; and to come back to the caravan, the Twaddell protest camp about an unfinished parade.[7] What these devices do beyond their spatial function, is present the construction and re-affirmation of social identity. They are as much real and physical, as symbolic and performative (Komarova, 2008). The ritualized parade claims urban space for its purposes and turns public space into an ethnic, political,

---

6   The 'Good Friday Agreement' or 'Belfast Agreement' as a major step in the Northern Irish peace process was signed on 10 April 1998. It was approved with a great majority in two simultaneous referendums in Northern Ireland and the Republic of Ireland in May 1998.

7   The Northern Irish writer Glenn Patterson describes the difficulties with the term 'community' in 'Don't mention the C-word':

> In order to take the sectarian heat out of our conflict (another C-word in need of examination) the labels Catholic and Protestant were first diluted by the addition of 'community' and then effaced almost completely as the Protestant and Catholic communities just became the Two Communities. But as soon as the Two Communities model was established, the singular form itself was altered: it became the fragment rather than the thing greater than the sum of its parts. (The Irish Times, 4 January 2014)

religious, cultural defined territory for like-minded citizens and as an exclusion zone for others.[8]

Policing the Twaddell camp and their daily attempts to march through the Republican area costs the taxpayer £40,000 daily, which for an impoverished area, seems like a waste of money. The Twaddell leaders blame the dissident Republican threat for the expense, besides, they argue 'what price do you put on your culture and human rights?' (*Belfast Telegraph*, April 2014).

Politically, one could see this protest in line with other long-term movements, from 'Occupy' to Tahrir Square (though the Twaddell protesters lack a revolutionary, liberating potential). Artistically, one could regard this stand-off as a 'socially engaged' action and visually potent performance. In its appearance and community involvement one could nearly read it (yet make no sense) as relational art practice. To go even further, its visual display is surprisingly similar to Mark Wallinger's 'State Britain' installation for the Turner Prize at Tate Britain, where the artist painstakingly recreated an anti-Iraq War camp previously located at the Houses of Parliament.[9] As an act of transition from real to symbolic, from action to representation, Mark Wallinger re-appropriated the objects and situation of a six-year-long political protest for the art world, raising 'challenging questions about issues of freedom of expression and the erosion of civil liberties in Britain today' (Tate Britain, 2006). What he inadvertently also raised were questions of the legitimacy of such transformations and the commodification of political activism through aesthetics.

For the Twaddell protesters, their day- and night-long sit-in is an expression of freedom as well: a campaign for loyalist culture and the right to express community identity; Protestant and British. But the Twaddell camp is not art, nor does it want to be. It is propaganda,

---

8   According to Komarova and McKnight (2013):

Urban space and claiming territory are central to the symbolism of parades. Individual parades are highly ritualised performances of the traditional 'custom and practice' of marching along clearly defined routes. Unionists' assertion of the right to parade and nationalists' contestation of a parade's route represent and perform a power struggle over territory (Bryan 2006, Cohen 2007). The enactment of parades and protests temporarily incorporates space into a performative practice (Cohen 2007) that contains the possibility of redrawing boundaries (Leach 2005). While these performative acts may not leave a lasting material imprint they are an integral part of the dynamics of continuity and change.
(Chapter 4.2 www.socresonline.org.uk/18/1/19.html)

9   For his Turner Prize nomination in 2007, the artist Mark Wallinger recreated peace campaigner Brian Haw's Parliament Square protest against the Iraq War: a meticulous reconstruction (not originals) of over 600 banners, photographs, peace flags and messages from well-wishers that have been amassed by Haw over five years, until he was removed by the police in 2006. See: www.tate.org.uk/whats-on/tate-britain/exhibition/mark-wallinger-state-britain

reactionary and, for many, intimidating. There is no future and no progression in its protest; it is a stand-off of a discredited ideology against the transition towards a 'shared future'. The Twaddell protest can't change its way, nor is it inventive enough to find new ones. It is an unwieldy protest, one which does not open new social and spatial relations. It is stuck.

COMMONS ROAD, BALLYKINLER

October 2009: a caravan is parked on the pavement of a crossing in the small coastal village of Ballykinler, a 40-minute drive south of Belfast. It is decorated externally with ceramic sculptures of birds and flowers and patterns of roses: an abundance of living room ornaments turned inside-out. The caravan combines the intimacy of a private home with a public display and purpose. It is the new, mobile community centre for the village: a communal meeting place, unfunded and unsupported by the local Council. This is an initiative by Anne-Marie Dillon, mother of seven children, local resident, artist, activist, feminist (listed in her own order of priorities). Her response when asked why she gets engaged, both personally and artistically, is convincingly simple: 'Just because we don't have a community centre doesn't mean we are not a community' (BBC, 2009). A statement and conviction that motivate most if not all of the many projects in Ballykinler by Anne-Marie Dillon and PS2.[10]

Once a week, sometimes more often, the caravan is crowded with ten, twelve women, most of them pensioners. They meet to talk, have a cup of tea, play bingo, listen to music, remember stories and invite others to tell them more. They do craft, plan car boot sales to raise money for a pensioners' day trip, for a girls and boys youth club, for mothers and toddlers, for the future. They have fun and carry out communal tasks at the same time. They care for the village and are, despite their age or because of it, drivers of social change. Perhaps, as Anne Querrien (2010) argued after visiting the village, they care

---

10   PS2 started to work together with Anne-Marie Dillon from 2009, just at the beginning of the mobile community centre. Since then most activities have been carried out together and with the support of PS2.

because they are women. For Christoph Schäfer (2010), the caravan goes way beyond its practical use and symbolic language:

> *What do you do in a country, where the classical routes of political self-organisation and militant collectivity have gone so far, for such a long time, that they have lost their integrity, their emancipatory potential has been all used up? A.M. Dillon and the Forever Young Pensioners suggest new ways, how to voice dissent, without treading down the same old beaten track. They constitute a parallel space of exchange, a centre on the move. The Pensioners style of 'aggressive cosiness' renders unspoilt forms of collectivity – the private tea party – accessible – as a source of political action. A winding rose – that has thorns.*
> (Schäfer, 2010: 338)

The mobile community centre caravan was in use (and sometimes still is) for more than a year. It was one phase and one formal construct in a long-term commitment by Anne-Marie Dillon, PS2 and other contributing artists and researchers, to engage with the residents and social environment of Ballykinlar. Their commitment led to a string of interventions, workshops and activities which were and are mainly concerned to propose and test forms of community space at a very basic, low-cost level, yet with plenty of fantasy, resilience and playfulness. Interestingly, it was the spatial need of the community to have a centre that triggered the actions and interventions, leading to new and changing 'built' situations and artistic and social outcomes. This process with its different spatial constellations can be viewed and analysed as a visible manifestation of the less visible social need to meet and communicate. As a process it did not develop linearly and steadily, instead it sometimes happened organically or ad hoc, erupting as re-action and protest to something, and at other times it was carefully planned and prepared. There were regular events (weekly meetings); seasonal events (village fair (Figure 5.2); summer trip; Christmas celebrations) and spontaneous actions (right of way protest; Bus Stop).

Figure 5.2 Village fair, Ballykinler village green, 2011
Photo: PS[2]

When measured against the criteria of socially engaged projects,
the community caravan seems to tick all boxes: it is creative, community-
centred, bottom-up, small-scale, DIY, cheap and mostly self-funded.
An near idyllic sheltered meeting place with the rose-patterned seats,
friendly pensioners and rural quietness. But it is not idyllic, nor is
Northern Ireland, nor the village.[11]

Ballykinler or Ballykinlar, depending on which of the two 'communities' one belongs to, is wedged between the Mourne Mountains,
the Irish Sea and, cutting off the access to the beach, a British
Army camp. The adjacent Abercorn Barracks has dominated the
village since 1902. The military provided many jobs, allegiances and
opposition, again depending on one's national/cultural identity. During
the 'Troubles', the army operated in Northern Ireland, but now they
prepare for deployments in Afghanistan and future areas of armed
conflict worldwide.[12]

11   In an interview for this text, Anne-Marie Dillon talked in connection to an early work, a cottage
out of cow dung and dust: 'This was a dark space, it exists all over Northern Ireland. It was brutal, a
brutal piece and that is exactly what I am working on in Ballykinlar: it is a brutal place.' Interview with
A.M. Dillon, Ruth Morrow and PS[2], June 2014.

12   In July 2014, the '2nd Battalion The Rifles' were relocated to an army camp in Lisburn, Northern
Ireland. The Abercorn Barracks and its grounds are now only used as training ground and many jobs
were lost in Ballykinler and nearby villages. How this will impact on the community remains to be seen.

The village is a condensed rural microcosm of Northern Irish society, history and politics, magnified through the presence of the army. So it's similar to interface zones in Belfast and its urban environment of segregated communities.

Northern Ireland is regarded now to be in a transitional phase of post-violent conflict. For nearly two decades, European 'Peace Funding' has supported community initiatives promoting a 'shared future' and respect. Public art was, until recently, mainly limited to visual art and mural projects. It developed a language and formats of community participation that is increasingly formulaic and packaged to produce a positive result. The expertise in peace-building strategies and initiatives is high, and one might argue, an industry based on funding in itself.

Within this context, 'space', as a social and built construct is only mentioned, debated and funded, if it is closely connected with the word 'shared'. Shared space is a key concept in politics and community relations, yet there are 'intrinsic problems in defining and shaping public space as "shared" and "civic" in cities, towns and villages that have experienced prolonged ethno-national conflict – both in terms of policy approaches to, and the practice(s) of, sharing space among communities' (Komarova, 2008: 4).

What this means for projects and initiatives with communities, is an overwhelming intentional or internalized tendency, to harmonize conflictual situations and negate differences in their outcomes. In simple terms, one could say, it produces rainbows, images of stereotypical hope, with little connection to the social reality. This is echoed and finds its equivalent in the critique by Claire Bishop of Bourriaud's relational theory where the 'artwork is presented as social interstice within which these experiments and these new "life possibilities" appear to be possible' (Bourriaud, 2002: 45). Bishop counters Bourriaud's concept of a harmonious, microtopian situation with its absence of friction, by referring to Laclau and Mouffe, who

> *argue that a fully functioning democratic society is not one in which all antagonisms have disappeared, but one in which new political frontiers are constantly being drawn and brought into debate – in other words, a democratic society is one in which relations of conflict are sustained and allowed for, not erased.*

Without antagonism there is only the imposed consensus of
authoritarian order – a total suppression of debate and discus-
sion, which is inimical to democracy.
(Bishop, 2013: 177)[13]

The mobile community centre or other projects in Ballykinler by
A.M. Dillon and PS² are never intended to harmonize social conflicts.
It is not social work, nor is it 'peace building', although it works with
social issues and some pedagogical understanding. It is artful and
playful intervention through constructed situations and actions; some
familiar, like a caravan or a village fair; some unfamiliar, like a caravan
for the public or a fair as contemporary museum. It is a work process
that finds and invents situations for conversations and negotiations,
and appropriate spatial forms for it to happen. And though the formal
appearance might sometimes look beautiful, or as Anne-Marie Dillon
critically says 'pretty to a degree it almost covers the brutality', the
work 'scratches the varnish of peace till cracks show' (Dillon, 2014).

This doesn't mean that the outcomes are better, socially or
aesthetically more significant. It is a creative position and work ethic
that require honesty and come with risks and setbacks. It is based
on a long-term commitment and on the fact that A.M. Dillon is a local
resident and permanently 'on-site'. Thomas Hirschhorn's terms of
'presence and production' can be applied to A.M. Dillon's role here,
as much as his rejection of the term 'social art':

I want to propose notions of my own because I can assess what
is involved and necessary to achieve 'Presence' and 'Produc-
tion'. I understand what it requires of me. However, I do not
know what 'community art,' 'participative art,' 'educational art,' or
'relational aesthetics art' mean. With the 'Presence and Produc-
tion' guideline, my aim is to answer the following questions: Can
a work – through the notion of 'Presence,' my own presence
– create for others the conditions of being present? And can my
work – through the notion of 'Production' – create the conditions
for other productions to be established?
(Lee and Foster, 2013: 371)[14]

---

13   It could be argued that the Twaddell protest in North Belfast is an act of suppressing debate
with its 'no surrender' policy.

14   It has to be stressed that Hirschhorn is internationally both present in communities and the
gallery/museum, a transmission and distribution which hardly exists in the case of Ballykinler – nor
would it be a motivation.

As much as the pensioner group in Ballykinler embraced and
'loved' the rose-patterned caravan (it became a model for a ceramic
flower-pot as part of a later project), it was not the first, nor the last
spatial situation of a community centre.[15] This aspect of change and
the various permutations of achieved and 'lived' spatial constellations
are important. Within their material and architectural limits, they are
both real and symbolic expression of (village) life. The first spatial situation for a community centre was a series of 'coffee mornings', where
A.M. Dillon placed chairs, sofa, tables at the side of the road. An
open-air living room prepared and decorated for 'guests'. It was a very
raw and naked protest, with a minimum of spatial definition, but high
in symbolic and political value, and as an artistic happening. When it
rained, 'community' didn't happen. Subsequently, the caravan, familiar
as a holiday home but unfamiliar as civic public space, was clearly an
'architectural' improvement, not least as shelter from the rain.

Yet the aim, for the pensioners, was a permanent space, a
community centre, a refurbished old building or a new, purpose-built
space, just as other neighbouring villages and towns had. With a
boarded-up, disused primary school in the heart of their village centre,
their long-term aim was to use the building as a community centre. It
would be big enough to incorporate many groups and activities, but it
was in public hands (the Education and Library Board) and slowly fell
into disrepair – reasons enough to act.

When a BBC Radio Ulster programme discussed the situation
of the pensioners, their 'protest' and use of a caravan as community
centre, the item was introduced with: 'They say they are using
pensioner power to shame the local Education and Library Board
into letting them use somewhere a little less mobile to meet in' (BBC,
2009). The wording captured a shift of the pensioners away from
the excitement of basic temporary situations towards a desire for
permanence, normalization: a proper centre, no longer nomadic. It
also captured the search for and conflicts of a community.

With the growing confidence that the women gained through
their collective actions, newspaper articles and visits by local councillors, the takeover of the empty school seemed the next, logical step.
Though the BBC programme did not open the doors to the school

15   As part of the 'UP-Down' project by PS² in 2010/11 pssquared.org/UP-Down.php, London-
based 'public works' developed a village object together with the pensioner group. The final product,
cast in ceramic and hand-decorated by the group, was a 'Rose Garden' flowerpot, an exact scaled
replica of the mobile community centre. It is now part of the 'international village shop' network, www.
internationalvillageshop.net/.

or a transfer of public ownership, the pensioners were given the use of an empty hair saloon, just opposite the previous caravan location, rent-free. The shop still remains the location of the 'Ballykinler/ Ballykinlar community centre' and is used by the pensioner group, a mother and toddler group, and two youth groups.

The 'protest' or 'adventure' for a community centre is, however, not over, though it has slowed down, at least as far as the pensioners are concerned. Their immediate need to have a fixed, warm community space is satisfied. Inverting Dillon's statement: 'Just because we don't have a community centre doesn't mean we are not a community', one could ask if the village now forms as a community because of the 'Ballykinler/Ballykinlar community centre' (BBC, 2009). Definitely not, but they are on a process towards becoming a stronger community, with all its disputes, common ground, shared concerns and passions. PS² intervened in this process through carefully planned yet low-funded art projects which fulfilled different roles: as art interventions, as academic research, as multidisciplinary contributions, all centred in the community. It is and was a mutual approach of giving and taking, of exchange, beneficial for all – or at least we hope so. Three examples of projects that illustrate the changing spatial aspects and formats:

—   Rhyzom workshop in Ballykinlar[16]
—   Transfer Test: student project about a conversion of the empty school into a community centre[17]
—   Village Fair (UP-Down)[18]

The Rhyzom workshop was located on the village green, used as both football pitch and Gaelic football playground.[19] Due to the lack of a bigger facility (the hair salon only became available several months

16   'Cultural production in rural environments and small towns' ran from 17–20 June 2010. As part of the EU-funded Rhyzom project, PS² organized a workshop with local and international artists and researchers in Ballykinler, including the community and Army. See: http://pssquared.org/workshop.php

17   Transfer Test was a five-day planning workshop by first-year students from both the undergraduate BSc Architecture and the Masters in Architecture course in the School of Planning, Architecture and Civil Engineering at Queen's University Belfast, as part of the 'Street Society' programme of live projects, 12–16 March 2012. See: http://pssquared.org/streesociety2012.php

18   The village fair (28 May 2011) was the final part of the 'UP-Down' project which included four different projects of art workshops with different individuals and groups of the village: the production of a film and cinema caravan; a local object (which became the ceramic caravan pot); the construction of a scrap metal mobile sculpture; a village newspaper and News website. February–May 2011. See: http://pssquared.org/UP-Down.php

19   Gaelic football is associated with Irish/Catholic culture, football with Protestant culture. Usually they do not share a common playground.

later), PS² placed an office container (cultural centre) at the edge of the pitch. Together with the caravan (community centre), it formed an extended community space not only for the two-day conference in Ballykinlar, but for the following month. The office container was in use not only by the pensioners, who liked the bigger space, but also by an informal mother and toddler group (who liked the safety of indoor and outdoor play possibilities on the pitch) and a youth group. This temporary, ad hoc constellation of container, fenced-off play area and caravan, satisfied, and at the same time stimulated, the need and desire for community space (Figure 5.3).

Figure 5.3 Rhyzom workshop, Ballykinler, village green, 2010
Photo: PS²

'Transfer Test' invited architecture students of Queen's University, Belfast, 'to propose ways of (self-help) renovation of the former Primary School and its potential future use as a community centre'.[20] The week-long project, with community consultations, site visits and research was highly productive and produced architectural models, plans and costs, indicating a phased, DIY-oriented process of adaptation. The outcome was presented to the community in Ballykinler as

20   Brief for Street Society, 2012: 'Transfer tests' – from closed school to community centre. See: pssquared.org/streesociety2012.php

well as to peer students and the wider public in Belfast. The project
not only demonstrated the old school in a new light – as a community
centre, but also increased the urge to achieve a take-over and to
equip the community with material and data. It sparked new ideas and
a renewed interest by the pensioners and sections of the community
to campaign for the school. Though the outcomes were handed over
to the press, local councillors and Northern Irish politicians, there
was, again, no opening of school doors. However, it led to an 'official'
consultancy report and Village Plan organized by the local government, demonstrating possibilities for a community centre, yet without
mentioning the existing work and struggle by the pensioners, artists
and researchers.

The Village Fair was the culmination of the 'UP-Down' project,
and the first fair for decades in the village. PS² picked up the tradition
of agricultural shows in rural areas in Ireland, which showcase farming
achievements, and re-used the format as a 'contemporary museum'
of the outcomes of the project workshops and village produce. A
cultural fair with bouncy castle and 'cinema caravan'; with a 'bike-
limousine' (Figure 5.4) and old-timer cars; with walking sticks and the
'ceramic caravan pot'; tea and sandwiches made by the pensioners
– sold from their caravan, and international food, cooked by army
wives. A DIY fair, self-organized, partly funded, non-profit, with all the
income going back to the involved groups. It was the biggest spatial
constellation yet in the use of common ground, marquees, caravans,
containers, open stalls. It was, for one day, a community centre, col-
ourful and mixed together. Since then it has become a fixed seasonal
event, though slightly more conventional but with the pensioners as
core organizers. This process also suggests the importance of the
symbolic value a space is given and, perhaps even more importantly,
the activity of people this space holds or enables.

Figure 5.4 UP-Down project:
bicycle-limousine workshop,
Ballykinler, 2011
Photo: PS²

What became clear through the various spatial projects discussed here was the incongruence between art interventions and
political and organizational community work. We are critically aware
of this shortfall and the fact that 'pensioner power' was toothless
when it came to committee meetings, applications and the slow
process of Council decisions. Though the group were and are major
stakeholders in the village, they are perceived as having 'no capacity'
and insufficient governance structures. Though the press and local
councillors took notice of the 'unusual' protest and activities in the
village, so far the community has achieved limited representation
and certainly no citizen control over decision-making processes that
impact on their lives. In short, the protest for a community centre
was not connected with a political protest that could connect and
work within the power structures. We had been part of a process
to raise awareness around social and architectural space but have
failed to focus on political space. While Claire Bishop suggests that
at 'a certain point, art has to hand over to other institutions if social
change is to be achieved: it is not enough to keep producing activist
art' (Bishop, 2012: 283). We think that it is as citizens, not artists or
architects, that we are more able to support the pensioners through
the appropriate administrative processes in order to achieve control
and ownership.

So how does this work speak to architecture? It certainly challenges conventional value systems that use permanence, quality of
materials, control of process and expense as measures of success,
since this work is temporary, cheap, and uses materials in an ad hoc
manner in largely improvised processes. But it is also working in
places where conventional architecture won't or can't go. The act of
making space, place and architecture is always contentious, but in a
highly territorialized society, such as Northern Ireland, building is both
intimidatory and vulnerable to intimidation. The spatial activities of
A.M. Dillon and PS[2], at times architecturally crude, don't just respond
to need – they also provide spaces to ask questions, challenge perceptions and test accepted positions, not only in relation to the world
around, but also to the individual worlds within. This is a creative
practice that initiates, enables and supports dialogue between diverse
actors in contested spaces; providing temporary shelter to social
relationships undergoing shifts in identity and/or re-configuration.
Such practice asks for patience, and abandonment of the idea of an
end point. Over time we have come to understand the work as a form
of improvised, socio-spatial rehearsal: architecture in the process of
becoming, still open for discussion and as yet inconclusive.

As part of the research for this text, we interviewed the pensioner group in the former hair salon. They looked at images from the past with great fondness, with their open-air sit-ins, the caravan, the Bus Stop, the village fair. 'It was good fun, it was brilliant', they concluded with some nostalgia (PS^2 interview, 2014). All in their seventies, they still want to have a bigger centre for the community, but feel left out by decision-makers and unsupported in their engagement by the wider local community. 'We are left to do it. The young ones don't. They have too much to do at home ...' The pensioners of course left their own homes several years ago, for a few hours a week, to drink tea, play bingo, care for the village and build a space of change; on the pavement; in a rose-patterned caravan; an empty hair salon and maybe, just maybe, in a refurbished school. But they are not stuck like their contemporaries on Twaddell Avenue, they are on the move, pulling and inspiring others to come with them.

REFERENCES

BBC Radio Ulster (2009) Wendy Austin: Interview with the pensioner group, A.M. Dillon, the Education and Library Board and a local councillor, *Talkback*, 16 December.

Belfast Telegraph (2014) 'Twaddell organiser Gerald Solinas: We shall not be moved until brethren get down that road', 28 April. Available at: http://www.belfasttelegraph.co.uk/opinion/debateni/twaddell-organiser-gerald-solinas-we-shall-not-be-moved-until-brethren-get-down-that-road-30222329.html (accessed 12 April 2016)

Bishop, Claire (2012) *Artificial Hells: Participatory Art and the Politics of Spectatorship*, London: Verso.
    (2013) 'Antagonism and relational aesthetics', in Kocur Zoya and Simon Leung (eds) *Theory in Contemporary Art Since 1985*, Chichester: Wiley-Blackwell, pp. 166–194.

Bourriaud, Nicolas (2002) *Relational Aesthetics*, Paris: Les presses du réel.

Dillon, Anne-Marie (2014) Interview with Ruth Morrow and PS², June 2014.

Good Friday Agreement, 10 April 1998, available at: www.gov.uk/government/uploads/system/uploads/attachment_data/file/136652/agreement.pdf (accessed 12 April 2016).

Komarova, Milena (2008) 'Shared space in Belfast and the limits of a shared future', in *Divided Cities/Contested States*, Working Paper No 3. Conflict in Cities and the Contested State, www.conflictincities.org/PDFs/WorkingPaper3rev_11.3.10.pdf (accessed 12 April 2016).

Komarova, Milena and McKnight, Martina (2013) '"We are watching you too": Reflections on doing visual research in a contested city', *Sociological Research Online*, 18(1): 19. Available at: www.socresonline.org.uk/18/1/19.html (accessed 12 April 2016).

Lee, Lisa and Foster, Hal (eds) (2013) *Critical Laboratory: The Writings of Thomas Hirschhorn*, Cambridge, MA: MIT Press.

Parades Commission for Northern Ireland Annual Report (2014) 31 March. Available at: www.paradescommission.org/getmedia/c4e4de29-3a2f-4eed-b021-985706d4a8a6/NorthernIrelandParadesCommission.aspx (accessed 12 April 2016).

PS[2] (2014) Interview with the pensioner group, Ballykinler, 3 June.

Patterson, Glenn (2014) 'Don't mention the C-word', *The Irish Times*, 4 January 2014.

Querrien, Anne (2010) 'The rhizome against desertification', in Doina Petrescu, Constantin Petcou and Nishat Awan (eds) *Trans-Local-Act Cultural Practices Within and Across*, Paris: atelier d'architecture autogérée, pp. 328–333.
Schäfer, Christoph (2010) 'Aggressive cosiness. embedded artists vs. interventionist residents', in Doina Petrescu, Constantin Petcou and Nishat Awan (eds) *Trans-Local-Act Cultural Practices Within and Across*, Paris: atelier d'architecture autogérée, pp. 335–338.

Tate Britain (2006) www.tate.org.uk/whats-on/tate-britain/exhibition/mark-wallinger-state-britain

6 – DECOLONIZING ARCHITECTURAL EDUCATION: TOWARDS AN AFFECTIVE PEDAGOGY

Pelin Tan

> *The relationship between education and the habit of the ethical is as the relationship without relationship between responsibility and the gift that we must imagine in order to account for responsibility.* (Spivak, 2012: 9)

Questioning architecture's social production in terms of pedagogy and its political and epistemic decolonization seems to me to be one of the most urgent issues in the field of architectural knowledge production. 'Social production' in architecture has been affiliated or understood as a normative, Eurocentric design practice for organizing society and cities since the twentieth century. Related themes in the social production of architecture include participatory design, social co-existences in different cities or architectural settings, and a field in which spatial practitioners have critically challenged the role of form, especially since the 1990s. The 'production' is multiple and social; it is in flux and relative. I argue that searching for radical and alternative pedagogies and methods is an important part of the social 're-produc-tion' in architecture for our current times. Architectural research that transverses and functions in both institutions *and* societies, directly, can play a role in transforming knowledge and public 'truth'.

My own position shifts between the fields of Sociology and Architecture. My living with the dilemmas of academic knowledge pro-duction and searching for alternatives coincide with the last 15 years of developments in global urban production and spatial practices. I teach at the Architecture Faculty of Mardin Artuklu University, officially in Southeast Turkey (unofficially in Northern Kurdistan), which was established by my colleagues five years ago. This position forced me to invent methodologies and alternative pedagogical modalities that could function also as a practice of decolonization. Here, I consider the practice of 'decolonization' in both extreme territorial conditions, as an epistemic angle and as a modernist theoretical category in the discipline of architecture. The basic principles for a decolonizing educational structure are, first, to construct non-hegemonic knowledge through collective processes and, second, to create an 'instituting practice' without remaining, or never fully reaching, the status of an 'institution'. Education is by default a fully instituting structure, where the institution itself becomes a machine that exists for the sake of sustaining itself. It is a form of colonizing pre-existing knowledge of all involved in the process: students and teachers alike.

What is a collective process in education? It is the destruction of the hierarchies of dualist structures between teacher and student, teaching and learning. Decolonizing education means collective self-teaching, learning by acting together, rejecting the gap between theory and practice, and deconstructing terms in education that are sustained by the institution, while preserving traditional knowledge from the earth and nature. The methodology, the syllabus and the content of *any* topic are the basis for a pedagogy.

Architectural education is often trapped in between architectural genres of specific territorial conditions and trans-local conflicts within form-concept relations that conservatively inform the syllabus and design studio programmes. Therefore, I feel it always requires two processes: first, to decolonize architectural knowledge from a certain hegemonic territorial condition, which that particular institutionalization process is attached to; and, second, to create a transversal methodology that goes beyond form and concept in design.

METHOD

A transversal methodology ensures a trans-local, borderless knowledge production that in a rhizomatic form reaches beyond topics of architecture and design to include citizenship, militant pedagogy, institutionalism, borders, war, being a refugee, documents/documenting, urban segregation, commons and others. Transversal practice here mainly refers to Félix Guattari's notion and practice, which he describes as '[N]either institutional therapy, nor institutional pedagogy, nor the struggle for social emancipation, but, which invoked an analytic method that could transverse these multiple fields (from which came the theme "transversality")' (Guattari, 1996: 121).

I understand the notion of transversality as a practice in which epistemic and theoretical categories are transverse, and replace each other. It is a practice that is very much embedded, bodily, in everyday life. The 'institution/instituting' is part of this, and so creating such a transversal practice also influences the political body of an institution and the way we are instituting. When I consider myself teaching in architecture, particularly as it involves different forms of production and representation of knowledge related both to small-scale design and yet at the same time larger, different levels of integrated disciplinary knowledge (sociology, sciences, art, etc.), I feel it is a powerful tool that could be taken further with students. Students' actions are part of this togetherness in the transversality of pedagogy.

The understanding of such a methodology is often affiliated with terms in alternative knowledge and pedagogy practice such as 'assemblage methods' or 'affective pedagogy'. Methodology is also a political tool that takes part in the process of knowledge production. Thus, the 'Assemblage Method', according to John Law (2004: 122):

> is the process of enacting or crafting bundles of ramifying relations that condense presence and (therefore also) generate absence by shaping, mediating and separating these. Often it is about manifesting realities out-there and depictions of those realities in-here. It is also about enacting Othernesses.

My understanding of Othernesses is informed by Levinas's approach to ethics. The teacher as colonizer in such a territory is in a problematic position, where assemblage methods can be a means to help create the needed radicalism with the colonized subjectivity; one in which my own colonizer identity is not based on fundamental justifications of a politically correct emancipatory act.

Following Law's statement in his (2004) book *After Method*, which mainly concerns critical approaches to method in the social sciences, can also reveal methodological problems in architecture research and its pedagogy. Both in design and conceptual frameworks, how can we understand the possibilities of creating such transversality that enacts Otherness, as teachers, as pedagogies? On the other hand, the term 'Affective Pedagogy' refers to Deleuzian mediations on Spinoza's concept of 'affect/affections' that is beyond the body, and assemblages of form have been described in a context for new methods in aesthetics: 'Affect is a starting place from which we can develop methods that have an awareness of the politics of aesthetics: methods that respond with sensitivity to aesthetic influence on human emotions and understand how they change bodily capacities' (Hickey-Moody, 2013: 92–93).

While there is not enough space here to elaborate on the intersection of assemblage methods and affective pedagogy, I can introduce some examples below, which may help to foster further discussions in architectural education, about its potentials in social actions. To do this, I will discuss a few examples from my own involvement in some 'instituting' practices and transversal methodologies as well as other examples of pedagogical practice that I follow.

In the graduate design studio that I co-direct with Bülent Tanju each autumn, we often struggle between producing the design project, as well as developing the conceptual background for it. Such a division is both ontologically and epistemologically sustained in design studios. Thus, in order to deconstruct it, we need a multiple, transversal methodology at both conceptual and functional levels that are inseparable in the process. *General Intellect: Labor in Architecture*[1] is a design studio in which we ask graduate students to read and think together about the literature of labour and alienation, within an autonomist Marxist perspective, as well as raise criticism on the working conditions of architects and designers. Most of the students trying to follow the graduate courses also have full-time jobs, either at architecture studios or in construction sites after hours. These conditions create for them a tangible involvement with the syllabus of our graduate architecture studio. During our course we conducted interviews and surveys on the working hours of architects, researched the spaces of freelance designers, along with gender differences in working conditions and the conditions of workers with architects on construction sites. The involvement of students in this process led them to create a collective called *Labor in Architecture*. They transformed their data and related information into an online digital mapping representation tool in 'graphcommon',[2] a website that makes public both their research process and a clear mapping of the labour conditions in architecture.

Another research project that is combined with a graduate seminar each spring term is *Forensik Mimarlık*, which observes and researches the territory around Mardin, an extreme war zone region. *Forensik Mimarlık* follows and examines issues such as migration, the 1990s civil war between the Kurds and the Turkish state, border practices and refugee camps, rural commons, the extrajudicial killings of the 1990s, dam constructions as surveillance and dispossession tools, and the autonomy of local municipalities. *Forensik Mimarlık*

---

1   'General Intellect: Labor Conditions in Architecture/Mimarlıkta Emek Ko ulları', Graduate Design Studio Project I, Autumn, Bülent Tanju and Pelin Tan, Mardin Artuklu University, Architecture Faculty. Available at: http://laborarchitecture.tumblr.com or http://graphcommons.com/graphs/78d3ab7f-31c6-47f5-b925-92df95558ad2

2   See www.graphcommons.com

research and graduate seminar are inspired by the forensic methodological research in conflict zones, led by architect Eyal Weizman and
his team.[3]

The methodological and theoretical concept of the 'forensic' developed in recent years by *Forensic Architecture*, as well as by others
such as Anselm Franke, has brought vital attention to the production
of public 'truth' in architecture. Returning to the Latin root of forensis,
Weizman observes the critical link between forum (as negotiation)
and forensics (as a methodology of examining crime):

> *Forensics is thus the art of the forum – the practice and skill*
> *of presenting an argument before a professional, political, or*
> *legal gathering. Forensics is in this sense part of rhetoric, which*
> *concerns speech. However, it includes not only human speech*
> *but also that of things.*
> (Weizman, Taveres, Schuppli and Situ Studio, 2010: 60)

In this context, architectural production and the presentation of
objects, things, testimonies and forms exist in multiple relations to
both the event and the space in which it occurred or is constructed.
'Forensics is thus concerned both with the materialization of the event
and also with the performance of the object within a forum' (ibid.: 60).

The research project that I established with my graduate students, *Forensik Mimarlık*, focuses on several actors such as human
rights activists, mayors and actors who are leading the production
of spatial development of Mardin and its region. The region, as a
traumatic zone of the past, intense civil war between the Turkish
government and the Kurdish movement, holds judicial incidents to be
analysed. The Human Rights Association of Mardin, which is involved
in investigating the extra-judicial killings and identifying forensics from
bones, is excavating the land around the region. *Forensik Mimarlık*
engages in the observation of how a territory, officially defined as
tabula rasa by hegemonic structures, needs to be analysed and
decolonized by research, and brings new conceptualizations with
concrete cases. The recent border politics between Syria, Iraq and
Turkey has led many refugees to flee to the southeast region of
Turkey, with the consequence of the expansion of refugee camps and
settlements in the region. *Forensik Mimarlık* worked with students to
research the camps, and as most of the students, as Kurds, speak the

---

3   See www.forensic-architecture.org

same languages as Arab immigrants, we were able to communicate with them directly. *Forensik Mimarlık* discussed instant architecture, emergency architecture and related conceptual discussions. *Forensik Mimarlık* research is also searching, pedagogically, to decolonize the language of architecture in this region. It is searching for future design proposals for this territory currently undergoing rapid urbaniza-tion. The *affective pedagogy* is part of this research, as it involves an instant involvement with the actors of the region.

DECOLONIZATION

The *Campus in Camps* initiative by *Decolonizing Architecture* (DAAR) in occupied territories in the West Bank, Palestine, is a different case of searching for an affective pedagogy. Decolonization methodologies in architectural pedagogy have been specifically situated and developed in disputed territories and cities. For instance, *Decolonizing Architecture* is 'an architectural collective that is dedicated to speculate on the reuse and transformation of colonial architecture'.[4] *Decolonizing Architecture* draws on the field of architecture, focusing on the reality of Palestinian refugees to create common spaces and perceive the notion of the 'camp' as a potential space beyond neoliberal citizenship and the dichotomy of public versus private space. *Decolonizing Architecture* collaborates with researchers, refugees, activists and civil representatives of different backgrounds to use militant urban and architectural research meth-odologies and identify common spaces in the refugee camps and former military buildings. Working with the inhabitants of the Fawar camp, for example, they have designed a small public space that was realized by young Palestinian refugees and families. A space for the exchange of everyday life experiences and local engagements can be the most important form of resistance against colonization. *Campus in Camps* run by youth in the Dheisheh refugee camp is an alternative pedagogical platform. This platform is based on several activities that take into consideration the refugee experience and the urbanization of camp practices, as well as wider concerns of education and methods of decolonization. Using social media tools as an expanding archive of sources for their activities, *Campus in Camps* enabled the creation of a new vision of education, by means of critical spatial practices.[5]

---

4   See www.decolonizing.ps/site

5   See www.campusincamps.ps

Campus in Camps has involved participatory engagement in three camps. The first is based in the Dheisheh refugee camp, an urbanized camp in Bethlehem city, in existence since 1948. The third generation of youth there, with architects Alessandro Petti and Sandi Hilal, created the Phoenix Center, that includes the Edward Said Library, which hosts talks and workshops with urbanists, spatial researchers and architects from abroad (Figure 6.1). The centre is a research place where different researchers meet and introduce their projects and their methodologies. *Campus in Camps* produces readers on pedagogy, on commons and on other related concepts that challenge these concepts in relation to their everyday life activities in urbanized camps.

Figure 6.1 *Campus in Camps*, Edward Said Library, March 2015
Photo: Ömer Faruk Gönenç

The second, Fawar camp, is more village-like and is located in the rural south of Hebron city. Again in existence since 1948, Fawar has a large population of women and children. *Campus in Camps* led to a long-term participatory design project to design a public square for the women, a project led by architect Sandi Hilal. The square is now a place for meeting, cooking and assemblies organized by the women (Figure 6.2). The camp is situated in a rural landscape and as a consequence, the women are not able to easily access urban spaces and the cultural activities there. Domestic privacy is also a strong concept here. This square, therefore, created a simple public space in which these women could participate in design decisions by virtue of its proximity to their domestic habitat.

Figure 6.2 Square, Al Fawar Camp, Director of Women Center, Ayat Al Thursan, February 2014
Photo: Pelin Tan

The third camp, Shufat, is like a little town squeezed in between the wall, built by the state of Israel in order to separate the Jewish satellite settlements and Palestinian settlements. Thus, the Shufat camp remains in an in-between situation resulting from land surveillance policy. *Campus in Camps* has collaborated with a girls' school in the camp, with the teachers who are running the school. In his article, 'Decolonizing Knowledge', architect and co-founder of the above-mentioned projects and practices, Alessandro Petti explains that in the first intifada, basic infrastructures were not available and gaining an education was not possible for children and young people. Self-sufficiency and collectively maintaining the commons became an important life condition for Palestinians in the occupied territories. Self-education and collective teaching became the tool of autonomy:

Theoretical knowledge was combined with one that emerges from action and experimentation. Learning became a crucial tool for gaining freedom and autonomy. People discovered that they could share knowledge and could be in charge of what and how to study … The classical structure, in which 'expert teachers' transmit knowledge and students are mere recipients to be filled with information, was substituted by a blurred distinction between the two.
(Petti, 2014)

Petti adds that such an educational practice became a tool of empowerment and emancipation, which, for Palestinians, is vital for decolonization under the state of Israel.

The term 'decolonization' in education is often used in discussions following the legacies of Fanon and Freire. This term became important as it signifies not only an institutional criticism but a search for alternative knowledge production in different colonizer–colonized structures. In the context of colonizer–colonized relations and subjectivities, 'decolonization' not only means resisting territorial occupation and violence but also transforming institutions, cultural products, approaches and values. Moreover, in the context of pedagogy, 'decolonization' basically signifies a non-institutional education where knowledge is produced and shared collectively. The university or academia is always considered the primary place for the production and dissemination of knowledge. Alternative structures and ways of producing knowledge, such as collective research and its representation via social media, are the main forms of non-institutional structures or 'becoming' institutions. Transversality is the practice that cross-creates and disseminates knowledge.

Such research processes and non-institutional structures can create a real effect and take part in the social-political transformation, both in formal institutions as well as in society itself. For example, the number of dams is expanding in Southeast Anatolia where our faculty is based. This reality is one of the main concerns in our graduate education, in which we take 'dam' as a building typology and spatial reality that is a colonizing strategy of the Turkish government, in order to dispose of the land (or dispossess the people from the land) and create surveillance tools, instead of ecological outcomes. As graduate students (architects and planners) observe and analyse this development, they are able to create a contra-knowledge of the role of such a spatial development that can create acts of decolonization in the near future.

Tuck and Yang (2012: 1) argue that 'decolonization' is a metaphor: 'The easy adoption of decolonizing discourse by educational
advocacy and scholarship, evidenced by the increasing number of
calls to "decolonize our schools," or use "decolonizing methods," or,
"decolonize student thinking," turns decolonization into a metaphor.'
The critical stance they elaborate in their article gives a deep
insight to help understand why we use this term in the context of
pedagogy. They continue: 'Decolonization as metaphor allows people
to equivocate these contradictory decolonial desires because it
turns decolonization into an empty signifier to be filled by any track
towards liberation' (ibid.: 7). For them, an anti-colonial critique and
decolonization are slightly different things. I think their critique helps
give a better understanding of the term. Yet the dualistic structures
of colonizer-oppressed subjectivities are more complex today and is
relative from territory to territory. In my opinion, using the word as a
metaphor still grants us emancipative power to reconsider our methodologies, the process-based research tools, the complex realities of
territories and the actors of the social production of architecture.

ARCHIVING

I claim that various methods of archiving, using new media tools
that open it up for public participation, are also an important part
of affective pedagogy. As new media tools advanced in design,
participatory research and common interactive knowledge building
became vital in the methodology of affective pedagogy. For instance,
a group of young architects have re-drawn the in-situ resistance
forms in and around Gezi Park, including the barricades during the
Gezi Park resistance, in the Occupy Gezi Architecture initiative. This
Istanbul-based collective *Architecture for All* (Herkes İçin Mimarlik)
created architectural drawings of ad hoc design structures in Gezi
Park and along the barricades in the Gezi Park resistance. During this
resistance there was a temporary mosque, a mobile food collective
run using simple materials and a tent, an open hospital, and so on,
which are examples of in-situ and instant architectures in Taksim
Square and Gezi Park (Figures 6.3 and 6.4). Straps were used to
represent the borders of each section in Gezi Park, marking the
function of the places; the straps expand or shrink according to
people's needs. In the initiative they claimed: 'We need new definitions for architecture in situations when architecture is removed from
architects. Each unique structure that we encounter in the streets and

Gezi Park has its own in-situ design and implementation process.'[6] Using common design tools to re-create the in-situ and affective experience of architecture, *Architecture for All* invents an embodiment through design methods, to preserve the affect of a spatial resistance but opens it for collective common practice.

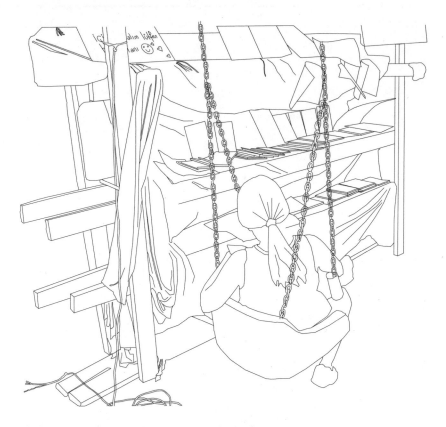

Figure 6.3 Gezi Park Library, drawing of Ad Hoc Design Structure
Drawing: *Architecture for All* (Herkes İçin Mimarlık)

---

6   See http://occupygeziarchitecture.tumblr.com

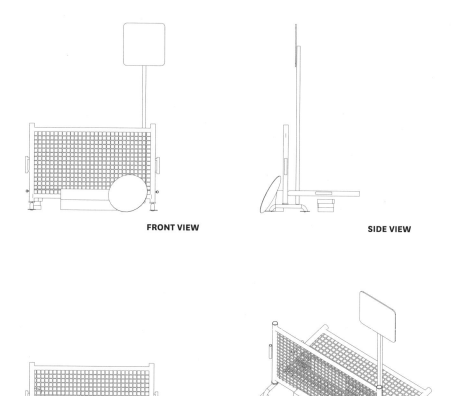

FRONT VIEW   SIDE VIEW

PLAN   AXONOMETRIC

Figure 6.4 Gezi Park Speaker's Point, drawing of Ad Hoc Design Structure
Drawing: *Architecture for All* (Herkes İçin Mimarlik)

Another project on archiving alternative architectural education models and the syllabus in history and from different geographies is *Radical Pedagogies: Action-Reaction-Interaction. Radical Pedagogies*, which is an ongoing, collective and open source research project run by Beatriz Colomina and her team[7] at Princeton University School of Architecture.[8] *Radical Pedagogies* displays a developed

7   The team includes PhD students Britt Eversole, Ignacio G. Galán, Evangelos Kotsioris, Anna-Maria Meister and Federica Vannucchi.

8   See http://radical-pedagogies.com

work in progress along with an interactive digital source and engagement from different parts of the world. The project unfolds the
different layers of the notion of alternative pedagogies in architectural
education, which the audience can relate to, not only as a data set
but also through their own experiences as students or teachers.
As an active, participatory archiving project, *Radical Pedagogies*
not only shares research on the alternative history of architectural
education but also poses questions on the genealogy of methodology
and the instituting practices of self-reflexive architecture education.
Such alternative pedagogies create unorthodox ways of thinking
and working with educational methodologies.[9] As an open source
project, it reveals for me basic questions in architectural education
and social production, such as 'what to teach?', 'in what ways?' and
'how such practices of constantly inventing pedagogies would affect
our "instituting" program in our faculties that we are running'. This
pedagogical radical method pushes us further in questioning knowledge production in architectural education: in which local conditions
and extraterritorial constraints, and following which traditions of
architectural history? Compared to the social sciences and other
fields, architectural education is more problematic, as the 'outside'
market of the neoliberal urban arena presses upon young students
and graduates. In addition, the fact of acquiring notions and referring
to social sciences, as we do, does not necessarily help in creating a
radical method within architecture, but rather keeps the focus on the
field of social sciences.

The radical questioning of the architectural discipline is deeply
rooted in architectural education, which still resists going beyond
studio work and the usual design methodologies to cross multiple
disciplines and consider trans-local territories. Today, the gap
between theory and practice has been challenged from a Deleuzian
perspective by social scientists who search for methodologies of
affective pedagogy and social engagements. As architecture education is increasingly influenced by social practice, this perspective
also has effects. Trans-disciplinary thinking, new media that provide
performative visual tools of representation, and engagements as a
militant researcher in everyday life in order to experience other 'knowledge' or the multiplicity of knowledge production, all urge us to alter
our research methods. Reformulating forms of reactions in syllabuses,

9   Orthodox means here a Eurocentric modern, architecture practice and history-driven education
in architecture faculties; which is common even in the architecture faculties of non-Western countries.

design studios or the politics of academic structures of architecture faculties will lead us to invent new pedagogies. Furthermore, not only established architects or studios/offices but many new alternative collectives are creating practices as a reaction to different territories and provide great potential for alternative design pedagogies for faculties, which is currently always dismissed. For example, my research collective *Forensik Mimarlik* is a tool that includes graduate students and researchers who together focus on the regional conflict and recent border issues, such as the process of refugee camps and dwelling practices of thresholds. This pedagogical practice therefore, has aims of both searching for instant methodologies of decolonizing education, as well as affective pedagogical tools to engage territorial realities at trans-local levels. In collaboration with *Campus in Camps* and Alessandro Petti, we are developing the tools of the spatial practices of decolonizing education, specifically setting up workshops that compare realities and cases between the conditions in the West Bank camps, Dheisheh, Al Fawar and Shufat and in Kobene and Southeast Turkey. Both communities, the youth of the camps and my graduate students from the Southeast region of Turkey are participating and developing mutual methods of analysis of the 'conflict territories' and are discussing architectural practices together.

In conclusion, discussions on affective pedagogy are not often related to questions of 'social reproduction' in architecture, with the exception of socially engaged architecture and participatory design practices. The question of how architectural knowledge and methodologies can create their own domain, within a non-institutional structure and be part of the transformation of society and politics depends in critical ways on new forms/formations of pedagogy in architecture. Forms, such as the ones I have introduced here are decolonizing and transversal; both critical facets of pedagogies capable of allowing participants to (re)produce their own instituting practices, from the university to society.

REFERENCES

Campus in Camps, available at: www.campusincamps.ps (accessed 24 April 2015).

Decolonizing Architecture, available at: www.decolonizing.ps/site (accessed 24 April 2015).

Fanon, Frantz (1963) *The Wretched of the Earth*, New York: Grove Press.

Forensic Architecture, available at: www.forensicarchitectureresearch.com (accessed 24 April 2015).

Freire, Paulo (1993) *Pedagogy of Oppressed,* London: Continuum. Graph Commons, available at: www.graphcommons.com (accessed 24 April 2015).

Guattari, Félix (1996) *The Guattari Reader*, ed. G. Genosko, Oxford: Blackwell.

Hickey-Moody, Anna (2013) 'Aesthetics and affective pedagogy', in Rebecca Coleman and Jessica Ringrose (eds) *Deleuze and Research Methodologies*, Edinburgh: Edinburgh University Press, pp. 79–95.

Labor in Architecture, available at: http://laborarchitecture.tumblr.com and http://staging.graphcommons.com/graphs/78d3ab7f-31c6-47f5-b925-92df95558ad2

Law, John (2004) *After Method: Mess in the Social Science Research*, London: Routledge.

Occupy Gezi Architecture, available at: http://occupygeziarchitecture.tumblr.com (accessed 24 April 2015).

Petti, Alessandro (2014) 'Decolonizing knowledge', available at: www.campusincamps.ps/democratizing-knowledge-production/, August (accessed 24 April 2015).

Radical Pedagogies, available at: http://radical-pedagogies.com (accessed 24 April 2015).

Spivak, Gayatri Chakravorty (2012) *An Aesthetic Education in the Era of Globalization*, Cambridge, MA: Harvard University Press.

Tuck, Eve and Yang, K. Wayne (2012) 'Decolonization is not a metaphor', *Decolonization: Indigeneity, Education & Society* 1(1): 1–40.

Weizman, Eyal, Tavares, Paulo, Schuppli, Susan and Situ Studio (2010) 'Forensic architecture', in Charles Rice, Adrian Lahoud and Anthony Burke (eds) *Post-Traumatic Urbanism: Architectural Design*, Chichester: John Wiley & Sons, Ltd, pp. 58–63.

FURTHER READING

Levinas, Emmanuel (1979)
Totality and Infinity, Dordrecht:
Kluwer Academic Publisher
        (1998) *Entre nous: Thinking
– of – the – Other*, New York:
Columbia University Press.

Tan, Pelin (2016) *Unconditional
Hospitality and Threshold
Architecture*, Barcelona: dpr-
barcelona.

7 – NEIGHBOURHOOD CLAIMS FOR THE FUTURE: FEMINIST SOLIDARITY URBANISM IN VANCOUVER'S DOWNTOWN EASTSIDE

Elke Krasny

This chapter is about the social reproduction of architecture as a resistant feminist practice at the urban neighbourhood scale. Architecture is not understood as a given or immobile object, but rather as the ongoing work of spatialized social relations. This work entails agency and positive change as well as counter-action and resistance. Both positive change and resistance are considered 'social reproduction work' in the development of urban neighbourhoods. This contention is explored through the example of the Downtown Eastside Women's Centre's (DEWC) involvement in the changing neighbourhood of Vancouver's Downtown Eastside over the past three decades. Social reproduction theorists like Silvia Federici and Mariarosa Dalla Costa have emphasized that reproductive labour is, for the most part, unpaid labour. It is also frequently referred to as hidden labour (Federici, 2012: 31). Histories of urban struggles and of feminist counter-planning, everyday feminist solidarity, practices of self-organization, urban activism, and right-to-the-city movements can, following this work, largely be understood as hidden labour that not only keeps the 'social reproduction of architecture' alive, but makes cities places of life, despite all the odds of rising inequality, vulnerability and precarity. Even though urban activism and right-to-the-city-movements make claims and demands visible, the better part of its social reproduction work remains hidden. It is mainly this hidden work that forges friendships, nourishes trust, instils hope, builds alliances, and supports resistance. Therefore, this chapter is also about hope and resistance focusing on the social reproduction of architecture as one that must be about feminist solidarity, one that is working across and between different claims and conflicts.

This chapter builds upon my 2011–2012 urban curatorial project,[1] *Mapping the Everyday: Neighbourhood Claims for the Future* that centred around a mapping of the claims and demands put forward by the DEWC since its inception in 1978 (Figures 7.1–7.3). The DEWC's claims can be understood as contributing to the development of the neighbourhood, and the social reproduction of architecture in (at least) two ways. First, articulating claims that influenced (or attempted to intervene in) the dominant planning and development processes, led in the main by the Simon Fraser University and the School for Contemporary Arts. These claims and demands informed (to differing degrees) the development and at the same time constitute a form of unrecognized labour. Second, the processes of collectively articulating claims and demands as the process of social solidarity and more importantly the everyday activities of the Women's Centre, foreground the *reproduction of spaces and relations that sustain the life of the neighbourhood* yet are mostly unrecognized.

Figures 7.1, 7.2, 7.3 (opposite page) *Mapping the Everyday: Neighbourhood Claims for the Future* installation view, Audain Gallery, Vancouver, 2011–2012
Photos: Kevin Schmidt.

---

1   Meike Schalk has written a seminal piece on the multifaceted social and political dimensions of urban curating. See Meike Schalk, 'Urban curating: a critical practice towards greater "connectedness"', in *Altering Practices: Feminist Politics and Poetics of Space*, ed. Doina Petrescu (London: Routledge, 2007) pp. 153–166. My own writing on urban curating includes: 'Het Verschil Maken: Strategieen in urban curating. Ma(r)king a difference: strategies of urban curating', in *OpTrek in Transvaal. Over de Rol van Pubieke Kunst in de Stedeijka Ontwikkeling. OpTrek in Transvaal. On the Role of Public Art in Urban Development. Interventions and Research*, ed. Veronica Hekking, Sabrina Lindemann and Annechien Meier (Heijningen: Jap Sams Books, 2010), 'In search of the present', in *In Search of Spaces of Negotiation*, ed. Kateryna Botanova (Kiev: ADEF Ukraine, 2012), pp. 134–141, and 'Urban curating: Jetzt Wi(e)der/Urban Curating: once again(st)', in *Die Kunst des urbanen Handelns/The Art of Urban Intervention*, ed. Judith Laister, Anton Lederer and Margarethe Makovec (Vienna: Löcker Verlag, 2014).

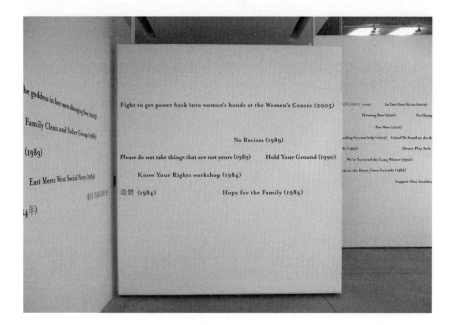

This hidden labour is public work, or put differently, it makes, what we call the public work. For practitioners of architecture, urbanism, research, theory, or curating, this means acknowledging the immense scale of hidden work necessary to make the (public) life of urban neighbourhoods. Although it is easy to critique social reproduction's hidden labour and its gendered nature, it is equally important, first, to open up new ways of thinking about social reproduction beyond the concept of waged labour (to acknowledge multiple economies and contributions) and, second, move it from the domestic scale of the household as it is normally understood to the urban scale of architecture, communities, neighbourhoods, and cities in order that we can more fully recognize the civic work involved in making neighbourhoods.

The project, and this chapter, posit 'social reproduction' as a field of 'transversal politics' (Yuval-Davis, 1999) and transnational feminist solidarity (Mohanty, 2003). It suggests that such approaches can result in the production of feminist urban infrastructure, i.e. built architecture or physical space, but also in counter-acting the dynamics of architecture that accelerate gentrification and cause evictions. This means working amidst contradictions that are not going to disappear but allow for agency only within the prevailing conditions of austerity, neoliberalism, neocolonialism, rising militarism, and new forms of sexualized and racialized segregation and exploitation. Therefore, the 'social reproduction of architecture' within these prevailing conditions needs to open up resistant spaces for feminist reproductions of space that are specifically anti-racist and emphasize the right to the city.

In the case of this project, *Mapping the Everyday*, the practice of 'urban curating' can also be seen as socially and spatially reproductive, involving aspects of 'hidden labour'. In this chapter, I introduce urban curating as a form of spatial practice before moving on to introduce the neighbourhood of the Downtown Eastside, and the importance both for this locality, and in general, of working with a 'transversal' and 'solidarity' approach to urban curating. I then introduce some of the elements of *Mapping the Everyday*, in the midst of its contradictory situation and history.

URBAN CURATING IN VANCOUVER'S DOWNTOWN EASTSIDE

Urban curating is an involved practice, working across and between differences amidst unresolved contradictions. Urban curating, as I understand it, is co-implicated in the work of social reproduction by way of alignments and collaborations. Analogous to social reproduction work, urban curating also has a non-hidden part that becomes public in the form of exhibitions in art and architecture contexts. In my own practice, I draw together critical urban studies, feminist thought, and the collaboration across urgent urban issues, contemporary histories of self-organization, politics of everyday life, and the fields of contemporary art and architecture.

Urban curating involves theory and practice, which are understood to be co-productive, co-dependent, and co-emergent. Urban curating that actively seeks to make itself part of the (hidden) work of social reproduction *moves across and between differences* in place and in time. There is a methodological analogy between my practice as an urban curator and my writing with my curatorial practice. As urban curating involves movements of 'across and between', these are also the movements of this chapter as it moves across and between theory and practice and between the DEWC and the Audain Gallery, the project's two architectural sites that are part of the same Vancouver neighbourhood. One of the sites does not surface in hegemonic urban histories or architectural monographs. The other site claims an important space in the city's history and equally in its architectural history. The social reproduction work of architecture, such as the work of the DEWC, does not necessarily lead to its inclusion in urban or architectural history. It does so in times of exception, moments of struggle, demonstrations and in this case, the articulation of specific claims and demands. Yet, this everyday work remains largely unnoticed and uncredited. It flies under the radar of the politics of recognition. Yet, the people performing this work credit each other, appreciate and value its importance and its scale.

The Downtown Eastside of Vancouver, one of the city's oldest neighbourhoods, boasts a long history of community activism and residents' resistance. For decades, the Downtown Eastside (DTES) has been marked by uneven development, neoliberal economics, gentrification, poverty, precarity, and violence. The Downtown Eastside Women's Centre (DEWC) is a self-organized feminist space dedicated to women's empowerment and fighting inequality. *Mapping the Everyday* included an activist, archival mapping of the history of the DEWC. It mapped the demands and claims put forward by the women of the Centre and took on the form of a text-based installation at the Audain Gallery. This 'horizon line' of demands (Table 7.1) and claims on the gallery's walls served as a backdrop when using the gallery space in its entirety as:

> [a] meeting ground for the production and sharing of different forms of knowledge. To achieve this, the collaborative project expanded to include the art collective desmedia, red diva projects, the art collective Coupe, Out of Bounds: Festival of Site-Specific Interventions, students from the School for the Contemporary Art at Simon Fraser University, and members of the Downtown Eastside community.[2]
> (*Mapping the Everyday*, 2011: 1)

2   This chapter will focus on the archival mapping and the complexities of the practice of transversal feminist politics and transnational feminist solidarity in the temporary alliance of the Downtown Eastside Women Centre, the Audain Gallery, and myself. An in-depth analysis and theoretical reflection of all the different artistic and activist contributions to *Mapping the Everyday: Neighbourhood Claims for the Future* exceed the scope of this chapter.

"All My Relations

Stop Violence Against Women (1980 –)
Our Hearts Go Out (1980 –)
In Loving Memory (1980 –)
Battered Women's Support Group (1980 –)
Take Back the Night (1979 –)
Banner Making Party (1982)
You are Not Forgotten (1982)
Create a Powerful Force of Change (1984)
East Meets West Social Party (1984)
Know Your Rights workshop (1984)
Hope for the Family (1984)
Support One Another (1985)
Role Models (1985)
Positive Parenting (1985)
Working Women's Drop-In – Ring Buzzer (1985)
A Chance for Women (1985)
We are the Seers, the Healers, the Warriors (1985)
The Common Woman is as Common as a
Common Loaf of Bread and Will Rise (1985)
Gather Together (1986)
Free Soup and Bannock (1986)
Take Back Your Power (1986)
Ongoing Social Action (1986)
No drugs or alcohol in the Centre. We don't want
a reason for the cops to come here! (1986)
See Some of the Strengths That You Did Not
Know You Had (1985)
All Women Band A Benefit Performance – all
proceeds to raise money for musical instruments
for our Sisters in Oakalla. Women's Event – At
the Centre. Free if you are broke.
Condoms, street Talk and Badtrick Sheets
Available (1986)
Gather Together (1986)
Take Back Your Power (1986)
Share Your Memories (1987)
Decrease the Grief (1987)
Bad Trick Sheets (1987)
Assertiveness with a Beat (1987)
Spruce You Up! Tie-dye to 50s music (1987)
Festival for Foods Parade (1987)
Grassroots Fundraising (1987)
Information and Support Sharing (1987)
No Way to Live (1988)
Take the Next Step (1988)
We Announce Our Solidarity (1988)
The Needs of Women Come First (1988)
Welfare Rates Under Attack (1988)
Tenants Rights Workshop (1988)
Becoming yourself through writing (1988)
Fight for Welfare Rights (1989)
Women's Right to Choose (1989)
Women's Forum (1989)
Willing and Able (1989)
No Homophobia (1989)
No Racism (1989)
Projects Collective (1989)
Fight City Hall (89-present)

On December 19th, approximately 2000 people
gathered at City Hall to protest rising rents and
growing homelessness (1989)
Red Road Warriors (1989)
Menopause Support Group (1989)
Clean and Sober Group meeting (1989)
Recovery (1989)
Family Clean and Sober Group (1989)
Please do not take things that are not yours
(1989)
Hold Your Ground (1990)
Sleeping Hummingbirds (1990)
We've Survived the Long Winter (1990)
Always Play Safe (1990)
Impossible Takes a Little Longer (1990)
Their Spirits Live Within Us (1990 –)
Justice for Missing and Murdered
Women (1990s)
Justice for Residential School Survivors (1990)
We are also always in need of clothes for
women (1990 –)
Campaign to Get Welfare Raised (1991)
Reclaiming Your Power (1991)
Aboriginal Celebrations and Ceremonies (1991)
Sisters in Spirit (1990 –)
The February 14th Women's Memorial March
Committee (1992 –)
We are committed to justice. (1992 –)
Tools for Change (1994)
A Safe Place for Women (1994)
Grief and Loss Support (1995)
Visualizing Workshops (1995)
Stop the War on the Poor! (1996)
Raise the Rates (1998)
Bad Date Sheets (1998)
Psychiatric Day Program (1999)
Healing Circle (1999)
Make a Wild Woman Out of You (1999)
Popular Education (1999–2003)
End Legislated Poverty (1999–2004)
The Learning Group (2000–02)
Learn how to make something from nothing
(stone soup) (2000)
Today in One Circle (2001)
Welcome Home (2001)
We Must Stand Together for Peace Justice,
Freedom and Equality (2001)
Honour our Sisters and Grandmothers (2001)
Join Us Women (2001)
Sisters Resist (2001)
Breaking the Silence (2001)
Positive Body Images (2001)
Appropriate Programming (2001)
There is joy in the struggle (2002)
Outings Rock Our World (2003)
University Access: Institute of Indigenous
Government Canada's First Nations College, in
Partnership with the DEWC – Tuition Free (2003)
Stop Police Violence (2003)
DTES, I Love (2004)
Stop Attacks on Women (2004)
Rise Up (2005)

Love and Support (2005)
Imagine the woman who honours the face of the
goddess in her own changing face (2005)
Fight to get power back into women's hands at
the Women's Centre (2005)
Donations Committee asking for your help (2005)
Pow Wow (2005)
Celebrate a New Beginning (2006)
Build Community (2006)
[first annual] Women's Housing March (2006)
This march is also being organized in solidarity
with our sisters in the Women Against Poverty
Collective in Toronto who on June 3rd are
organizing a housing takeover in Toronto to draw
attention to the links between safe housing and
women's ability to live free from violence. We are
joining together from Toronto to Vancouver to
demand safe, long-term affordable housing for
women to be made available immediately
Our Own Voices: of Pain and Hope (2007)
Vigil and March to Honour Women (2007)
Stop All Forms of Violence Against Women:
End Patriarchy! (2007)
Power of Women (2007)
Safe Housing for Women (2007)
An Open Letter to Mayor Sam Sullivan and City
Council from Women in the Downtown
Eastside (July 2, 2007)
DTES Community Meeting at DEWC – Men
Welcome. Open to All Concerned DTES
Residents and Community Members (2007)
March for Women's Housing and March Against
Poverty! Elders, Youth, Men Welcome Bring
Drums and Your Friends (2007)
Stop Child Apprehension, Support Mothers (2008)
We Demand an Inquiry into the Missing
Women (2008)
People Are Dying (2008)
Social Housing, Healthcare and Childcare
Now! (2008)
No More Evictions and No More Condos! (2008)
Stop Criminalizing the Poor (2008)
End Global Hunger and Poverty (2008)
Affordable and Safe Housing Now! (2009)
Stop Ticketing and Arrests Under Project Civil
City (2009)
Fight Rapid Hotel/SRO Closures and
Evictions (2009)
Stop Police Brutality (2009)
Housing Now (2010)
In Our Own Voices (2010)
No Olympics on Stolen Native Land! (2010)
People Before Olympic Profits (2010)
Survival, Strength, Sisterhood: Power of Women
in the Downtown (2010)
Our Lives, Our Voices: Downtown Eastside
women find healing through narrative (2010)
Respect Your Elders (2011)
We will be marching to demand action on
women's safety (2011)

Women's Coalition of the Downtown Eastside:

Women's Safety 24/7 Women's Coalition of the
Gone but not Forgotten (2011)
Downtown Eastside is a newly formed network
of women-serving organizations and women's
groups in the Downtown Eastside of Vancouver,
Coast Salish Territories (2011)
Stop the Pantages Development (2011)
Boycott Sequel 138 (2011)
Gentrifuckation (2011)
Housing For All (2011)
Social Housing, child care and health care
for all! (2011)
No more evictions and no more gentrification in
the Downtown Eastside! (2011)
Stop criminalizing the poor! (2011)
DTES is Not for Developers (2011)
Many Paths of Our Resistance (2011)
Participant Groups in the Missing Women's
Inquiry Pressure Premier Clark to Ensure Access
and Justice (2011)
Committee Announces Non Participation in
Sham Inquiry (2011)"
(Mapping the Everyday: Neighbourhood Claims
for the Future, exhibition, 2011–2012)

Table 7.1 List of initiatives

The agenda of the DEWC and the curatorial intent shaping *Mapping the Everyday: Neighbourhood Claims for the Future* intersect issues of urban justice, urban transformation, anti-racism, politics of recognition, politics of commemoration, and transnational feminist solidarity:

> *High levels of violence, homelessness, addictions and poverty characterize the Downtown Eastside community, and women and children are particularly vulnerable to exploitation, injustice and injury. Founded in 1978, DEWC is one of the few safe spaces within the Downtown Eastside exclusively for women and their children.*
> (Cecily Nicholson, email correspondence with the author, 11 August 2011)

From a theoretical perspective, *Mapping the Everyday: Neigh-bourhood Claims for the Future* and its activities of alliance building (Figure 7.4) within the social reproduction of architecture draw upon the concepts of transversal politics as described by Nira Yuval-Davis and upon the work of Chandra Talpade Mohanty, in particular, her critical insights on what is needed for feminist practice at the beginning of the twenty-first century. The 'social reproduction work of architecture' is concerned with the reproduction of bodies and space. Bodies have to be reproduced both over time and in space. Much of this work remains hidden, some of this work, as manifestations, protests or community meetings underline, makes this hidden work publicly visible. (Yet one should add that a lot of this visible work still remains unpaid and precarious labour.) Its processes of alliance building and resistance are bound up with the 'politics of recognition' (Taylor, quoted by Yuval-Davis, 1999: 97) and the politics of commemoration. *Mapping the Everyday* followed the principles of 'transversal politics' that, according to Nira Yuval-Davis, are based on the following. First, 'standpoint epistemology, which recognises that from each positioning the world is seen differently', second, 'difference by equality' and third, 'a conceptual differentiation between positioning, identity, and values' (Yuval-Davis, 1999: 94). These principles were put into practice throughout the project, and as much as the curatorial intent was about alliance building and establishing relations and connections, it was equally about acknowledging the many different borderlines crossing such a project, both from within and from the outside.

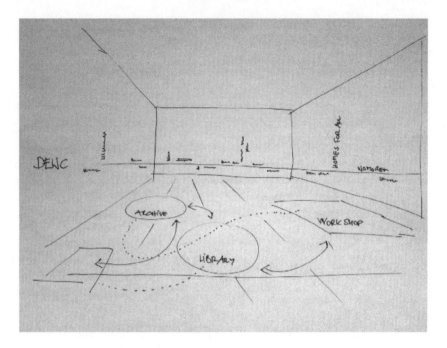

Figure 7.4 *Mapping the Everyday: Neighbourhood Claims for the Future* sketch showing the alliances and collaborations

> *Feminism without borders is not the same as border-less feminism. It acknowledges the fault lines, conflicts, differences, fears and containment that borders represent. It acknowledges that there is no one sense of a border, that the lines between and through nations, races, classes, sexualities, religions, and disabilities, are real – and that feminism without borders must envision change and social justice work across these lines of demarcation and division.*
> (Mohanty, 2003: 2)

Urban curating is necessarily plural in nature, not one thing, but many. It seeks to nurture support and temporary alliances. 'Hence decolonization, anticapitalist critique, and solidarity. I firmly believe an antiracist feminist framework anchored in decolonization and committed to an anticapitalistic critique, is necessary at this time' (ibid.: 3).

THE IMPORTANCE OF WORKING WITH DIFFERENCE AND SOLIDARITY IN VANCOUVER'S DOWNTOWN EASTSIDE?

The DEWC and the Audain Gallery were the two venues connected through the people involved in *Mapping the Everyday: Neighbourhood Claims for the Future.* These two venues are in walking distance of each other; the DEWC is located at 302 Columbia Street at Cordova, the Audain Gallery at 149 W Hastings Street. One could argue that walking the short distance is already part of the social reproduction of architecture. Bodies moving through other spaces, crossing thresholds, opening doors, making themselves present in different territories, are part of the transversal politics and its recognition in space. The two sites are part of the same neighbourhood, yet they are set apart by the economies of power and influence. Vancouver has often been described as a city of neighbourhoods. 'The City of Vancouver is made up of a number of smaller neighbourhoods and communities; however, not everyone agrees on all of the names and boundaries of these areas.'[3] It is commonly understood that the neighbourhood, in the context of urban planning, is taken for granted. Yet what actually makes a neighbourhood remains largely unclear. One might argue that neighbourhoods are in fact effected by the social reproduction of architecture, in that neighbourhoods come into being via the hidden work produced by all the social relations necessary to then self-identify as part of the neighbourhood. Locating the DEWC and the Audain Gallery in the shared context of the same neighbourhood acknowledges the invisible and visible borderlines cutting through a neighbourhood and the fraught relations between unequal neighbours. The arrival of the downtown campus of the Simon Fraser University and the Audain Gallery are accelerating gentrification. On a practical and a theoretical level, the means of resistance have to be nourished to effectively allow for the survival of the neighbourhood and its social reproduction against the onslaught of gentrification wrought in part by new architecture, such as the Woodward's Building in which the Audain Gallery is located.

In the fall of 2010, Simon Fraser University's School for the Contemporary Arts and the Audain Gallery moved to the DTES Woodward's Building. This is a landmark building fraught with historical significance, struggles, and occupation. Originally built in 1903 for the Woodward's Department Store, the building stood empty after

---

3   See http://vancouver.ca (accessed 3 December 2013).

Woodward's bankruptcy in 1993. In fact, it was the 2002 housing occupation that actually triggered the redevelopment.

> *In 2002, radical anti-poverty activists occupied the site of the former Woodward's department store, located in the centre of Vancouver's impoverished Downtown Eastside in what became a high-profile protest over gentrification, government cutbacks and homelessness … Highly politicized Woodsquat activists invoked a language of rights, social justice and insurgent citizenship. The City obtained an injunction, compelling the protesters to remove the encampment.*
> (Blomley, 2011: 1)

In 2004, the City of Vancouver selected Westbank Projects/Peterson Investment Group as developers for the project. The architectural design was undertaken by Henriquez Partners Architects. It includes 'market' and 'non-market' housing units and an extensive addition to Simon Fraser University's downtown campus. In 2006, the Woodward's complex, except for its oldest original part, was demolished.

Sociological analysis and urban scholarship have devoted a lot of attention to the processes of gentrification. In the burgeoning literature on gentrification, the co-implications of contemporary art and of university campuses as drivers of urban redevelopment and gentrification processes, have been worked out.[4] Therefore, the specific situation of the Audain Gallery bringing together *both* the contemporary art and a university campus in the midst of a major process of gentrification warrants hesitation and doubts regarding the politics and the ethics of alliance building with its neighbours.

> *Since Simon Fraser University's School for the Contemporary Arts and the Audain Gallery moved in the fall of 2010 to the Downtown Eastside of Vancouver, often described as the poorest postal code in Canada, questions of gentrification, representation, site-specificity, and research ethics have become crucial.*
> (Bitter, in *Mapping the Everyday*, 2011: 1)

---

4   Examples of gentrification efforts and urban renewal/or new urban development based upon universities and campus buildings abound. An example from the 1950s is the University City in West Philadelphia. A more recent example is the 2013 Campus of the Vienna University of Economics and Business that includes buildings by Hitoshi Abe, Peter Cook and Zaha Hadid, among other star architects.

Alongside the term neighbourhood, the term community[5] has also
been widely used to describe different groups constitutive of social,
spatial, economic, ethnic, or sexed difference in the urban topography. Distribution of difference is constitutive of uneven development
and vice versa, uneven development is constitutive of the distribution
of difference. Both marked and unmarked borders negotiate the
territories of difference. Even though publicly accessible, the Audain
Gallery is part of the security system of the Simon Fraser University.
Visitors entering the gallery space must pass guards behind their
glass windows in the security booth and guards doing their rounds in
the Woodward's building. The community of students passes easily;
the community of women from the Downtown Eastside Women's
Centre garners the guards' attention. Upon entering the Downtown
Eastside Women's Centre, one sees a woman working the reception
counter and feels the need to introduce oneself as a person new to
the Centre and its community. At the gallery, a guard monitors the
comings and goings of the visiting public. At the Women's Centre, a
table next to the reception desk makes one stop. Here, a number of
items such as candles or small memorabilia are displayed to commemorate the people who did not survive the last weeks or months.
These objects demand attention, they remind visitors to respectfully
commemorate the dead who are part of the everyday life in the
Downtown Eastside.

The entanglements of activism, contemporary art, university
campus architecture, gentrification, and neoliberal urbanization are
what *Mapping the Everyday: Neighbourhood Claims for the Future*
has made itself part of (Figure 7.5). The project took place with
awareness of the ways that critical and feminist practices have been
incorporated into capitalism as well as the neoliberal logics that pose
threats to alliances and solidarity. This in turn, comes with a long
history of feminist debates over the politics of representation and
the politics of recognition with regard to ethnic, economic, cultural,
sexual, religious, or bodied differences. Differentiation and solidarity
are therefore to be understood within the politics (and economics)

5   Community has warranted a lot of theoretical and philosophical attention. Jean-Luc Nancy,
Alain Badiou, Giorgio Agamben and Chandra Talpade Mohanty, to name just a few, have written
extensively on community. Neighbourhood, on the other hand, has until now remained strangely
under-theorized, even though neighbours are constitutive of interdependent spatial and social urban
relations. In both urban planning and urban analysis, definitions and descriptions of neighbourhood
remain rather imprecise and inadequate. Neighbourhood intersects local and global scales and
allows for an understanding of cities not in their totality, but in their parts and specific particularities.
Neighbourhoods in different cities might share more commonalities than adjacent neighbourhoods in
the same city.

that are their underlying structure. At the same time, this analytical understanding must not impede curatorial feminist agency and activist alliances. The contemporary feminist paradigm of transversal politics, as described by Nira Yuval-Davis, and of transnational feminism, as developed by Chandra Talpade Mohanty, offers not only a strong commitment to practice, at all times respectful of difference, but also a strong theorization of this very commitment. This allows us to conceive of the co-existence of differentiation and solidarity. Such a concept is foundational for the urban curatorial work of *Mapping the Everyday: Neighbourhood Claims for the Future.*

Figure 7.5 Collective Futures in the Downtown Eastside: forum and discussion led by the desmedia collective in Vancouver in the exhibition *Mapping the Everyday: Neighbourhood Claims for the Future*
Photo: Sabine Bitte

RECOGNIZING UNEQUAL POWER RELATIONS AND COLONIAL LEGACIES IN THE NEIGHBOURHOOD

From a curatorial perspective, the project relied on the critical and de-colonizing activation of formats that are implied in the colonial legacy of cartography and historiography. 'There are three key components in this collaboration: the archive, the map, and the library.'[6] These components are formal, foundational, and conceptually important. If we situate these components in a genealogy of the history of ideas, we can see that their purpose is to collect, store, and convey different forms of knowledge.

> The archive, the map, and the library have long been part of a set of governmental strategies of organization and consolidation. If read from another vantage, however, these strategies allow people to see how 'seeing like a state' functions. In other words, this alternative view makes it possible to see the inner operation of the state in the production and reproduction of hegemonic power. Ultimately, this view is double – the ways of viewing the state offers, while also seeing alternative ways of viewing that have been excluded by the state. This doubled viewing is profoundly dialectical. ... Social movements, protest groups, emancipatory education movements, feminist collectives, and others have taken up both sides of this dialectic strategically. (Krasny, in Mapping the Everyday, 2011: 2)

In order to avoid the pitfalls of representational reductionism or discursive colonialism, an urban curatorial project like Mapping the Everyday: Neighbourhood Claims for the Future has to rely on differentiated agency based upon a praxis of attentiveness, care, and listening. Chandra Talpade Mohanty has critically analysed 'discursive colonization on the lives and struggles of marginalized women.' (2003: 230). What was at stake in Mapping the Everyday: Neighbourhood Claims for the Future was the inherent danger of reproducing unequal power relations inextricably connected with the historic legacy of

---

6   In the context of this chapter, the archive and the map are central. The third component resulted in a new mobile library for the Downtown Eastside Women's Centre. A number of workshops realized by women of the Centre and students of the School for the Contemporary Art of Simon Fraser University resulted in a collection of books covering a wide range of themes and subjects from poetry to law, from self-help to Vancouver's history. Following a suggestion of Sabine Bitter, who was the curator of the Audain Gallery at the time, the design for the mobile library is based on historic furniture that was part of the Simon Fraser University campus at the time of the Simon Fraser University Strike in 1968.

colonialism, contemporary strategies of urban research and artistic production with regard to the politics of recognition and the distribution of
knowledge, and the spatial effects of gentrification. In 2011, Vancouver
commemorated its 125th anniversary. Even the city's name, named
after George Vancouver, bears witness to the city's colonial history:

> *Dispatched to the region by the British in 1791, Vancouver*
> *conducted an exhaustive cartographic survey and has been*
> *represented as the 'true discoverer' of the coast. ... this*
> *reconnaissance induced and supported a range of imperial and*
> *colonial practices. Vancouver's work played a central role in the*
> *creation of a system of imperial inscription that primed the coast*
> *for colonial intervention.*
> (Clayton, 2000: 371)

Mapping the Everyday: Neighbourhood Claims for the Future was
part of a number of projects officially funded by the City of Vancouver
to commemorate the 125th anniversary of Vancouver. It became
important to critically relate the artistic and curatorial practice of mapping, used to create a timeline of demands of the Downtown Eastside
Women's Centre, to the history of cartography and its colonial implications. Moreover, it is of importance to commemorate the spatial politics
at stake in the practices of the anniversary commemoration, particularly
in the knowledge that the city of Vancouver is on unceded land:

> *Only in 2014 Vancouver city council has unanimously voted to*
> *acknowledge that the city is on unceded Aboriginal territory.*
> *Mayor Gregor Robertson declared a 'Year of Reconciliation' last*
> *summer, in the hopes of building new relationships between*
> *Aboriginals and Vancouverites ... 'Underlying all other truths*
> *spoken during the Year of Reconciliation is the truth that the*
> *modern city of Vancouver was founded on the traditional*
> *territories of the Musqueam, Squamish and Tsleil-Waututh First*
> *Nations and that these territories were never ceded through*
> *treaty, war or surrender,' reads part of the motion from the city.*
> (Meiszner, 2014: online)

Astutely aware of the implications of contemporary art and university campus architecture in gentrification processes, on one hand, and
the dangers of discursive colonization, on the other hand, I arrived at
the curatorial suggestion of mapping the claims and demands that the
women of the DEWC have put forward since its inception in 1978.

These claims bear witness to the ongoing social reproduction work carried out by the women of the Centre. These claims put this hidden work into words. They name it. 'The DTES communities' profound sense of the logics and strategies of representation is expressed in the common use of the demand "Nothing About Us Without Us"' (*Mapping the Everyday*, 2011: 1). Respecting this demand and working together accordingly was the premise for the alliance and the mapping process. Even though no formal archive has ever been established, the Centre has kept records and copies of the newsletters the women have issued regularly since 1978. These served as the basis for the mapping. A series of workshops at the DEWC inspired the formation of an ad-hoc group by the women of the Centre and created the opportunity to work through materials. The group consisted of Terri Marie, Karen Lahey, Debbie Ventura, Dalannah Gail Bowen, Sue Zhao, Sara, Ramona, Pat Haram, Audrey, Joan Morelli, Shurli Chan, Stirling, Stella August and Beatrice Starr. Drawing from the Centre's archival materials, the women organized their claims and demands chronologically and thematically, in the process revealing patterns of change and continuity. These claims and demands addressed issues of poverty, violence, and uncertainty. Equally, the claims and demands are the shortest possible versions of intensified descriptions of what the women demanded from themselves, with regard to the social reproduction work they perform both on a daily basis and in times of crisis, exception, and increasing pressure.

As a physical site, the Centre continues to withstand removal. As a social site, the Centre provides support, and inspires hope. The social reproduction of architecture is addressed on a number of levels in the practice of the DEWC and in the temporary alliance built between the women of the Centre, the Audain Gallery, and myself as artist-in-residence/urban curator. The collected claims bear witness that the Centre is part of the neighbourhood's history as site, supportive of solidarity and friendship between indigenous women, Chinese women, and other women. The claims manifest the Centre's resistance through the women's counter-actions against neoliberal urbanization, gentrification, and austerity measures. The timeline also demonstrates that for over 30 years the Centre has been part of larger and global discussions of feminism, indigenous cultures, colonialism, poverty, urban justice, and housing rights. Not only have the women created a physical space in which support and friendship can be lived and practised on an everyday basis, they also continue to manifest their physical and political resilience and resistance in their daily movements to and from the Centre in the city of Vancouver, in their marches and demonstrations, in neighbourhood meetings, and, in alliances with others, both with communities or people from the neighbourhood and from afar. All this taken together is part of the immense scale of (hidden) labour of the social reproduction neces- sary for their survival and for the resistance of the neighbourhood. The right to the city, expressed as the women's right to the neighbour- hood, has both public and personal dimensions.

> Mapping the Everyday *foregrounds women of the Downtown Eastside's capacity to affect social transformation via sustained resistance to, and rearrangement of multiple, relational modes of ruling apparatuses and regulatory bodies including police, court and legal systems, the service industry, business, education, and media. Open to the voices and everyday actions of community members, the collaborative efforts subvert the representation of women in the downtown eastside as victims, fixed or pacified, and as abject components of a still-colonial and patriarchal gaze.* (Nicholson, in *Mapping the Everyday*, 2011: 3)

Knowingly entering into the entanglements and inherent relations between economic globalization, the legacy of colonialism, neoliberal gentrification, contemporary art and new campus buildings, chal- lenges any naïve, complicit or uncritical temporary alliance. Yet, one cannot let these conditions result in the postulation of the impossibility of such alliance. Affective relations, trust, friendship, and resistance are in turn supported through a temporary alliance of transversal feminist politics and feminist transnational solidarity. Through such a temporary alliance built by urban curating, a space like the Audain Gallery can be transformed by way of the 'social reproduction of archi- tecture'. Together, we turned the space of the Audain Gallery into a public interior, enabling and making manifest a feminist alliance for the social reproduction of space/the reproduction of a social space:[7]

> *A transversal feminist politics and a transnational feminist prac- tice depend on building solidarity across the divisions of place, identity, class, work, belief, and so on. In these very fragmented*

---

7   An in-depth description and analysis of the formal and aesthetic appearance of the installation and the assemblies, meetings, reading groups, and performances exceed the scope of this chapter. Suffice to say, that my curatorial intent firmly rooted the conceptual aesthetics and research in the legacy of conceptual feminism within contemporary art practice in its activist dimension. Both appearance-wise and conceptually, projects like Lucy Lippard's c. 7.500 or Martha Rosler's If You Lived Here inspired *Mapping the Everyday: Neighbourhood Claims for the Future*.

times it is both very difficult to build these alliances and also
never more important to do so. Global capitalism both destroys
the possibilities and offers up new ones.
(Mohanty, 2003: 250)

In concluding, I want to invoke categories like trust, respect,
friendship, and mutual support in order to advocate an urban curatorial
practice that makes itself part of the social reproduction of architecture
moving across and between hope and resistance, precarity and
vulnerability. Within the time and the space of a temporary alliance,
differentiation and solidarity move in tandem with conflict and hope. The
social reproduction work of architecture, even though largely hidden
work, proves it can provide platforms for transversal feminist politics
and sustained transnational feminist solidarity withstanding the continued legacies of coloniality, and the precarization of bodies and space.

REFERENCES

Blomley, Richard (2011) *Rights of Passage: Sidewalks and the Regulation of Public Flow*, New York: A Glass House Book.

Clayton, Daniel (2000) 'On the colonial genealogy of George Vancouver's chart of the Northwest Coast of North America', *Ecumene: A Journal of Cultural Geographies* 7(4): 371–401.

Federici, Silvia (2012) *Revolution at Point Zero: Housework, Reproduction and Feminist Struggle*, Oakland, CA: PM Press.

Krasny, Elke (2010) 'Het Verschil Maken: Strategieen in urban curating. Ma(r)king a difference: strategies of urban curating', in Veronica Hekking, Sabrina Lindemann and Annechien Meier (eds) *OpTrek in Transvaal. Over de Rol van Pubieke Kunst in de Stedeijka Ontwikkeling. OpTrek in Transvaal. On the Role of Public Art in Urban Development: Interventions and Research*, Heijningen: Jap Sams Books.
   (2012) 'In search of the present', in Kateryna Botanova (ed.) *In Search of Spaces of Negotiation*, Kiev: ADEF Ukraine.
   (2014) 'Urban Curating: Jetzt Wi(e)der/Urban Curating: once again(st)', in Judith Laister, Anton Lederer and Margarethe Makovec (eds) *Die Kunst des urbanen Handelns/The Art of Urban Intervention*, Vienna: Löcker Publishers.

Mapping the Everyday: Neighbourhood Claims for the Future, Audain Gallery SFU Woodward's, November 17, 2011–February 25, 2012, brochure printed on the occasion of the exhibition by the same name, with contributions by Sabine Bitter, Elke Krasny and Cecily Nicholson.

Meiszner, Peter (2014) 'City of Vancouver formally declares city is on unceded Aboriginal territory', *Global News*, 25 June. Available at: http://globalnews.ca/news/1416321/city-of-vancouver-formally-declares-city-is-on-unceded-aborginal-territory/ (accessed 3 December 2015).

Mohanty, Chandra Talpade (2003) *Feminism Without Borders: Decolonizing Theory, Practicing Solidarity*, Durham, NC: Duke University Press.

Schalk, Meike (2007) 'Urban curating: a critical practice towards greater "connectedness"', in Doina Petrescu (ed.) *Altering Practices: Feminist Politics and Poetics of Space*, London: Routledge, pp. 153–166.

Yuval-Davis, Nira (1999) 'What is transversal politics?' *Soundings* 12(summer): 94–98.

FURTHER READING

Deutsche, Rosalyn (1996) *Evictions: Art and Spatial Politics*, Cambridge, MA: MIT Press.

Fraser, Nancy (2009) 'Feminism, capitalism and the cunning of history', *New Left Review* 56(March–April).
    (2013) *Fortunes of Feminism: From State-Managed Capitalism to Neoliberal Crisis*, London: Verso.

Lefebvre, Henri (1991) *The Production of Space*, Oxford: Blackwell.

Mohanty, Chandra Talpade (1991) 'Under western eyes. feminist scholarship and colonial discourses', in Chandra Talpade Mohanty, Ann Russo and Lourdes Torres (eds) *Third World Women and the Politics of Feminism*, Bloomington, IN: Indiana University Press.

Zukin, Sharon (1989) *Loft Living: Culture and Capital in Urban Change*, New Brunswick, NJ: Rutgers University Press.

8 – IS "TACTICAL URBANISM" AN ALTERNATIVE TO NEOLIBERAL URBANISM? REFLECTIONS ON AN EXHIBITION AT THE MOMA

Neil Brenner

1.

What can "tactical urbanism" offer cities under extreme stress from rapid population growth, intensifying industrial restructuring, inadequate social and physical infrastructures, rising levels of class polarization, insufficiently resourced public institutions, proliferating environmental disasters and growing social unrest? The recent MoMA exhibition on *Uneven Growth* (MoMA 2014–2015) aimed to explore this question through speculative interventions by teams of architects whose remit was to make design proposals for six of the world's "megacities"–Hong Kong, Istanbul, Lagos, Mumbai, New York and Rio (Figure 8.1). The exhibition has provoked considerable debate about our contemporary planetary urban condition and, more specifically, about the capacities of architects, urban designers and planners to influence the latter in progressive ways.

Figure 8.1 MoMA Uneven Growth exhibition
Photo: *aaa*

Such a debate is timely, not least because inherited paradigms of urban intervention—from the modernist-statist programs of the post-war epoch to the neoliberalizing, market-fundamentalist agendas of the post-1980s period—no longer appear viable. Meanwhile, as David Harvey notes in his comment on the MoMA exhibition, "the crisis of planetary urbanization" is intensifying. Megacities appear to be poorly equipped to resolve the monstrous governance problems and social conflicts that confront them. Under these conditions, Harvey grimly declares: "We are ... in the midst of a huge crisis—ecological, social, and political—of planetary urbanization without, it seems, knowing or even marking it" (2014: 29).

Against this foreboding background, can "tactical urbanisms" provide tractable solutions, or at least open up some productive perspectives for actualizing alternative urban futures? Despite the cautiously exploratory tone of its curators' framing texts in the exhibition catalogue, the MoMA project on *Uneven Growth* articulates a strong set of claims regarding the potentials of tactical urbanism (Bergdoll, 2014; Gadanho, 2014). In the various documents associated with the exhibition, the notion of tactical urbanism is presented as a robust interpretive frame for understanding a variety of emergent urban design experiments in contemporary megacities. Just as importantly, MoMA curator Pedro Gadanho explains his choice of the concept as a basis for stimulating debate and practical experimentation regarding possible future pathways of urban design intervention, and above all, as a means to promote "social justice in the conception and appropriation of urban space" (Gadanho, 2014: 23). As the search for new approaches to organizing our collective planetary urban future gains increasing urgency, these broadly affirmative discourses around tactical urbanism demand critical scrutiny. This chapter confronts this task, and in so doing, engages with some of the broader questions regarding the capacities of architecture/design as a means of (re)producing and transforming space with which this volume is concerned.

2.

In the exhibition catalogue, Gadanho and several other internationally influential curators and urban thinkers frame their understanding of tactical urbanism. They offer a variety of contextual reflections and interpretative formulations to explicate its essential elements. Several points of convergence emerge:

— Tactical urbanism arises in the context of a broader governance crisis in contemporary cities in which both states and markets have failed to deliver basic public goods (such as housing, transportation and public space) to expanding urban populations.

— Tactical urbanism is not a unified movement, but a general rubric through which to capture a broad range of emergent, provisional, experimental and ad hoc urban projects.

— Tactical urbanism is mobilized "from below," through organizationally, culturally and ideologically diverse interventions to confront emergent urban issues. Professional designers, as well as governments, developers and corporations, may participate in and actively stimulate tactical urbanism. But its generative sources lie outside the control of any clique of experts or any specific institution, social class or political coalition.

— Tactical urbanism proposes immediate, "acupunctural" modes of intervention in relation to local issues that are viewed as urgent by its proponents. Its time-horizon is thus relatively short, even "impulsive" and "spontaneous." Its spatial scale likewise tends to be relatively circumscribed—for instance, to the park, the building, the street or the neighborhood.

— Specific projects of tactical urbanism are said to evolve fluidly in relation to broader shifts in political-economic conditions, institutional arrangements or coalitional dynamics. These qualities of malleability and open-endedness are widely praised in discussions of tactical urbanism, generally in contrast to the comprehensive plans, formal-legal codes and rigid blueprints that were characteristic of modernist-statist projects of urban intervention.

— Tactical urbanism generally promotes a grassroots, participatory, "do-it-yourself" vision of urban restructuring in which those who are most directly affected by an issue actively mobilize to address it, and may continually mobilize to influence the evolution of methods and goals. For this reason, tactical urbanism is often presented as an "open-source" model of action and as a form of "reappropriation" of urban space by its users.

Most of the commentators involved in *Uneven Growth* present tactical urbanism as an alternative to both modernist-statist and neoliberal paradigms of urban intervention, for instance, because it is grounded upon participatory democracy; because it aims to promote social cohesion; and because it is not formally pre-programmed in advance or "from above." However, it is the opposition of tactical urbanism to modernist, comprehensive forms of urban planning that is most cogently demarcated in the wide-ranging narratives associated with the exhibition. Modernist-statist modes of urban intervention, it is argued, have receded due to the ideological ascendancy of neoliberalism and the associated "disassembling of nation-states" (Sassen, 2014) since the 1980s. To the degree that some elements and offshoots of that tradition are still being mobilized in the megacities of the developing world via holistic, comprehensive planning and "top-down action," they are often "entangled in inefficient politics, corrupt bureaucracy, and economic insufficiency" (Gadanho, 2014: 18). Tactical urbanism is thus presented as a potential palliative for urban problems that state institutions and formal urban planning procedures, in particular, have failed to address adequately.

Despite the affirmations of many of the contributors to *Uneven Growth*, it is less obvious as to how the projects associated with tactical urbanism could counteract neoliberal urbanism. Especially in light of the stridently anti-planning rhetoric that pervades many tactical urban interventions and their tendency to privilege informal, incremental mobilizations over larger-scale, longer-term, publicly financed reform programs, it seems reasonable to ask in what ways they do, in actuality, engender any serious friction against the neoliberal order, much less subvert it. In some cases, tactical urbanisms appear more likely to *bolster* neoliberal urbanisms by temporarily alleviating (or perhaps merely displacing) some of their disruptive social and spatial effects, but without interrupting the basic rule-regimes associated with market-oriented, growth-first urban development, and without challenging the foundational mistrust of governmental institutions that underpins the neoliberal project.

The relation between tactical and neoliberal forms of urbanism is thus considerably more complex, contentious and confusing than is generally acknowledged in the contributions to the debate on *Uneven Growth*. As Table 8.1 illustrates, it cannot simply be assumed that, because of their operational logics or normative-political orientations, tactical interventions will counteract neoliberal urbanism. No less than five specific types of relation between these projects can readily be imagined, only two of which *might* involve a challenge to market-fundamentalist urban policy. There are at least three highly plausible scenarios in which tactical urbanism will have either negligible or actively beneficial impacts upon a neoliberalized urban rule-regime.

1. *Subversion.* Tactical urbanism interrupts the logics of growth-first, market-oriented urban governance and points towards alternative urban futures based on grassroots democracy and social justice.

2. *Reinforcement.* Tactical urbanism alleviates some of the governance failures and disruptive consequences of neoliberal urbanism, but without threatening its grip on the regulatory framework governing urban development.

3. *Entrenchment.* Tactical urbanism internalizes a neoliberal agenda (for instance, related to a diminished role for public institutions and/or an extension of market forces) and thus contributes to the entrenchment of neoliberal urbanism.

4. *Neutrality.* Tactical urbanism emerges in interstitial spaces that are neither functional to, nor disruptive of, the neoliberal project. It thus co-exists with neoliberal urbanism in a relationship that is neither symbiotic, parasitic nor destructive.

5. *Contingency.* Tactical urbanism opens up a space of regulatory experimentation that, under certain conditions, contributes to the subversion of neoliberal programs. But, in other contexts, with many of the same conditions present, this does not occur. The impacts of tactical urbanism on neoliberal urbanism are thus contingent; they hinge upon factors extrinsic to it.

Table 8.1 Five types of relations between tactical and neoliberal urbanisms

Tactical urbanism may be *narrated* as a self-evident alternative to neoliberal urbanism; but we must ask: is this really the case, and if so, how, where, under what conditions, via what methods, with what consequences, and for whom? Clarification of these issues is essential to any serious consideration of the potentials and limits of tactical urbanism under contemporary conditions.

Neoliberal urbanism is not a unified, homogeneous formation of urban governance, but represents a broad *syndrome* of market-disciplinary institutions, policies and regulatory strategies (Brenner *et al.*, 2010a, 2010b). While certainly connected to the ideology of free market capitalism, this syndrome has assumed deeply variegated political, organizational and spatial forms in different places and territories around the world, and its politico-institutional expressions have evolved

considerably since the global economic crises and accompanying geopolitical shocks of the 1970s. Across all the contextual diversity and
evolutionary mutation, however, the common denominator of neoliberal
urbanisms is the market-fundamentalist project of activating local
public institutions and empowering private actors and organizations to
extend commodification across the urban social fabric, to coordinate
a city's collective life through market relations, and to promote the
enclosure of non-commodified, self-managed urban spaces.

As Teddy Cruz succinctly notes in his contribution to the *Uneven
Growth* catalogue, all this has promoted the "shift from urbanizations
benefitting the many into models of urban profit for the few" (2014:
51). Whereas the idea of "urbanizations benefitting the many" broadly
corresponds to the now-discredited megaprojects and programming
techniques of statist-modernism, the promotion of "urban profit for the
few" has been the predominant tendency since the 1980s, at once in
the older capitalist world, the former state socialist world and across
most of the postcolonial and developing world. Despite plenty of
variegation, resistance, contestation and reregulatory pushback, this
tendency has persisted, and even intensified, through the many waves
of industrial restructuring and financial crisis that have ricocheted
across every zone of the world economy since that period, including
since the most recent "Great Recession." The patterns of "uneven
growth" that are under scrutiny in the MoMA exhibition must be
understood as its direct expressions and outgrowths.

It is, then, neither the contemporary urban condition "as such,"
nor the inefficiencies of modernist-statist urban planning, that have
most directly triggered the problems to which contemporary forms of
tactical urbanism are responding. Rather, contemporary tactical urbanisms are emerging in contexts that have been powerfully ruptured and
reshaped by historically and geographically specific forms of neoliberal urbanization, based on the class project of restricting "the right to
the city" (Lefebvre, 1968) to the wealthy, the elite and the powerful,
and reorienting major public investments and policy regimes in ways
that prioritize that project above all others. Despite its pervasive
governance failures, its powerfully destructive socio-environmental
consequences and its increasingly evident ideological vulnerabilities,
neoliberalism continues to represent the taken-for-granted "common
sense" on which basis urban development practice around the world
is still being forged. The question of how designers might contribute
to alternative urban futures must thus be framed most directly—and,
from my perspective, a lot more combatively—in relation to the apparent resilience and elasticity of neoliberal forms of urban governance.

One important consequence of these observations is the proposition that the architectural and design disciplines could significantly
enhance their capacity to make durable, progressive urban interventions by engaging more systematically with questions of *institutional*
(re)design—that is, the systems of collectively binding rules that
govern the production, use, occupation and appropriation of space.
The latter are arguably as essential to the broad visions for future
megacities proposed in *Uneven Growth* as the tactical, acupunctural
projects of infrastructural and physical reorganization with which
the bulk of the exhibition is concerned. Indeed, in the absence of an
aggressively re-asserted role for governmental institutions—publicly
funded through an equitable tax regime; democratically legitimated
and publicly accountable; legally regulated and transparently
monitored; and oriented towards the public interest—it is difficult to
imagine how the tactical urbanist proposals put forward in *Uneven
Growth* could ever accomplish larger-scale, longer-term impacts.

Herein lies a potentially serious contradiction. The anti-statist,
anti-planning rhetoric of many tactical urbanist interventions may, in
practice, erode their capacity to confront the challenges of upscaling
their impacts. To the degree that advocates of tactical urbanism frame
their agenda as an alternative to an activist role for public institutions
in the production of urban space, they are at risk of reinforcing the
very neoliberal rule-regimes they ostensibly oppose. This is in no
way to suggest that tactical urbanist projects should ignore the
serious deficits of state action in contemporary megacities. On the
contrary, the critique of how market-oriented state policies (including
privatization, deregulation and liberalization) erode public institutions
in favor of privatized forms of urban appropriation is essential to any
counter-neoliberal, reregulatory project. Just as important, in this
context, is the collective demand for more extensive public support for
key dimensions of social reproduction—the essential infrastructures
associated with housing, transportation, education, public space,
health care, and so forth. The point here, then, is simply that there are
deep tensions between the project of finding viable alternatives to
neoliberal urbanism and a tradition of urban intervention that tends to
distance itself from state institutions.

In his contribution to the *Uneven Growth* catalogue, Teddy Cruz offers a hard-hitting formulation of the major challenges associated with that endeavor among architects and designers:

> *Without altering the exclusionary policies that have decimated a civic imagination in the first place, architecture will remain a decorative tool to camouflage the neoconservative politics and economics of urban development that have eroded the primacy of public infrastructure worldwide ... the major problems of urbanization today ... are grounded in the inability of institutions of urban development to more meaningfully engage urban informality, socioeconomic inequity, environmental degradation, lack of affordable housing, inclusive public infrastructure, and civil participation.*
> (2014: 51)

This is precisely the dilemma: how can tactical urbanisms do more than serve as "camouflage" for the vicissitudes, dislocations, and crisis tendencies of neoliberal urbanism? Cruz's formulation underscores one of the key conditions under which it might begin to do so: through the re-imagination of design, not simply as a "decorative tool" or formal set of techniques-for-hire by the ruling classes, but as a basis for asking critical questions about contemporary urbanism, and as a set of collectively shared, creative capacities through which to "coproduce the city as well as new models of cohabitation and coexistence to advance agendas of socioeconomic inclusion" (Cruz, 2014: 51). This goal cannot be realized simply through the redesign of specific physical sites within the city; it also requires the creation of "a new role for progressive policy, [and] a more efficient, transparent, inclusive, and collaborative form of government" (ibid.: 55). In other words, the pursuit of alternative urbanisms requires the creation not only of new urban spaces, but of new state spaces as well.

3.

These considerations yield a critical perspective from which to examine some of the design proposals for contemporary megacities that are on display in *Uneven Growth*. MoMA curator Gadanho's remit to the six design teams was not only to propose a tactical intervention for a specific megacity—"acupunctural outlooks on how change for the better could be induced in diverse urban contexts"—but, in so doing, to offer a new perspective on what a socially engaged architecture might look like. We must thus consider the exhibition materials at once as possible scenarios for a future urbanism, and as visions of how the design disciplines might use tactical approaches to contribute to their realization. Even if they harness the speculative capacities of design, then, the proposals on display in the exhibition are clearly not meant to be pure fictions—they are presented as critical tools "to reflect upon the problems of today" (Gadanho, 2014: 23, 16).

Only some of the design proposals featured in the exhibition respond effectively to this remit. While the exhibition's theorists broadly agree on the contours of a tactical urbanism, there is evidently considerable confusion regarding the meaning and implications of this notion among the designers themselves. Although all of the design scenarios are presented under the shared rubric of tactical urbanism, some bear little resemblance to an acupunctural, participatory, open-sourced intervention. Indeed, several of the design proposals involve large-scale megaprojects and landscape transformations that could only be implemented through a powerful state apparatus; they are difficult to envision as more than partial outgrowths of tactical methods. Meanwhile, other design proposals are consistently framed within tactical parameters, but yield a vision of the urban future that appears entirely compatible with most versions of neoliberalism. Such interventions may be "tactical," but they totally bypass the intricacies of exploring real alternatives to the currently dominant system of market rule.

A number of the proposals circumvent questions of implementation entirely, offering decontextualized design "solutions" to the pressing problems of megacity development, for instance, regarding water scarcity, insufficient land for housing, transportation bottlenecks or issues of energy supply. Because they bracket the formidable constraints associated with implementation under a neoliberalized rule-regime, these design scenarios remain at a purely hypothetical level—visions of an alternative universe that are utopian in the literal sense of that word; they are located *nowhere*. They put the capacities of design thinking on display, often with striking visual flourishes, but with considerably less traction than if the conditions for their actualization were seriously interrogated.

Among the contributions to *Uneven Growth* that most directly attempt to mobilize tactical interventions as part of a broader assault on neoliberal urbanism, the scenarios elaborated by the Mumbai design team (URBZ/Ensamble-POP lab), the Istanbul design team (Atelier d'Architecture Autogérée [*aaa*]/Superpool) and one of the New York City teams (Cohabitation Strategies, CohStra) are particularly generative. Notably, each does so through an engagement with the housing question, which has been a fundamental terrain of design intervention and political struggle throughout the history of capitalist urbanization. In confronting this well-trodden terrain, the teams illustrate how an expanded vision of design—as a set of combined capacities for spatial intervention, social empowerment and political critique—can contribute to the ongoing struggle for alternative urbanisms.

The Mumbai proposals by URBZ/Ensamble-POP lab mobilize tactical interventions to protect so-called "slum" neighborhoods such as Dharavi and Shivaji Nagar from the massive land development pressures associated with Mumbai's extensively neoliberalized, financialized economy. This is a multifaceted proposal, perhaps reflecting the different positionalities of the project teams in relation to the slum itself (URBZ is a group of activist designers with strong roots in Mumbai's poor neighborhoods, whereas the POP lab is based at MIT). At its core, the project presents a series of incremental design strategies to promote an alternative vision of the "slum" as a space of productivity, creativity and ingenuity—a "*tabula pronta*," in the team's formulation, rather than a *tabula rasa* that can be readily razed to make room for new zones of single-function mass housing. Instead of imposing a new prototype from outside, the designers propose to enhance spatial practices that already animate those neighborhoods—specifically, the integration of residential spaces with work spaces or "tool houses." By supplying a model of up-building that enables residents to construct new platforms for work and everyday life above their homes, and by creating a network of "supraextructures" on a plane stretched like a "magic carpet" above the rooflines, new possibilities for endogenous local economic development and social interaction are envisioned. The developmental potentials thus unleashed would, the designers propose, serve as strong counterpoints to dominant ideologies of the slum as a space of backwardness and pathology, while also stimulating the elaboration of a less polarized growth pattern across the metropolitan fabric.

Thorny questions remain, of course, regarding the degree to which the proposed tactical interventions could protect the most strategically located neighborhoods from land development pressures, especially in the absence of a broader political movement that questions the model of market-driven urban growth to which Mumbai's growth coalition committed itself following the liberalization of the Indian economy in the 1990s. Through what institutional mechanisms and political coalitions could tenure security be attained by slum dwellers living in zones of the city that are considered attractive by growth machine interests? As Neil Smith pointed out some time ago, when local government institutions align with development interests to exploit such a "rent gap" in the urban land market, organized resistance is likely to be met with considerable vilification, if not outright repression (Smith, 1996). There is no doubt, however, that design has a fundamental role to play in defending vulnerable populations and neighborhoods against further disempowerment, dispossession and spatial displacement. The proposal for Mumbai by URBZ/Ensamble-POP lab very productively puts this issue on the exhibition's agenda. It will hopefully inspire other designers to take up this project in other megacities, in collaboration with local inhabitants, local social movements, and non-governmental organizations that share their concerns.

While the design proposals presented by the Istanbul and New York teams contain important architectural/morphological elements (pertaining, for instance, to buildings, infrastructures and neighborhood districts), their creative radicalism is strongly rooted in models for new institutional arrangements that would empower each city's low- or middle-income inhabitants to occupy, appropriate and regenerate spaces that are currently abandoned, degraded or being subjected to new forms of vulnerability. In the New York context, the CohStra team focuses on a variety of interstitial or underutilized spaces in the city core—from vacant lots and abandoned buildings to various kinds of lower-density housing provision—in order to propose an alternative framework for land ownership (community land trusts), housing provision (mutual housing associations), building management (cooperative housing trusts), and household financing (community credit unions). In the case of Istanbul, the Atelier d'Architecture Autogérée's design proposal targets the mass housing complexes that were constructed for the burgeoning middle classes during the post-1990s period by Turkey's Housing Development Agency, known as TOKI, which are predominantly located in more peripheral districts within Istanbul's rapidly urbanizing metropolitan territory. Here, the designers propose to retrofit existing TOKI housing ensembles, and their immediate landscapes, in ways that facilitate new forms of communal self-management by the inhabitants—including, as with CohStra's proposal for New York, community land trusts and local credit unions, along with other forms of collectively managed infrastructure such as community farming and gardens, fisheries, workshops, green energy sources, and repair facilities (Figures 8.2 and 8.3).

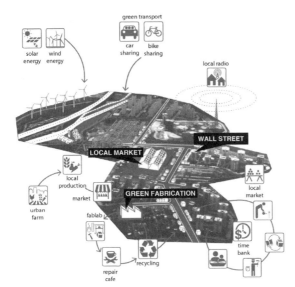

Figure 8.2 KiTO neighborhood strategy, by *aaa*

Figure 8.3 KiTO posters for actions, by *aaa*

As with the Mumbai team's proposal, each of these tactical interventions is framed as a response to a specific, immediate set of threats to urban life that have been imposed by the neoliberal growth model in the city under consideration—the "crisis of affordability" for working New Yorkers; and the destabilization of the model of middle-class consumerism that had been promoted in Istanbul through TOKI mass housing. Notably, however, CohStra and the Atelier d'Architecture Autogérée move beyond a defensive posture in relation to such issues, offering instead a vision of how the spaces that are being degraded under neoliberalized urbanism could become the anchors for an alternative vision of the city as a space of common life and collective self-management. In both projects, the site of design intervention is viewed as a *commons*, a space of continuous, collective appropriation and transformation by its users. Both teams offer a vision of this commons as a *process* to which designers can contribute in fundamental ways, not only by elaborating spatial proposals for the reorganization of housing functions or other dimensions of social reproduction, but by re-imagining how such basic institutions as private property, profit-oriented real estate investment, urban land markets, and municipal bureaucracy might be transformed and even superseded to serve social needs, to empower urban inhabitants, and to contribute to the creation of a genuine urban public sphere.

Although the Istanbul and New York projects are presented in tactical terms, they are clearly intended as more than fleeting acupunctural interventions. Part of their appeal is precisely that they offer a model of tactical urbanism that may be aggressively upscaled and converted into a city-wide counterforce to the neoliberal model. Initially offering a kind of protected enclave for a vulnerable population, each project is then meant to be transformed into a generalizable alternative to the specific forms of housing commodification and accumulation by dispossession that have underpinned "uneven growth" in their respective megacities. It is this reflexive attempt to connect the methods of tactical urbanism to a double-edged redesign of urban spaces *and* institutions that makes these teams' proposals effective as tools for envisioning alternatives to the neoliberal city. In thus proceeding, however, the proposals by the Atelier d'Architecture Autogérée and CohStra move beyond the realm of tactical urbanism: rather than being a focal point for investigation as such, the latter becomes a kind of launching pad for envisioning and enacting a "politics of space" (Henri Lefebvre)—that is, a political strategy of large-scale sociospatial transformation.

Here, too, of course, the inevitable questions of implementation loom on the horizon. How can this vision of the commons (and of common*ing* practices) be realized when the dominant class interests in each megacity continue to promote a profit-oriented, speculation-driven growth model? Where are the social forces and political coalitions that could counteract that model, and would they really opt for the level of collective coordination and communal sharing proposed by these design teams? How can local alternative economies be protected from incursions by profit-oriented producers, who may (for instance, through economies of scale, or more rationalized forms of labor exploitation) be able to offer more affordable or desirable products to cash-strapped consumers? Designers cannot answer these questions, at least, not among themselves; they can only be decided through political deliberation, public debate, and ongoing struggle. But, because CohStra and the Atelier d'Architecture Autogérée took the fundamental step of integrating such political-institutional considerations into their spatial proposals, they productively contribute to that process. Just as importantly, their proposals also articulate a more socially engaged, politically combative vision of what the design disciplines have to offer the urban public sphere in an era of deepening inequality and highly polarized visions of our global urban future.

4.

Given the difficulties that some of the design teams appear to have had with the tactical urbanism framework, one cannot help but wonder whether it offered them too narrow a terrain, or too limited a toolkit, for confronting the vast challenges that are currently emerging in the world's megacities. MoMA curator Barry Bergdoll anticipates this conundrum, noting the gap between the "modest scale of some [tactical] interventions" and the "dimensions of the worldwide urban and economic crisis that so urgently needs to be addressed" (Bergdoll, 2014: 12). In the face of these challenges, one can hardly reproach the teams that opted to venture forth with big, ambitious proposals rather than restricting themselves to mere "tactics."

But here arises a further contradiction of the *Uneven Growth* project. A pure form of tactical urbanism would have to be systematically *anti*-programmatic; it could only maintain a consistently tactical approach by resisting and rejecting any movement towards institutionalization. Yet, to the degree that the tactical design experiments on display in *Uneven Growth* articulate a broader vision of urban transformation, they necessarily hinge upon the (eventual) articulation of a comprehensive vision of the whole. The generalization of tactical urbanism will thus entail its self-dissolution or, more precisely, its transformation into a project that requires longer-term coordination; stabilized, enforceable, collectively binding rules; and some kind of personnel assigned to the tasks of territorial management—in other words, *planning*. We thus return to the supposedly discredited, outmoded terrain of statist-modernism, the realm of big ambitions, large-scale blueprints, elaborate bureaucratic procedures and comprehensive plans, in opposition to which the precepts of tactical urbanism are generally framed. Even if one prefers tactical methods over those of top-down bureaucracies (or, for that matter, those of profit-hungry developers and transnational corporations), it would seem that a serious discussion of large-scale territorial plans, institutional (re)organization and political strategies of implementation is unavoidable, at least if the goal is seriously to envision a future for megacities that is more socially and spatially just, democratic, livable and environmentally sane than our present global urban condition.

For anyone sympathetic to tactical urbanism *and* the project of large-scale, progressive urban transformation, this contradiction is probably unavoidable. Can it be made productive? Perhaps the radical potential of tactical urbanism lies less in its role as an all-purpose method for designing urban futures, than as a radically democratic counterweight to institutional systems, whether state-driven or market-dominated. Some of the most valuable contributions in *Uneven Growth* serve this very purpose: they point towards the possibility that, rather than being instrumentalized for social engineering, political control, private enjoyment or corporate profit-making, the capacities of design might be remobilized as tools of empowerment for the users of space, enabling them to occupy and appropriate the urban, continually to transform it, and thus to produce a different city than anyone could have dreamt up in advance.

But even in this maximally optimistic framing of tactical urbanism, the "big questions" regarding how to (re)design the city of the future—its economy, its property and labor relations, its spaces of circulation, social reproduction and everyday life, its modes of governance, its articulations to worldwide capital flows, its interfaces with environmental/biophysical processes, and so forth—remain completely unresolved. As MoMA's Department of Architecture and Design continues its productive engagement with urbanism, let us hope that such questions will stay on the agenda, and that the creative capacities of designers can be harnessed to confront them with all the critical force, political imagination, and systematic vision they require.

REFERENCES

Bergdoll, Barry (2014) "Preface," in Pedro Gadanho (ed.) *Uneven Growth: Tactical Urbanisms for Expanding Megacities*, New York: The Museum of Modern Art, pp. 11–13.

Brenner, Neil, Peck, Jamie and Theodore, Nik (2010a) "Variegated neoliberalization," *Global Networks* 10(2): 182–222.
     (2010b) "After neoliberalization?," *Globalizations* 7(3): 327–345.

Cruz, Teddy (2014) "Rethinking uneven growth," in Pedro Gadanho (ed.) *Uneven Growth: Tactical Urbanisms for Expanding Megacities*, New York: The Museum of Modern Art, pp. 48–55.

Gadanho, Pedro (2014) "Mirroring uneven growth," in Pedro Gadanho (ed.) *Uneven Growth: Tactical Urbanisms for Expanding Megacities*, New York: The Museum of Modern Art, pp. 14–25.

Harvey, David (2014) "The crisis of planetary urbanization," in Pedro Gadanho (ed.) *Uneven Growth: Tactical Urbanisms for Expanding Megacities*, New York: The Museum of Modern Art, p. 29.

Lefebvre, Henri (1968) *Le droit à la ville*, Paris: Anthopos.

Sassen, Saskia (2014) "Complex and incomplete: spaces for tactical urbanism," in Pedro Gadanho (ed.) *Uneven Growth: Tactical Urbanisms for Expanding Megacities*, New York: The Museum of Modern Art, p. 41.

Smith, Neil (1996) *The New Urban Frontier*, New York: Routledge.

9 – SOFTWARE AND SPATIAL PRACTICE: THE SOCIAL (CO)PRODUCTION OF SOFTWARE OR SOFTWARE FOR SOCIAL (CO)PRODUCTION?

Phil Langley

The practice of architecture is conditioned by our technology, from drawing boards and pencils through laptops and screens, to sensors and networks, yet the mediating nature of this technology often goes unacknowledged. Perhaps this relationship with the 'tools of our imagination' (Piedmont-Palladino, 2007) was easier to ignore in the past, but the need to engage with the effects of software on our behaviours (and vice versa) should no longer be in doubt. While the social nature of the scientific laboratory has been described by sociologists of science such as Latour, and the significance of non-human devices in the production of knowledge identified and documented (Latour and Woolgar, 1986), the same is not true of spatial design practice and its relationship with digital technology. We have definitively moved beyond the false paradigm of 'Computer Aided Design', in which skeumorphic[1] software packages echoed the functionality and reinforced the behaviour of the drawing board, but where we have moved to is less certain.

The current discourse around spatial design and digital technology includes speculations on smart cities (and, by dubious extension, smart citizens) and the rise of the so-called 'internet of things'. Each of these two strands focuses on a 'near future' vision of ubiquitous computing in our urban environments that, in their most optimistic form, suggest significant reductions in waste and energy use, increased efficiency of transportation and communication infrastructures and even of democracy itself. Such optimism, should of course, be treated with caution – not least as it poses the question, by whose measure can these changes be described as 'improvements'? But

---

1   The term skeumorphic relates to objects whose design has been principally derived from the required functionality of an earlier object. A more general example of skeumorphism would be a digital watch that displays on its screen the rotating hands of an analogue watch.

software is already central to the design and documentation of buildings and cities. It is used for 3D, 4D (even 5D)[2] modelling as well as
for complex simulations and analyses of virtual environments. At the
same time, it is becoming more important in the operation of those
environments once they have become material. Most significantly
here, the use of particular software, at certain stages of design and
operation is becoming more and more prescriptive, placing significant
demands on building designers and users.[3] The practice of spatial
production is firmly situated in a new digital reality in which software
can no longer be seen as merely a tool.

Software itself is always social, either actively so through the
interactions of developers, or more passively through the historic
layering of code which makes use of previously written code.[4] I am
concerned specifically with using an idea of 'social coding' as a way
of challenging mainstream ideas of what software in spatial design
practice should be and what software should do. We need to develop
alternative approaches and explore new relationships between
ourselves and our technologies. I want to examine software itself as
a legitimate site of study – what is software actually made 'of'? – and
in particular the culture of software (Fuller, 2003, 2008). What is the
social agency of software and how can this be used in both the social
(co)production of software and the development of software for social
(co)production? In order to answer this, I will use the ontological
framework of the 'post-human', and in particular Donna Haraway's approach (Haraway, 2003), as a way of re-casting ourselves in relation
to our technologies. Additionally, I will look to the radical development
of 'queer technology' (Blas, 2006, 2008), as a design methodology

---

2   3D is, of course, model geometry and 4D is time simulations carried out using that geometry.
'5D' represents another layer of socio-economic data applied to the model and typically refers to
cost modelling.

3   I am writing this in the context of a significant change to mainstream architectural practice in
the UK, which is in the process of being implemented, the effect of which will be to determine the
means of digital production within architectural offices and, by extension, schools of architecture
throughout the country. In April 2016, the UK government implemented procurement standards
that require all projects funded by central government to be delivered using complex BIM (Building
Information Modelling) software that is currently only available as a closed, proprietary product.
This will determine the way in which much of the built environment will be designed, described
and documented. Leaving aside the detailed implications of prescribing the use of such software
specifically, which is worthy of a separate discussion, this enshrining of behaviour highlights precisely
the fallacy that software is merely a tool. This is software as a method of control.
See www.bimtaskgroup.org

4   For an example of 'Social coding', see the widely popular coding sharing platform 'github',
available at: https://github.com

for software and technology, which encourages a 'destabilisation' of the normative binaries and dichotomies. These two strands set an alternative horizon for our engagements with technology and through an example of my own practice, this chapter aims to explore these implications.

DIGITAL COMPANIONS

In Haraway's Cyborg Manifesto, the ontological notions of 'human' and 'non-human' are destabilised and the oppositional distinctions between human (or animal) and machine instead become 'leaky' (Haraway, 1991). These cyborg formations imply blurriness at the boundaries of categorisation and suggest a complex, co-evolutionary process rather than a simple combinatory one. Haraway's cyborg is not created though mechanical couplings between entities from closed categories, but rather the dynamic topological relationships across blurred edges that create new, but inherently unstable (virtually, materially, temporarily) entities. Haraway develops her concept of the cyborg into an idea of a 'companion species' that represents a further 'synthetic de-centralising' of the natural and the artificial (Haraway, 2003). The cyborg destabilises any notion of categorisation to such an extent that 'species' can no longer be treated in isolation and requires a particular understanding of co-evolution:

> It is a mistake to see the alterations of dog's bodies and minds as biological and the changes in human bodies and lives, for example, in the emergence of herding or agricultural societies as cultural, and so not about co-evolution.
> (Haraway, 2003: 31)

For Haraway, the fate of the 'dog' and the 'human' have become so intertwined that any hierarchy between the two is flawed and the individuation of species becomes redundant. Furthermore, her notion of 'co-evolution' requires a non-deterministic approach to such relationships. Haraway's cyborgs and companion species outline a post-human condition in which we are placed in a dynamic topological relationship with/as 'companion species' that we make and remake, at the same time that they make and remake us. While Haraway is specific about dogs in her manifesto, it seems to me to be interesting, relevant and useful to extend this concept to an idea of a 'digital companion species'. Such a digital companion would not be an embedded 'productised' device or 'assistant', but instead would be an ever-changing presence, over which we can exert influence and which, in turn, can influence us. A 'digital companion species', one that follows a process of co-evolution, would be more reflective of the variable agencies of software.

THE SOCIAL AGENCY OF SOFTWARE

Our machines are disturbingly lively and we ourselves frighteningly inert.
(Haraway, 1991: 152)

Everything I do appears to be somehow mediated by digital technology and not just the kind of cognitive expansion afforded by personal networked devices such as smart phones. In my professional work, the software I use or create does not merely act as a tool offering me a way to carry out an already defined task in a more efficient way, it does not provide a short cut to a pre-known destination. It also carries its own logic that mediates my activity and in doing so exhibits its own agency. At it most simplistic, the software can be seen as having 'secondary agency', extending that of its creator into the realm of the user, so that the creator is able to act as a 'guiding hand' to those that deploy the software. This description is, at first glance, an attractive one. It allows me, first, as the user of software, to critique the expectations of its use in practice and, second, as a creator of software, implies that I can 'influence' the practice of others. But it isn't that simple.

The notion of the 'secondary agency' of software implies a deterministic relationship between creator and user – or, as these terms are modified in Mackenzie's ontology of software, originator and recipient (Mackenzie, 2006).[5] Instead, the agency of software is relational – it has a variable capacity to mesh with other actors within new contexts (Mackenzie, 2006; Kitchin and Dodge, 2011). Kitchin and Dodge use climate change modelling to illustrate this definition of the agency of software. The complex simulations carried out to predict the effect on the Earth's atmosphere – a huge, collaborative scientific undertaking – are distilled into single digit temperature increases across the whole globe, that are deemed to be either acceptable or not during political negotiations. In this case, the simulation model – the software – is not carrying the agency of its creators. Instead it is demonstrating its capacity to affect as part of a

---

5   The full ontology is as follows: 1. Code as index; 2. Originator; 3. Recipient; 4. Prototype.

relational system.[6] 'The models analyse the world, the world responds to the models' (Kitchin and Dodge, 2011: 30).

Mackenzie describes the edges of each part of his software on-tology as fuzzy and states that what is important is that 'the patterns of relations that unfold in the neighbourhood of software are agential' (Mackenzie, 2006: 17). That is to say, that each of the entities in the ontology may act on any other at any given moment, depending on circumstance. Furthermore, this describes software not as a stable entity with its own discrete agency, but rather as something that only ever exists as part of a larger formation that includes both its past 'origins' and its future 'destinations'. Furthermore, software doesn't just appear, as Mackenzie states:

> *Someone or something codes it; there is an originator. Whether the originator is a programmer, webmaster, corporation, software engineer, team, hacker or scripter, and regardless of whether the originator's existence can be forgotten, sanctified or criminalized, software originates somewhere.*
> (ibid.: 14)

In this way, the software is not acting on something or someone, instead its effects are co-produced between the fluid, interchanging roles of 'originator' and 'recipient'. I would go further in the definition of 'originator' to include those whose use of proprietary software becomes a tacit approval of its functionality and in some way perpet-uates it. By this description, we are all originators of software and we are all already involved in its (co)production.

In her book, *Close to the Machine*, Ullman provides a first-person account of the messy nature of software development and, by extension, software. Her narrative, based on her own experiences as a professional programmer, reveals the relational agency of software through the social intra-actions of the 'code', 'originators', 'receivers' and 'prototypes', and she provides specific testimony on the social nature of software. Ullman talks particularly about writing code, when it is at its most unstable, and in doing so offers an alternative de-scription of the 'discipline' of programming as a dynamic (rather than procedural) process, that has no meaningful beginning or end. 'It has

---

6   This illustration of the agency of software can also be seen at the scale of a building, where complex environmental simulations carried out at the design stage to predict the internal conditions are simplified to single letter performance ratings – A, B, C, etc. – determined by regulatory bodies, denoting 'overall' success or failure.

occurred to me that if people really knew how software got written I'm not sure they'd give their money to a bank, or get on an airplane again'[7] (Ullman, 2013: 2).

Code is always on the 'verge of disappearance' or collapse, precisely because it is relational and co-evolving. It barely works and without nurture and care, it will begin to deteriorate and break down. Functionality is lost as the 'ecosystem' which it inhabits changes and it becomes less and less intelligible as the code loses contact with those who created and understood its unique idiosyncrasies.

'QUEER' TECHNOLOGY

The F/LOSS (Free/Libre Open Source Software) movement, in which the term 'free' refers not to the cost but the users' freedom to study, modify and distribute the software, provides a broad framework for other ways of producing software (and has, of course, influenced many other discussions on copyright and ownership). This breadth includes both the creation of free alternatives to closed, propriety software[8] as well as more radical propositions. Artist and writer Zach Blas has made one such radical proposition which he describes as Queer Technologies (Blas, 2006, 2008). Blas's approach has developed from the wider discourse of queer theory, in which the term 'queering' is used not only in relation to groups such as gay, lesbian and transgender but can also be understood as a performative act against dominant perceptions and normative systems. For Blas, this includes a design methodology that embraces 'uselessness' as a way of challenging the ways in which software is considered to 'work' and is able to disrupt the normative binary by working across them. This queering of software is achieved through questioning the very function of functionality. As Blas says:

> *I think Queer Technologies wants to work in the interstices of useful and useless, or to find new uses through the useless. Importantly, this is not about deconstruction, it is about use, about doing something, experimenting with new ways of doing and making things happen.*
> (Interview with Zach Blas, n.d.)

---

7   I would also add 'design a building' to Ullman's statement.

8   Examples include the image editing software GIMP, which offers an alternative to Adobe Photoshop (www.gimp.org/index.html) or Open Office in place of Microsoft Office (www.openoffice.org).

Artist Željko Blaće works with this approach and takes the queer operating system as a paradigm for proposing other ways of doing software that challenge the normative systems of productivity and digital technology. Blaće's project for a Queer OS is an ongoing exploration of speculative proposals and prototypes, carried out through a series of collaborative events and workshops. Blaće places significance on the act of creative inquiry (rather than the technical activity of writing code, for example) and thus provides a platform for wider participation in the social, economic and political debates that surround software.[9]

The queering of software offers a strong design approach for those working with, as well as on, software. Rather than seeking to chase the supposed functionality of proprietary norms (something that could be said of F/LOSS projects such as Open Office), queerness allows for a more creative process of exploration that addresses the social nature of software and goes further than the very general aims of the F/LOSS movement and provides a specific software design methodology.

'SOCIAL' MEDIA

While these approaches might help inform 'small-scale' technological interventions such as coding on a personal computer, for instance, how can they help us also engage with the kinds of networked computing that have become so pervasive? More so than so-called 'cloud' storage systems for music or video files which are typically operated 'on demand' by the user, social media systems represent a perverted kind of digital companion that is always on, always operating, always connecting. Facebook, Twitter and other social media software provide not only a platform for our own, directed communication, but a means of aggregating content from others, sometimes our known contacts but also from unsolicited sources, such as advertisers or other 'curated' content.[10] Its function as a direct communication

---

9   A 2014 workshop by Željko Blaće on the Queer OS was held in Brussels in 2014, hosted by arts-lab *Constant*, as part of their GenderBlending workshop http://constantvzw.org/site/-GenderBlending,190-.html. The discussion during the workshop included general proposals to change the skeumorphic features of normative operating systems such as files and folders as well as specific queer 'functionality' such as discontinuous communication systems (i.e. receiving a message via one account and replying via another), as a way of combating digital surveillance.

10   Social media corporations are also not averse to 'curating' this content in order to manipulate users. Facebook was revealed to have managed the flow of positive and negative news stories to users' news feeds in order to control their emotions: www.theguardian.com/technology/2014/jun/29/facebook-users-emotions-news-feeds

platform has made social media an often reported feature of political uprising and protest in many countries around the world (Castells, 2012; Gerbaudo, 2012). Manuel Castells claims that networks, which for him are the dominant mode of organisation of our society, are controlled by those who can program the networks and can switch the networks. Here, to program is to set the goals of the network, whereas to switch is to connect different networks and share those goals. In his words:

> If power is executed by programming and switching networks, then counter-power, the deliberate attempt to change power relationships, is enabled by reprogramming networks around alternative interests and values and/or disrupting the dominant switches while switching networks of resistance and social change.
> (Castells, 2012: 9)

Castells advocates a direct challenge to the mechanisms of power through the re-programming of its networks and disrupting dominant switches, urging us to occupy the medium of communication. Castells even goes as far as to claim the Occupy movement was being born digital, which suggests that characteristics of these protest movements have been irrecoverably altered by the use of social media.

These broad claims of the significance of social media in the facilitation of collective action are, perhaps, overly simplistic (Gerbaudo, 2012). Amidst the understandable optimism that many protest movements have created (as well as the undoubted additional 'functionality' that global communication networks in general provide), there is, at least for me, an accompanying concern at the suggestion that the success of such movements may rest on the continued use of a technology that lies so far outside of the influence or control – commercially, politically or materially – of the protagonists.[11] And, of course, the widespread use of social media by those who wish to challenge existing power structures has led to increased scrutiny of digital communication by governments worldwide. The ability of global

---

11   One striking example that makes visible this power imbalance is a tweet sent during the 'Green Revolution' in Iran, in 2009. 'ALL internet and mobile networks are cut. We ask everyone in Tehran to go onto their rooftops and shout ALAHO AKBAR in protest #IranElection' https://twitter.com/mousavi1388/status/2156978753. The message was sent by a supporter of the reformist politician Houssein Mousavi who stood for election during the contested 2009 elections that precipitated the uprising. The 140-character message encapsulates the fragility of our access and the impermanence of these networks during what was, ultimately, an unsuccessful opposition movement.

security services to spy on the mass of emails, calls, messages, tweets, likes, favourites, etc. has brought into sharp focus questions around our relationship with such platforms, the commercial interests that supply them, and the government agencies that oversee them. Nevertheless, there is something appealing in Castells's optimism of the potential for social media, and the direct link he makes to the occupation of the material and the virtual: 'They build their projects by sharing their experiences. They subvert the practice of communication as usual by occupying the medium and creating the message' (Castells, 2012).

@SIMULATIONBOT

Using the conceptual framework of post-human de-centring of the natural and synthetic, alongside the social agency of code and using some of the aspects of queering technology, I would like to offer a prototype for software for social (co)production, in terms of spatial design practice. The @simulationBot project is an attempt to advance an alternative strand of open source software for spatial design that does not attempt to duplicate the functionality of existing, proprietary platforms such as those used for complex geometry modelling or data management. Instead, I am suggesting other types of interface and interaction with design and software that develop, rather literally, the idea of a (digital) companion species and in some way attempt to 'occupy the medium'.

The @simulationBot is a kind of 'twitter bot',[12] a computer program that automatically 'tweets' in response to certain stimuli. It is a prototype project that appropriates three familiar characteristics of the micro-blogging platform Twitter – 'liveness', 'hashtagging' and 'geo-location' – to propose an alternative idea of software for spatial design (Figures 9.1 and 9.2).

---

12   See http://en.wikipedia.org/wiki/Twitterbot

Figure 9.1 Photos by workshop participants

Figure 9.2 Design 'hacks' by workshop participants

A twitter bot, which typically runs continuously on web servers, can be used for various purposes, including spamming users. Depending on their complexity, the twitter bot can respond in many different ways but it typically is not based on any AI (artificial intelligence) system and its behaviour is mostly 'hard-coded',[13] for example, bots may automatically re-tweet the post of another user. More complex bots tweet about events on other platforms, for example, @parliamentedits posts any changes to Wikipedia pages made from an IP address inside the UK Parliament building.[14] Regardless of the specifics of the behaviour, the bots offer a novel way of 'occupying the medium', working within the constraints for the platform as con-

13   Hard coding refers to the act of embedding data and/or data structures into a program, rather than being able to generate it dynamically. For example, the file path to a user's documents folder on a personal computer would be hard-coded into the operating system. While it is not necessarily 'bad' (and is, in fact often necessary), hard coding can result in fixed software behaviours.

14   See https://twitter.com/parliamentedits, or https://gist.github.com/Jonty/aabb42ab31d970dfb447, or www.theguardian.com/technology/2014/jul/30/how-to-find-out-when-uk-politician-edits-wikipedia-page

trolled by their corporate owners, but also extending the functionality of those platforms beyond that which its originators had intended. In doing so, twitter bots are able to appropriate not only the software but also the networked hardware that support them – data centres, mobile and wireless communications and the personal computing devices of Twitter users. The bots are still fragile – they can only function while Twitter allows programmers access to their platform through the API[15] and as long as the platform itself is left switched on – but it is still a more extensive 'reprogramming' of the network in which not only the message is altered, but also the medium.

The behaviour of my own digital companion – @simulationBot[16] – was developed to employ not only the underlying functionality of the Twitter platform, but was also designed in opposition to other characteristics that have developed as part of the wider exploitation of Twitter. The technology of social media platforms provides a very simple method of 'content aggregation', but they do not, in themselves, provide a reliable format for the content itself because we as users, don't view ourselves as 'content' generators.

It is common to see, both in academic research as well as in contemporary news media, visualisations of Twitter data, sometimes represented on a map, or aerial photograph. This is typically produced from a static data set, 'scraped' from the posts of unsuspecting users some time after an event has occurred. In this kind of arrangement, the Twitter users are merely passive suppliers of data to an unknown outside observer, rather than active participants in the process. As a consequence of this imbalance, the data set itself is severely undermined. While there is no such thing as a 'complete data set', this kind of data set is particularly flawed when represented in a generalised way. At a population scale, it is unlikely that the demographics of all Twitter account holders will ever be 'representative' and nor will those tweeting at any given moment be representative either. And at the scale of a single tweet, it requires active use of the geo-locative functionality of each user's device and rigorous use of the hashtag mechanism to make a tweet in any way machine-readable.

---

15   The API, or the Application Programming Interface, is a set of protocols that determine how publicly exposed software components can interact and how developers can use them to create their own outcomes. The API is controlled by the principal 'originators' of a piece of software and the depth of its functionality can vary widely. Furthermore, changes to the API can result in previously functioning software becoming obsolete.

16   The twitter bot simBotBETA @simulationBot was created using www.processing.org and the libraries www.twitter4j.org and http://unfoldingmaps.org/. Source code for @simulationBot can be found at www.github.com/phiLangley

The @simulationBot project is about altering our interaction with the software of Twitter in order to create an alternative 'social' assembly and was created using these fundamental principles:

—   The 'digital companion' is not merely an outsider and should be an active member of the social network.
—   The 'digital companion' must be, in some way, present and visible, rather than remote.
—   The data has to be made actively and not collected passively.
—   The data must be re-presented in real time.

The @simulationBot was developed for, and during, a series of workshops intended to question the nature of software and code in spatial design practice.[17] In the final experiment participants were asked to explore the city centre of Sheffield and propose 'hacks' – which are a sort of 'micro' design intervention – which they would tweet about, using photos and text, as well as hashtags and their GPS location (Figure 9.2). The tweets were collated in real time by the @simulationBot, which produced a live map of data, indicating the individual and group activity that was projected at the event venue as well as re-tweeted to the dispersed participants. So, the @simulationBot acts as our digital agent within the system. As members of the group send tweets from the locations across the city, they receive notification from @simulationBot about the activities of other members of the group. The map of the tweets was not only built in real time, but also shared in real time, as snapshots were shared in the communications of the @simulationBot (Figure 9.3).

While operating in this way the @simulationBot is no longer only exploiting the infrastructure of social media – GPS-enabled devices, sending and storing text and media across communication networks – but rather is beginning to modify it. The usual method of directed interface from the service provider – targeted ads, curated content, and so on – is replaced with a 'digital companion' participating in the activity as well as enabling it.

---

17   The simBot workshop was part of 'The Whole School Event – Designs on our City' which took place in February 2014, and was organised by the Sheffield School of Architecture (SSoA), University of Sheffield. The workshop, entitled 'open data in the city' was carried out with Dr Mark Meagher, of SSoA, and included student participants from across SSoA. See https://architecture. dept.shef.ac.uk/ssoa_news/?p=1812

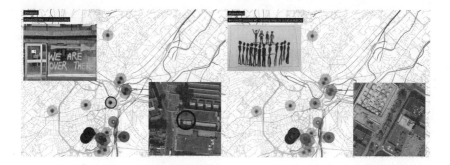

Figure 9.3 Maps created by @simulationBot and Phil Langley

SOFTWARE AND SPATIAL PRACTICE

It is clear to me that, as architects, our relationship with our technology is central to our practice. The unstable agencies of software
show that we cannot consider it a neutral tool in the production of
space. The behaviour of software affects the process of design and,
similarly, software should be affected by the type of design process
that we want to adopt. Software cannot simply be deployed in order
to realise a designer's wishes. Instead, to work with software and
technology should be a reflexive practice in which the relations
between designer and the software are made and remade. The
idea of social (co)production of space is not yet part of mainstream
architectural practice and it seems unlikely to me that software that
is developed for that mainstream would be wholly applicable to
this other approach. The @simulationBot is a very simple attempt
to propose other types of software that may be (co)produced for
spatial design. We need alternatives that are not just different in
terms of access – 'open' rather than 'closed' – but are distinctive in
functionality. The very notion of functionality must be re-examined and
the queering of technology offers a convincing design methodology
for both understanding and critiquing existing software and proposing
others. Code is an unstable material, from which sturdy algorithms
and software emerge. While stability is seen as a prerequisite for
software to be successful, perhaps we shouldn't aspire to it. The
problematic hardware and software assemblies of networked communication technology, for instance, represent a level of stability that we
cannot realistically hope to replicate, so perhaps we shouldn't even
try. Rather, it is in the messiness of code where we can co-evolve
with our own digital companion species, species which have agency,
which have behaviour, which 'affect' and are 'affected'.

REFERENCES

Blas, Z. (2006) *What is Queer Technology?* Available at: www.zachblas.info/publications_materials/whatisqueer technology_zachblas_2006.pdf
(2008) *Gay Bombs: User's Manual, Queer Technologies.* Available at: http://www.zachblas.info/wp-content/uploads/2016/03/GB_users-manual_web-version.pdf
(n.d.) Interview with Zach Blas. Available at: http://rhizome.org/editorial/2010/aug/18/interview-with-zach-blas/ (accessed 28 February 2015).

Castells, M. (2012) *Networks of Outrage and Hope: Social Movements in the Internet Age*, Cambridge: Polity Press.

Fuller, M. (2003) *Behind the Blip: Essays on the Culture of Software*, Brooklyn, NY: Autonomedia.
(2008) *Software Studies: A Lexicon*, Cambridge, MA: MIT Press.

Gerbaudo, P. (2012) *Tweets and the Streets: Social Media and Contemporary Activism*, London: Pluto Press.

Haraway, D. (1991) *Simians, Cyborgs and Women: The Reinvention of Nature*, London: Free Association Books.

(2003) *The Companion Species Manifesto: Dogs, People and Significant Otherness*, 2nd edn, Chicago: University of Chicago Press.

Kitchin, R. and Dodge, M. (2011) *Code/Space Software and Everyday Life*, Cambridge, MA: MIT Press. Available at: http://site.ebrary.com/id/10479192

Latour, B. and Woolgar, S. (1986) *Laboratory Life: The Construction of Scientific Facts*, ed. J. Salk, Princeton, NJ: Princeton University Press.

Mackenzie, A. (2006) *Cutting Code: Software and Sociality*, New York: Peter Lang.

Piedmont-Palladino, S. (2007) *Tools of the Imagination: Drawing Tools and Technologies from the Eighteenth Century to the Present*, New York: Princeton Architectural Press.

Ullman, E. (2013) *Close to the Machine: Technophilia and its Discontents*, London: Pushkin Press.

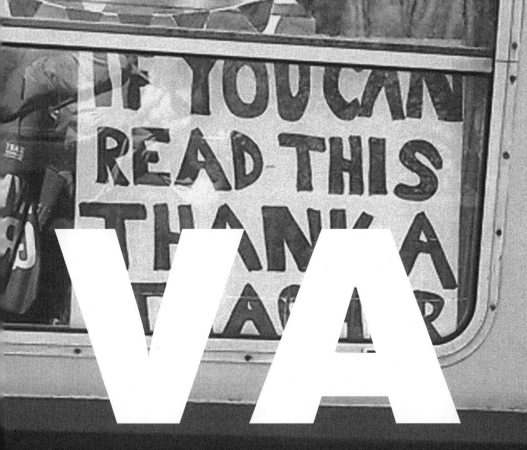

LOW-COST (COMPARED T
CURRENT MOD

? 2.6 PEOPLE = HOUSHOLD

520 EURO/MONTH (BE06kr
(~ 450€

15.3% HOUSING + UTILITIES (

73% CREDIT FOR HOUSE (ENERGY, WATER, H

5% HIPOTEKA (EUROPE
60%)

140.000 ___ -TENANTS/PODSTAVA

12% APA___MENTS

4.9% KAN___ ___ 30 YEARS
60D ___ ___R → 190%

1.000€/PERSON → HOUSHOLD
(+ GRAY ECONOMY ?) 2.600€

80€ = HOUSING + UTILITES

80€ × 12m × 30y = 28.800€/30 YEA

12-15m2 MIN/PERSON

(26) 31-39 m2 (+ COMMON SPACES)

PASSIVE HOUSE → 15€ UTILITIE

65€ → ZADRUGA/CO-OPERATI
TAKES CREDIT (0.2%)

MAINTANANCE + WORK OF CO-OP → 15€

10 — DIVERSE ECONOMIES, SPACE AND ARCHITECTURE: AN INTERVIEW WITH KATHERINE GIBSON

Kim Trogal (KT) — Could you tell us about 'community economies' and how you think community economies might influence architecture?

Katherine Gibson (KG) — The way we are using the term 'community economies' is quite specific. What we are trying to enact with the terms is this recognition of *being in common* – the notion that we are interdependent with each other as humans and with the non-human environment. A community economy is really trying to act on that interdependence in an ethical manner, in a manner that includes care for the other in the practice of surviving, which is what economies are about. How that happens is going to be quite specific in different places, but it would influence architecture, because architecture is, in my lay terms, a kind of framework for living – the built environment, the infrastructure in which one lives. The idea that you could bring a sense of 'in common' into the practice of architecture produces all sorts of challenges. We could break down those challenges into what sort of materials do we use, and in terms of those materials, what's their relationship to the natural environment from which they are derived? Or, how have they been produced and by whom, around the world?

So, in every element, in design, in building practices, in the infra-structures that might support buildings, questions of interdependence could be brought to bear. That would be different to the way in which architecture has developed in a monocultural, capitalist economy, in which you are thinking about various kinds of productivity of returns and extractive relationships with the environment, without necessary consideration of its own well-being.

That's an abstract argument, but on the other side of that, I think architecture offers a lot for enabling us to live more ethical, economic lives. There is an enabling aspect of the built environment – to allow collectivity, or sharing, or to allow care to be enacted, which is going to be important. What that means in practice is something that I can see *aaa*[1] is trying to think through and experiment with.

---

1   *aaa* is the atelier architecture autogérée (the Studio for Self-Managed Architecture). *aaa* is a collective platform which conducts explorations, actions and research concerning urban mutations and cultural, social and political emerging practices in the contemporary city. *aaa* was founded in 2001 by Doina Petrescu and Constantin Petcou, see www.urbantactics.org

Doina Petrescu (DP) — Do you think a particular type of architecture can also influence and support community economies? Can it work both ways?

KG — Yes, I think it can. It has to be a symbiosis. So much of what is stopping us from enacting more community economies are the durable structures in which we are living: the things that are standing in the way of being able to simply share consumption items, the way in which our houses are all individuated. We can't share our washing machines, we can't easily car share or have collective living with collective environments and also some kind of separate family space. Obviously there have been examples where this has been tried and a specific architecture has emerged, whether it's in a kibbutz, collective housing, or feminist experiments with the collectivisation of domestic work in the nineteenth century that Dolores Hayden documents in her book (Hayden, 1981). Clearly there have been attempts to try to build a different kind of built environment, in which different kinds of enactments of care can take place, but at the moment, we are reliant on these examples to imagine how architecture could be used more effectively to influence and shape community economies.

I would like to see a huge diversity in architectural styles. I don't think there is a sense in which one style is more appropriate to a community economy than another. I'd rather see there being a range of different kinds of styles that would attend to different kinds of needs in society.

KT — Whilst architecture might support forms of sharing and collaboration, but do you know of examples working the other way around, where community economies are used in the processes of making buildings or maintaining them?

KG — I think if you unpack any building, you probably find diverse economies in them. The examples that come to mind, like the kind of house building that goes on in communities, say, in the Philippines that I am familiar with, there is a whole range of different materials that are accessed. Some are bought on the market, like the iron sheeting for the roof, but other things are taken from nature whether it's the natural fibres or bamboo structures, and then the labour processes they use to build the houses are a mixture of craft work by individuals, or families working together. Really when it comes to raising the building, the whole community comes together and offers volunteer labour as part of a time-honoured tradition. I think this has followed through into developed countries like barn raising in New England, for instance.

If you think of all the elements of a diverse economy, there are different kinds of transactions, using different kinds of market, some of them are more mainstream, capitalist markets, others could be transactions with craft producers or nature itself and different kinds of labour practices that are used, different kinds of financing, whether it's community lending or using a bank loan. If you start to attend to diverse economic practices, you can see that probably many build-ings have enrolled a lot of different kinds of practice. If you look at the life of a building, a house, for instance, in Australia, it might have been built by a developer under very capitalist relations of employment and so on, with sub-contractors and potentially, slave labour, illegal labour. But over the life of that building, families then modify buildings, they change them, they sell them, they put their own labour into them and the outcome is very much a mix, a whole range of different kinds of economic practices. We can unpack any building in terms of its diversity. If we don't explore, we can see a building as just industrially built. But once you start to recognise diverse economies, there's an opportunity to think which parts we might do differently or where might we start to honour the labourers that are involved, the environ-ments that have given rise to the materials in different ways.

DP — How each part creates value and *what kind of value*?

KG — Yes, and how that value can have a life, what is its future? How will it transfer to the next generation? So much building is done for the now, not for the future and yet we live in a society where we inherit things from the past that were built under very different condi-tions of production; feudal, other capitalist forms of production, and so on, and we are still enjoying the benefit of those buildings. There is something wonderful about seeing these buildings as an inheritance, and also an inheritance for the future generation, and that's something that is lacking a lot in the building that is going on at the moment, it's very short term.

There's another side to that, which could be the need for more short-term or transitory building, so there is not only one form of temporality that I'd want to support. Again, that would be another way of looking at diversity, the kinds of temporalities that buildings can tap into, and what the needs are that would be met by that.

KT — Do you think that the diverse economies you work with produce different spaces, rather than necessarily architecture? We wondered if there are examples from your work, or other examples you find inspiring?

KG — That's an interesting question because certainly I think we could argue (and I'm sure many people have) that different kinds of economic formations produce different kinds of built spaces. We just have to look to socialist economies in the post-war period and the built environments that emerged out of state planning, whether you call it state capitalism, or communism. One of the things that really struck me between Hong Kong and Manila was the very different built environments that emerged in those booming Asian cities. We have Hong Kong, where British colonialism and social policy played a major role in the built environment, and Manila where American colonialism and then nationalism were very much dominated by the free market.

To start to think what spaces diverse economies would produce, I think what we would need to do, is look back at how those spaces are also produced by diverse economies. Diverse economies are always with us, it's just that we don't see them. So, in Manila, for instance, there is diversity in people building their own shacks on rivers as well as capitalist corporations building high-rise buildings right next to them, because there is no regulation at all. Whereas in somewhere like Hong Kong, you've got an incredible level of social housing and public transport in that country, although many people would see them not as the best housing in the world, the level of provision is amazing. It's gone along with strong state support at the same time as having informal markets, at the base of large social housing high rises and, of course, capitalist-oriented high-rises for the financial sector, and so on. So I think what we have around us is the product of diverse economies, but we need to unpack them, so the question on my mind would be, if we wanted to build spaces informed by an ethic of care and an ethic of a community economy, what might they look like?

The examples I could point to would be ones such as the town of Mondragon, in the Basque region, which has grown up with the development of the worker-owned cooperatives and the economic base of that particular region. They are very much built on principles of the old Spanish towns, with the squares still intact, where people meet and gather every day. There are still high-rise apartments that in the past were quite modest apartments, and most people lived their social life outside of the apartment on the street. I think that is probably changing. I was amazed to see these apartment buildings with supermarkets in their basements, so people could easily get to do their provisioning, but right next to, juxtaposed with these old town squares and preserved buildings from the past. It's still a very modern landscape in that sense, and with nature all around with these wonderful mountains. It did make me think about how this environment reflects cooperative values and solidarity principles.

My overall point is that every space is itself diverse and we need to appreciate that first and then think about how we want to shape space to enhance the kind of relations of interdependence that are key to building a community economy.

KT — We are interested in the way in which your practice, and the work of the Community Economies Collective[2] (CEC) is a place-based practice. You are working at different scales, neighbourhood or urban, sometimes regional. This question of interdependence you raise, of course, it brings into play many different kinds of scales, but how is the issue of scale important in your work? Do community economies exist at a more local scale, and, if so, how can one scale it up?

KG — I'd see it as a misunderstanding to regard community economies as only ever a local intervention. It's definitely true that a lot of the work that's been done by people associated with the community economies collective has been related to community-based interventions and local development. That's one of the features of the work, that sense of engagement with people trying to rethink their economy and what their economic pathway is. But the community economies approach, which is just reframing 'the' economy and re-centring our focus on ethical relationships and diverse economic practices, is applicable across all scales. In fact, there are people that are working with it now as a framework, who operate at a national scale, even a global scale.

Our new book, *Making Other Worlds Possible: Performing Diverse Economies* has some chapters that elaborate that perspective (Roelvink, St. Martin and Gibson-Graham, 2015). The chapter by Maliha Safri and Julie Graham is talking about the 'global household', for instance. You could start to look at the labour and the caring that's done in households and the way that households are now international in a way, because of the remittance flows and labour

2   The Community Economies Collective (CEC) and the Community Economies Research Network (CERN) are international collaborative networks of researchers who 'share an interest in theorizing, discussing, representing and ultimately enacting new visions of economy.' Their projects have grown out of J.K. Gibson-Graham's feminist critique of political economy. See www.communityeconomies.org/Home

flows all around the world that are supporting households. There are already diverse economic practices that are making the global household work, but there are ways in which we could recognise this more in public discourse around economies, for instance. One of the other chapters by Marianna Pavlovskaya talks about the USSR before the fall of the Soviet system and the ways in which we can start to think about diverse economies at a national scale that were both suppressed and articulated in that social formation. So I think there is a way in which our work can be applied at all scales. How we then enact the politics around that scale is a question.

Clearly, the reframing is important. What we've pointed to in our work is how national statistical authorities are starting to document things like caring labour, unpaid labour and voluntary labour. So already we're starting to see aspects of diverse economies at a national scale. How we act on that visibility to try to produce environments and contexts in which community economies can be supported is another thing.

The question, or issue of scaling-up, we've addressed in a number of ways. One aspect of the scaling-up, or diffusion of innovation, such as the idea of a community economy, is through language, which is something that can spread. It scales up immediately if it's picked up and is used across space. So we're being very careful when we're trying to develop a different language of economy that can be spoken in different places.

Your question brings up the question of what do we mean by 'scale-up'? The way we are thinking about it more recently, I suppose, is in terms of different technologies, and metrics and measurements, and that's one way you can pick up a technology and it can be applied at all different levels and scales, and so on. If that technology is something like an accounting system that pays attention to surplus or pays attention to the value of things created by nature that's unremunerated, and so on, then that's a way of spreading that vision of interdependence that's starting to help people see it influencing their practice. So that's very different from saying 'Oh, let's set up a little community economy, a social enterprise right here' and let's see if social enterprises could be done around the world. In a way, we're moving to a meta-theoretical level with the notion that languages and technologies are mobile. How they get placed in any particular environment is probably going to take on a different character according to the different needs.

DP — With *aaa* we were also concerned with this. On the one hand, we are prizing the local, but at the same time we were working a lot with this notion of trans-local, as a way of scaling-up. We considered this might be a way of being connected or of creating networks that go beyond the local in which what is local is recognised and preserved, all the specificity of what's happening in a place. Yet at the same time there are other things that could be mutualised at a larger scale, which could be tools that could be shared, knowledge can be shared.

KG — Yes, the technologies that you are creating for ecological living are ones that can be transferred as well. I mean, every local is itself global, if you start to do the 'diverse economy inventory',[3] you'll see how one place has got relations connecting it all around the world. Keeping that in mind is important, because otherwise you get pigeon-holed as localist and particularist, as if you are only doing something that's going to help a specific community. It is a real challenge for us to make those connections all the time between what's going on in one place and how this might be some kind of, well, 'prototype' is probably not the right word. And it's not something to be replicated either, it's something that would spread through distributed networks. Yet it needs the involvement of policy frameworks that can recognise what's being done and set up the regulatory frameworks that will allow it to spread.

DP — These are networks to be created and maintained, it won't spread naturally. It needs to be done in a kind of continual negotiation between the scales, for which you need facilitators.

KG — This is why some geographers abandon the notion of scale as they find it boxes people in too much. The way we have those nested boxes, local, national, as if they are 'Russian dolls' that you open up and there's another one inside, and then another one inside. There's a lot of critique about that at the moment and we are still searching for a language that starts to talk about trans-local connections and transversal flows. I think we're at a point where we can work with these ideas, but it's not easy to produce a systematic language for what is meant.

---

3   See Chapter 6 in *A Postcapitalist Politics* (Gibson-Graham, 2006) or www.takebackeconomy.net for theoretical and practical guides to conducting a Diverse Economy Inventory.

KT — In thinking about the language that you've been developing, more conservative movements in the US and the UK (e.g. Big Society) use similar terms to community economies, which encourages volunteering, community-led initiatives, and so on. We are wondering how community economies might be distinguished from that approach?

KG — It's a familiar kind of reaction to our work, because of the language. Just the term 'community', which is always taken over by the state in all sorts of nefarious ways, whether fascist or neoliberal. So we have to be very careful when we use this language and I think that the rise of neoliberal discourse and the ideological project of neoliberalism has had a major impact on governance and governance practice. The ideologues would say it's about de-regulation, but then the others would say that it's just a different kind of regulation, re-regulation, populism, and so on. Through these different kinds of neoliberal arts of governing, obviously the market has been a primary one, 'let the market decide', and the shift to individual responsibility as something that should be privileged, and so on. Under that logic, everyone should be 'pulling themselves up by their bootstraps', volunteering, sharing and caring. The way that language is drawn into this neoliberal project is a worrying one. It's one where people see the projects that we've been involved in as somehow positively feeding into those neoliberal projects, or being corrupted by them, and so on.

We take a position that there is a difference between the ideological project, the 'big society', 'the Third Way' or whatever, and the actual practice of the arts of governing that might then be rolled out. There's an opening there, for many things to happen. When there's a vision, I think, of a community economy, there is a way in which these things can be perhaps used in a way that is quite against the ideologues' vision of how policy should be rolled out.

A good example is a paper we found quite interesting, by James Ferguson, who talks about the ways in which the South African state started to move towards this neoliberal project, which would use the market to decide that everybody can get their social bonds and do what they want with it, rather than the provision of social welfare services (Ferguson, 2010). What he documents is that it gave rise to a whole load of diverse markets, people started to have money to do different things and it allowed them to start to develop small businesses, cooperatives, other kinds of things. So the actual practice that occurred was quite open to all sorts of different kinds of initiatives and ethics to be enacted. It wasn't this seamless, lining-up of ideology and practice, that often people assume will happen.

This means that in every instance we need to start thinking about how these partnerships or forms of responsibility can be enacted to practise some kind of ethics of interdependence versus say, a practice of individualism, an 'I'll just do my thing and too bad about the rest of you.' The language of active citizens, partnerships and possibilities, which is all part of the Big Society project, can also be a language of community economy, and I don't think we can assume there's auto-matically going to be this co-option, which is a lot of people's worry. The reason to work against co-option, or the only way we can work against co-option, is to have a more constant analysis of what's going on, and not assume that there is a one-size-fits-all solution. From a community economies point of view or from a neoliberal point of view, there will always be contestation here. We need a way to talk about the technologies that we are using, to try to create more sustainable livelihoods, or ethically oriented livelihoods, or care for the planet. The worry is there, cutbacks to funding, for example, that puts limits on community economy experimentation. But, we (Julie and I) have always argued against that kind of tendency that critical scholarship has, of lining everything up into one formation, such that it then debilitates politics. This is where our analytical skills have to be used, so we can recognise the danger, and also recognise the language – we don't have to be beholden to it. There are multiple ways of governing and acts of governance, that we need to be developing for community economies and work within the framework that we've got.

People often ask us 'Where does the state relate to your work?', our approach is to say, well, the state is diverse. There are many different elements, policy-making frameworks, departments, and so on. Rather than seeing the state as always speaking with one voice, we proceed with finding those spaces within policy-making and within government that are open to the kind of advances or innovation this kind of practice can produce. States are contradictory. If you start from that perspective, that things don't line up, it allows you to start then using your analytical skills to find strategically, where you can move, who you can move with and how.

DP – In your future work, what do you still want to know, to do or to achieve? What is the future of work on community economy?

KG – Well, there's lots of work going on in different directions within the collective. On a theoretical level, there's an interesting engagement in what is going on between our work and the work of actor-network theorists. We are trying to look at the assemblages that community economies are or take the form of, and how those assemblages and the technologies they involve could be shaped. This is adding another language into our work, which until now has been more focused on the agency of collective subjects, who are largely human. We're starting to say, how do we talk about agencies across that notion of assemblages, with others, and communities, whether it's technological or non-human, and so on?

In practical terms, that's led to a research project around the social innovations that groups of collective agencies are producing, that are enabling them to start to do business differently, or start to do community development differently. I think we've always marshalled lots of examples to pull out what the ethical content is, and we haven't gone back for more ethnographic discussions with people, to understand what are their ethos, how they are embodying and practising these ethos and ethics, what are the techniques of accountability, or ways of relating to suppliers or kinds of finances that will help them to do this kind of work and enact these kinds of economies. We are interested to do more engaged work co-producing knowledge with people who are experimenting in all sorts of ways, particularly in collective ways.

I'm interested in using mapping as a way of helping to produce those figure-ground shifts for people, in lots of different ways. So they start to be interested in the project of building on a reframed economic knowledge to open up opportunities. I think there's work going on, at lots of different levels. Some people in the Community Economies Collective are able to talk to policy-makers about this work and are starting to have more of an engagement with government agencies around these kinds of practices. At the moment their work has been more with provincial governments and national governments and their various policies. My colleague Stephen Healy has been to a UN meeting around social enterprise and solidarity economies, so there is obviously an interest at a global level too, and an emergence of different kinds of economies that have social values at their core, so I think there is scope for more involvement.

Our most recent book *Take Back the Economy*, is very much a popular book, so there's some going back now and trying to reconnect with various academic debates. We're torn, most of us, because we want to do this more in the world, in partnership as well. But I think there's a lot of exciting work going on across the group and then also very exciting connections with other groups like yours, where that will help us to develop a lot more, to have conversations outside our group as well.

KT and DP — Thank you!

REFERENCES

Ferguson, James (2010) 'The uses of neoliberalism', *Antipode* 41: 166–184.

Gibson-Graham, J.K. (2006) *A Postcapitalist Politics*, Minneapolis, MN: University of Minnesota Press.

Gibson-Graham, J.K., Cameron, Jenny and Healy, Stephen (2013) *Take Back the Economy: An Ethical Guide for Transforming Our Communities,* Minneapolis, MN: University of Minnesota Press.

Hayden, Dolores (1981) *The Grand Domestic Revolution: A History of Feminist Designs for American Homes, Neighborhoods, and Cities*, Cambridge, MA: MIT Press.

Roelvink, G., St Martin, K. and Gibson-Graham, J.K. (eds) (2015) *Making Other Worlds Possible: Performing Diverse Economies,* Minneapolis, MN: University of Minnesota Press.

11 – CARING: MAKING COMMONS, MAKING CONNECTIONS

Kim Trogal

This chapter aims to open up some questions around care[1] and the production of architecture and space. I consider both the spatiality of care and how care *as a practice* might involve working with different concepts of space. Following feminist thinkers and activists, especially Maria Mies, Veronika Bennholdt-Thomsen, Silvia Federici and architect Leslie Kanes Weisman, I explore how such concepts have, historically at least, structured dominant value systems that marginalise and disavow care labour. Through this discussion I want to make a case for the importance of including care within our understandings of architectural production, to highlight a critical yet often unseen relationship between space, architecture and care.

While spatial concepts have implications for care, care is also something that produces *spaces and relations*. It is a form of spatial production. I turn to practices of collective care to consider how they have produced different architectures, as well as different spatial concepts and practices, such as commons and mutual aid. In Nel Noddings' terms, these forms of care makes 'circles', namely, we care for those close to us and care exists in a 'circle' of proximity (Noddings, 1984). For this reason, I look at how contemporary spatial practices work *beyond the proximate* and create 'care chains' in Nodding's terms. I ask how can care make transversal[2] connections in spatial practice, how can care create connections *across* diverse social and cultural groups. I also consider how care might make 'trans-local' connections, to avoid becoming territorially exclusive or localised practices.

---

1   Care is a common word that we all know but one that can mean quite different things at different times. It is an emotion (to care about someone), it is an activity (to take care of something), it is a form of labour and feminists have developed it as a name for a specific kind of ethics. Caring, as an everyday activity, does not at first glance seem to be directly connected to architecture.

2   The concept of transversality is Guattari's and I elaborate it a little below, see also Guattari (1984) and Genosko (2009).

THE SPATIALITIES OF CARE AND INTERDEPENDENCE

One way to think about care is as a form of labour, in which one person or a group of people are looking after or supporting another. With care, we have relations of interdependency. Political theorist Joan Tronto suggests that the question of 'who is caring for who?' is probably the biggest political question there is:

> *Because the provision of care in human society has almost always proceeded by creating rigid hierarchies (castes, classes) by which some are able to demand the services of others, care has basically been of little interest to those in positions of power. The exclusion of care from politics grows out of an unwillingness to look at care on its own terms. ... care is a complex process that ultimately reflects structures of power, economic order, the separation of public and private life and our notions of autonomy and equality.* (1995: 12)

When we make 'who is caring for who?' central, we reveal hierarchies, dependencies and exclusions. What is important from the fields of architecture, planning, urbanism, and so on, is that the question of 'who is caring for who?' is part of a spatial dynamics at multiple scales, from global, regional, in neighbourhoods, in our homes to the scale of microscopic organisms. The spatial dynamics of care are part of what is usually called the geography of uneven development, or reductively put, in our current mode of development, we only have advancement or 'progress' in one place, at the expense of others in other places.

As prominent geographers have long argued, 'space matters', that space, and the ways we make space, have a dialectical relation with society (Massey, 2005; Smith, 2008; Soja, 1996). Across many disciplines, and in architecture and geography especially, feminists have shown how relations of care and dependency are structured along spatial conceptions, such as the dichotomies of city/country, home/work, public/private, so-called Global North/Global South. These dichotomies, feminists argue, function with exploitative divisions of labour, specifically care labour and reproduction.[3] While the terms of the dichotomies are not discrete in lived experience, they are

---

3   Leslie Kanes Weisman has argued that the spatial dichotomies that support exploitative or dominating gender relations are placed in a masculine-feminine dichotomy. 'Feminine' spaces, including reproductive and servile ones, are connected by association and are often situated behind, below, left, back, or generally concealed (Weisman, 1992: 11).

often deployed in discourse as though they were, both in general and in urban policy. The dichotomies of home/work, Global North/Global South belie their complexity and support 'perverse subsidies'.[4]

In the fields of architecture and design, we are perhaps more familiar with the idea of dependency in material terms. Architects and designers work with concepts such as ecological footprints[5] and are working increasingly with chains of material dependency, of material flows, including urban agriculture, waste and construction materials. However, there are other forms of dependency that are equally unsustainable, which we don't tend to recognise, neither as designers nor citizens. In *World City*, Massey draws attention to work on health inequality, in particular, research into the migration of skilled workers like nurses and midwives, from low- to high-income countries. Such research shows the inequity of access to health care, leaving countries in sub-Saharan Africa with very low numbers of midwives and very high rates of infant and mother mortality (Mensah *et al.*, 2005, cited in Massey, 2007: 175). Many factors contribute to this but there can be no doubt, this is one resulting factor from our economic model and lack of social sustainability, which is displaced to different, poorer regions.

We tend to deal with these problems through charity and benevo-lence, but it doesn't stop because the problem is structural. Midwifery is a very literal example of care giving and my argument here is not around this specific problem but to point to a broader question of value. Care is not only carried out by midwives and nurses, but can include all the people who make our cities and regions liveable: teachers, cleaners, youth workers, community workers, the people who remove your rubbish, people who grow your food for you, and so on (Figure 11.1). This is why it is important. This is what is called today a 'crisis of care', that we cannot actually re-produce and maintain the society in which we live.

---

4   Namely, these terms and discourses obscure the relations of actual dependency and our perceived notions of dependency: a dominant group (potentially associated with class, race, gender or geographical region) that is subsidised and dependent on a weaker one, constructs a situation where the weaker one is regarded *as* the dependent. Examples of this are to be found literally everywhere, the mother seen as dependent on another's wage or welfare payments, or the financial aid, for instance, sent to 'developing' countries. Each payment sets those in a position of perceived dependency (from the Western perspective or from the wage perspective), but with the land, resources and labour of the country that supports the West, it is the relation of actual dependency that is obscured (Massey, 2007: 175).

5   A city's ecological footprint shows the amount of resources that city consumes. It shows the physical area it takes to produce and maintain those resources, in order to allow the city to function in its current state. The total ecological footprint for London, for example, is over 34 million global hectares, which is an area over 200 times the city itself. The main contributors are electricity and fuel use for housing and food (Environment Agency, 2012).

Figure 11.1 'If you can read this thank a teacher' poster displayed in the window of a canal boat, Regents Canal, Hackney, February 2011
Photo: Kim Trogal

Advocates of a feminist ethics of care have strongly argued against the myth of individual independence. We are all cared for by others at certain moments in our lives, and most of us will care for others at some point too. As Richard Sennett (2004) has argued, the condition of dependence whether occurring naturally or constructed, has acquired a shameful status.

Care, then, is not a call for autonomy, that each person or place should be more independent or self-sufficient but is to question the very notion of autonomy and to recognise that care structures our world. If relations of care and interdependency are structured along spatial conceptions, which spatial concepts can we use (and perform) that are more attuned to care? In feminist political economy, thinkers like Silvia Federici, Maria Mies and Veronika Bennholdt-Thomsen have pointed to the commons as one such space (Federici, 2004; Mies and Bennholdt-Thomsen, 1999).

COLLECTIVE CARE AS POTENTIAL COMMONS

There are different kinds and concepts of commons, but in its most traditional form, commons are frequently understood as shared spaces or resources that are neither public nor private. They are shared and held in common, a form of ownership or responsibility *made through use rather than as a property relation*. Commons are both material (such as a fishery) and immaterial (like language). In their historical and traditional forms, commons are/were essential to reproduction and livelihoods, they provided subsistence. Historians connect their privatisation with the separation of (wage) labour from other life activities, and feminists thus show that it is in the money-economy that housework and reproductive tasks ceased to be viewed as 'real' work (Federici, 2004: 25).

In contrast to the isolation of reproductive work in spatial dichotomies, commons are the spaces, physical or virtual, of alternative economies and economies that are more reciprocal. There are practices of care that belong to commons and commoning practices, such as forms of responsibility, of sharing, of reciprocity, of democratic organisation and of welfare. However, *care as a practice can be said to produce commons too.*

Some built examples of collective care can be found in Dolores Hayden's seminal work, *The Grand Domestic Revolution* (1981). In this book she pieces together some of the lost history of women's work in architecture and offers numerous examples from the 1800s and early 1900s in which women and men experimented with the socialisation of domestic work. In these cases domestic work was organised within a collective, rather than on an individual household basis, and took place at the scale of: housing blocks or estates; neighbourhoods; at municipal level or even at a national level. As domestic work was socialised, new kinds of domestic workspace, cooperative forms of organisation and architectures were developed:

> *In order to overcome patterns of urban space and domestic space that isolated women and made their domestic work invisible, they developed new forms of neighbourhood organisation including housewives' cooperatives, as well as new building types, including the kitchen-less house, the day care centre, the public kitchen and the community dining club.*
> (1981: 1)

To glance at this example of cooperative housing in Letchworth (Figure 11.2), there is perhaps not anything special to be seen architecturally. On closer inspection, it becomes apparent that it is very different to what the majority in the UK would expect or demand for their own homes. In some cases, it is quite challenging, the plans look ordinary until you realise there is no kitchen in each dwelling, it is elsewhere. To live in these places means to live very differently, to the lives we know and consider normal.

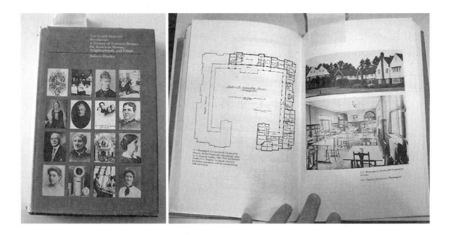

Figure 11.2 Dolores Hayden's Book, *The Grand Domestic Revolution*, alongside an example from her analyses of Cooperative Housing in Letchworth
Photos: Kim Trogal

In *The Grand Domestic Revolution*, there are examples of new types of organisation *and spatial organisation*, public kitchens, day care centres, cooperative laundries. In this case, design, architecture and planning were very much part of this movement. However, as Dalla Costa and James (1975) argue, communal facilities like public kitchens cannot be a spatial project alone, otherwise they simply risk becoming the site of low-paid work for women outside the home, without actually challenging the notion of work or wage. What is important in projects based on *collective* 'shadow-work'[6] such as childcare or domestic work, and subsistence work such as agriculture, is that they must challenge the validation of different forms of labour and challenge the separation of the monetary economy from domestic ones. The examples in Hayden's book are no longer in existence, but they are a vital part of the history of the collective spaces of care. Her book is still important and 30 years after it was published, it still provokes interest. In 2009, Casco Office for Art, Design and Theory

---

6   'Shadow-work' is Ivan Illich's term, which in fact *excludes* agriculture and subsistence work, it is unpaid work whose 'performance in the condition for wages to be paid'.

   I call this complement to wage-labour 'shadow-work'. It comprises most housework women do in their homes and apartments, the activities connected with shopping, most of the homework of students cramming for exams, the toil expended commuting to and from the job. It includes the stress of forced consumption, the tedious and regimented surrender to therapists, compliance with bureaucrats, the preparation for work to which one is compelled, and the many activities usually labelled 'family life'.
   (Illich, 1980: 1–2)

in Utrecht, began a long-term programme of projects, research and exhibitions called *The Grand Domestic Revolution: A User's Manual*. As part of their research, they interviewed Hayden to ask her if we could talk of a Grand Domestic Revolution today (Choi and Tanaka, 2010: 37–52). Her answer was no, as she argued that while there are small interventions, there is *no movement*. There is no feminist movement today concerning domestic work as there was in 1970s and neither is there anything like the scale of the movement of the eighteenth and nineteenth centuries that is documented in Hayden's book. But today, there are other movements generating and working with alternative economies, such as the ecological movement. Here we find experiments with different forms of exchange, like time banks as well as Local Exchange Trading Schemes (LETs), and different forms of collective and commoning practices, such as gleaning as well as urban agriculture and gardening.[7] These are perhaps opportunities and possibilities for a new 'grand domestic revolution'.

While care may potentially produce commons, what is also notable is that commons involve a different kind of care than the kind we are usually familiar with. Caring is often typified by dyadic relations (e.g. parent–child; nurse–patient; teacher–student) and thus consists of chains of people (you care for your mother, who cares for her neighbour, and so on).[8] Commons are a form of care that historically existed within a group or community of people, as did practices of mutual aid. They could both be considered in Nodding's terms, as care circles. What differentiates the two perhaps, among other things, is their relation to space.

CARE THROUGH OBJECTS AND EVENTS: MUTUAL AID AS COLLECTIVE PRACTICE OF CARE

Mutual aid is the name given to the process when people voluntarily work together or pool resources for mutual benefit. It is something done for others but also for oneself. In his classic work on the subject, Kropotkin argued that different human societies all invented mechanisms and rituals to maintain mutuality and collective life. He showed how, over several hundred years coinciding with industrial capitalism,

---

7   Similarly, Federici, Dalla Costa, Mies and Bennholdt-Thomsen have all pointed to urban agriculture (agriculture, that in Dalla Costa's words is the labour that 'sustains life for everybody') as possible locations for new commons (Dalla Costa, 2007; Mies and Bennholdt-Thomsen, 1999; Federici, 2005).

8   The concept of care circles and care chains is taken from Nel Noddings (1984).

such practices were heavily regulated against. He cites for example, until 1884, in France, it was forbidden to form groups of more than 19 people. In England, between 1760 and 1844 over 4,000 Acts of Parliament were passed to remove all traces of common ownership of land and possessions (Kropotkin, 1987: 180–207). The Combination Laws also prevented people from organising themselves, making unionism illegal.

What Kropotkin showed is that even when such laws are made and commons enclosed, mutual aid takes place through other institutions (ibid.: 197–198). What is interesting is that these practices survived longer as they were attached to objects and events. For example, in rural regions of Southern France, Kropotkin tells of wine growers who formed associations, consisting of between 10 and 30 growers, who had a steam-powered water pump in common ownership. There was thus a network of people attached to this object, which moved across private space. The group or part of the group would cooperate in such a way that each vineyard could be irrigated. There are many examples like this across the world and I mention this one precisely because it was considered ordinary. The point is that it is the object and the task that connect, rather than the space.

Kropotkin suggests another example, in regions of Germany, people would help to build each other's houses, using timber from the common forest. Sometimes there would be a fete or an event, which was a call for aid. On that day, everyone participated in the building of another person's house. Again, this was common and it was often the custom that whoever was being helped had to throw a feast for everybody. If they did not feed the others well, it was considered extremely bad-mannered as everyone had had a day of hard labour (1987: 197–198).

In the example of the vineyards, a network is mobilised by a task and a commonly owned object, and in the example of the house, a network is mobilised by the construction of private property. These examples are interesting from an architecture and design perspective. It suggests that the actual space may be of less importance than the community and practices associated with it, which can continue to be supported through common objects or activities rather than spaces.[9] It also suggests that private spaces, buildings and their care can still support common or mutual practices.

---

9   This corroborates the findings of action research by aaa in their Eco-Box project (Petrescu, 2010).

Historical examples of mutual aid could be interesting for designers, both as a way of working against a hyper-individuality as well as something useful to know when we have a widespread loss of public (state) space. From a design point of view, I wonder what kind of contemporary objects and events could be invented? And what would it take to sustain them?

We have a contemporary form of mutual aid in the time bank movement, which sometimes also shares objects, as well as time. One example, local to me, is *Haringey Green Bank,* who as part of their time banking scheme are building a tool bank, a library of equipment for gardening. The objects are held by the time bank and individuals may borrow them, but a condition of their use is that they are not for private use, they may only be used for community projects. While a spade, or other commonly owned gardening tool is perhaps not that remarkable in itself, as someone with a design background, I start to wonder what would it take for these tools to become more interesting in terms of the structures that exist around them. Is this a framework in which you can start to have new common objects of mutual aid?

The example of mutual aid being the way in which people built their houses is also interesting. Most of us are unlikely to undertake this kind of endeavour today. We are unlikely to build someone else's house without official remuneration or written agreement. But again it doesn't stop us asking what it would take, because what makes it difficult to really imagine something today is that in order to partici-pate you need very high levels of trust and stability in a group.

As Marilyn Friedman (1993) says, we extend a special privilege to those we care for and we tend to care for those who are close to us. A community of mutual aid was one such circle of proximity, because there are limits to care. You can't care for everyone and everything all the time. Historically this was physical proximity, if you lived in the village or had commoners' rights. Time banking may be reminiscent of a historical form of community, one that is geographically based. But how are we to deal with this question of proximity and develop forms of care that do not bring territorial operations of space, which the historical commons and mutual aid would have been tied to? How can we understand the 'circles' of care that exist now, and make new ones, but not allow them to become exclusive structures? How to extend beyond the circle without undermining trust or stability?

CARE THROUGH TRANSVERSAL, TRANS-LOCAL CONNECTIONS

To start thinking about what kinds of connections can exist both *within and between localities*, a common proposition is that small initiatives need to be networked together. Jeanne van Heeswijk is certainly someone who practises care and her work provides one example of how to think about the question of 'circles' and connections. One of her best-known projects is the *Blue House* in Ijburg, Amsterdam, which has been described as a collective research project and a networked practice.[10] Ijburg is a newly built, large suburb of Amsterdam that was planned to contain 18,000 new homes for 45,000 residents (O'Neill, 2011). In collaboration with the architect Denis Kaspoori and the artist Hervé Paraponaris, they created a framework for artist residencies over a four-year period. A condition of the residencies was that artists had to engage with the locality and part of their brief was to create new models of sociality. The *Blue House* ran alongside the phased construction of the suburb, so the estate was partially inhabited for a number of years until the building work was complete.

With each of the projects, and in total there were some 900 for the *Blue House*, different networks of people were involved. Each intervention, object and use had a community of people attached to it to make it work. They are all groups with different timescales, some overlap, sometimes people are part of different groups at the same time.

While Heeswijk is very much engaged with the locality in which she is working, she also works with an international network of artists. She traces some of this network on her website where she really acknowledges all the contributions made. She recognises all the people it took to make it happen and recognises things that are not normally considered work, such as moral support. Through her website you can see the group a project brings together and, if you have enough patience, you could trace where people have multiple affiliations to different projects.

---

10   Heeswijk was effectively self-commissioned and inaugurated the *Blue House* herself. She negotiated for one of the dwellings to be taken off the market and donated to the community for four years. She called the dwelling the Blue House, as a play on van Gogh's Yellow House and Frieda Kahlo's blue house, as meeting place for artists, a hosting place for artists to stay. See O'Neill (2011).

Another example of working with trans-local networks is the *Rhyzom* project, organised by five partners: Agency in Sheffield; Public Works in London; PS[2] Belfast; *aaa* in Paris, and Cultural Agencies in Istanbul. Each of the partners set up field trips and workshops to help explore some of the questions they had emerging from their own local cultural practices. What maybe differentiates this work from other forms of networked practice is that rather than connecting individuals from an art network to a specific locality, here an art/architecture/academic network of friendship is used *to connect local groups to one another.*

In a lecture, Ruth Morrow, one of the participants in *Rhyzom*, gave an example of an exchange between *Oda Projesi* from Istanbul and the *Forever Young Pensioners* in Ballykinler, with each presenting their group and experiences to the other (Morrow, 2012). She emphasised the significance of the *mutual qualities of the exchange and connection.* For *Rhyzom*, each of the groups organised workshops and visits for the others, with the aim of 'setting up connections and networks of production and dissemination' (*aaa*, 2010). So a network of friendship established the initial project, but each workshop enabled relations to be extended a little, making new connections each time: 'performing a rhyzom' as *aaa* say (2010: 21).

The *Rhyzom* network now has a life in *Eco Nomadic School*, a project that I have been involved in.[11] Here the network is mobilised to test the mutual teaching of ecological practices, sharing of skills and experience between different groups (Figure 11.3). In October 2011, as part of a 'live project'[12] a group of Masters students in architecture from the University of Sheffield organised a public workshop for the network. Over two days the students organised a variety of different activities, walks, lectures, discussions, brainstorming as well as informal aspects, like a meal. Through the workshop the students organised, other connections began to be made. This led to the later involvement of other groups, specifically members from *Incredible Edible*, in the second workshop in Brezoi, Romania. A connection and presence which would otherwise never have taken place.

---

11   The project has four main partners, Agency in Sheffield; *aaa* in Paris; *myvillages* in the Netherlands and Germany and the Foundation for Community and Local Development in Brezoi, Romania.

12   Live Projects are part of the curriculum of Masters students at the Sheffield School of Architecture. They are six weeks long and students are required to work in groups for 'live' situations, working with real clients, and so on.

Figure 11.3 *Eco Nomadic School* visit to the Odaie, in the mountains outside of Brezoi, Romania, January 2012
Photo: Kathrin Böhm

Bringing in Guattari's concept of 'transversality in a group', one can start to see that the kinds of relations both within and between groups in these projects have particular importance. Understanding that institutions contribute to the creation of certain kinds of subjectivity, Guattari introduced the notion of transversality. Transversality means (crudely put) to overcome the structures and routines that have become sedimented in practices and make new kinds of connections and subjectivity. In his case, within the psychiatric clinic, roles and relations are highly structured, such as the doctor–patient relation or medical staff–service staff relation. Artist Susan Kelly describes transversality like this:

> Broadly speaking, Guattari used the term transversality as a conceptual tool to open hitherto closed logics and hierarchies and to experiment with relations of interdependency in order to produce new assemblages and alliances ... A movement or mode of transversality explicitly sets out to de-territorialise the disciplines, fields and institutions it works across.
> (Kelly, 2005)

Projects like *Rhyzom* and *Eco Nomadic School* follow something of a transversal approach. They bring together different constellations of people: community activists, community growers, local residents into relation with those in academia, in art. It is not simply a 'bridge' between the civic realm and academia/arts institutions, but rather aims to produce mutual relations. In *Eco Nomadic School*, for example, in one context participants are 'teachers' or experts, yet in another they participate as students, and roles are reversed. These projects demand a repositioning of the self in relation to others, putting oneself in different roles and contexts.

My experience in *Eco Nomadic School* has changed my preconceptions about the nature of trans-local connection, care and dependency. Initially I felt that trans-local connection should resolve issues regarding our material dependencies, questions of food, energy, and so on. But this experience (for me) has emphasised that an important connection between places is maybe not (only) material, but also about immaterial connections. Projects like this can make not only trans-local connections, but also transversal ones, creating the context in which your ways of seeing are altered through exposure and connection to those who live differently.

Gibson-Graham also bring in the idea of immaterial trans-local connections in their work. They make special reference to shared languages in order to help create a shared imaginary as well as building community through shared knowledge (Gibson-Graham, 2006). This is surely something that universities can contribute to and indeed they do through an initiative like *Eco Nomadic School*. Through the platform one can enter into another circle and learn from them.[13]

Considering the long-term nature of connections is important, as *Blue House*, *Rhyzom* and *Eco Nomadic School* are all projects with defined timeframes. What can make them sustainable? Here it becomes clear that both connections and commons, circles and chains need care themselves, they need to be looked after.

Following feminist approaches, I have tried to elaborate some of the spatial aspects of care and consider some of the ways that care can produce different architectures and different spaces. I think to bring care into understandings of the 'social production of architecture' means

---

13   This is also very much the case with Kathrin Böhm's work, particularly in her work with Public Works and their project 'International Village Shop'. See her contribution to this volume as well as 'International Village Shop'.

considering the paradigms in which things are both produced and 'taken care of'; it means considering the spatiality of interdependence and care.

I have tried to consider how practices of care work with concepts of space and how those concepts operate alongside, and even produce, value systems. I think making care central introduces the necessity of valuing different kinds of labour, contributions and activities. I have suggested some possibilities of how this might be done architecturally, through the spaces of collective care, or practices such as commoning and mutual aid. The trans-local practices in connected disciplines of art (Heeswijk) as well as the cultural networks and teaching and research practices of *Rhyzom* and *Eco Nomadic School*, also suggest *transversal* forms of care between groups and places. The examples I chose here also importantly make reference to other contributors to this volume. This is to acknowledge that many contemporary practitioners are *already practising care*. Just as other practices of care risk being hidden, taken for granted and undervalued, an important point is to recognise them as crucial kinds of action, which help make our world(s).

REFERENCES

aaa (2010) *TRANS-LOCAL-ACT: Cultural Practices Within and Across*, 1st edn. Paris: aaa/peprav.

Choi, Binna and Tanaka. Maiko (2010) 'You ask me if there is another "Grand Domestic Revolution" going on right now, and the answer is... an interview with Dolores Hayden', in *The Grand Domestic Revolution Goes On*, Utrecht: Casco Office for Art, Design, Theory and London: Bedford Press, pp. 37–52.

Dalla Costa, Mariarosa (2007) 'Reruralising the world', *The Commoner* 12: 111–118.

Dalla Costa, Mariarosa and James, Selma (1975) *Power of Women and the Subversion of the Community*, 3rd rev. edn, Bristol: Falling Wall Press Ltd.

Environment Agency (2012) 'London's ecological footprint', 21 August, available at: www.environment-agency. gov.uk/research/library/ publications/115654.aspx.

Federici, Silvia (2004) *Caliban and the Witch: Women, the Body and Primitive Accumulation*, New York: Autonomedia.

(2005) 'Women, land-struggles and the valorization of labor', *The Commoner* 10, available at: www.commoner.org. uk/10federici.pdf (accessed 1 January 2011).

Friedman, Marilyn (1993) *What Are Friends For? Feminist Perspectives on Personal Relationships and Moral Theory*, Ithaca, NY: Cornell University Press.

Genosko, Gary (2009) *Félix Guattari: A Critical Introduction*, London: Pluto Press.

Gibson-Graham, J-K. (2006) *A Postcapitalist Politics*, Minneapolis, MN: University of Minnesota Press.

Guattari, Félix (1984) *Molecular Revolution: Psychiatry and Politics*, Harmondsworth: Penguin Books.

Hayden, Dolores (1981) *The Grand Domestic Revolution: A History of Feminist Designs for American Homes, Neighborhoods, and Cities*, Cambridge, MA: MIT Press.

Illich, Ivan (1980) *Shadow-Work*, Cape Town: University of Cape Town Press.

International Village Shop, available at: www.international villageshop.com/about/ (accessed 10 May 2012).

Kelly, Susan (2005) 'The transversal and the invisible: how do you really make a work of art that is not a work of art?' *Republicart*, available at: www.republicart. net/disc/mundial/kelly01_en.htm (accessed 12 May 2012).

Kropotkin, Petr Alekseevich (1987) *Mutual Aid: A Factor of Evolution*, London: Freedom Press, pp. 180–207.

Massey, Doreen (2005) *For Space*, London: Sage.
    (2007) *World City*, Cambridge: Polity Press.

Mensah, Kwadwo, Mackintosh, Maureen and Henry, Leroi (2005) *The 'Skills Drain' of Health Professionals from the Developing World: A Framework for Policy Formulation*, London: Medact.

Mies, Maria and Bennholdt-Thomsen, Veronika (1999) *The Subsistence Perspective: Beyond the Globalised Economy*, trans. Patrick Camiller, London: Zed Books.

Morrow, Ruth (2012) 'Being at hand', lecture given as part of the Social Production of Architecture series, University of Sheffield, March.

Noddings, Nel (1984) *Caring: A Feminine Approach to Ethics and Moral Education*, London: University of California Press.

O'Neill, Paul (2011) 'The Blue House', in Paul O'Neill and Claire Doherty (eds) *Locating the Producers: Durational Approaches to Public Art*, Amsterdam: Valiz, pp. 17–61.

Petrescu, Doina (2010) Keynote speech 'Gardeners of the Common', presented at the Sexuate Subjects, UCL, London.

Sennett, Richard (2004) *Respect: The Formation of Character in an Age of Inequality*, Harmondsworth: Penguin.

Smith, Neil (2008) *Uneven Development: Nature, Capital, and the Production of Space*, 3rd edn, Athens, GA: University of Georgia Press.

Soja, Edward J. (1996) *Third-Space: Journeys to Los Angeles and Other Real-and-Imagined Places*, Oxford: Blackwell.

Tronto, Joan (1995) *Caring for Democracy: A Feminist Vision*, Utrecht: Universiteit voor Humanistiek.

Weisman, Leslie Kanes (1992) *Discrimination by Design: A Feminist Critique of the Man-Made Environment.* Urbana, IL: University of Illinois Press.

12 – TRADE AS ARCHITECTURE: PUBLIC REALMING THROUGH TANGIBLE ECONOMIES

Kathrin Böhm

I am an artist with an interest in architecture and economy as two realms where our sense of possible societal and commoning relations are shaped through everyday activities. Even though I work and present myself as an artist, I prefer to think of myself as a builder or a dealer who acts within and across everyday situations, and whose work is set out to extend collective practices of spatial and economic production.

I use the term public space in relation to its use, accessibility and the collective claims made on it, and therefore in its broad meaning of being a space that is open to the general public, with numerous access points and low thresholds. In this chapter, economic activities are regarded as a means to re-produce public space, and architecture is understood as the socio-spatial structures we inhabit and model. Neither are third-party provisions or remote concepts, but public realms, which we shape and influence through the ways we organize action and cultural interaction. The making of space and the running of our economy are things we are involved in on an everyday basis.

I have chosen to write about three particular projects by Myvillages,[1] in which practices of collective production and forms of trade are a means to extend and create localized public realms. These public spaces are networked and interlinked with publics elsewhere, for instance, a rural community in a different country or 'the art world' at the other end of town (Figures 12.1–12.3).

---

1   Myvillages is an international artist group founded in 2003 by Kathrin Böhm (the UK), Wapke Feenstra (the Netherlands) and Antje Schiffers (Germany).

Figure 12.1 2016 Company Drinks Range (group photo)
Photo: Jennifer Balcombe. Courtesy of Company Drinks

Figure 12.2 Rural Women's Economies Workshop (group photo), Eco Nomadic School, Frensdorf, 2013
Photo: Kathrin Böhm

Figure 12.3 Village Produce (group photo), International Village Shop, TENT, Rotterdam, 2011
Photo: Wapke Feenstra

01

The drinks shown in Figure 12.1 are the bottled outcomes of a new community enterprise called *Company: Movements, Deals and Drinks* (*Company*). The range of beverages includes eight different sodas: one DIY cola, a green hop beer and several cordials. The ingredients were all picked and made by different groups and communities who live in the east London Borough of Barking and Dagenham. The drinks were produced between March and September 2015, traded in the autumn with the profits reinvested to further develop and grow this public endeavour. *Company* connects east London's history of going fruit and hop-picking in Kent with the set-up of a new community drinks enterprise. The traditional 'hopping' epoch spans from roughly 1850 to 1950 with mainly women and children spending the late summer months on farms to pick hops, get fresh air and to earn some extra money. *Company* revisits this history through re-vitalizing and altering practices of communal picking and drinks production and trade, for more details, see www.c-o-m-p-a-n-y.info

02

In Figure 12.2, the women on the steps in front of the communal 'House of the Farmwoman' in the village of Birkach in Southern Germany are from nearby and from faraway places such as Berlin, Budapest, Oslo,

Paris, Brezoi, London and Rotterdam. The group met for a two-day
mixed programme on rural women's economies as part of the ongoing
Höfer Goods project, which is linked to the broader activities of the *Eco
Nomadic School*.

Höfer Goods are new annual products developed collectively by
Kathrin Böhm together with the Höfer Women and external guests. As a
starting point, they take local histories and resources and their function
and aesthetics are informed by past and current practices.

Eco Nomadic School (2011–ongoing) is the result of a collaborative
pan-European research programme called Rhyzom (2008–2011),
and the organizers and partners include atelier d'architecture (Paris),
Myvillages, Agency (Sheffield), public works (London), FCDL (Brezoi),
PS² (Belfast) and Platform Garanti (Istanbul), see also Chapter 11 in this
volume. For more details, see www.rhyzom.net/nomadicschool/

03

In Figure 12.3, the homemade jams, knitwear and newly developed
collective products fill the stalls and counters of the *International Village
Shop*, a trans-local infrastructure which instigates the production of
new collective goods with rural communities, alongside the set-up of
temporary and permanent trading posts. The shop and the public counter
form the place where new and existing products from geographically and
culturally dispersed rural communities meet, the Höfer Frogbutterspoon
meets the new Fufu Bowl from the Ghana village of Ekumfi Ekrafo, the
Northern Irish Caravan Pot meets the Swiss Ittinger Ei, Russian hand
brooms meet Frisian horse milk.

The *International Village Shop* has been set up as a joint
initiative by Myvillages, public works, Grizedale Arts and Somewhere
in 2007. The shop is now run by Myvillages. For more details, see
www.internationalvillageshop.net

The group photos are introductions to collectivities, which are linked
to the production and exchange of goods and knowledge, and the construction of new local and trans-local public spaces. The constellation of
each photo results from the focal activity of each project; going picking/
Company, learning/*Eco Nomadic School*, trading/*International Village
Shop*. As formats and concepts they represent alterations of familiar
spaces or organizational forms such as a business, a school or a shop.

On their own, the images don't explain the social, geographical
and economic complexities that are going on beyond the photographic
framing of a moment. Narrated, they offer detailed stories of why they are
group photos of *new* collectivities and new public spaces. The group of

drinks is made by a local community that doesn't reassemble the community from the same place, who went picking 60 years ago. The original hop-pickers were English working-class communities, and the groups in the black-and-white photos of the time consist mainly of females and their extended East End families. The new family of drinks not only represents a dramatically changed local community but also a different way of meeting and working together in the same spaces, be it the farm or the neighbourhood. The once important and often dominant family links are tentatively replaced by other links, interests or desires, such as a longing for social situations, collective adventures and shared productivity. The making, consuming and trading of drinks both represent and facilitate changing collectivities. As both tangible and consumable goods, the drinks can be just a simple commodity, but they can also be an agent for economic and cultural changes, and the making of new public realms.

The goods in the *International Village Shop* also play an ambivalent game, between being a straightforward commodity, the embodiment of a particular collectiveness as well as being a local product in an international network. Each good represents a particular rural locality while participating in the shaping of a new trans-local cultural space. Locally, the actual collective development and making of the goods open up new spaces for collective reflection, invention and action. Within the international trading network of the shop, the goods allow for new inter-rural neighbourhoods on the shop counter, while at the same time presenting a culturally confident and ready-to-trade interface with urban audiences.

The three projects are all medium- to long-term ones and have their own reproductive elements and cycles. *Company* is set up as an annual cycle of drinks production. It starts with the fruit-growing season and intensifies during the trading season in late summer and autumn. The knowledge gathering and exchanging aspects of *Höfer Goods* are linked to the *Eco Nomadic School*, which has been touring a number of European local projects and partners since 2010, with regular partners providing a continuous growth of social relations and applicable knowledge and skills exchange. The *International Village Shop* is open-ended and functions through continuous production and trade across geographically dispersed local projects and temporary and semi-permanent shop manifestations.

LOCALIZED COLLECTIVE PRODUCTION AND PRODUCTS AS EMBODIMENTS

Production chains are often removed from everyday experiences and the actual making of things becomes a mystery (like architecture and the economy in general). The making of things is something that is done for us by others, leaving us with a single role at a single moment in time: that of consumer or user.

Both in *Company* and *Höfer Goods*, it is key that the possibility and technicality of making something are deconstructed and *made public*. The different steps to reach a product are made accessible as activities to become involved in, from developing a brief for a product, to preparing, processing and packaging. The projects have their own cyclic or perpetual dynamic, e.g. *Company*'s production/distribution/reinvesting chain is organized along the local growing season, with large social events in summer and autumn and a quieter period each winter. The different stages and moments of each project are collectivized by making them publicly accessible at any point, so that the productive and re-productive activities become a generator of shared common space. The products are embodiments of a collective ambition and the trade allows for spatial extensions into a larger general public realm.

The starting point for the new development and production of goods is always a community and their environment as a localized lived and spatial reality. Community is a possibly heterogeneous group, which shares a link to one place, this could be the population of a village or landscape, the staff of a factory or the users of a community centre. Myvillages works with 'the local' in cultural terms; the making of a particular landscape and the actual current activities and interests in that place. We are interested in the fluidity and ambiguity of what local means in regards to territory and identity and are particularly interested in the tangible closeness and immediacy of the local, where narratives and everyday activities can be pinned down fairly precisely. The local as an actual social and spatial framework allows for a self-positioning, where ideas and possibilities can be tested in the here and now. 'Local' is often used as a strategic term to focus and at the same time ask questions about the place we work and live in.

There is of course a dark side to the local, for example, widespread tendencies to use it as an attribute that excludes newcomers, or a general romanticization of a dead but well-remembered local culture, which therefore constitutes a resistance to recognizing the local as something in transition, which can change radically. The local also carries restrictions in scale and Greg Sharzer in his (2012) book, *No Local*, stresses the fact that without a critical understanding of the internal drives of larger, and often globally dominant systems, such as capitalism, the potential for small-scale local initiatives remains limited. Besides the current euphoria when it comes to anything local, he hints towards a hidden pessimism potentially inherent in the concept of localism, which assumes that we cannot make fundamental change at this level. However, towards the end of his book Sharzer refers to Gibson-Graham in their request to see 'capitalism as fragile, [so] we can create politics with a new kind of dispersed collective action that [does] not depend upon the organized revolutionary agendas of more established radical politics' (Sharzer, 2012: 126).

All the projects presented here work towards the recognition of still existing or new public realms as the place where you can get involved in collective and communal endeavours and therefore in societal, economic, spatial and political dynamics. In a recent interview, Kamila Shamsie defined public space as a place in any city in which everyone has the right to be present (Shamsie, n.d.). A widely differing range of people come together in these spaces in which they must learn to share, a quality Shamsie believes, is one of the great virtues of public space. Katherine Shonfield's concept of 'public time' is also important here and explains the necessity of having access to, and being able to experience 'public' in durational terms (1998). Her argument is that *time spent in public, this can be waiting for a bus, sitting on a train, walking up a street, allows us and forces us to understand ourselves in relation to others in the same place*, and she argues that the quality of society's public time reflects directly its current democratic state.

Company, *Eco Nomadic School* and *International Village Shop* have and make different public times, and use goods and products to pin the 'public' down as something that has been collectively achieved and can be shared. Even though the collective action in the three projects structure themselves around cycles of (re)production, the actual and tangible outcomes play an important role. The moment when the product is presented and launched in public is very often the moment when the ambition to create new public spaces becomes clear.

Company refers to a historic period when east London families, mainly women and children, would go hop-picking to Kent, with their involvement in the production chain of beer-making clearly being reduced to two moments: the harvest (of the hops) and the consumption (of the beer – mainly done by their male family members). The ambition of *Company* is to make the remaining parts of the drinks production chain accessible, from picking to bottling, trading and making profits, with different roles being on offer at different points. Here the products, the actual drinks, represent their collective history and possibilities for new communal forms of production, and at the same time they are also just commodities with a clear function, to be bought because someone is thirsty and wants to have a drink, or share one with others.

The group photo of all the different drinks we made is important in its diversity and represents new possible social and productive constellations. The historic hop-picking photos show extended East End families, mainly the female members and children. The group photo of the drinks we make now represents very different communal, but not family-bound, bonds and possibilities. The label and narrated stories of each drink explain who went picking and what, where and how the production was carried out. Each drink's chain involves different groups of individuals, who either came together through their mutual interest in the project, such as the former hop-pickers, individuals who join local foraging tours or kids who drop in for the cola workshops, or those who have temporary bonds, such as the students of the local college or existing women's groups.

In a similar way, with all products, the drinks are rooted in histories of manufacturing and the semiotics of the product itself are as an everyday object and usable item. The making of drinks, including beer, was for a long time a home-based process, which got outsourced to external manufacturers (small local breweries), which then grew in scale to industrial complexes and moved elsewhere. Dagenham, for example, is well known for its industrial heritage with Ford cars being the most prominent, a fact that often overshadows the other industries that were first established and then grew large there, including among others R. White's Lemonade. Both the area's rural links (the area being farmland and market gardens) and its industrial heritage (with a wide range of manufacturing and employment) are still recognizable and important aspects of a local identity, but without any immediate function or opportunity (as land is not cultivated and the industries have moved away). The semiotics of the different drinks and their individual cultural meaning are something to be slowly revealed through the project as it continues.

The *Höfer Goods* are not based on one product range but vary in their outputs and refer in broader terms to the history and capacity of what post-agricultural villages produce today, in terms of goods and lived culture. In the case of Höfen, it is the women who are involved in the invention and making of new product. The collective informing-ourselves, knowledge and skills exchange is also part of the *Eco Nomadic School*, a trans-local and pan-national project. In workshops and seminars we address questions of rural women's economies, traditional forms of labour, and local and regional production and manufacturing facilities. The product development process starts with an open question and the product can be anything. The products that have been made since

2006 range from frogbutterspoons,[2] tinned clay to machine-made lace. The produced objects are key to the project, and while wordings like 'product' and 'good' reflect their everydayness, the objects also become actors and, as Latour describes it:

> As soon as we allow [non-human objects] to enter the collective in the form of new entities with uncertain boundaries, entities that hesitate, quake and induce perplexity, it is not hard to see that we can grant them the designation of actors. And if we take the term 'association' literally, there is no reason either not to grant them the designation of social actors.

If the relations between things stand in for relations between people, then the objects are non-human participants: 'The goods themselves bring their socialities and networks of dependence into visibility, creating conditions where the politics behind the journeys can be revealed.'[3]

NETWORKED ACTIVITIES AND THE ARCHITECTURAL

> We need to place what we know within a structure, which in turn enables us to make sense of our knowledge.
> (O'Neill, 2006: 12)

All social structures have spatial conditions and the making of new relationships will shape new spaces. The relationships made through the collective and productive enterprises of the projects described here weave spatial realities between the often very different places in use. They link parks to community centres, farms to a soda workshop, a training kitchen to a playground, a factory to a coffee table, a local archive to a hop-garden, slowly revealing the three new community buildings in their making, the shop, the school, the company.

These structures, or architectures, need to be more foregrounded within the general current cultural discourse of relational practices, which often focuses on the socio-geographical or socio-political rather than the actual physical spatialities and qualities. The spatialities in use are rarely confined to one place or building. They are often complicated,

---

2   The Frogbutterspoon is a product developed by Kathrin Böhm, MyVillages and the women of Höfen as part of the *Höfer Goods* series. It is a cream spoon, which also functions as a knife and a stamp. It is made from porcelain and refers to 'frogs', which is also the nickname of the villagers. See www.internationalvillageshop.net/products/butter.spoon

3   Miranda Pope in her unpublished essay on *Company*, referring to Latour (2007: 75).

spreading across places and times, experienced by individuals or groups, on- and off-line. They are multiple and messy spatialities which constitute our everyday experience and which we travel through in very fluid ways, moving from private social space to public online, from intimate public to professional private, and so on. However, when it comes to describing the everyday use of space, our language seems much more limited than the realities we experience. We mainly rely on terms which refer to the static and the built, such as the square, the school, the mall, the park, the corner, the office, and so on, rather than temporary realms with often unclear boundaries.

It is this limitation in readily available language, paired with a general shift towards a global culture where mobility, connectivity and dispersed sociabilities dominate, which Lane Relyea addresses in his (2013) book, *Your Everyday Art World*. Here he reflects on a general loss of the architectural, which he regards as a danger to further lose control over one's own means. For example, the shift from production to project, which characterizes the current art world also means that 'the figure of the network begins to appear less like defiance and more like the latest answer to capitalism's constant need to overcome and reinvent itself' (Relyea, 2013: 9).

The question he poses is how current cultural practice and socially engaged art in particular can remain critical and engaged, without being swallowed up by what has become a general global socio-cultural phenomena, following the dynamics of digitalization, globalization and neoliberalism where everyone becomes an ever-more spread-out decentred actor (or 'omnivore', as Relyea puts it). A networked society where everyone can adapt supposedly active relations to production and the imposed concept of the 'pro-sumer' (marketer-speak for professional or 'producerly' consumers) dilutes any self-driven collectivity. He also points to the danger that the current project might be too determined and embedded within purely social flows and networks and shift away from the architectonic, which to a certain degree is crucial in achieving and practising collectivity.

The understanding of collective space is essential in understanding collectivity, which is more than just a group of people but a group that does something together in a place at a time. To become aware, use and adapt surrounding and remaining public spaces and facilities (or make them temporarily public) is structural to the projects described in this chapter. They are a practised counter-action to Relyea's warning of a loss of architectonic. The use of space is the immediately tangible element, even though the actions start with social relations. To declare the social, cultural and economic actions in our projects an act of making architecture is political and suggests collective constructions, which adapt the realities of types of buildings that are familiar to us (the shop, the school, the company) to explore and practise alternatives.

'This is the shop and the shop can be many things' (or school, or company …) takes away the polarizing and inherent hierarchical nature of existing formats and buildings, and makes it explicit that they are formats to play with and adapt from different directions and adapt to many contexts and goals. Since most public or publicly accessible structures are being more and more defined by capitalist economic thinking, an adaptation of these structures also means imagining and re-introducing other economic concepts (Gibson-Graham, 2013). This goes hand in hand with Gibson-Graham's call for more intentional economic activities, where non-capitalist imaginaries can come to live and be practised in order to confront, change or re-organize capitalist social relations.

Space itself remains, however, immediately accessible for private or public use and it has always been an urgent question to ask *who is going to shape our lived spaces.* Space remains the location where we 'culture' our everyday, and if we only use it to do remote socializing via social media, then it becomes one type of space, one where we rely on means produced by others to function. How can we regain capacity? By simply using it, and by extending and tactically adapting the user formats, which are normally suggested to us by the dominant capitalist urban planning, such as, for example, the *flâneur* or the coffee shop user who frequents the urban plazas or the shopper/consumers who flow across retail and cultural offers. To become aware, the use and adaptation of the surrounding and remaining public spaces and facilities (or making them temporarily public) are structural to the projects described in this chapter.

Company set out to shape a new productive public realm which combines collective action driven by a desire to socialize with an economic cycle of production and trade. The word 'company' carries this triple meaning already, and combines the social, spatial and economic. It signifies a commercial business and its premises and at the same time, the condition of being with others. To temporarily relocate to the Kent countryside without their husbands not only allowed the women during the hop-picking years to take on different roles (money-earner, independent, rule-makers), it also provided one of the few income opportunities for women at the time. I use the *Company* project as an example here, as it is set up as a cycle of various activities with the aim of reproducing a possibility for 'good company' but also of growing into a business and commercial enterprise. It roots itself in the history of going hop-picking *en masse*, which was more than just an economic activity born out of sheer necessity. The scale and reminiscence of 'hop-picking' times carry many narratives that go beyond its primary function, which was to provide temporary labour for the hop farms and therefore the production of beer (external gain). It seemed to carry a second, more internal function, which was to give the working classes the opportunity to spend time together away, in the countryside (an activity normally reserved for the middle and upper classes) while also making some money. Or, as one of the former hop-pickers recalls: 'It wasn't just about the money, but about being in good company.'

Miranda Pope, in her essay on *Company*, points towards Foucault and what he calls 'subjugated knowledge', a set of knowledge 'insufficiently elaborated'. Understood in this way, 'going picking' created social situations that generated knowledge around a set of subjectivities not normally taken into account within the economic cycle of production. In this specific case, the knowledge generated by the working class. Through the process of *Company*, including workshops, talks, visits, picking and making, participants' reminiscing about the hopping days often revealed a longing for a different being together and making together. It has been deeply touching to meet so many people who have been hop-picking. The ways they express what they liked about it suggest that it is much more emotional and complex, and close to a basic human desire as words like 'working holiday', 'summer in the fields', 'some extra money' or 'good fun' would describe.

Richard Sennett talks about the capacity for cooperation (which he sees as embedded in human nature) as something we need to craft in order to prosper in social and societal terms (Sennett, 2013). Without wanting to over-romanticize the hop-picking days, it is clear that something in the collective memory is carried forward with a longing, and subsequently so is the desire to recreate it, or recreate situations for this collective experience to exist and develop again. What is interesting about the surviving memories is that they hint towards a special collectiveness brought to life through these annual trips, which is closely linked to an existing working-class culture but at the same time seems to extend it further. Many remember it as a 'time capsule' with other rules, a temporary matriarchal society with freedom to roam for the children. One man talked about a certain autonomy which he embraced, another women spoke about camaraderie, fun and freedom.

Bev Skeggs, in her talk, 'Value beyond values', quotes David Graeber as saying that 'there is a certain communism of the senses at the root of most things we consider fun' (Skeggs, 2013). Relyea's term 'essentialising' culture (instead of subjectifying or deconstructing it) might be useful here, and *Company* is trying to reconnect to what was 'good company' during the hop-picking days by organizing and facilitating collective and productive moments, such as going picking, making drinks, sharing stories. *Company* links a broadly positive collective/group experience from the past (hop-picking) and explores its particular positive qualities and values, allowing them to be reproduced as a social and economic reality in today's circumstances.

My own longing for collective structures and public spaces doesn't necessarily come from a social longing, from not wanting to be alone, but from an appreciation of the fact that a certain 'everyday togetherness' has power which needs to be recognized in order to also make it an emancipatory or political force. I enjoy self-organized, collective situations (as the opposite of imposed collectivities), which shift everyday productive or reproductive labour (such as cooking, preparing food, picking, washing, cleaning) from a purely private event to something public.

The company, shop and school described in this text demarcate the public realms for this. They are structures under construction with many access routes and low thresholds. Their maintenance is high and should be, since they are structures of long-term future investment, built with the communal and collective values we manage to bring together.

REFERENCES

Gibson-Graham, J.K. (2013) 'Economic meltdown, or what an iceberg can tell us about the economy', essay published for Trade Show, Eastside Projects, Birmingham.

Latour, Bruno (2007) *Politics of Nature*, Cambridge, MA: Harvard University Press.

O'Neill, Gilda (2006) *Lost Voices*, London: Arrow Books.

Relyea, Lane (2013) *Your Everyday Art World*, Cambridge, MA: MIT Press.

Sennett, Richard (2013) *Together: The Rituals, Pleasures and Politics of Cooperation*, London: Penguin.

Shamsie, Kamila (n.d) 'Shared spaces with Kamila Shamsie', available at: www.publicspace.org/en/post/kamila-shamsie (accessed 6 July 2015).

Sharzer, Greg (2012) *No Local*, Alresford: Zero Books.

Shonfield, K. (1998) *At Home with Strangers: Working paper 8: Public Space and the New Urbanity* (Richness of Cities). London: Comedia in association with Demos.

Skeggs, Beverley (2013) 'Values beyond value? Is anything beyond the logic of capital?', lecture 17 October, LSE, London. Available at: www.lse.ac.uk/publicEvents/events/2013/10/20131017t1830vSZT.aspx. Also *The British Journal of Sociology* 65(1) (2014): 1–20.

FURTHER READING

Ainley, R. (ed.) (2001) *This Is What We Do: A Muf Manual*, London: Ellipsis.

Böhm, Kathrin and Pope, Miranda (eds) (2015) *Company: Movements, Deals and Drinks*. Heijningen: Jap Sam Books.

Bourriaud, N. (2002) *Relational Aesthetics*, Dijon: Les presses du réel.

Khatib, Kate, Killjoy, Margaret and Mcguirre Mike (eds) (2012) *We Are Many*, Oakland, CA: AK Press.

Lefebvre, Henri (1991) *The Production of Space*, trans. Donald Nicholson-Smith, Oxford: Blackwell.

Massey, Doreen (2005) *For Space*, London: Sage.

public works (2006) 'If you can't find it, give us a ring', Birmingham, available at: http://www.public worksgroup.net/2009/01/27/ if_you_cant_find_it.pdf

Raunig, Gerald (2007) *Art and Revolution*, Los Angeles: Semio-texte.

Rollig, Stella and Sturm, Eva (eds) (2002) *Dürfen die das?*. Vienna: Turia und Kant.

Sholette, Gregory (2011) *Dark Matter*, London: Pluto Press.

Shonfield, K. (2001) 'The lived and the built', in R. Ainley (ed.) *This Is What We Do: A Muf Manual*, London: Ellipsis.

13 – METROPOLITAN COMMONS: SPATIAL COMMONING IN BERLIN'S GROßER TIERGARTEN AND TEMPELHOFER FELD

Sandra Bartoli and Mathias Heyden

SPATIAL COMMONING, PUBLIC SPACES AND WHAT IS AT STAKE IN BERLIN

If the notion of the commons is ground-breaking in creating societal places at large for all species (Gibson-Graham and Miller, 2011),[1] then we argue that commoning, as a form of activity, is most importantly *propositional*. This activity includes not only a permanent negotiation of old and new commons, but also a continual caretaking role and struggle to guarantee its long-term existence.

Here we relate commoning to the practice of taking civic responsibility for claiming public space and maintaining it, and in doing so two relevant qualities of such space unfold: the first recognizes that the efforts for democratization almost always take place on open public space; the second is that there is a newly expanded definition of public space. Namely, in the current rampant urbanization in which cities and regions, rural and urban habitats, nature, technology and infrastructure merge (White and Wilbert, 2009),[2] open public space is potentially the vessel and test-bed of radical integrative forms of use, production and reproduction as well as of human and non-human

---

1   J. K. Gibson-Graham and Ethan Miller redefine the notion of economy where community, understood as in 'being-in-common', includes human and more-than-human species. Economy is therefore the shared domain of a 'multispecies community' interlaced with 'politics, ethics and the dynamics of social and ecological interdependence' (2011: 2).

2   Damian White and Chris Wilbert address new notions of urban natures, new environmental politics, to which they give a necessary update, by using instead the term 'technonatures': 'what we call "nature" is not necessarily degraded by being mixed with humans, and ... social life has always been constituted through diverse foldings and unfoldings – of ecologies, cultures, technologies, and diverse nonhuman others' (2009: vii).

ecologies, setting forth relevant commoning trajectories for present and future commons.[3]

Berlin is a city where it is possible to interpret several trajectories of spatial commons; for instance, in its long history of struggles for civil rights, common goods and rights to the city's space; the workers movement of the late nineteenth century; the beginning of public housing in the 1920s; the collectivization of private land during the rebuilding of the city in the post-war years; the continued presence of counter-cultures and queer cultures; and in the recent debates on public and common goods brought about by 'urban pioneering' and other similar bottom-up place-making practices.[4] In the face of a seemingly unstoppable real estate sell-out, expanding building boom and inadequate politics of the municipality, open public space is more than ever the territory where what is at stake in Berlin is most visible.

This chapter focuses on two case studies that constitute out-standing and precious place-making in Berlin, although they manifest themselves in very different ways. These are respectively Berlin's oldest and newest open public spaces: Großer Tiergarten and Tempelhofer Feld, respectively. In these cases, public space is not only being re-claimed, but also, as practices that raise the question of spatial commoning, they further the idea of *metropolitan commons*.[5] While trying to contribute to the discourse and fight for the right to the city in the face of ruthless politics and derailed economics in Berlin, these case studies can also be a contribution to overcoming a crisis of imagination, which often seems to underlie the desperate mindsets of many citizens of today.[6] To explore this contribution to

3   Open public space does not automatically constitute commons; in the classic definition commons are not privatized resources and are the responsibility of and cared for by groups of people – the commoners. The following case studies, Tempelhofer Feld and Großer Tiergarten, are maintained by the Berlin municipality, but because of their size, history, qualities and uses, they both carry multifaceted aspects of commoning. Because of their characteristics of space and use, we refer to them not only as urban but also as metropolitan commons, valuing their aspects of commoning as novel exciting challenges, harbingers of large-scale commoning yet to come: 'commoning-trajectories'.

4   In East Berlin, since the 1960s, there had been total collectivization of the city, while in West Berlin, the city was administered through public/public, public/non-profit, and more recently public/private partnerships, in which governmental formulas necessarily needed a 'strong' government, which regulated the institutionalized common goods almost exclusively through top-down politics and administration. This form of government always encountered stark critique, and was involved in the past 25 years with the privatization of common goods, which rendered obsolete the 'commoning' integral to these public resources.

5   See footnote 3.

6   If we are talking about citizens, we first of all are talking about members of civil society. However, we also include members of other societal realms, whether in politics or the administration, economics or science, etc.

metropolitan commons and indeed show what a metropolitan commons might be, this chapter draws particularly on the work of David Harvey, Silvia Federici and Donna Haraway.

In his book, *Rebel Cities* (2012), David Harvey states that the fight for the right to the city, in the definition coined by Henri Lefebvre, needs to be theorized and practised along with the notion of urban commons. Particularly relevant to Großer Tiergarten and Tempelhofer Feld is the matter of scale, as Harvey critically points out that most of the research on the commons evaluates smaller groups of people and as such it deals 'only' with bits and pieces of cities and regions in which the notion of commoning is operating well. Subsequently, he discusses how far commoning might work on a larger scale such as the city, the region, the country or the world, concluding that by extending the scale, some level of top-down governance is still necessary, while helping to cultivate transparent and mutual cooperation between the various small-scale commoners.[7]

Our exploration of metropolitan commons follows Silvia Federici (2004, 2010), who, in combining a feminist perspective with a left-wing approach towards subsistence, use, production and reproduction, emphasizes the notion of the body. In exploring metropolitan commons, while we begin with the body in place-making, we particularly question which bodies are intended. Following Donna Haraway (2003, 2008), we discuss the radical entanglement of species in these places, perhaps a commons in itself in the web of interdependence which sustains all organisms.

On Sunday, 25 May 2014, more than 700,000 citizens voted for the law proposed by 100% Tempelhof,[8] against the Berlin municipal government's plan to develop massive housing and office building schemes, and to build the Berliner Zentralbibliothek (the Berlin central library) on the site of the former Tempelhof airport. The majority of the people who took part in the referendum about the development of this outstanding inner-city area voted to leave this site, a public property, empty of buildings, as a 'void' to be developed gradually and as a park only.

---

7   Discussing the matter of large-scale commons, Harvey points to the American anarchist and libertarian socialist, Murray Bookchin, and his book *From Urbanization to Cities: Toward a New Politics of Citizenship* (1995), which advocates the decentralization of society, an ecologically driven libertarian socialist municipalism, arguing, for example, for face-to-face and assembly democracy.

8   100% Tempelhof was the slogan used in the public petition for the referendum about a law to maintain the newly acquired accessible public property as one public space. To declare this public land 100% free of any new building development, in the aftermath of the closure of Tempelhof inner-city airport, ultimately meant opposing the vast real estate development drafted by the Berlin municipal government.

It is here where the urgency for a radically democratic debate about public spaces in Berlin is most intensely experienced.[9] The reasons for this vote are many, but the most important in our view is that the people in Berlin expressed an increasing awareness to determine the present and future of the city's spatial commons.

At the same time, parallel to this popular claim for Berlin's newest and largest open space, Großer Tiergarten, the oldest and historically most prominent park, has become Berlin's major platform for mass events. The site for large rave and techno parties in the mid-1990s such as the internationally known *Love Parade*, is now the location of the world soccer championship's *Fanmeile*, the anniversary of the Fall-of-the-Berlin-Wall, New Year's Eve celebrations, and many other recurrent promotional events such as Mercedes Benz fashion week. Such events present an increasing top-down management and development, leading to a steady appropriation of this public space by the Berlin city council and the German government, and ultimately by private companies and global players.

Meanwhile the people using this great park in the inner-city site on a daily basis, are increasingly left out of the debates about its management and development. In Großer Tiergarten, the notion of Berlin's spatial commons is hardly discussed, even though a great number of citizens not only appreciate this open space but are actively taking care of it. In fact, numerous groups of volunteers, such as amateur and professional ornithologists, dendrologists, conservationists and many others engage with this place with different aims. The park is an ancient body, its space, use and users are interwoven to the extent of transgressing practices of heritage, ecology, humanism and urbanism on this same territory. From this point of view, a case study of Großer Tiergarten can contribute to the current discourse on the contemporary definition of commons in general, and of spatial and metropolitan commons in particular.

---

9   In parallel to the widely discussed resistance of Kotti & Co and their allies, a tenant initiative that fights against the privatization and gentrification of former public housing.

GROßER TIERGARTEN

One way to understand Großer Tiergarten[10] in Berlin as a place of commoning is by starting to recognize the transgressions[11] that take place there. Tiergarten is a heritage park as well as an ecological biotope, a wild forest as well as a space of human leisure and mass events, and thus it simultaneously transgresses all these definitions. Tiergarten to some extent shows what the urban realm can become: a place of extreme coexistence and inclusion. Functional zoning is here exchanged for the rule of contingency, under which territories and jurisdictions (of species) are constantly and creatively negotiated, overlapping and shifting.[12]

Transgressing heritage
Rewriting urban history is an effective form of power. In the past 25 years of Berlin's urban development, the municipal government's re-newal plans have mainly been based on the reproduction of nineteenth-century city morphologies, while other temporal layers were simply dismissed or even actively erased. The reductionist approach of these heritage practices toward constructed historical identities and authen-ticities of public spaces is, in the case of Tiergarten, transgressed.

Originally a swampy forest along the River Spree, Tiergarten existed before the city of Berlin was founded. Now it provides a lens for a model of simultaneous history where all the history of Berlin is contained: a marshy wooded area of the glacial valley, the chosen ground for royal hunting game, a dense forest with carved-out Baroque rooms, a landscape park, a stage for Nazi parades,

---

10   Großer Tiergarten is the full name of the park, but it is commonly known as Tiergarten. For simplicity from this point on in the chapter, we refer to it by its shortened name.

11   Rem Koolhaas introducing the 14th Architectural Biennale in Venice in 2014 asked: 'If future norms of society will be dominated by the mantra of sustainability, convenience and security as opposed to *liberté, egalité, fraternité,* the question is where remains the space for the creative process of transgression?' Koolhaas' question offers a framework for a constructive notion of transgression to address the Tiergarten, a uniquely wild and cultured construct, which, while crossing the borders of canonic urban categories, requires yet new trans-disciplinary definitions. In fact, the intrinsic transgression (of urban categories) in which this park exists, defines an unprecedented model of human and more-than-human history entwined within the city. This particular definition of Tiergarten's transgression was first adopted by Sandra Bartoli in her concept of the international symposium *Tiergarten, Landscape of Transgression (This Obscure Object of Desire),* which she organized at Haus der Kulturen der Welt in Berlin in 2015, under the aegis of the Department of Urban Design and Urbanization TU Berlin.

12   In a creative process of constant redefinition of boundaries, this form of spatial as well as epistemological transgression recalls Haraway's definition of 'natureculture' and the 'hybrid', transgressing classic binary oppositions.

a battlefield in the Second World War, a provider of firewood and farming land in the post-war state of emergency, completely replanted in the 1950s, and turned wild in the 1970s and 1980s (Wendland, 1993). Its inception cannot be pinned to a singular epoch, rather, its true heritage might lie in the consideration and representation of all times at once. Recent attempts by the Berlin municipality to stress the reconstruction of Baroque elements, such as straight allées and a formal water basin, are in stark contrast to the park as a whole: its multilayered nature defies any imposed inception.

Transgressing ecology

Models of spatial commons for a possible and joyful future are necessarily biodiverse, allowing extended sharing not only by humans but comprising all species. Tiergarten, because of its impenetrability, over-abundance of plants, relative solitude and lack of funding for a strictly manicured park, is a better host of biodiversity than many of the large, urban parks such as Central Park in New York or Hyde Park in London. This forest grown on a wetland of glacial origins, inspired a young Alexander von Humboldt to research and collect mosses and lichens.[13] It was destroyed after the Second World War, with the cutting down of more than 200,000 old trees to procure firewood during the severe winters of 1946 and 1947. In the late 1950s, the replanting was led by the Director Willy Alverdes, who deliberately took care of the ecological aspects, envisioning a forest healing itself together with raising the morale of the Berlin population, by interlacing layers of grasses, bushes and trees in complex plant communities (Lesser-Sayrac, 1996). Much of the massive and undisturbed vegetation growth was the result of this plan, between 1960 until 1989, the area being contained on its east side by the Berlin Wall.[14] The inclusive ecology of Tiergarten lies in its inherent commoning nature, and works with the sensibilities of accepting, managing and guaranteeing the juxtaposition of high biodiversity, multilayered use and heritage in the same landscape.

---

13   In February 1789, a 19-year-old Alexander von Humboldt wrote to a friend telling him about his study of nature through his walks in Tiergarten (Jahn and Lange, 1973). This is also quoted in *Der Große Tiergarten* by Maria-Sofie Rohner and Angela von Lührte (2009), a remarkable botanical history of Tiergarten.

14   One particularly biodiverse area developing into a dry grassland and forest (Rohner, 2011) was contained by the Berlin Wall on one side and by a busy road called Entalstungsstrasse (the forerunner of the planned autobahn extension of the Westtangente, replaced in 2007 by the Tiergartentunnel). Birdwatchers and nature lovers were frequent visitors to this area, and used to call it *Regenwald* ('The Rainforest') (interview in Tiergarten with former Park Director, Christoph Schaaf, 2 September 2013).

Transgressing anthropocentrism

Tiergarten offers a view on extended and multiple forms of autonomy as an inherent characteristic of spatial commons. Tiergarten is in fact much more than a park serving human necessity and pleasure. Its autonomy from the strictly human takes many forms and scales: as an example, its considerable size reaches a critical mass that affects the entire climate of the city, establishing a cooling core which attracts winds channelled from the south through the Park am Gleisdreieck, the Tempelhofer Feld, and other open spaces (Horbert *et al.*, 1993). Tiergarten's size, together with its critical biomass, makes it nearly 'incommensurable',[15] establishing a level of autonomous existence for this place, which becomes extraterritorial and therefore self-regulatory.

The act of claiming and that of maintaining a territory in constant negotiation are essential characteristics of spatial commons, not only among humans but more importantly between species. Tiergarten is shared by many creatures: the animal realm encroaches with the human and vegetal, so sovereignty over the territories is always overlapping.[16] Falcons, buzzards, foxes, hedgehogs, beavers, humans and a rich variety of plant societies use this place throughout the year; the boundaries of their territories are constantly and necessarily shifting. This kind of interdependent regulatory quality is also essential to an expanded definition of commons as resilient from a future trajectory. That the Tiergarten exists on its own rules is no surprise: in the city and yet beyond the human, and in this way perhaps more than the city. Its size, incomparability and density ensure that the anthropocentric notion of a constructed park, as this is in fact the case, can also coincide with an exceptional place of extreme natural autonomy.

---

15   The adjective incommensurable, 'not-measurable', is in this case used to address a strictly perceptual characteristic of some large parks, reflecting on the understanding that to be able to measure a space, as an example by walking it, equals to 'contain it in one's mind': one of the keys to a humanistic and anthropocentric understanding of the world at large.

16   Maria-Sofie Rohner undertook an extensive survey of Tiergarten, twice, in 2006 and in 2011, and, commissioned by the nature conservation department of the city, prepared a report about the change in the conditions of existing red-listed plant biotopes and fauna-flora habitats, after the building activities which comprised an extensive reconstruction of historical paths, irrigation systems in a dry grassland habitat (!) and a Baroque basin. The report demonstrates evidence of the destruction of rare biotopes, a true loss for the east side of Tiergarten, a section that until the cleansing heritage practices of 2006 had hosted a real convergence of civilization and wildness, with precious red-listed high grass meadows, rare birds, sun-bathing people, and all of this just a few metres from the Brandenburger Tor. Rohner's report is a contribution to the draft of a new management plan for Tiergarten (Landesbeauftragte für Naturschutz und Landschaftspflege, Berlin, 2011).

Transgressing planning

Tiergarten defies dominant modes of planning by allowing highly differentiated cultures of appropriation, which are essential to a spatial commons as understood as practices of use. Tiergarten is possibly one of the most 'commonized' public spaces in Berlin. Its constituent lack of functional zoning leaves all areas open to inter-pretation. Planned but not divided into functions, one of the rules for spatial interpretation is, for instance, contingency, where use is never predetermined, but is open and flexible, dependent on the spatial qualities of the different areas. Practices of use in Tiergarten are very diverse, and some also are very old, for example, there has been a tradition of gay cruising near the *Siegessäule* (Victory Column) for over a century or the extended naturism taking place nearby and in different locations across the park.

Tiergarten has been the location for many mass protests, both today and in the past. But most importantly, Tiergarten describes the changes in the conditions of use and the production of public space in the city, which have been dominated by commercialization, especially in the past two decades. Currently the park is under significant development pressure, arising from the highly controlled neighbouring areas, such as the government district (including the Reichstag and the Brandenburger Tor, all stormed by tourists), the many embassies under heavy surveillance, and now the recently built districts for luxury apartments. Another striking example of change in the general understanding and dealing with the use of public space in Berlin is the establishment of the *Fanmeile* (the football 'Fan Mile') after the 2006 World Championship (Figure 13.1) to an almost permanent *Festmeile* ('Party Mile') on Strasse des 17. Juni in the middle of Tiergarten. Currently the *Festmeile* hosts a large number of celebratory and commercial events, all year long. New plans are pending that aim to optimize and better control Strasse des 17. Juni, which will affect Tiergarten, including a new, more powerful lighting system, a massive underground infrastructure for water and electricity to feed public viewing and general fairs, and the proposal for a tall permanent fence all around Tiergarten for crowd control, and loudspeakers in case of mass panic.

Figure 13.1 Tiergarten, *Fanmeile* during World Championship, 2014
Photo: Sandra Bartoli

Nonetheless, Tiergarten, as it is today, continues to be a place of science fiction richness, nurtured by 'collaborative entanglements' of species, trans-disciplinary biologies, 'a string figure tying together human and non-human ecologies' (Haraway, 2014). This is, freely adopting Haraway's words, the place where species meet. Such is the extraordinary coexistence and interdependence of wildlife, plants and humans, present, for example, in naturists lingering in dry, long grass fields, right across from the Brandenburger Tor or near the busy roads of the Victory Column; in the empathic and respectful interaction with the place of quiet birdwatchers in order to sustain a multitude of wild birds; in the activism of many amateurs and experts in dendrology, who monitor the state of growth of ancient and young trees; in old rhododendrons, overgrown yew bushes and marsh grasses that provide privacy for sex in the gay cruising area and concealment for the make-shift tents of homeless people. Tiergarten transforms not only the relationship of people to other species, but has the power to reformulate identities and create new roles in their contribution and connection to a city understood as a biodiverse construct at large. Empathies, interdependencies and emerging collaborations constantly mingle in this place. Tiergarten has not only the potential to be a catalyst for rebooting a new understanding of integrative urban life, but also because of the transience of its physical appearance alternating in wild growth, construction, destruction and replantation, continues to produce a more genuinely urban and richer paradigm of the city (Figure 13.2).

Figure 13.2 Tiergarten, picnic in the forest, 2013
Photo: Sandra Bartoli

TEMPELHOFER FELD

Unlike Tiergarten, Tempelhofer Feld is not an old and multilayered body in the heart of the city, and consequently it has a different public significance. The former airport is Berlin's newest, large-scale open public space, and it is for many reasons the major site for the current debate on Berlin's future development. Located in the south of the inner city, its neighbours are both densely populated areas and less dense suburban areas. As such, the development of the 300+ hectares of public land can be understood as prototypical for Berlin's present and future.

The novelty of Tempelhofer Feld is explored here through the lenses of creative rejection and civic transformation, challenging the ordinary understanding of what is urban, and in these ways it can be seen as a metropolitan common. The recent referendum about the development of this outstanding inner-city area must be understood as a decision that opposes politics and administration, and at the same time claims, maintains and subsequently designs open public space through the means of everyday use, urban pioneering and city-wide political activism.

One reason for the massive, regular use of Tempelhofer Feld is the fact that some of the adjacent neighbourhoods critically lack open spaces. The former airfield is easy to reach either by foot, bike, public transport or car. Even more importantly seems to be the large scale of the site, which attracts not only its neighbours but people from all over Berlin, as well as a national and international public. Under the grand open sky, the space is predominately characterized by the two former runways and the network of roads that connect them to the former airport building and other facilities (Figure 13.3). Entering Tempelhofer Feld feels like stepping onto an inner-city utopia, an inner-city island that has lost its functions and does not yet have new ones.[17]

Figure 13.3 Tempelhofer Feld, landing strip, 2013
Photo: Sandra Bartoli

---

17   The site in the course of history was farmland, a military field and occasionally a location for fairs, sports and play. It became an airport in the 1920s. Currently it could be interpreted as 'derelict land'. Instead it magnificently proves it can function as a public park; without the characteristics of a conventional park. Its size alone makes it difficult to define. More than 300 hectares nearly without footpaths, with the few large infrastructure roads left over from the airport, lacking trees, covered in high grasses, this space reads almost as a plain, somewhere outside of town.

Interestingly, the former high security fence, which is still standing, contributes to this reading. The site is accessible only through a couple of gates that are opened at sunrise and closed at sunset. Additionally, the management company, Grün Berlin GmbH, a city-owned company, has security patrols regularly on duty, while also taking care of infrastructure, safety, cleaning and information, and verifying the proper use of the inner and outer areas.

The inner area, about 200 hectares, is defined as a natural habitat of protected flora and fauna, where people are almost absent. The surrounding outer area, about 100 hectares, is characterized by the former airfield 'taxi-way'. Here almost any kind of human use contingent to an open field can take place.

Its relevance for us is not in the exploration of a multitude of uses, but in the interdependency between the centralized management by Grün Berlin GmbH and the various cultures of spatial appropriation. As a metropolitan common, the former airport must be understood differently from smaller, more traditional commons. The matter of scale needs to be addressed critically in terms of caretaking and struggle; in this case of large-scale commons, this endeavour is worth pursuing gradually, experimentally, slowly focusing on a future perspective.

Subsequently, the management by Grün Berlin GmbH can be understood as both an obstacle but in many respects also as a support structure, until the time when an agreement is reached on a citizen-based way of developing and managing the former airfield.[18] Constrained by the results of the referendum, Berlin's Department for Urban Development and Environment started a participatory process, which invites engaged organizations, initiatives and citizens to discuss the development and management of the 300+ hectares of open space.[19, 20]

The issues involved in this process relate to top-down politics, for instance, the fact that the site is administratively shared by different districts: Kreuzberg-Friedrichshain (to the north), Tempelhof-Schöneberg (to the west and the south), and Neukölln (to the east and the south). Nevertheless the Berlin municipal government considered the site too strategically important to be developed and

---

18   See footnote 6.

19   See www.stadtentwicklung.berlin.de/umwelt/stadtgruen/tempelhofer_feld/index.shtml

20   The crucial question is how far this participatory process will succeed not only in generating a city-wide consultation of citizens but also in making the citizens into the decision-makers for the management and development of the park.

managed by district authorities alone and installed two publicly
owned companies to be involved: the above-mentioned Grün Berlin
GmbH, which is responsible for the open spaces, and the Tempelhof
Projekt GmbH, which is responsible for the airport building and other
facilities. This outsourcing causes multiple problems, for example,
until the referendum, the Berlin municipal government was planning to
keep one-third of the open space, about 100 hectares, for large-scale
housing and office building schemes, while the district authorities,
without being consulted, were confronted with full master-plans
supplied by the two companies.[21]

The privatization of the master-planning processes, and the lack
of critical consideration of the combined effects of gentrification and
the housing crisis, were among the most important matters addressed
by political activists.

Another outstanding aspect which recommends Tempelhofer
Feld as a metropolitan commons are the 'urban pioneers' who
developed practices of commoning on this public land. They are
perhaps the main force acting here, creatively rejecting top-down
planning, and contributing to the civic transformation taking place on
Tempelhofer Feld.

Located in the outer area, there are hundreds of gardeners
engaged in the Allmende-Kontor, a community garden project,
which is one of the most outspoken commons projects in Berlin, and
probably one of the most media-covered, bottom-up projects in Berlin
in recent years (Figure 13.4). But other outdoor activists are enriching
the place. Besides various sports projects, ranging from cycling
and other more unusual wheeled devices to sport programmes and
classes of all kinds, one finds various alternative educational and
cultural initiatives, and more community gardens.

---

21   The site is not the first area of this kind subject to neoliberal politics. Since the fall of the Wall,
the Berlin municipal government has increasingly outsourced similar large-scale master-planning
assignments to publicly owned companies. Even though these companies are city-owned, their main
agenda is profit-oriented that actively moves away from the focus on the broader public good and
well-being of all Berlin citizens.

Figure 13.4 Tempelhofer Feld, community garden project 'Allmende-Kontor', 2016
Photo: Sandra Bartoli

Sixteen urban pioneer projects resulted from an open call
launched by the Berlin Department for Urban Development and
Environment. One could imagine that with this gesture, the Berlin
municipal government was reaching out to citizens who wanted to
make use of the former airport. However, it seems that applicants
who critically questioned the municipal government's planning affairs
were easily dismissed. Nevertheless, even the selected projects, and
especially the Allmende-Kontor garden, contributed hugely to the civic
contestation of the municipal government's plans. To a certain extent,
the various urban pioneers proved that a self-made city is possible,
and it can be done as a form of spatial commoning.

Ironically even the highly contested fence round the site could be
understood as a support structure for learning about spatial commons
at various scales. After the airport closed down in 2008, protests
arose, demanding the dismantling of the fence. The fence is a concrete act of control by the Berlin municipal government, who never
publicly stated what would happen with this piece of public land.
Instead it continued to propose constantly changing master-plans,
none of them of a truly consistent participatory nature. At the same
time, it is the same fence, in the form of a concrete spatial definition
of a very large undefined field, that made Tempelhofer Feld grow in
the awareness of the people to become their public park, and through
this to challenge politics and the administration.

While transforming the site into an open public space and a spatial commons, it was also the understanding of this airport as a cultural commons that made the majority of people vote to oppose the municipal government's master-plan. The symbolic significance of this site is particularly important when we remember that this was the major hub for bringing the necessary goods into the city, when the Soviet Union cut off West Berlin from West Germany in 1948–1949 in the blockade of Berlin.

Additionally, another argument follows David Harvey (2012), concerning the surplus value of a city's growth, which is generated by the everyday activity of all its citizens, and as such it must be shared by all, everybody being potentially a commoner. Accordingly, the increasing quality of life in the neighbourhoods adjacent to Tempelhofer Feld can be understood as a product generated by all its inhabitants, and thus the resulting physical as well as metaphysical surplus value must be understood as a common good.[22]

In consequence, this is the suggestion to discuss the future of the former airport not separately from its adjacent neighbourhoods but to include them in the urgently needed debates about how to theorize, plan and build for a renaissance of a spatial commoning, to develop an environment that is truly democratic, and socially, ecologically and economically just for all living species.

TWO PUBLIC PLACES, TWO PUBLIC PRACTICES: COMMONING-TRAJECTORIES FOR THE FUTURE?

One can say that civil rights are always fought in and because of public space. It is still on public turf that citizens' rights are negotiated to begin with. Tempelhofer Feld and Tiergarten are very different places, but they share many aspects that are fundamental to what constitutes the power of public space and the potential for spatial commoning, essential to the life of the city.

Within this paradigm, the recent events of Tempelhofer Feld are paramount: the people of Berlin refuse to comply with the logic of densification and forthcoming gentrification. This is not only against the trend for almost total sell-out, introduced in the 1990s and promoted starting with the twenty-first century led by the Berlin

---

22   The simple question remains for whom the increase of quality of life is generated, or better, how to guarantee it without discrimination. In fact, the low-rent districts (of centuries-old left-wing tradition) near the former airport are in the process of being gentrified, the beginning of this process is marked by the opening of the Tempelhofer Feld as a park.

municipal government, but also is against 'common sense', given that
the demand for housing in Berlin is currently very high. The results
of this referendum demand that Tempelhofer Feld should stay free,
advocating a slow and reflected development that hopefully responds
to the well-being of all people in Berlin.

The struggles over Tiergarten are not as overt as in the case of
Tempelhofer Feld. Nevertheless this is also a highly contested public
space that has a long history of civil rights protests. For instance,
the famous 'In den Zelten'[23] was a location established in the mid-
eighteenth century for leisure pursuits, but also as a venue for mass
debates. More recently the Berlin Pride Parade[24] takes place here.
But Tempelhofer Feld and Tiergarten have more qualities than just
being open public spaces: *they are territories that instigate a higher
level of civil agency.* What they have in common is their 'extraterritorial' quality: they are both exceptionally large, Tempelhof is 355 hectares, and Tiergarten is 210 hectares, and both possess a degree of
immeasurability in terms of human perception of space. They possess
nearly independent legislation by themselves, a *zona franca.*

Tempelhofer Feld appears an endless and wide expanse, a field
with prairie-like qualities. It has a direct connection to the sky and an
empowering open view of the city skyline, giving the sense of being
'on top of the world', while its boundaries are blurred in the distance.
As such, Tempelhofer Feld appears to be an almost infinite space.

Tiergarten, on the other hand, is defined by a dense and multilayered vegetation, due not only to a lack of financing, but also as
the consequence of a deliberate decision in the 1980s, when the
cutting down of the fast-growing trees (in order to leave more space
for the slow-growing ones) was opposed by the Berlin municipal
government's political intention to re-establish a primeval forest, an

---

23   'In den Zelten' ('in the tents') was the name of a street (today John-Foster-Dulles-Allee) on the
north side of Tiergarten, and it referred to a series of marquees selling refreshments to the visitors of
Tiergarten. These were the initiative of refugee Huguenot families who in 1745 received permission
from Friedrich II to open their businesses here. With 'In den Zelten' Tiergarten became also a place of
political gatherings and debates.

24   In West Berlin, the Christopher Street Day demonstration for gay rights took place on 30
June 1979. Since then this parade starts each year in the street Kurfürstendamm, in the district of
Charlottenburg, and traditionally reaches its final destination at the Großer Stern, the roundabout
with the Victory Column, in the middle of Tiergarten, where public talks, parties and dance raves go
on late into the night.

Ur-wald.[25] The result was a park with the spatial qualities of a rich and unruly overgrown forest.

Tiergarten's users linger in a semi-wild forest with scattered long shady meadows and dark streaming waters. Always open, it is approachable day and night, thereby nurturing a long tradition of the illicit: prostitution, homosexual and heterosexual cruising, naturism, the presence of unauthorized and temporary signs to express discontent in politics. Homeless people use this place as their home. Even unwanted animals roam loose here, for instance, turtles or escaped Canadian geese and mandarin ducks, animals not local to the Berlin region, are thriving in this place among the native species. The list is long, everything seems to be allowed to exist in the shadow of this rich and unruly overgrown forest.

The use of Tempelhofer Feld, on the other hand, differs drastically. This site, completely contained by a fence, is closed at night. A regulated zoning of use is applied which determines the specific areas for barbecuing, for cultivating vegetables, fruits and flowers in urban farming clubs; other areas are preserved for the survival of wildlife (skylarks), or for flying kites. The former landing strip is perfect for biking, inline-skating, and other sporting activities. Tempelhofer Feld in its vast scale suggests the absence of the urban: people sit and lie in the high grasses of this open field, evoking ancient bucolic scenes. Tempelhofer Feld, in its current use as a utopian construct of arcadian aspirations, free from developers' plans, is a luxurious way to play Robinson Crusoe in the middle of the city; in this case, however, Robinson has an iPhone and a state-of-the-art carbon-frame bicycle. Tempelhofer Feld is by now the closest thing to what Archigram once envisioned as a plug-in city, but without the fanciful service sockets of David Greene's RockPlug, LogPlug, and TreePlug.[26]

Tiergarten is a sort of matrix for a spatial commoning of Berlin where Berlin's existence can be traced back in time and projected forward in a radical act of sharing open space while including all kind of species. On the other hand, Tempelhofer Feld is a place-making site where citizens are currently experimenting with new ways of

25   In the late 1970s and early 1980s, ecological awareness and sensibility were high in West Berlin when the government drafted a survey map (1979) of all ecological biotopes existing in the city (in the west). The history of this process is also partially covered in the dissertation by Sonja Pobloth (2008).

26   The compelling Rockplug, Treeplug and Logplug were part of a project conceived in 1969 by David Greene of Archigram, for a series of high-tech infrastructures, camouflaged in pastoral semblance and ambiguously non-disruptive of the landscape's general appearance; these were buried networks serving a nomadic and (auto)mobile society enjoying an uninterrupted idyllic scenery.

producing and reproducing Berlin by claiming, maintaining and thus designing their own open public spaces through everyday use, urban pioneering and city-wide political activism.

This understanding of Tempelhofer Feld and Tiergarten alongside the notion of the spatial commons introduces both sites as exemplary open public spaces in a much larger context. In the face of dramatic political and environmental crises, periodically aggravated by financial and economic crashes, the applied approaches and instruments of a reparative nature have inadequate results. Within the growing call to challenge the imagination to act in a fundamentally different way, Tempelhofer Feld and Tiergarten represent examples that contribute to rethinking the meaning of the public and spatial commons and commoning in society at large.

REFERENCES

Bookchin, Murray (1995) *From Urbanization to Cities: Toward a New Politics of Citizenship*, London: Cassell.

Federici, Silvia (2004) *Caliban and the Witch: Women, the Body, and Primitive Accumulation*, Brooklyn, NY: Autonomedia.
(2010) 'Feminism and the politics of the commons', in K. Van Meter, C. Hughes, and S. Peace (eds) *Uses of a Whirlwind: Movement, Movements, and Contemporary Radical Currents in the United States*, Oakland: AK Press.

Gibson-Graham, J.K. and Miller, Ethan (2011) 'Economy as ecological livelihood', in K. Gibson, D. Bird Rose and R. Fincher (eds) *Manifesto for Living in the Anthropocene*, Brooklyn, NY: Punctum Books.

Haraway, Donna (2003) *The Companion Species Manifesto: Dogs, People, and Significant Otherness*, Chicago: Prickly Paradigm Press.
(2008) *When Species Meet*, Minneapolis, MN: University of Minnesota Press.
(2014) 'Anthropocene, Capitalocene, Chthulucene: staying with the trouble', lecture, Arts of Living in a Damaged Planet Conference, Aahrus University, Denmark, 9 May.

Harvey, David (2012) *Rebel Cities*, London: Verso.

Horbert, Manfred *et al.* (1993) *Karte Klimafunktionen*, Berlin: Umweltbundesamt.

Jahn, Ilse and Lange, Fritz G. (eds) (1973) *Die Jugendbriefe Alexander von Humboldts 1787–1799*, Berlin: Akademie Verlag.

Lesser-Sayrac, Katrin (1996) 'Willy Alverdes: sein Werk als Gartenarchitekt und seine Verdienste für den Großen Tiergarten in Berlin', in *Der Berliner Tiergarten: Vergangenheit und Zukunft, Landesdenkmal Berlin*, Berlin; Schelzky & Jeep, pp. 34–54.

Pobloth, Sonja (2008) 'Die Entwicklung der Landschaftsplanung in Berlin im Zeitraum 1979 bis 2004 unter besonderer Berücksichtigung der Stadtökologie', doctoral thesis, TU Berlin.

Rohner, Maria-Sofie (2011) *Aktualisierung von Biotoptypen, Rote-Liste-Arten und FFH- Lebensraumtypen der Rasen, Wiesen und Säume auf seit 2006 durch bauliche Maßnahmen veränderten Arealen als Beitrag zu einem Pflegewerk im Großen Tiergarten*, Berlin: Landesbeauftragte für Naturschutz und Landschaftspflege, Berlin.

Rohner, Maria-Sofie and von
Lührte, Angela (2009) *Der Große
Tiergarten – Botanisch-
historische Exkursion in Berlin-
Mitte am 1. Juni 2008*, Berlin:
Verh. Bot. Berlin.

Wendland, Folkwin (1993) *Der
Großer Tiergarten*, Berlin: Gebr.
Mann Verlag.

White, Damian F. and Wilbert,
Chris (eds) (2009) *Technonatures:
Environments, Technologies,
Spaces, and Places in the Twenty-
first Century*, Waterloo, ON:
Wilfrid Laurier University Press.

14 – SOCIAL PROPERTY AND THE NEED FOR A NEW URBAN PRACTICE

Gabriela Rendón and Miguel Robles-Durán

> *The property in the soil–that original source of all wealth–has become the great problem upon the solution of which depends the future of the working class.*
> (Marx, 1869)

To give up all existing and future urban land to developers and land-lords is to surrender all of society's elementary sheltering needs to one privileged class of speculators. This was the urban tragedy of the late twentieth century; the pervasive naturalization of private property rights over the housing rights of most of the world's population.

Despite this tragedy, the twentieth century saw, for a brief period, the social dictates of many modern states in favor of guaranteeing a large portion of urban land in the control of public entities, for the purpose of benefiting society at large. No doubt swayed by the contentious arguments of the nineteenth and early twentieth centuries against private property by influential public figures like Proudhon, Marx, and Bakunin, who, together with massive social movements, con-structed the basis of the international urban struggles which marked this period. These struggles confronted many state policies with active experiments in other forms of land tenure beyond private property. This was the period that gave rise to the idea of "social property," gradually defined by the appearance of many variations of housing cooperatives, living communes, squatting collectives, common spaces, and public land reserved for its enjoyment and use by all citizens alike. It is under these political conditions that architecture, planning, and their connected urban disciplines were at last beginning to contribute to a restructuring of space that benefited most members of society. This was in sharp contrast to the previous centuries, where the purpose of these experts was to serve the will and desires of the landed elites.

For this short time, the proliferation of urban disciplines and their traditional services made social sense. Democratic societies were envisioning a common wealth project and the trained technicians used their skills to help materialize its demands to the best of their disciplinary capacities. Progressively, a large number of architects and planners began to design spaces commissioned in the name of

public good. Ethically, there was very little to question these types of
social commissions, which demanded no less than the envisioning
of never before seen forms of public housing, of schools, hospitals,
cultural spaces, community centers, transportation networks, and
recreational infrastructure. The urban professionals, who were actively
taking part in these state-driven projects, had very little reason to
move outside the trades imposed by their disciplinary boundaries.
Public entities were taking care of structuring the economic, political,
and social processes needed to develop, manage, and sustain such
projects. *The production of a socially just urbanity demanded the
design and coordination of incredibly complex processes, where the
architect or planner mostly played the singular and specific role of
giving physical form to them.* There was a clear social relevance in
the tradition of urban disciplines, which for a brief period could have
been seen as analogous to any respected form of social service.

As the post-war twentieth-century ideals gradually morphed
into the consolidation of the global neoliberal project, first, with
the election of Margaret Thatcher as Prime Minister of the United
Kingdom in 1979 and soon followed by the election of Ronald
Reagan as the President of the United States in 1981, the active
roles of architecture and planning gradually returned to their original
purposes: both the representation of elitist power and as sets of
knowledge that effectively aided in the concentration of individual
wealth. The complex array of bureaucrats and public professionals
that once had designed, coordinated and sustained the economic
and political processes that supported the expansion of social
property, slowly gave way to the neoliberal need to extract private
rent from everything where human sweat is involved. This meant that
private property needed to be re-emphasized as the urban principle
for economic growth. New political and financial instruments that
could liberate property from public holding into speculative trade had
to be designed and implemented, and, importantly, all the previous
commitments to secure urban land for general social well-being
were disregarded as inefficient and producing a damaging public
debt. Many states succeed in this transition and others continue
this trajectory at a slower pace, but almost all the world, in one way
or another, has promoted the kind of speculation made possible by
private property as a principal engine of economic growth.

In the twenty-first century, at a time where the richest 1 percent
of the world's population own more than 48 percent of the total
global wealth (Credit Suisse Research Institute, 2014: 11), private
property (temporary or permanent) is hardly questioned. Moreover,

it is promulgated as the given natural law that establishes the ruling principles for urban ordering, growth and landed wealth accumulation. Armies of urban professionals, from architects and planners to engineers, work to give visual form to these principles, while in the name of protecting society's universal consent for private property, the privileged class of speculators *design the urban processes that can guarantee its reproduction.* But, "if indeed private property in land is based upon such a universal consent, it evidently becomes extinct from the moment the majority of a society dissent from warranting it," (Marx, 1869). As Marx pointed out, it is this critical failure in the social reproduction of space that will continue to define our urban futures. It will do so unless we, the army of urban professionals, begin to infiltrate the political and economic decisions and the transformative urban processes that are normally out of reach of the myopic disciplinary knowledges that have demarcated the so-called design specializations over the years. *In order for urban disciplines to be socially relevant again, they have to radically transform into the many roles that the early twentieth-century alliance of public servants performed, coordinating communities, designing economic models, writing and advocating new policy, bending property laws, developing new property models, training inhabitants, defending vulnerable dwellers, and co-creating new community management systems, all of this before thinking of its physical representation as architecture or a urban scheme.* Why? Because these are the processes that allow the production and sustainability of more just urban environments and most states have stepped back from performing this social role. Today the disciplinary precise ways of practicing just help consolidate the expansive visions and territorial expressions of the greatest dispossession of urban wealth in history. For those of us with stronger, socially minded consciences, it is time to rethink what a professional practice should do in the contemporary context.

SOCIAL PROPERTY AND THE DEVELOPMENT OF COOPERATIVE HOUSING TRUSTS

This way of looking critically at the current condition of urban practice was one of the main drivers for us to found a professional organization, which could begin to propose socially relevant modes of operation. The collapse of Lehmann Brothers in September of 2008 gave us the final nudge, making us realize that a different kind of urban practice was urgently needed. Cohabitation Strategies (CohStra) began operating then, as a cooperative for socio-spatial design and development.

Among the many critical urban conditions that CohStra has been able to work on, challenging capitalist conceptions of private property has been of primary importance to us, which we have done by developing community-controlled, permanently affordable housing models. After several projects in Europe and South America, in late 2011, we began to explore this possibility in one of the most aggressive urban environments imaginable: New York City. We figured if it was possible to develop social property in that city, then it would be possible anywhere in most of the world.

Envisioning new housing paradigms amidst the housing crisis may be overwhelming and sometimes disempowering for communities in large urban areas dominated by profit-driven development, as in New York City. Nevertheless, there are few places with such powerful tools and assets as those owned by New Yorkers particularly for the following reasons:

— They hold one of the most valuable housing legacies of the country.
— They have lived in collectivity for centuries.
— They have struggled to reform housing legislation.
— They have consolidated the largest public housing authority in America.
— They have succeeded in regulating nearly half of the rental housing stock.
— They have occupied the neglected city and reinvented it through the creation of housing cooperatives.

Unfortunately, profit-driven forces have taken over the city, suppressing progressive action, luring local authorities to overlook such an invaluable housing legacy, and promoting an exclusive city for only a few. Lavish buildings, holding units with seven-digit values rising side by side with an unprecedented number of homeless (men, women, families, and children) are but one of the outcomes. This engineered crisis has caused indignation to all those excluded, and asserted the need to create alternative ways to produce our neighborhoods and cities.

The "creative destruction," as Harvey (2008) asserts, is not exclusively taking over central city areas. In fact, real estate speculation, massive illegal displacements, and other predatory practices are plaguing working-class and low-income districts. Homes have turned into precious design objects, cash machines, financial assets, and numbers in spreadsheets for architects, slum landlords, developers, and city officials respectively. *The city has become a battleground, and to survive it is critical to envision alternative property and housing paradigms that assist in the production of anti-speculative, accessible and just districts.*

To achieve this, it is worthwhile revisiting the city's housing legacy and identifying available instruments. For instance, it is worth scrutinizing the community and tenant-led housing programs that aim for the rehabilitation of neglected and vacant city-owned properties, along with other types of self-management practices that took place during the 1970s and 1980s. The Sweat Equity, Urban Homesteading, Community Management, and Tenant Interim Lease programs, for example, emerged in response to the striking landscape of vacant buildings throughout the city, and the initiatives led by low-income groups to take over and rehabilitate those spaces through organized efforts. These grassroots practices evolved into local and federal, community, and tenant-led programs addressing not only the thousands of neglected properties but also the deficit of public-housing provision and the ongoing decline of inner-city neigh-borhoods, especially communities of color. While the landscape has changed from dilapidated tenements to luxurious apartments, some of the principles of these programs, such as sweat equity and mutual aid, are still fundamental for communities and tenant control over land. Indeed, most of the buildings that were rehabilitated during this period, which were transferred to tenants and community manage-ment organizations or became limited-equity housing cooperatives, are still important assets for low-income groups.

Unfortunately, most of these programs have been gradually eroded. Housing policy and programs that focus on the welfare of people have increasingly been replaced by approaches benefiting the real estate sector and promoting economic rather than community development.

These approaches have marginalized the provision of housing for very low-income and low-income households, and have abandoned any sort of urban processes that imply community involvement. Re-cent housing plans and programs have provided an insufficient supply for the demand, and usually the affordability of the units is limited due to the lack of instruments enforcing affordability in perpetuity.

THE COOPERATIVE HOUSING TRUST PROGRAM: A NEW HYBRID MODEL FOR THE PRODUCTION OF PERMANENT AFFORDABLE LIVING, WORKING, AND LEARNING SPACES

The production of permanent affordable housing and just districts, providing local access to spaces for production, cooperation, and knowledge exchange can be achieved by doing the following:

— challenging the hegemonic model of property;
— sharing skills, responsibilities, and resources;
— considering collective demands rather than individual interests.

Undoubtedly, the support and commitment of all government levels are primarily required, as well as local political will.

The *Cooperative Housing Trust Program* is envisioned as a pilot program using existing instruments for land management and housing development, while considering the social, spatial, and political complexities of New York City. After five years studying the politics of development and displacement in the city, and the organizational and political power of community groups, we started conceiving a path back to the social property that has been lost, but that can be regained through a collective effort.

The ownership model that we have envisioned aims to provide permanent affordable housing choices and, at the same time, to mitigate the effects caused by recent policy approaches that transfer responsibilities and resources to the private and the non-profit housing sector, without requiring the inclusion of community stakeholders and potential tenants in the decision-making process. It intends to offer tenants and neighbors a voice and ownership in the processes of producing their own living, working, and learning environments. We have known for a long time that while the private housing sector has adopted "gentrification and displacement in the name of development" as a policy in this city, the non-profit sector has been busy getting funds and negotiating land to counteract the effects produced by such processes. However, getting resources has not been easy since subsidies increasingly favor developers, and public funds and programs require a competitive process that is often influenced by the non-profit leaders' political influence. Rivalry between non-profits serving the same jurisdiction has often been an issue that prevents a number of things: first, collaboration and openness between non-profits addressing similar issues; second, innovative and tactical

approaches to assist in the ongoing battle between powerful developers and resourceless communities; third, the creation of transparent
and participatory processes for residents and community stakeholders; and, finally, the creation of local coalitions to envision, participate
in, and campaign for pathways leading to alternative housing models
providing social, economic, and spatial justice.

The envisioned *Cooperative Housing Trust Program* acknowledges these facts by proposing a hybrid tenure framework. Unlike the
current affordable-housing options, this model is not fully owned and
managed by a public entity or a non-profit entity, nor by a cooperative
housing corporation. This housing model is planned, financed, developed, managed, and owned collectively by all of these entities alongside community stakeholders and residents. The co-ownership is one
of its key characteristics. Since housing cooperatives (particularly
limited and non-equity cooperatives) face financial difficulties when
rehabilitating and constructing new housing, this model proposes the
development of housing cooperatives sponsored by the public sector
and co-managed by public representatives, community stakeholders,
and cooperative members. The great majority of the shares would be
public initially and decrease over time until becoming marginal. The
shares granting ownership, management and control over the cooperative would divert from public to collective once the development
is fully paid and the cooperative members have built the required skills
to operate the maintenance and financing of the property.

This housing model combines some of the organizational and
legal frameworks of community land trusts, housing cooperatives, and
other mutual aid associations, as well as some of the principles of
the tenant and community-led housing programs, which have already
created affordable housing alternatives and preserved low-income
communities in New York City. The proposed hybrid ownership model
is comprised of a fourfold structure: a Community District Land Trust,
a Mutual Housing Association, a District Credit Union and one or
more Cooperative Housing Trusts (Figure 14.1).

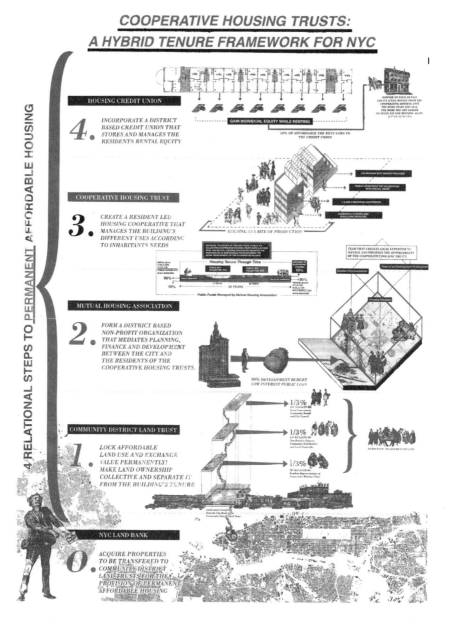

Figure 14.1 Cooperative Housing Trust: a hybrid tenure framework for New York City
Image: Cohabitation Strategies

A Community District Land Trust (CDLT) has been conceived to acquire properties located in a circumscribed area (the community district) on behalf of the community and to hold them in trust for the development of Cooperative Housing Trusts.[1] The CDLT would provide 99-year renewable leases for exclusive use in accordance with the terms of the trust. This district-based CLT has been designed as an independent non-profit, sponsored by the city and managed by a tripartite board with equal representation from public authorities (including the municipality, the local city council office, the community board, and so on); non-resident community stakeholders; and residents.

In the last few decades, non-district-based Community Land Trusts have been coveted by community-based organizations, housing advocates, and activists in order to preserve and develop permanent affordable housing. However, and despite their efforts, communities have faced all sort of difficulties in acquiring properties in large urban centers. Real estate values are high and expertise in financing and management is not always found among community members. Thus, in order to facilitate the acquisition of properties, members of the CDLT (a cohort of people with diversified expertise and resources) and the Mutual Housing Association (explained below) are committed to identifying abandoned or neglected properties, including those holding tax arrears, legal or environmental problems, and to search for the owners. Traditionally, neglected properties would be transferred to responsible landlords, non-profits, or private corporations, with the assistance of the local government, either by negotiation or by law. In this case a CDLT would be the first option for these sorts of transfers to ensure the provision of permanent affordable housing in those properties. The acquisition of land can be accomplished also through non-profit land banks, public concessions, donations from re-zoning processes, and agreements with the current owners.

The New York Land Bank Act, aiming to combat blight and vacancy in urban areas within New York State, was signed in 2011. A number of Land Banks have been activated in the State since then. In the case of New York City, it is critical to implement a city-based, non-profit land bank with strict by-laws. For instance, we propose that the acquired land should be transferred exclusively to CDLTs for the preservation and development of affordable living, working, and learning spaces.

A district-based Mutual Housing Association (MHA) has also been proposed to develop, finance, and operate the Cooperative

---

1   The difference between a Community Land Trust (CLT) and the proposed Community District Land Trust (CDLT) is the property area. A CLT may own one or more properties, adjacent or dispersed in the city. In this case, the proposed CDLT owns properties within the limits of community districts, therefore, we can call it district-based.

Housing Trusts for an interim period. In order to sustain cooperatives over time, it builds up local expertise to manage and preserve the affordability of the cooperatives. The MHA's role is:

— to draft a district housing plan according to local needs and priorities to rehabilitate buildings or develop new land provided by the CDLT;
— to pull together an organizational structure comprised of experts outside and within the community;
— to develop and operate the cooperatives;
— to train local people in construction, maintenance, and management skills to run the properties, so that when ownership passes to the cooperative, members can take control and make their own decisions.

THE ECONOMICS OF THE COOPERATIVE HOUSING TRUST PROGRAM

The majority of the capital cost of each Cooperative Housing Trust, about 90 percent, is sponsored by the local government, while the planning and management costs, about 10 percent, are provided by the MHA. This fee guarantees the cost of the first development phase: research and planning. The seed money (10 percent) could be granted by a private foundation; financed by a private entity with a low rate of interest; collected through crowd funding (community members) or other private and public contributions, and can be raised prior to initiation of construction. The public investment in the development is projected to be fully amortized over time, approximately 40 years. During this period, the city gradually transfers its shares to the cooperative while keeping 10 percent in perpetuity. During the first 40 years, cooperative members pay a monthly fee to cover the financing, operational costs (maintenance, real estate taxes, etc.) and to contribute to a mutual housing fund. Once the development is fully amortized, the cost of the monthly fee drops and a small portion is set aside to finance future cooperatives (seed money). These cooperatives encourage collective control among those with lower incomes while providing long-term reliability in meeting the supply of permanent affordable housing and in maximizing the benefits of public funds. These cooperatives are structured with equity limitations, imposing restrictions on speculation or rent increases by requiring that members leaving the cooperative must transfer the units back to the cooperative.

The Cooperative Housing Trusts (CHTs) have been envisioned for the rehabilitation, repurposing, and construction of abandoned, vacant, and underutilized properties, such as residential buildings, industrial sites, and lots. There are hundreds of neglected and vacant properties in the peripheral Community Districts in New York City. The main purpose of this new model of housing is to provide and preserve permanent affordable housing through shared management and ownership. The hybrid tenure of these cooperatives not only means the combination of public and collective ownership; this model offers different housing types and sizes for singles, couples, small and large families, as well as particular and co-housing accommodations. Co-housing units offer affordable housing opportunities to large families or households with special needs, such as single parents or seniors, who often require mutual aid and companionship. This option includes private rooms and shared facilities, such as kitchens, bathrooms, play rooms, living and working spaces. The units target households with different income brackets, from 40 to 80 percent of the local median household income. Last but not least, tenure may be short- or long-term. A number of units are set aside to house families or individuals who need special support and housing for a specific period of time. These units are part of the 10 percent public share, so they are owned by the local government in perpetuity.

Besides guaranteeing permanent affordable housing, this co-operative model aims to encourage the active participation of residents in the construction, maintenance, and administration of the building. Cooperative membership requires residents to participate in the cooperative's decision-making through the cooperative board, whose seats are not restricted to residents but also includes representatives from the MHA and local public authorities to keep the interest of residents and the community at large (10 percent of votes). Job training in different areas is promoted in this model, as is sharing skills with other cooperative members within the property in which they live, as well as other neighboring cooperatives. Sweat equity is of great value. The equity generated by working for the benefit of the CHT may be exchangeable for lease subsidies, espe-cially for those households with greater needs, or can be saved in the cooperative fund. Tenants leaving the units may get a return for their involvement throughout the years.

The Housing Credit Union is a member-owned financial coopera-tive, with the aim of providing financial services to community mem-bers and operating the housing mutual fund. A small portion of the monthly rent fee is put aside, transferred to this fund and saved for community members leaving the cooperative. A proportional equity of their work and engagement during the leasing term in the cooperative is given back to them when they leave.

THE (RE)PRODUCTION OF SOCIAL PROPERTY AND THE URBAN PRACTICE

Collective property, despite its marginal presence in large urban areas, represents spaces of resistance that have emerged out of long-term struggles. These spaces, which are neither private nor public, have been constituted as a means of survival; to fight against urban decline; to prevent homelessness; to preserve low-income communities; to provide shelter and services that neither the market nor the public sector will supply. Community Land Trusts and Housing Cooperatives (limited equity or non-profit) occupy an important space in cities to preserve affordable housing and equitable communities (Figure 14.2). Unfortunately, they have not reproduced and have even declined in recent years, despite the colossal efforts that low-income and vulnerable groups have made to keep these assets.

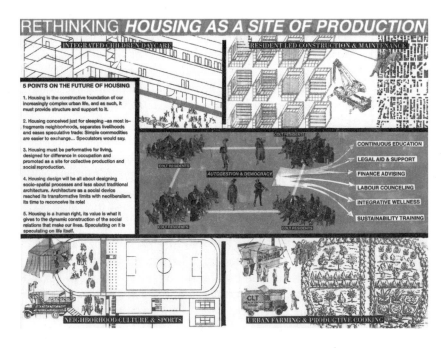

Figure 14.2 Rethinking housing as a site of production
Image: Cohabitation Strategies

The reproduction of social property today requires hybrid models of ownership and long-term alliances across different sectors, disciplines, and government levels. The Cooperative Housing Trust Program is one alternative that explores the possibilities that can be formulated by using existing public instruments and funds, as well as developing hybrid structures of property and housing, involving local groups with the political and organizational power to produce change. Undoubtedly, urban practice needs to be completely re-defined in order to co-produce spaces where people can (re)produce themselves, their cities, and their livelihoods. We are convinced that it is still possible to imagine new forms of living, even within the oppressive capitalist context that many believe we cannot escape and thus should surrender to.

In the West, since the early twentieth century, housing has gone through two main general paradigms, first, the transfer of public power, money, and resources to the government for it to decide on how its citizens should live, this direction can be categorized as the welfare paradigm. The current paradigm began when the transfer of public power, money, and resources began to shift towards private corporations, private developers, and the financial industry in general. We can refer to this as the neoliberal paradigm. Our proposal belongs to neither of these two, which ultimately trusts in the slow, grassroots formation of a new paradigm, where the transfer of public power, money, and resources is funneled back to collective enterpris-es giving them the right to build the city as their hearts desire. This, also, is how David Harvey (2008) defines the right to the city:

The right to the city is far more than the individual liberty to access urban resources: it is a right to change ourselves by changing the city. It is, moreover, a common rather than an individual right since this transformation inevitably depends upon the exercise of a collective power to reshape the processes of urbanization. The freedom to make and remake our cities and ourselves is, I want to argue, one of the most precious yet most neglected of our human rights.

REFERENCES

Credit Suisse Research Institute
(2014) *Global Wealth Report*,
October.

Harvey, David (2008) "The right
to the city," *New Left Review* 53:
23–40.

Marx, Karl (1869) The Abolition of
Landed Property. Memorandum
for Robert Applegarth
December 3 1869. Available:
https://www.marxists.org/archive/
marx/works/1869/12/03.htm

15 – AFFORDABLE HOUSING IN YOUR LIFETIME?[1]

Ana Džokić, Marc Neelen and Ana Vilenica

In January 2013, Belgrade's daily newspaper *24 Hours* published an article stating: 'It is possible to get an apartment in Belgrade even three to five times cheaper than the average – for 300 to 500 euros per square meter. Citizens can get such apartments under the condition that they join forces and practically become developers of a building they will later on live in. Members of the initiative "Who Builds the City" firmly believe that this is achievable' (Krkić, 2013). Although the article had 169 'likes', it featured a number of comments, all stating that in today's Serbia such a proposal is hardly achievable, outright impossible or simply utopian.

What makes this unbelievable for *24 Hours*' commentators? Especially if we know that over the last half-century, the citizens of Belgrade have proved themselves rather hands-on in resolving their housing issues and able to manage with rather modest budgets, regardless of the political and economic conditions surrounding them? Since the end of the 1960s, during the heyday of socialist Yugoslavia, citizens who were somehow left behind by the guaranteed 'societal housing',[2] which was provided as a basic right, decided to take matters into their own hands on a rather impressive scale. This resulted in the emergence of, for instance, Belgrade's suburb of Kaludjerica,[3] currently recognized as one of the largest informal settlements in the Balkans. Equally, during the disastrous 1990s and the disintegration of Yugoslavia, it became clear that citizens were on their own in resolving their existential needs and many did so through

---

1   This chapter draws on information, ideas and plans gathered and developed through Smarter Building's working sessions, as well as parts of the text 'Smarter Building' ('Chytrejší staveni', in Czech), written by Ana Džokić and Marc Neelen, with Marko Aksentijević, Nebójša Milikić, for the architecture magazine *ERA 21*, issue December 2013, Prague, and the article 'From Survival Strategies to Housing for All' ('Od strategija preživljavanja ka stanovanju za sve', in Serbo-Croatian), written by Ana Vilenica, Ana Džokić and Marc Neelen, for the magazine *Nepokoreni grad*, issue 4, November 2014. The authors are members of the Smarter Building initiative, Belgrade.

2   Societal housing was financed through collective housing funds, invested in by the workers of individual socialist companies in Yugoslavia. It therefore differs from 'public housing' in that it was not directly provided by the state.

3   Belgrade's suburb Kaludjerica today officially houses over 30,000 inhabitants, largely in brick and concrete buildings erected without legal building permits.

direct action, by extending buildings informally, even constructing new suburbs, much like Kaludjerica's pioneers had done decades before.

However, what makes it unbelievable today is, first of all, an inability to articulate the interests of individuals and social groups *as common, collective interests*. Although without any hard evidence, two decades of erosive economic instability and the harsh shift to a society based on dispersed individuals who are left to figure out their survival on their own terms, but also those forced to return or stay with primary or extended family, have generated citizens for whom issues of desired, chosen or negotiated collectivity remain rather abstract, overwhelming and untested in real life. Second, the prospect of entering the domain ruled by ruthless 'investors', profiteers, developers, or as many would say 'sharks', makes the attempt to find an alternative additionally unimaginable.

This is the condition of resolving one's housing situation, and one that is accompanied by a lifetime of mortgage debt, and the normalization of housing construction as a solely profitable activity, done according to a simple and one-sided model: the developer profits, and we are in debt. Therefore, 'establishing a new, not-for-profit and solidarity actor in the field of housing is not just a technical, but also extremely sensitive political issue',[4] wrote the editors of the Croatian magazine, *Defiant City* responding to *Pametnija Zgrada (Smarter Building)*, a project we co-initiated with the Who Builds the City[5] platform at the end of 2012. Since then, this initiative has engaged numerous professionals, activists and citizens in a search of a model of affordable, collectively devised housing.

This chapter is about our search to discover what affordable housing in Belgrade could entail today, to re-examine possible collective action in this field, and to create the conditions for such action to emerge. To those familiar with architectural and artistic practices engaging with the wider politics of space, it may not come as a surprise that *Smarter Building* originates from within the cultural field, but steps out of it to intervene in the norms of the current market-determined housing model. *Smarter Building* is driven by a group of individuals coming from the edges of their professions of cultural production, architecture, political science, who are also personally affected as long-term subtenants in an unregulated rental market, living nomadi-

---

4   *Nepokreni grad*, volume 4, November 2014, available at: http://maz.hr/files/ng-casopis-4.pdf

5   Who Builds the City (Ko gradi grad) platform was started in Belgrade in 2010 by Marko Aksentijević, STEALTH.unlimited (Ana Džokić, Marc Neelen) and Cultural Center REX (Nebojša Milikić, Dušica Parezanović), registered as a citizens association in 2016.

cally or with traumatic experiences of real estate traps, all determined to take on a topic that has been left unanswered by developers, the magic of the market, but also by politicians and syndicates.

ENTER THE HOUSING MARKET

In 2009, just before the global economic crisis hit Serbia, apartment prices per square metre in the more affluent areas of Belgrade had sky-rocketed to fictional heights, from 2,500 to 4,000 euros.[6] A fourth-floor studio apartment, 41 square metres, in the vicinity of New Belgrade's Arena, for example, would sell for 123,000 euros at that time.

While apartment prices in Belgrade have significantly dropped in the last few years, this has not resolved the burning housing issue. Knowing that the average monthly net income is about 425 euros,[7] and that a small apartment in Belgrade costs around 1,400 euros per square meter,[8] it is obvious why an estimated 150,000 people have an unresolved housing situation.[9] If we add to this the fact that 15 per cent of apartments are overpopulated, and another 15 per cent of apartments are constructed from non-solid materials (Petrović, 2013), these figures become even more alarming. Equally, those who have managed to buy an apartment during the last decade, now struggle under the burden of heavy mortgages.

This is the reality for us, for our colleagues and friends, and for the generations following those who euphorically bought up the apartments that made up the stock of societally owned housing in Serbia at the beginning of the 1990s. At that moment, the state nationalized this housing stock overnight, and subsequently privatized them. This was the beginning of the real estate market in Serbia, with the now private apartments turned into commodities. With this, the cycle of societal involvement and collective investment in housing was brought to an end and has not returned in any significant form since. Today, private apartments account for 98 per cent of the housing available in Serbia (Palgo Centar, 2010).

Today's construction market is highly unregulated and frequently situations have arisen in which one and the same apartment was sold

---

6   B92.net, 17 February 2009.

7   The average income in Belgrade in August 2014 was 50.645 Serbian dinars. Cekos.rs.

8   24sata.rs, 1 September 2013.

9   According to the Tax Administration of the Serbian Ministry of Finance data for 2013.

twice or even multiple times, and its 'owners' lost the considerable sums invested. In the wake of this, associations like '1000 Mistreated'[10] have formed, who represent people camping in half-finished buildings, and sometimes even seizing them from the so-called developers in order to finish them on their own. If we add that socially, subsidized rental accommodation basically does not exist, the contours of the challenge become visible.

A HOUSE IN YOUR LIFETIME?

Are you interested in building a decent apartment in Belgrade at 300-400-500 euros per square metre without getting yourself into debt and unpayable loans, living in impossible conditions, or waiting for your relatives to move to the countryside or to Heaven? Impossible?[11]

It was with this announcement in one of the leading newspapers at the end of 2012, that *Smarter Building* took off to reflect on a way to realize apartments that would be available to a large number of those who do not have one, or cannot afford one under the current economic conditions. At the same time, the rise of the European credit crisis, with slogans like 'You will not have a house in your fucking lifetime'[12] on the streets of Barcelona, gives a wider perspective to the scale of today's housing problem created by real estate speculation. In Spain, the impossible mortgage situation pushed people onto the streets or to suicide (Human Rights Watch, 2014),[13] while millions of newly constructed houses stand empty for years. Two decades ago, the issue of housing was expelled from the agendas of governments and urban planners and landed in the hands of real estate developers with little societal consideration. But recently, the housing issue has started to affect citizens in a wider European context and coalesces not just around problems but also

---

10   The citizens association 'Hiljadu oštećenih'' (in Serbian) has been formed in response to the practices of the company Delta Legal in Belgrade's neighbourhood Filmski grad, Košutnjak.

11   Advertisement by Who Builds the City in the daily newspaper, *Danas*, December 2012.

12   'No vas a tener una casa en la puta vida' (in Spanish) was already a slogan of the campaign V de Vivienda that started in 2006.

13   See, for instance, Human Rights Watch, *Spain: Rights at Risk in Housing Crisis*, 27 May 2014. Available at: www.hrw.org/news/2014/05/27/spain-rights-risk-housing-crisis (accessed: October 2014).

potential ways out of the problem. This is visible in the newly emerging social-urban-political movements in Spain, for example.[14]

This does not mean that in addressing this challenge, experiences and approaches from other contexts can readily be introduced
or put into action. *Smarter Building* starts from a position that we
need to move beyond existing norms and models of the unattainable
apartment purchased on the market. The norm that 'prescribes' how
we come to own or rent an apartment is a social construct, not a
natural fact, and therefore it is open to change by making it affordable,
and importantly, disentangling it from unsustainable debts, economic
and social enslavement, poverty and gender-based dependence.[15]
However, to do so, current norms need to be changed, rather than
'overwritten' by realities imported from elsewhere.

From its inception, the initiative has been open to people seeking
to jointly engage, in a 'smarter' way, by planning and designing
collectively, investing their time, knowledge, skills and financial
resources responsibly, and building 'intelligently'.[16] Willing to discover
if the 'impossible' can be reached instead, about thirty of us decided
to give it a go. Among the motives to join were predominantly
existential reasons, a lack of our own living space and an awareness
that 'mortgages take us into slavery', or professional interests among
architects, while what united us was an overarching political concern
that 'this issue has to be addressed'. However, it would demand that
we should be 'persistently crazy and courageous'[17] on the way.

Smarter Building introduces the format of public working sessions
to discuss, self-organize and construct a prototype of a collective
housing solution that can serve as a model (Figure 15.1). Through

---

14   According to Flesher Fominaya (2014):

*It is impossible to understand Podemos without taking into account the crisis and the
social response to the crisis in the form of the Indignados/15-M movements and related or
constituent movements such as the remarkably successful Platform for those Affected by
Mortgages (PAH) and the Movement for the Right to Housing.*

See also Colau and Alemany (2014) and chapter 18, this volume.

15   Women in particular are in a more vulnerable situation. For instance, in cases of domestic
violence, they often decide to stay with their partner, as otherwise they would have no economic base
to live independently.

16   In a twist on the notion of 'smart house', 'Smarter Building' suggests that housing should
– through a collective process – be much more a social response, rather than delving into smart
materials and energy efficiency.

17   Quotations from the participants at the first working session of *Smarter Building*, December 2012.

a number of such sessions,[18] the group has started to dissect the pricing of housing, explore forms of direct democratic decision-making, outline the legal aspects of a collectively run organizational model, and imagine possibilities for introducing the notion of equality to a society largely based on inequality. The workings of these sessions reveal an interesting pattern: faced with a particular issue like ownership structure, people who joined would at first dominate the issue based on the current norms, 'proven' experience or knowledge given by their professional background (architectural, legal, financial, etc.), before slowly surrendering to the insight that their views might be entirely rewritten.

Figure 15.1 Working table, drafting statute of a 'smarter' housing cooperative
Photo: Ana Džokić and Marc Neelen

WHERE DOES THE SMARTNESS RESIDE?

The politically sensitive aspect of this and similar approaches emerging across Europe comes from the possibility of (re-)claiming the production of housing by citizens. Thus, taking it out of the realm of

18   Seven 'working tables' took place at Cultural Center Rex from December 2012 to September 2013.

profit-making and cutting out the middlemen – developers, investors, real estate agents, contractors and, ultimately, the bank. Another aspect concerns eliminating the commodification of housing, which otherwise makes it prone to speculation. This means a radical departure from the current housing construct.

Although *Smarter Building* did not start from a prescribed idea of how the housing and its organizational model should be, the cooperative form soon came forward as a legal and organizational entity for people to perform a collective endeavour. On one hand it is a known organizational form, which has been present in Serbia from 1870,[19] when the first housing cooperative was formed, and it was practised in socialist Yugoslavia, parallel to the much more common model of societal property.

During the last twenty years the format of the housing cooperative has not been given any support by state legislators in Serbia.[20] Being sidelined, it has degenerated, slipped into market practices and consequently is mistrusted. Although it is clear that the status of cooperatives needs to be revised, the reformulation of the Law on Cooperatives has been stuck in procedures for the past few years.

A 'smarter' cooperative would unavoidably question issues of profit and ownership. If profit (financial, but also symbolic or other, less 'measurable' forms) and ownership were the principles that brought us to the impossibility of having our housing resolved in the first place, it is obvious that a 'smarter' model would try to counter it. Individual ownership can be addressed by skipping the idea of private property of the apartments, transferring the ownership of the housing stock to the cooperative, while its members – the cooperants – become renters (through monthly rent) or users (through a one-time or series of successive opt-in fees) at an affordable price, agreed through the assemblies. To restrict the possibilities of profit-making, this model limits price rises once the apartment is completed. When someone wants to move out, their investment is returned but profit cannot be extracted – in this way the possibility for new people, who are in a similar situation, to enter is consistently maintained.

In addition to its organizational model, the *Smarter Building* group developed the budgetary framework needed for the construction and financing, which is based on a solidarity economy between

---

19   As stated by Suzana Jovićević, Secretary General of the Union of Housing Cooperatives of Serbia, at *Smarter Building* working table, March 2013.

20   For a view on the current status of cooperatives in Serbia, see Milojković (2009).

economically unequal participants. This implies the exclusion of investors and market-based ways of giving credit,[21] and instead relies mainly on the resources of the group itself. The model envisions the substantial reduction of utility costs by building apartments with high energy efficiency (to the PassivHaus standard[22]); and the reduction of costs of both construction materials and labour through a collective approach. This relies on: self-construction and do-it-ourselves techniques whenever possible (even by devising a production line for the main construction elements); the reduction of installation costs (sanitary and kitchen equipment) through joint purchase; the optimization of apartment sizes, so that certain features will become part of community life (such as the common laundry room, guest room, but also a social centre or a common working space, etc.).[23]

The structure provides for only 20 per cent of members who are able to immediately invest the necessary sum by selling their previous inadequate dwellings, while 80 per cent of the apartments are intended for people for whom they would otherwise be unattainable, including those with no income[24] and those who are homeless.[25] Those who engage in this endeavour can choose how to contribute: whether through investment in advance, long-term monthly repayments or (partly) through their own work. The calculation is made in relation to statistical data, according to which the average monthly household income is 518 euros, and according to which it is not possible to expect that household to spend more than 15 per cent[26] or 80 euros on rent and utilities per month (Figure 15.2). In reality, for those who are just entering the housing market, the norm exceeds this amount several times.

---

21   In November 2014, during a working session with Goran Jeras, one of the initiators of the newly formed ethical bank 'ebanka' in Zagreb, the potential of the cooperative to attract the necessary starting capital under its own conditions, and not necessarily dictated by others, such as commercial banks, opened.

22   For more information on the PassivHaus standards, see www.passivhaus.org.uk.

23   The next level of challenge will be the relation between spatial settings and forms of dependency and social conditioning. For instance, how floor plans could liberate or disentangle us from certain patterns or certain behaviours. There is an exceptional potential to explore the ways in which we are conditioned by the perception or imaginary of the 'proper' apartment, or the 'proper' building, street, neighbourhood and so on.

24   There are 17.6 per cent officially registered unemployed in Serbia, while in reality this figure is much higher, B92.net, October 2014.

25   According to the 2011 census, homeless people make up a drastic 10 per cent of the Serbian population, which relates to primary and secondary homeless. See Bobić (2014).

26   Information and Statistical Office of the City of Belgrade (2012).

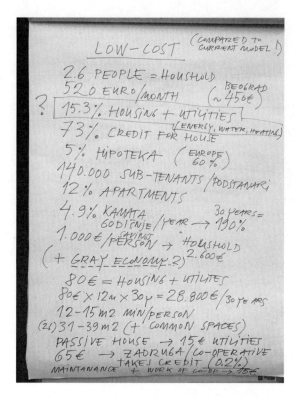

Figure 15.2 Establishing the price point for affordable housing Photo: Ana Džokić and Marc Neelen.

ENTER THE POLITICAL DOMAIN

For this approach to become more widely implemented and move beyond a prototype made by a group of determined citizens, it is necessary that municipalities, cities or the state recognize the importance of such a model of housing and offer land for use under favourable terms or without compensation (Figures 15.3 and 15.4). This would significantly lower the fees for urban land and create the conditions for construction loans on a non-commercial (no- or low-interest) basis. All of these issues spurred the group to the challenge of lobbying political actors. In order to achieve better visibility and verify certain assumptions that the group developed, part of the team responded to the 2014 architectural competition MILD home, announced by Belgrade's municipality Savski Venac. The scheme was selected as one of the three equally awarded proposals,[27] which opened the way for possible talks and negotiations with political actors.

27   The competition entry 'Nova moba za ovo doba' and its details (in Serbian) can be found at: http://kogradigrad.org/nova-moba-za-ovo-doba.html.

Figure 15.3 Expedition to possible construction sites, city centre
Photo: Ana Džokić and Marc Neelen

Figure 15.4 'Land for sale', expedition to possible construction sites, periphery
Photo: Ana Džokić and Marc Neelen.

One of the potential problems of this negotiation lies in the possible side effects that the housing model can produce. The introduction of a not-for-profit housing model and construction below market prices directly threatens the territory of developers and their potential customers. The potential danger lies in the pressures investors place on political actors and the consequent introduction of new measures for the protection of market conditions. Equally there is a danger that overtaking the obligations of the state might tame potential social rebellion, and that such cooperative models might partially normalize the lack of societal responsibility, bringing no fundamental resolution to the systemic housing problem.

On the other hand, there is also a risk in the potential labelling of the *Smarter Building* initiative as being 'too subversive', in that it openly critiques the prevailing (peripheral-capitalist) economic-political system and its ideological mechanisms, and that this might endanger the necessary institutional support.

Finally, it is important to emphasize that the key obstacle to the initiative brings us back to the essential struggle of trying to introduce a new actor in the field of housing, the citizens themselves. Following the first contours of *Smarter Building* being made public through the media, in May 2014, the Serbian Prime Minister publicly presented a new initiative aimed at alleviating the unbearable situation of austerity measures. It is an initiative for the construction of 50,000–100,000 affordable housing units at a price similar to that targeted by *Smarter Building*, around 400 euros per square metre. The apartments would be built exclusively by commercial developers, on state-owned and state-provided land, while accompanied by guaranteed non-interest loans. The proposal came with a note that this is a task that only foreign investors, such as those from the United Arab Emirates,[28] have the capacity for.

A PEEPHOLE INTO A POSSIBLE FUTURE

While *Smarter Building* has provided us, the group behind it, with a sense of capability, of vitality in what we feel we can contribute today, it also has pointed to the loops in history one can hardly avoid recognizing, when, for instance, looking back to the birth of the co-operative movement some 150 years ago, or the first citizens-driven housing initiatives that followed a short while later across Europe. At that time, a lot of the movements were concerned about re-inventing social reproduction, by setting conditions anew. But equally it was about acknowledging the struggle it would entail, at times necessary, to be pushed from unlikely places, coalitions and practices. Today, with *Smarter Building* and similar initiatives, we are on the way to entering other relationships, ones different from the relations we are used to and conditioned by. It is a trajectory that leads us along instances that sharply remind us of the marginal position we might

28   In the light of the wider bilateral agreement between the two governments on investments in Serbia, such as the privatization of the national airline and the flagship development project, Belgrade Waterfront, worth over 3 billion euros.

currently take, but moreover, it confirms that a gang of 'persistently crazy' enthusiasts could rewrite an episode here, transforming what was deemed utopian into the possible, therefore piercing peepholes through the current reality, towards a possible future. In itself this is an immensely empowering experience, an experience greatly needed today. While the issue of housing often turns out to be a secondary one in local struggles, what is necessary is that this important structural matter of social reproduction is appropriated again as an inseparable part of the dynamics of political action towards making housing accessible to everyone.

REFERENCES

Bobić, Mirjana (2014) 'Beskućnici (Homeless)', Belgrade: Statistical Office of the Republic of Serbia.

Colau, Ada and Alemany, Adrià (2014) 'Mortgaged lives: from the housing bubble to the right to housing', *The Journal of Aesthetics & Protest*. Available at: www.joaap.org/press/pah/mortgagedlives.pdf (accessed November 2014).

Flesher Fominaya, Cristina (2014) 'Spain is different: Podemos and 15-M'. Available at: www.opendemocracy.net. 29 May 2014. (accessed November 2014).

Human Rights Watch (2014) *Spain: Rights at Risk in Housing Crisis*, 27 May 2014. Available at: www.hrw.org/news/2014/05/27/spain-rights-risk-housing-crisis (accessed October 2014).

Information and Statistical Office of the City of Belgrade (2012) 'Statistićki godišnjak Beograda', Belgrade.

Krkić, M. (2013) 'Kako do tri puta jeftinijeg stana', *24 Sata*, 13 January. Available at: http://arhiva.24sata.rs/vesti/ekonomija/vest/kako-do-tri-puta-jeftinijeg-stana/70976.phtml.

Milojković, Gordana (2009) 'Zadrugarstvo: Nekad bilo u Srbiji', *Biznis & Finansjie*, October. Available at: http://bif.rs/2010/04/zadrugarstvo-nekad-bilo-u-srbiji/.

Palgo Centar (2010) *Socijalno stanovanje. Prikaz stambenih politika Srbije i odabranih zemalja Evrope*. Belgrade: Izdanje Palgo centar i Urbanisticki zavod Beograda.

Petrovic, Mina (2013) 'Serbia', in Josef Hegedus, Martin Lux and Nora Teller (eds) *Social Housing in Transition Countries*, London: Routledge, pp. 244–261.

Džokic, A., Neelen, M., with Aksentijevic, M. and Milikic, N. (2013) 'Chytrejší staveni' ['Smarter Building'] in *ERA 21*, issue December 2013, Prague.

Džokic, A., Neelen, M. and Vilenica, A. (2014) 'Od strategija preživljavanja ka stanovanju za sve' in *Nepokoreni grad*, issue 4, November 2014.

16 – POPULAR BRAZILIAN ARCHITECTURE IN THE MAKING – OR THE POWER OF PRODUCTIVE CONSUMPTION

Rainer Hehl

> The "making" in question is a production, a poiesis–but a hidden one because it is scattered over areas defined and occupied by systems of "production" (television, urban development, commerce, etc.), and because the steadily increasing expansion of these systems no longer leaves "consumers" any place in which they can indicate what they make or do with the products of these systems. To a rationalized, expansionist and at the same time centralized and clamorous, spectacular production corresponds another production, called "consumption."
>
> The latter is devious, it is dispersed, but insinuates itself everywhere, silently and almost invisibly, because it doesn't manifest itself through its own products, but rather through its ways of using the products imposed by a dominant economic order.
> (de Certeau, 1984: xxi)

POPULAR ECONOMIES

Against the belief that globalization would render the world a homogeneous and generic field controlled by market interests, urban realities round the world remain diversified and locally specific. Under the reign of a globalized economic order, with an estimated one-third of the urban population now living in "informal cities" (UN Habitat, 2011: 30), urban production can be seen as increasingly generated by popular masses and processes beyond formal control.

If city growth in the future will be predominantly driven by urban informality, parallel governance, and self-organization, the question is whether these sub-systems represent alternative models for urban production or if they are rather integral components of the dominant economy. In view of the advance of informal urbanization, how can we consider the production by people, as expressed in localized, counter-cultural projects, in the context of a dominant, globalized market system (Figure 16.1)?

Figure 16.1 Informal commerce added to the generic model of Brazilian mass housing. Parauapebas,
Brazil, 2010
Photo: Rainer Hehl

The case of the metropolis in Brazil gives us an insight into how
popular culture is affecting the market economy and vice versa. While
urban production in Brazil is determined by both generic standardized
models, on the one hand, and uncontrolled informal growth, on the
other, the notion of "popular production" represents a further category
forming the middle ground, where the generic and the specific meet.
But who exactly are these popular producer-consumers? Who are the
population groups that are sustaining the popular economy?

In Brazil, the composition of what can be understood as the
"popular masses" has drastically changed during the past ten years,
mainly due to transformations of income distribution. With the
emergence of the lower-middle class, which represents the biggest
segment of Brazilian society today, low-income populations are
increasingly gaining access to consumer goods. These new consumers are now considered the main target for future market expansion
and the drivers for economic growth. While the purchasing power
of the emerging lower-middle class is increasing, the aspirations of
these populations follow and adopt the consumer patterns of the
upper classes. The massive growth in demand for consumer goods
such as air conditioning, cars, and flat-screen televisions will not only
significantly worsen the ecological footprint, they will affect the value
chains of small-scale commerce and production, turning the popular

economy into an arena for corporate interests. For example, in Brazil, large retailers and the food industries see the favelas as the biggest potential area for further market expansion, replacing micro-commerce with products that are exactly tailored to the needs of specific user groups. The change in consumer-producer patterns also impacts the articulation of the urban realm, turning buildings and public spaces into objects of speculation while favoring the production of surplus value over use value. It remains to be seen if these emerging markets will just follow the mechanisms of an unfettered free market, or if they will manage to move towards a more equally distributed reproduction of architecture and public space, with a fair allocation of resources for all.

COLLECTIVE MOBILIZATION

Nobody expected anything radical would happen on that day. According to official media on 20 June 2013, 1.2 million people filled Rio de Janeiro's streets, raising their voices for democracy and participation. A wide range of Brazilian society, young people, popular movements, and enraged citizens demonstrated against the operating mode of an established system, which does not take enough care of the people's needs. In its whole history, Brazil had never seen a similar mobilization of protesters on this scale, making claims for public interests. What was the motivation for the uprising of the masses and this sudden explosion of huge, collective energy? Whether the protesters were clamoring for thorough action against state corruption or for more investment in education, social security, and public transportation, one message was clear: from now on things have to change.

What can be interpreted as a rising concern for collective interests and civic consciousness is connected to the fact that Brazil has become a middle-class country. The revolt against the current political system expresses the gap between the promises of an emerging world power for economic betterment, and the everyday reality of the average Brazilian who has to struggle with dysfunctional public services and the inefficiencies of a corrupt government. While it is questionable if the protests so far have brought about significant changes, the demonstrations certainly revealed that the composition of society, the ways in which collective interests are negotiated, and the social body of which contemporary capitalism is formed, have all changed.

Are we facing here a new phase of the urban revolution? If we look at the claims that have been put forward by the majority of the protesters, it seems that the current economy provides neither the guarantee for private welfare nor the equal distribution of common goods. Even though the fair distribution of wealth remains one of the fundamental demands of democratic societies, the value production of current systems is hardly questioned. What Maurizio Lazzarato, referring to Gabriel Tarde's work, termed "inconsumable commons" describes how civic societies are relying on common resources that cannot be provided by the market, including "knowledge, language, science, culture, art, information, forms of life relations with oneself, others and the world, etc." (2004: 199). Considering the economy, not only as the (re)production of ownable goods and services, but the particular life-world complex within which desires, beliefs, language, signs, sensibilities of community circulate, the point of resistance cannot rest on the mere re-measurement and re-attribution of wealth, but must work upon the transformation of the very forms of life that subtend such practices.

THE TROPICALIST COUNTER-CULTURE

Brazilians lived through a similar moment 45 years ago during the takeover by the military regime, when 100,000 people occupied public spaces, fighting against state oppression and the introduction of the dictatorship. They sang in the streets "Tomorrow has to be another day" (amanhã há de ser outro dia), a line of a song written by the Brazilian singer-songwriter Chico Buarque, associated with the music genre MPB, Música Popular Brasileira. The street protest gave rise to the formation of Tropicália, which soon became known as an ephemeral, but high-impact movement. Led by MPB artists, including Gilberto Gil, Caetano Veloso, and others, Tropicália was about the appropriation of local and foreign music styles in order to relativize the prevailing notions of authenticity in Brazilian music. Tropicália intended to turn the collective energy as it emerged from the protest into an artistic movement, but it also claimed to undo age-old categorizations, such as high and popular culture. Oscillating between the artistic avant-garde and mass culture, the movement radically altered the field of popular music, creating new conditions for the emergence of ec-lectic and hybridized experiments. It also defined an inaugural moment for a broad range of artistic practices and behavioral styles identified as "counter-cultural" during the period of military rule. Until now, Tropicália has been considered a key movement in cultural production in Brazil, addressing the creation of a collective identity across the whole spectrum of Brazilian society, at a time when the country was experiencing increasing political repression and social segregation.

Even though the Tropicalist movement was strongly rooted in local practices, it was also promoting a certain kind of transnational identity by adhering consistently to international pop culture and hybridizing Brazilian music styles with foreign influences. In this sense, Tropicalism was understood by its followers as "*superantropo-fagia*," a revision of the cannibalistic ritual that aimed to incorporate the enemy's forces. Based on the rituals of certain indigenous tribes, the cannibalistic practice of "*antropofagia*" was used by the Brazilian Modernist avant-garde in the 1920s in order to create their own "Brazilian" identity out of the Modernist movement that was taking place at that time in Europe. Unlike the early Modernist attempts to appropriate the cultural advance of the former colonizers, the Tropicalists were more interested in the making of popular culture, rather than introducing the notion of the popular into the artistic language of the cultural elite. Within the wide range of MPB, the Tropicalist sound was invented for the avant-garde as well as for the consuming masses. As a matter of fact, the popularity of its proponents is still transgressing the boundaries between classes and nationalities today. When Gilberto Gil released his album entitled "Refavela" in 1977 and included the lines in his song: "The refavela reveals the paradoxical Samba school, quite Brazilian in its accent—but international in its language,"[1] the claim for cross-cultural exchange is expressed in the paradox of being rooted in different value systems at the same time.[2]

In line with Andrade's slogan, "Only Anthropophagy unites us,"[3] the Tropicalist mind-set wasn't only open to devour foreign cultures but it also practiced the reverse process, engaging in the "powerful sense of being devoured" (Oiticica, 1992: 124). It was by embracing

---

1   Original line "A refavela / Revala a escolar / De samba paradoxal / Brasileirinho / Pelo Sotaque / Más de língua internacional."

2   Similarly, Brazilian artist Hélio Oiticica reclaimed Anthropophagy with a show that he organized in 1967 featuring several pieces by young Brazilian artists, including his own work entitled "Tropicália," which was later adopted as the name of the whole movement. With his inaugural presentation Oiticica intended to extract "from individual creative efforts the principal items of these same efforts, in an attempt to group them culturally" (Oiticica, 1967). The message of the operation was clear—the gathering of collective forces was meant to designate the creative will of a culture in the making. With a spatial arrangement of the specific milieu that he experienced in the favelas of Rio de Janeiro, Oiticica imagined in his installation a re-founding of Brazilian culture by drawing from a peripheral position. Rather than just decontextualizing the favela experience within the museum space, his installation Tropicália involved translating images of "Brazilianness" in order to be internalized and re-deployed by cultural producers.

3   Oswald de Andrade's manifesto, which starts with the lines "Only anthropophagy unites us. Socially. Economically. Philosophically." was first published in *Revista de Antropofagia*, No. 1, São Paulo, May 1928. English translation by Maria do Carmo Zanini in 2006.

the differences of the Other that the Tropicalist movement opened the path for a dialogue between high and low culture, between the aspiration for the avant-garde by the cultural elite and the fragmented and heterogeneous body of the popular masses. Cultural production was understood as a project that reaches far beyond the boundaries of class distinction and national identity, the reproduction of collective space being anchored in an anthropophagic practice of a culture in the making. Moving from forms of political resistance to cultural practice, the Tropicalist movement managed to expand the field of counter-cultural practice. While breaking down the boundaries between mainstream and oppositional action, it also introduced another kind of value production. Whether counter-cultural practice is considered here as the only remaining alternative for continued resistance to the repressive regime or as sheer phenomenon of artistic expression, Tropicália provided another vision of cultural identity by incorporating creative counter-cultural practice within the predominant conditions of an emerging mass culture.

CONSUMER-PRODUCERS

Back then, it was rather clear against whom or what to resist. In the face of governmental repression, whether this applies to the military regime or to the dominating order of the police state, it was easy to identify the enemy.

If we look at the current situation, things today are much less clear-cut. While power is exercised and operated by an economy that ensnares us in a fine weave of dependencies, it is actually quite hard to find an oppositional position. Can we truly fight against dominating corporate interests while at the same time being consumers that guarantee the operational mode of the current economic system? Are there still alternatives that can be developed within or against the operating system of market-driven interests? Are the popular masses just subject to a consumer culture that is following the preconditioned behavioral patterns of the globalized market economy?

Michel de Certeau states in his book, *The Practice of Everyday Life*, that the operational models of popular cultures cannot be confined to the past, the countryside, or primitive peoples. They exist in the heart of the strongholds of the contemporary economy. By defining the main field of popular action within the framework of the prevalent economic system and related modes of production, de Certeau positions the consumer as a crucial actor in the process of the formation of cultural identity. With an emphasis on the various "ways of using the products imposed by a dominant order" (1984: xxi), the rituals of everyday practice are considered the main driver for the resistance to an imposed order. Rather than questioning the constitution of established power constellations, de Certeau is interested in the question of what the consumer finally does with consumer products and whether consumerism can create its own local identity by emphasizing the fact that acculturation is mainly determined by individual and collective appropriation.

POPULARIZATION

In reality, a rationalized, expansionist, centralized, spectacular and clamorous production is confronted by an entirely different kind of production called "consumption" and characterized by its ruses, its fragmentation (the result of the circumstances), its poaching, its clandestine nature, its tireless but quiet activity, in short by its quasi-invisibility, since it shows itself not in its own products (where would it place them?) but in an art of using those imposed on it.
(de Certeau, 1984: 31)

In order to illustrate his claims, de Certeau refers to the practices of certain indigenous Indian cultures in the face of the dominating order of Spanish colonization. What turned the suppressed people into creative consumer-producers was namely the fact that the "Indians often used the laws, practices, and representations that were imposed on them by force or by fascination to ends other than those of the conquerors" (ibid.: 31). The subversion of the ruling power was exercised without leaving the system—the procedures of consumption could "remain other" by making the prevailing order function in another register. Against the generic logic of market-driven consumerism, de Certeau opposes a process of "popularization" while addressing the question of what the end-users finally make out of the commodities that are offered to them.

The act of creative appropriation becomes most obvious in the contemporary context when we look at the parallel modes and tactics as deployed within the conditions of urban informality. In line with de Certeau's argument, the lessons from the favelas can be found in the various ways the formal system is diverted in order to adapt to the conditions of local characteristics and the necessities of everyday life. Instead of just being a subversive regime that creates an alternative reality according to its own rules, informality complements the formal system by introducing new value chains that are adapted to the specificity of the local milieu. While urban informality can also be seen as just another kind of manifestation of the neoliberal market logic, the reinvention of the everyday will only be achieved through the ruses and tactics of popular appropriation.

EVERYDAY TACTICS

If strategic maneuvers can be described as calculations of power relationships deployed by subjects with will and authority (a business, an army, a city, a scientific institution), a tactic refers rather to "the art of the weak"—or in the words of de Certeau:

Lacking its own place, lacking a view of the whole, limited by the blindness (which may lead to perspicacity), resulting from combat at close quarters, limited by the possibilities of the moment, a tactic is determined by the absence of power just as a strategy is organized by the postulation of power.
(1984: 38)

Accordingly the ways in which tactics are exercised are intrinsically related to the notion of time. Inscribed in specific timeframes, tactics are therefore always operating "within the enemy's field of vision," whereas strategies depend on spatial logics and territorial claims in order to be effective. The absence of a proper locus is what makes a tactic weak and vulnerable, but also flexible and adaptable to the dynamics of a constantly changing reality.

Popular tactics are still present within the public realm of the Brazilian streetscape and most efficient when it comes to finding a way out of the regulations imposed by the public authorities. Invented by popular ingenuity, the *cavalete*, a device that serves as a mobile market stand, embodies all the virtues of popular Brazilian street culture. The components of the foldable system—sticks from scrap wood, aluminum hangers and a bunch of screws—are assembled by local manufacturers and only distributed at specific selling points in the streets. The elegance of the construction results from the most important functionality of the system. Once the controlling public authorities are around, the *cavalete* construction can be dismantled in seconds in order to swiftly eliminate proof of any illegal activity (Figure 16.2). Or think of the *camelôs* (street vendors) who appropriate the space of public transportation, those who sell candies wrapped in bundles hanging from a hook, which eventually hangs from the handles inside

public buses. The ingenuity of the attachment system seems just
stunning. It's not only the practicality and simplicity of the hanging
version of a candy stand that makes the solution so convincing, it is
also accompanied by a certain elegance in the unconventional use of
the laws of gravity, constantly poised for flight should the vendor need
to flee from the police.

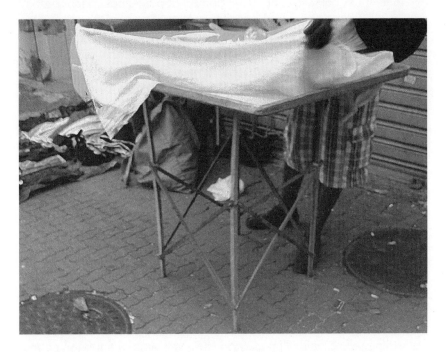

Figure 16.2 The table-stands (cavaletes) used by street vendors in Rio can be dismantled
spontaneously as soon as the police arrive, Rio de Janeiro, 2012
Photo: Julian Schubert

SHOCK OF ORDER

As the tactics of the popular economy are considered subversive
to the established formal order and corporate interests, the popular
culture of street vending in Brazil is increasingly subject to restriction
through new laws and regulations concerning their use in public
spaces. The policies recently introduced in Rio de Janeiro, on the
pretext of sanitation and security, ban a great deal of the popular
street culture for the sake of public order. The operation *Choque de
Ordem* (shock of order) set in motion in 2009 by the City of Rio de
Janeiro in collaboration with the Special Secretary of Public Order
(SEOP) and the municipal cleaning company (Comlurb), is based on

the conviction that the streets of Rio have to be cleaned up in various ways. This involves increasing trash collection, shutting down illegal commercial activities, such as unlicensed vans and street vendors, and enforcing laws relating to public decency. With the enforcement of order, informal street activities and spontaneous pop-up selling points are prohibited in favor of a more formalized, corporate economy. In its most pervasive logic, the control of public space for corporate interests was exercised during the World Soccer Championship in 2014. As a consequence of contractual agreements between FIFA and the municipal governments, a special commercial zone was set up around the soccer stadiums. The proposed legislation prohibited the sale or display of any merchandise at the "Official Competition Venues, in their immediate vicinities or in their main points of entry," without FIFA's express permission.

The contracts illustrate the spatial strategy behind the dominant market forces very clearly. While popular products are increasingly the subject of corporate protection, the appropriation of urban spaces through everyday practices is suppressed in favor of very specific processes of social engineering. As a result, public space ceases to be a place for popular economies and local production. The FIFA example, however, shows how forms of life produced by popular livelihoods are subjected to standards and regulations, which allow global capitalism to operate *without obstacles and constraints*. Under this arrangement, informality is accepted as long as it guarantees the provision of cheap labor. As soon as the subaltern masses are turned into consumers, their productive forces are controlled and incorporated within market logics. If popular culture still aims to enter the public realm, what kind of tactics have to be invented that are able to cope with the perfidious strategies that favor corporations?

THE FUTURE OF URBAN INFORMALITY

If urban informality provides the domain where appropriation tactics are deployed, it can actually be considered a counter-model to the prevalent commodification of public space. But what happens when it comes to the production of new homes? Do spatial appropriation and auto-construction represent a viable solution for massive urban growth, or does informality just stand for the incapacity to deal with the challenges of urban growth?

There is no doubt that the massive advance of urban informality is causing major problems to the urban system as a whole, whether it relates to pollution in open sewers, a lack of garbage collection or offenses by criminal organizations. However, if we look at the generic repetition of standardized housing units provided by governmental programs, the outcome of formal solutions to the housing deficit fails to meet their ambitious goals. While access to urban services is still lacking, it is mainly due to the mono-functional character and the rigidity of low-income standards that newly built social housing complexes turn into ghettos. In order to undo the lack of diversity and adaptability, informal extensions built by the inhabitants themselves remain the only alternative for users to adapt their own living conditions. Even though informality helps to compensate for insufficient standards and to transform the generic layouts into neighborhoods, the question is whether the primitivism of generic production can be suspended by the primitivism of informal construction. Instead of just complementing the insufficiency and low quality provided by the market system with improvised structures, another take on the relationship between generic and specific seems to be necessary. What if generic production could be conceived by anticipating its future transformation—and what if informal appropriations could be coordinated in order to be able to formulate the collective project of the city? Wouldn't it be possible then to establish a popular building culture between the operating systems of generic and informal production that is able to mediate between different modes of city making?

POPULAR BRAZILIAN ARCHITECTURE

It might be pure coincidence that another event happened on June 20, 2013, in Rio de Janeiro, in immediate proximity to the crowds demonstrating at Praça Tiradentes. In the middle of a sudden outburst of collective discomfort, the APB collection, research on "Popular Brazilian Architecture" was presented to a local crowd. Specific elements of Brazilian spaces were held up against the generic model of Brazilian mass housing, "Minha Casa, Minha Vida" (My House, My Life) (Figure 16.3). With the eye of an outsider to Brazilian informal culture, a team of researchers collected examples of building elements, street activities, construction methods, floor plans, public furniture and other components that seemed to make a fundamental contribution to the richness, vitality, and creativity of Brazilian spaces (Figure 16.4). The APB collection was elaborated as a generative language, which opposes abstract formal design methods and instead favors empirically acquired knowledge, based upon observation and experimentation, promoting a radical belief in self-generated urban production and based on centuries of adaptations, transformations, and trials. With a deep interest in the modalities of everyday practice, the APB collection presented tools that provide what is needed to enable Brazilian popular cultures, and to help reinvent them at the same time.

Figure 16.3 Low-income settlement established by the Brazilian social housing program, Minha Casa, Minha Vida, Parauapebas, Brazil, 2010
Photo: Rainer Hehl

Figure 16.4 Guard securing the exhibition 'A.P.B' at Studio-X during the protest, Rio de Janeiro, 2013
Photo: Julian Schubert

Against the backdrop of the turmoil surrounding the APB event, even government officials realized there was an urge for change. But what exactly has to be transformed so that the social reproduction of popular architecture can become a strong actor in the processes and negotiations of city making? As counter-proposals to the inability of the current urban economy to produce cities rather than market-driven developments, the spatial tactics of Brazilian Popular Architecture could only deploy its transformative potential if integrated within the formal framework of state politics, and if its practices were strengthened within the logic of market forces. What has been termed by de Certeau as 'productive consumption' then might go beyond the impact of tactical maneuvers leading to significant social change, as it also affects consumer patterns, behavioral norms, and cultural production.

Half a century ago, the Tropicalist movement transformed the traditional notion of popular production in Brazil into an open process of cultural creation. The application of "popular architecture" within the current protocols for urban production could have a similar impact in the context of the social transformations that are happening today. Whether we look at the experimentation of collective action in the streets of Rio or at the emerging interests in APB (Arquitetura Popular Brasileira), June 20, 2013 marked the beginning of a new era for popular movements in Brazil, but it also offered the opportunity to rethink design practice as a powerful tool for the reproduction and reinvention of popular culture beyond class segregation, the privatization of common goods and the domination by corporate interests and, eventually for the realization of a truly popular Brazilian architecture.

REFERENCES

de Andrades, Oswald (1928) *Manifesto*, *Revista de Antropofagia*, No. 1, São Paulo, May 1928. English translation by Maria do Carmo Zanini in 2006.

de Certeau, Michel (1984) *The Practice of Everyday Life*, Berkeley, CA: University of California Press.

Lazzarato, Maurizio (2004) "From capital-labor to capital-life," *ephemera* 4(3): 187–208.

Oiticica, Hélio (1967) "Esquema geral da Nova Objetividade Brasileir," exhibition catalog, Museo de Arte Moderno, Rio de Janeiro. Translated into English in Hélio Oiticica (1992) "General scheme for new objectivity," in *Hélio Oiticica*, exhibition catalog, Rotterdam and Minneapolis: Witte de With and Walker Art Center.
    (1992) "Tropicália," in *Hélio Oiticica*, exhibition catalog, Centro de Arte Hélio Oiticica, Rio de Janeiro.

UN Habitat (2011) *The State of the World's Cities 2010/2011: Bridging the Urban Divide*, London: Earthscan.

17 – TENT CITIES, PEOPLE'S KITCHENS, FREE UNIVERSITIES: THE GLOBAL VILLAGES OF OCCUPATION MOVEMENTS

Peter Mörtenböck and Helge Mooshammer

> *Because between us we have all the resources we need.*
> (Tent City University, Occupy London)

CAMPING AND THE QUESTION OF COMMON PROPERTY

Tahrir Square, Puerta del Sol, Zuccotti Park, Gezi Park – names of public squares such as these have in recent years become synonymous with political protest. Rather than being referenced to a particular moment in time, a set of actors or an ideological orientation, these protests are identified by their urban manifestations. While some years have passed since the peak of the movements of the squares in 2011 – from the Arab Spring and the Spanish Indignados to the global phenomenon of Occupy – together, they have helped to establish a model for forcing the concerns of marginalized and disempowered groups onto the public agenda. The continued deployment of this model can be seen in the ways in which various forms of civil disobedience and unrest, such as the wave of protests on Kiev's Maidan or the resurgence of Occupy Central in the course of the Hong Kong electoral reform 2014, have recently claimed public squares as their place to demand change and develop alternative alliances (Figure 17.1).

Figure 17.1 Occupy Central, Hong Kong, 2011
Photo: Peter Mörtenböck and Helge Mooshammer

The right to political participation such uprisings call upon is made manifest through occupying central nodes in the visual and spatial domains of the social world. Rather than merely passing through space and leaving its surfaces untouched, these protests employ an array of tactics to demonstrate the potential permanence of resistance. Key to their political currency is their attachment to urban life and their insistence on non-defiance until some change has been achieved. These endeavours entail not only an encroachment on symbolic space – the use of banners, placards, performances or mock statues to propose alternative significations – but also the (re)production of a whole set of infrastructures that help to sustain the presence of protest: from the provision of food, sanitation and medical care for the bodies that occupy these squares to a range of social and cultural means to further the political milieu of the protest – libraries, theatres, ad-hoc exhibitions, pop-up galleries, assembly spaces as well as communication and media platforms, ranging from on-site radio and press corners to social media and outreach tools. Discussing the implications of a spatial realization of alternatives, our concern here is the relationship between the symbolic reach and political impact of these contemporary forms of protest, on the one hand, and the dynamic re-production of occupations as sites of collective negotiation, on the other.

The rapid spread of the Occupy Movement in autumn 2011 – from Occupy Wall Street, and Occupy London to Occupy Frankfurt and Occupy Central – provides a rich tapestry to study this particular tactic of political resistance that centres on the transformation of public space into a political commons. The tool of choice was the collective power of bodies, who occupied parks and squares, demonstrating a unity of cause and a shared determination not to vacate these spaces as long as they felt they were being denied scope for political action. The occupation claims the space it opens up by simultaneously and literally blocking it. We are dealing here with a paradoxical figure that produces a political commons and in which tents, kitchens and classrooms play an at times comprehensible and yet also surprisingly central role.

Although the temporary occupation of squares and parks basically requires nothing more than the concerted action of human bodies assembling at a particular place at a specified point in time, it nevertheless makes a difference whether the aim of the occupation is met solely by its realization, as is generally the case with flash mobs, or involves a long-term goal. 'The purpose of Occupy Wall Street is to occupy Wall Street', as film director Michael Moore entitled his commentary in *The Nation* in March 2012, in which he emphasized the compelling connection between, on the one hand, the occupation of Zuccotti Park and all such occupations and, on the other, the symbolic space of the international financial might embodied in Wall Street (Moore, 2012). In the long term, Occupy aimed to establish a global network of interconnected spaces whose scope extends far beyond the act of physical occupation and whose alteration cannot be merely a question of intervention in material arrangements. However, in itself, physical occupation – the animation and organization of the architecture of a space – is a question of the concrete configuration of bodies and thereby also of the technologies that protect, nourish and provide for these bodies. Since Occupy was not only about the demonstration of strength through the act of assembly but also the political potential of the insistence on the continuance of this assembly, these technologies are an indispensable element of the action.

Even before the beginning of the actual occupations, tents had already turned up in the oft-quoted call by the anti-consumerist Canadian magazine and blog *Adbusters* on 13 July 2011 as a central tool of spatial occupation. Indeed, the two phrases 'Are you ready for a Tahrir moment?' and 'Bring a tent' seemed to assume an automatic connection between the tent and occupation. A tent is more than merely an object providing a temporary domicile: it manifests the intention to abide, both as a gesture with which the time span of an action is signalled and as a mobile space that is part of the establishment of an encampment. Together, these two aspects open up a political repertoire in which the tent encampment emerges as a combination of field and event, action and community. Simultaneously open and closed, enduring and fleeting, controlling and liberating, the camp represents a form of spatial praxis whose determinant feature is its own indeterminacy – its ambivalence in relation to what it produces and what it itself already is. This indeterminacy at the level of spatial production is continued in the indeterminacy of the camp as a social and political mechanism. The camps of the movements of the squares, with their improvised forums, rituals, rhythms and architectures, suggest a politics in which what is produced always represents a potential for a series of further movements and phenom-ena. The collective articulation of the camp in numerous gatherings, mutual assistance and collectively organized actions is thus a continuous process, one that entails the exploration of the possibility of a twenty-first-century social and political movement (Grusin, 2011). Camps, whether those of the protest movements of our time or other camps that have been established for purposes of protest, resistance or autonomous organization, are thus not only sites of discussion and deliberation but also non-stop experiments in a form of cohabitation based on community and trust.

In order to distinguish themselves from existing forms of associ-ation, camps also need to mark an 'elsewhere' in a spatial respect, whether as the historical other of the town and its citizens in the form of the military camp and soldiers located outside the town walls, or in political-legal terms as a space outside the prevailing legal order in which other forms of sovereignty are practised, for instance, through the exercise of military, police, foreign or autonomous power. Camps thus displace and locate, intertwining these two moments such that their occupants become included in their exclusion. In this way, they intensify their difference from dominant logics of order, while also inspiring, as illustrated by particular historical sites, the encroachment of one organizing principle on another. In ancient Rome, for example, the *Campus Martius* initially served as a field and a military exercise ground and later as a meeting place for the Senate, as a venue for theatre performances and triumphal processions, and as a site for baths, monuments and obelisks. The ancient Mars Field thus constitutes a site inscribed with different orders and programmes, a site of overlays, contaminations and dislocations in which various influences generate their respective action spaces. A different field of interaction between city and camp emerged in the work of Leon Battista Alberti, who, in the fifteenth century, cultivated the idea that military camps should be understood as the 'plant nurseries of the cities'. The general principles of urban order and control generated by this conception led to the construction of colonial planned cities but can also be seen during the twentieth century in the military structure of refugee camps, transit housing and hut barracks.

This military origin of the camp, its ambivalent nature and the comprehensive influence of principles of spatial order had conspicuous consequences for the development of protest camps in the twentieth century, for their territorial and strategic organization of protest, for the forms of resistance they offered, and for the security and extension of controls over self-organized structures. At all important locations of the Occupy Movement, camps were set up that included the infrastructure, tents and kitchens typical of an occupation in order to provide for a lasting engagement. However, whereas in modern warfare camps are usually established in secure locations behind the front line and provide battlefield support from a distance by supplying ordnance, holding new material for the front in readiness, and providing food and quarters for soldiers, in the case of the recent occupation movements, the tents themselves formed the front line in the occupiers' struggle to stay where they were. The most vehement challenges coming from police and local authorities were not directed at the protest as such or at protests taking place on the street in front of banks, town halls and company headquarters, but at the tents, tarpaulins and other materials ensuring that the movement could stay put.

On the one hand, this had to do with the local relocation of the front line: after the site at which the protest was directed – New York's Wall Street – could not be physically occupied by Occupy Wall Street, nearby Zuccotti Park was selected and provided a point from which the movement's protest marches repeatedly streamed in the direction of Wall Street. On the other hand, the movement's gatherings in public space were also informed by the idea of the formation of a new social constitution, the development of economic principles and the exploration of mechanisms of direct democracy. The site where this process could take place and where a solidarity community united by a collective political aspiration could take shape was thus not Wall Street but the movement's camp itself. It was not the campaigns, protests and demonstrations conducted at multiple locations against the richest 1 per cent but rather the camps of the Occupy Movement that represented the decisive tool in the struggle against the despised system. They provided a testing ground for the emergence of a new community from a collection of fundamentally different individuals outside the influence of established social institutions. The fact that in this context trust was established between disparate people and groups, and collective decisions were shaped by the sense of a newly formed community meant that the camps were more than merely bases of operations. At the same time, they constituted educational sites, forms of political theatre and incubators of an unfolding organizational culture (Snyder, 2011). The framework for this evolution was provided by the interplay of political forums, working groups and actions with an improvised infrastructure of signs and banners, laptops and generators, kitchens and libraries, medical facilities and tents.

CAMPS AND THE PERMANENT STATE OF EXCEPTION

When Zuccotti Park was occupied in September 2011, the police initially banned tents, braced tarpaulins and similar constructions. Even tarpaulins held up by the occupiers themselves to protect laptops and other technical devices from the rain were confiscated. It was not only the tents themselves that were constantly subjected to detailed monitoring by inspectors from the city administration but also all other components and mechanisms involved in the establishment of the camp. For instance, on several occasions, fire services and police confiscated gas and diesel generators used in various camps to produce heat and electricity, as well as portable toilets, microphones and amplifiers. However, the collective ingenuity of the activists quickly produced practical alternatives. Confiscated diesel generators were often replaced with bicycle-driven devices, sound systems with 'human microphones', Portaloos with eco-toilets, and banners fastened to poles with slogans on pizza boxes. Escape routes required in case of fire frequently had to be cleared after being encroached on and the assertion of regulations pertaining to emergency response procedures led to repeated spatial restructuring of the camps of the Occupy Movement. This dialogue of measures and counter-measures generated a specific architecture of resistance, with which the borderlines of the confrontation were continuously constituted and their frameworks were mirrored in spatial terms. The micro-urban structures of the Occupy camps thus formed a reference image of their respective environments, one made up of a unique composition of bodies, material, structures, intensities, sounds, movements, rhythms and extensions – a step-by-step urbanization of the site in which spontaneous ideas, encounters, agreements, interventions and ruses drove action and generated new scenarios.

In this process, questions of security, health and hygiene developed into primary arguments made not only by the activists but also political decision-makers. Whereas for one side the issue was ensuring the safety of the camp before the onset of winter through an improved and durable infrastructure, criminal incidents in the camp and reports of poor security and hygiene repeatedly played into the hands of the other side as it endeavoured to conquer political terrain piece by piece. Apart from smaller two- and three-man tents, the town-planning working group in Zuccotti Park brought in several large frame tents at the start of November, which were used for specific purposes such as the women's tent exclusively reserved as a sleeping and discussion space for women, a measure resulting not least from the sexual assaults that had taken place in the park up until that point. Mayor Bloomberg's statements in the media at this time regarding the newly erected group of tents remained tentative, no doubt due to the fact that Brookfield Office Properties had still not insisted on a strict application of the guidelines governing the use of the park. The end result was that by the onset of winter a small space devoted to essential medical services had expanded into a meticulously negotiated and intricately dovetailed camp architecture extending from an information area and religious space in the north-western corner across the actual tent encampment of the occupation and a kitchen and first-aid area in the centre of the site to the library, art and media zone on the camp's eastern side.

This accentuated spatialization of the protest not only generated more protection for all those participating in it but at the same time made the symbolic and physical presence of the protest itself clearly readable (Hailey, 2009: 25). Moreover, the adversarial camp that the police had erected on the edge of the park occupation became equally readable. Its core was the SkyWatch operations platform, a mobile watchtower equipped with reflective glass, spotlights and cameras that could be extended to a height of 8 metres (Sheets, 2011). The panoptic design of these surveillance machines inevitably leads to associations with Foucault's concept of the disciplinary society and the mechanism of self-discipline, based on the inter-nalization of behavioural norms in situations in which people do not know when they are being observed. Indeed, it is not difficult to see the clean-up actions begun in the camp in November, the numerous self-imposed regulatory measures and the many rules identified by the occupiers themselves and coordinated with the authorities as elements within a larger image of the encampment, one that includes the police watchtowers and the metal fence with its police-controlled entry and exit points that was erected around the park in the course of the occupation. In effect, Occupy Wall Street positioned itself within a camp formed and monitored by the police. Internally oriented activities pertaining to welfare, intermediation and discipline within the camp were largely left to the occupiers, who also diligently decorated the boundary fence with ornamental objects and placards. Whereas due to the complex legal status of the park, the occupation was able to manifest itself spatially and develop a camp almost in accordance with the prevailing laws, at the same time it made itself vulnerable to external supervision. Step by step, it internalized forms of supervision originating from outside the camp, which were ultimately able to enclose, destabilize and capture it.

The elastic geography of the camp that made it possible for the protesters' concept of autonomy to seamlessly dovetail with the efforts of the state and its security forces to exert control had less to do with the specific development of the occupation of Zuccotti Park than with the typological condition of the camp in itself. The unintentional transformation of a protest camp into a policed camp shows how easily the state of emergency aspired to by the occupation could be applied to the occupation itself. Seeking out an urban space for occupation in which the laws governing public space are largely abrogated and erecting a camp on this site, i.e. a kind of space whose typology is already inscribed with the conditions of the state of emergency, creates a situation in which the point is quickly reached where the assertion of political sovereignty becomes particularly easy – where the distinction between public and private is abrogated and, as argued by Giorgio Agamben, 'a force of law without law' can come into operation (2005: 39). The covert concern of many institutional operations directed at the Occupy Movement was not the territorial control of parks or squares but rather the maintenance of the state of emergency as an organizing principle of a seemingly ubiquitous social crisis, whether in the micro-urban structure of the Occupy camp or the structure of urban development as a whole.

KNOWLEDGE AS RESISTANCE: KITCHENS, LIBRARIES AND UNIVERSITIES

The mainspring of spatial diversification in the Occupy camps focused on here was the desire for a common search for answers in an egalitarian environment. These arenas show how in oscillating movements between ideas and spatial praxis a political commons was generated – not as a thing or asset and not as a quantifiable process, but as a mouldable social relationship between an assembled group and the environment it has claimed (Harvey, 2012: 73). Intellectual and physical nourishment, specially invented recipes, well-networked preparation and alternative forms of enjoyment, served as catalysts of a globally dispersed, experimental sociality. Through a process of discussion, the question of who cares for the community was replaced by that of how care is provided and who requires care. It was thus neither an abstract image of the public sphere nor the clear contours of an occupied space but the concrete experience of shared and repeatedly reframed situations that played the decisive role in the global village of the Occupy Movement. In this sense, Occupy constituted a unique constellation and will not be repeated in the same way. However, the elements involved in it continue to exert an effect: the networks of indebtedness and state control and beliefs in the need to justify or challenge them – and not least the spatial structures in which the experiences and narratives of Occupy (like those of other political struggles before it) have been inscribed.

The task of supplying food literally assumed a central place in many Occupy camps, including in the Occupy Wall Street camp. The People's Kitchens established in the camps usually occupied a central location, from where they could supply food for the activities encircling them while also constituting an informal meeting point for everyone in the camp. At the beginning of the occupation of Zuccotti Park, dishes consisted above all of casseroles brought by activists, salads prepared on-site, pizzas delivered as donations and other dishes provided by individual supporters. Providing support for the occupied parks and squares with all kinds of homemade food constituted an important point of contact for many people, above all in the early weeks of the occupation – a declaration of solidarity with the concerns of the Occupy camps. However, already early on, the People's Kitchen in Zuccotti Park began to relocate food preparation to a soup kitchen in the east of New York, where Occupy Wall Street could prepare hundreds of meals daily without having to deal with the exigencies of the occupied space. This formation of a food-preparation network had decisive effects on the situation following the clearing of Zuccotti Park. In 2014, the kitchen was still supplying hundreds of meals a day in Manhattan, where every weekend the Occupy People's Kitchen was erected on Union Square to hand out food.

Communicating and 'representing' the movement to the outside world also took place at other points in the camps of the Occupy Movement. In the larger camps, media and public relations work was usually conducted in special information areas, near to which legal advice was often offered and entire libraries emerged. The most comprehensive collection of books and journals associated with Occupy was located in the northeast corner of Zuccotti Park, where in November 2011 up to 9000 publications were available, supervised for the most part by professional librarians. In a time when libraries are disappearing from urban public life, the libraries of the Occupy Movement signalled the vital importance of this form of public space. The motive driving the spontaneous emergence of these 'People's Libraries' has less to do with the propagation of a targeted corpus of literature than with the formation of a community of readers, a social bond forged by reading, reflection, discussion and conversation. The communicative focus of the Occupy libraries thus emphasizes the role of the library as a building block of the community. It not only attests to the necessity of the struggle against the disappearance of public libraries but also situates the library as an important space in the struggle of the Occupy Movement against the disappearance of alternatives to the purely economic. As a mobile library including an online catalogue, the Zuccotti Park People's Library continues to embody this idea and is supporting different Occupy meetings and events with what could be salvaged of the collection following the clearing of the park.[1]

Apart from the open programme offered by such people's libraries, the Occupy Movement's concern with education was manifested above all in the numerous courses, workshops and seminars held in various self-founded, free universities. In the run-up to Occupy's emergence, student protests around the world sparked by opposition to tuition fees in 2009 and 2010 had already led to a broader discussion on the connection between education, privatization, speculation and indebtedness. The financial burdens and indebtedness faced

1   During the clearing of Zuccotti Park on 15 November 2011, police removed 5000 books in garbage trucks. 1275 were later retrieved, but of these only 839 were in a readable condition. See online: http://peopleslibrary.wordpress.com/2011/11/23/packed-press-conference-documents-ruins-of-over-3000-books/

by many students subsequently led them to engage in Occupy and to focus in particular on the issue of educational alternatives. The result was a rapid emergence of blogs, e-zines, meeting points and networks in which information was disseminated and discussions started. Initiatives such as New York's *Occupy University*, Boston's *Free School University*, London's *Tent City University* and *The Art School in the Art School* took this discussion a step further, in that they, as the education arm of the Occupy Movement, developed alternative formats entailing free education for all. Offering a thematic spectrum ranging from poetry to radical economics, a number of these universities held up to 500 seminars and workshops, whether in the meeting tent of an Occupy camp, on city squares, in private dwellings or in occupied bank and school buildings. While anyone who wished to could teach, numerous university teachers also made themselves available to contribute to this particular facet of Occupy's political programme. Featuring speakers such as Manuel Castells, David Harvey and Vivienne Westwood, the *Tent City University* in the Occupy London camp in front of St Paul's Cathedral presented one of the most radical experiments in terms of the endeavour not merely to imitate educational formats but repeatedly to develop alternatives that sought to combine other content with new formats. This approach inspired the foundation of a 'Bank of Ideas' in an occupied building owned by the Swiss bank UBS not far from the second London Occupy camp on Finsbury Square (Figures 17.2 and 17.3), and subsequently a 'School of Ideas' in an empty school building a few hundred metres away, where courses in alternative citizenship were held for neighbourhood children.

The unfolding of social and cultural relations in protest camps creates a space that supports, focuses and expresses spontaneous utterance and assembly. The emphasis here is not first and foremost on the territorial dimension of the occupied space but on the spatial *praxis* of the camp, which helps repeatedly to generate new and useful tools for the movements. From this perspective, the many specialized spheres of protest camps, such as kitchens, libraries, medical service and media points, can be described as collectively structured fields of action that constitute a networked form of cultural praxis and for whose activities self-elected working groups can feel responsible.

Figures 17.2 and 17.3 Occupy
Finsbury Square, London, 2012
Photos: Peter Mörtenböck and
Helge Mooshammer

Adopting a condition of occupation, whether it be physical, legal
or intellectual, is without doubt a question of the space being occupied. Spaces prohibit or allow their adoption just as acting subjects
facilitate or hamper the adoption of the condition of occupation.
However, the subjective adoption of such a condition is not only a
spatial question but above all a question of duration, persistence and
abidance, and not least a question of renewal, change, emergence,
growth and catalysing. As Walter Benjamin argues in his theses on
the concept of history (2010), challenging the permanence of the
state of emergency requires insight into the parallel existence of
multiple times. Such a layered, non-homogeneous temporality, through
which we enter into a range of affective attachments, confronts the
collective situation of the occupation with temporal disjunctions,
that is, with disjunctions that organize experiences differently. The
endeavour to break into this structure, reorganize experiences and

achieve a collective orientation therefore constitutes the focus of progressively self-empowering occupation movements (Adams, 2011, 2012). However, this progressive self-empowerment is more than merely a process. It is a type of collective action whose fleeting contours are oriented less to the actually perceptible than to a range of imperceptible qualities and potentials. It is precisely at this point of the empowerment of bodies and subjects, in the reality of its potential, that, as Brian Massumi argues, the decisive force of a movement is expressed, in a relationally activated preparedness for what may come about (2011: 43). In itself, the temporal quality of the moment in which the movement of the squares has begun to unfold and, city by city, has been infused with the idea of a new cultural dynamic, already shows the degree of force that can be mobilized when a movement detaches itself from the static image imposed upon it, when it begins to break through the sclerotic relational patterns of perception, affect and action and replaces them with a collective delineation of the conditions for future possibilities and movements (Figure 17.4).

Figure 17.4 Occupy Frankfurt, 2012
Photo: Peter Mörtenböck and Helge Mooshammer

REFERENCES

Adbusters (2011) '#Occupy-WallStreet', 97 (Post Anarchism), September/October.

Adams, Jason (2011) 'Occupy time', *Critical Inquiry*, 16 November 2011, available at: http://critinq.wordpress.com/2011/11/16/occupy-time.
    (2012) *Occupy Time: Immediacy and Resistance After Occupy Wall Street*, New York: Palgrave Macmillan.

Agamben, Giorgio (2005) *State of Exception: Homo Sacer II.1*, Chicago: University of Chicago Press.

Benjamin, Walter (2010) 'Über den Begriff der Geschichte', in Walter Benjamin, *Werke und Nachlass, kritische Gesamtausgabe*, vol. 19, Berlin: Suhrkamp.

Grusin, Richard (2011) 'Premediation and the virtual occupation of Wall Street', *Theory and Event*, 14(4): supplement.

Hailey, Charlie (2009) *Camps: A Guide to 21st Century Space*, Cambridge, MA: MIT Press.

Harvey, David (2012) *Rebel Cities: From the Right to the City to the Urban Revolution*, London: Verso.

Massumi, Brian (2011) *Semblance and Event: Activist Philosophy and the Occurrent Arts,* Cambridge, MA: MIT Press.

Moore, Michael (2012) 'The purpose of Occupy Wall Street is to occupy Wall Street', *The Nation*, 14 March.

Sheets, Connor Adams (2011) 'Occupy Wall Street latest target of controversial NYPD surveillance units', *International Business Times*, 9 November.

Snyder, Gwen (2011) 'Campaign vs. encampment', *Occupy! An OWS-Inspired Gazette*, 3 (15 December).

18 – TACTICAL PRACTICES OF CREATIVE DISSENT

Ana Betancour

Global protests, as we have witnessed since Seattle in 1999,[1] and more recently during student protests in London and Rome, not to mention mass mobilizations in North Africa, France and the major cities of Spain and Greece, show us that a critique of capitalist globalization is both possible and urgently necessary (Figure 18.1).[2] Grassroots social movements have catalysed a process of democratic renewal and, it is suggested, led to a redefinition of global civil society. These massive assemblies and initiatives of social engagement became platforms from which more formalized movements such as the political party *Podemos* emerged in 2014 and *Barcelona En Comú* in June 2014 which recently won the municipal elections in Barcelona (May 2015). This chapter contends that these mobilizations and renewal have also fuelled a re-imagining of both the production and distribution of culture and the modes of working in artistic and spatial practices.

Figure 18.1 Genova Libera/ Free Genoa, demonstration against the G8 meeting in Genoa, Italy, July 2001 Photo: Oriana Eliçabe, in Global Resistance

1   In Seattle, a mass mobilization took place at the end of November 1999 (N30), in protest and to coincide with the World Trade Organization meeting the same date.

2   This refers to the anti-globalization mobilizations in London (June 1999), Prague (September 2000) Gothenburg (June 2001), Genoa (July 2001, see Figure 18.1), Barcelona, and the historically unprecedented demonstrations opposing the Iraq War, which brought nearly 20 million people from over sixty nations onto the streets on the same day, 15 February 2003. Between 2001 and 2003, photographer Oriana Eliçabe followed and photographed the anti-globalization demonstrations and actions that took place during the international summits in Genoa, New York, Barcelona, Cancun and others.

The aim of this chapter is to explore these alternative modes of working and their impact on and challenge to the social production of urban space and architecture. In this chapter I will introduce three specific examples of artistic activist practices, carried out in Spain during the years 2006–2014: *Realidades Avanzadas* (Advanced Realities), *TAF!* (Taller de Acción Fotográfia, the Photographic Action Workshop) and finally the mappings of *IMC/Indymedia Estrecho*. The practices, in particular, their acts of representation and visual cultures, are *tactical practices of creative dissent*. Tactical practices here include political art, art activism, collaborative art and direct actions of civil disobedience; such specific artistic networks manifest in a process of interaction between a multitude of actors and spaces within the city. By drawing on ideas of tactical media, these practices suggest possible expansions of the notion about what a social architecture driven by involvement and grassroots participation could be. This will include collaborative art projects being organized at the intersection between public art and new social movements (NSM).[3] The focus will be on the depiction of these projects as conflicts, reactions and responses, namely their dissenting relation to urban processes of urban regeneration, gentrification and privatization. In the process, the questions asked here are: Which modes of action are in operation? What tactics are being used by these artistic practices in an attempt to reveal and subvert the structures of power and processes of gentrification?

A closer examination of these modes of action and the ways of working developed by certain collaborative art projects, social movements and direct actions, will not only trace a shift in the role of artistic work but it might also offer some insight into the tools and tactics that could be introduced to resist the deleterious effects of these contemporary models of urban development. The role of artists as social and spatial instigators in these processes could show us other possibilities of understanding urban space and architecture from a social and participative perspective beyond the traditional ways of how to approach, respond to and create urban change.

---

3   The term new social movements (NSM) indicates a heterogeneous range of collectives that include anti-militarist, anti-authoritarian, autonomous groups, ecologists, human rights and women's rights groups, as well as many other groups opposing neoliberal politics.

DIRECT ACTION, CAMPS AND
COMMUNICATION SPACE

In order to understand some of the background as well as the tactics used today in the recent *15M*[4] mass mobilizations throughout Spain in 2011, it is perhaps important to mention the *V de Vivienda* (H for Housing)[5] campaign that started five years earlier. In May 2006, an anonymous email message was sent around Madrid, calling for a spontaneous sit-in. Following the massive turnout and success of the action, the *Assembly for Housing and against Precarity* (*V de Vivienda*) was created (Figure 18.2). Its purpose was to articulate the struggle for the right to access decent housing and work, and it operated under a slogan that countered precariousness and specu-lation: 'Housing is a right and not a business.' This local grassroots campaign has acquired a significant political role, becoming part of a larger social movement. Social networks, connecting groups and individuals – using direct action, demonstrations, assemblies, work-shops, public talks, open-air screenings, photographic campaigns and performances – have been rapidly organized in order to make visible the existing conflicts and housing situation. These actions function as a political platform creating a heterogeneous and diverse multitude with no political party behind them, reclaiming the streets as a common space for direct representation.

---

4   15M is shorthand for the demonstration that took place on 15 May 2011, in which thousands of people participated in a march against public health cuts, convened by a platform of the indignant and outraged, including collectives in favour of the right to decent housing and families under threat of eviction, workers, students and university workers in protest against cuts in higher education. The demonstration developed into an open-air camp in Plaza Catalonia, at the centre of Barcelona, in parallel to the simultaneous demonstrations and outdoor camps in Plaza del Sol in Madrid and similar activities in other Spanish towns. This was organized and coordinated through social media, especially on Twitter: see #yeswecamp, #spanishrevolution, #acampadas and other blogs: www.yeswecamp.net/ (accessed 10 June 2011).

5   See http://www.sindominio.net/v/ (accessed 20 April 2011).

Figure 18.2 Sentada, V de vivienda/sit-in, in the campaign V de Vivienda, Barcelona, 2006
Photo: Oriana Eliçabe

Realidades Avanzadas[6] (Advanced Realities) was an artistic project that developed as part of the social movement around *V de Vivienda*. This project had its origins in a film, a mixture of fiction and candid camera footage, that revealed the intertwined relationship between developers and financial institutions. Made available via You-Tube, La Caixa (one of the largest banks in Catalonia) raised a legal challenge to the film and it was quickly censored, citing the reason as breach of copyright laws. The film's withdrawal by YouTube led to massive protests and wide dissemination through alternative websites in Spain. This gave rise to a series of performances and public events, resulting in another film, an election, and a call to create a world record – a public mass shout out for the right to housing. The performance was carried out in the public spaces of Barcelona, which transformed the symbolic square of Plaça St Jaume[7] into an interactive theatre stage and a space of protest. The performance was like a television show, in which a moderator organized the audience to perform a collective public 'loud shout', which was measured on an interactive 'shout-meter'. The project was initiated by *Teatro Conservas*[8] in collaboration with the *Enmedio*[9] art and activist collective

6   See https://conservas.tk/?s=Realidades+Avanzadas&submit=Buscar (accessed 20 April 2011).

7   The square Plaza St Jaime, in Spanish, and the more commonly used Catalan name for the square: Plaça St Jaume, is the main square in Barcelona, the symbolic heart of political power in Catalonia as well as the seat of the regional government of Catalonia and the regional delegation of the Spanish Government.

8   *Teatro Conservas*, a theatre located in Barcelona, produces performances, festivals, media acts and public events. See http://conservas.tk/ (accessed 20 April 2011).

9   *Enmedio* is a Spanish artist-activist collective and social platform working with art projects and interventions in public space; their projects explore ways of using art as a tool of social transformation and collective performances. See www.enmedio.info (accessed 20 April 2011).

and members of the former collective *Las Agencias*.[10] These actions were intended as media events and explored the means of making an impact on public debate as well as functioning as catalysts for wider social and cultural processes.

Thousands of people have continued to claim the right to adequate housing and the *V de Vivienda* campaign has established a network of actions and a visual campaign across various cities in Spain. Some of these tactics can be found in the *15M* movement demonstrations and *acampadas*.[11] These open-air camps serve as examples of decentralization and coordination to generate a shared identity via symbolic membership of an anonymous political community, while challenging the traditional forms of political representation. As a result of their fast, fluid positioning and temporality, assemblies in the squares and open-air camps are increasingly transforming the way we think about and make built environments.[12] Through new ways of organizing and structuring space starting with social processes, direct democracy, new ways of communication and collective participation in the construction of these urban spaces, they also become an early indicator of mobility and political flux, mapping a local and global political landscape.

COLLABORATIVE PRACTICES OF SELF-REPRESENTATION

The eviction statistics in Spain are shocking. Since 2007, some 400,000 families have lost their houses. In 2012 alone, there were 532 evictions per day. *TAF!, Taller de Acción Fotográfica*,[13] the

10   Established in 2000, the collective Las Agencias emerged out of a series of open workshops as part of a programme of events at MACBA, the Contemporary Art Museum of Barcelona. In the first year of activity, these permanent public workshops produced more than twenty projects, fourteen tactical workshops and five longer-term projects. The workspace also hosted the headquarters of the anti-World Bank Summit Campaign (2001) and Indymedia Barcelona. From these tactical workshops emerged various art-activism projects. The aim was the construction of images of the activists by the activists themselves, functioning as counter-images to the prevailing representations of activists spread by the corporate mass media.

11   *Acampadas* is a Spanish word and means open-air/outdoor camps and camping. It has also become the name defining the movement of recent occupations of public squares in Spain. See http://acampadabcn.wordpress.com/ (accessed 2 November 2011).

12   Charlie Hailey, in *Camps: A Guide to 21st-Century Space* (2009) examines the space and idea of the camp as a typology and defining dimension of twenty-first-century life that register the struggles, emergencies and possibilities of global existence.

13   Orianomada: www.orianomada.net/en/taf/ with Enmedio: www.enmedio.info/taf/ (accessed 27 March 2014).

photographic action workshop, uses photography as a tool for social change and direct intervention in public space. *TAF!* gives a face to these statistics through the use of photography and defines images as a tool of social transformation. The projects aim to empower people affected by the crisis and to create a strong media impact, particularly by using social media for dissemination. The project in collaboration between *TAF!* and with PAH (*Plataforma de Afectados por la Hipoteca,* the Platform of People Affected by the Mortgage Crisis), a broad social movement of people who have been or are on the point of being evicted from their homes, have made a strong impact in Barcelona and Spain through the use of social media. *TAF!* take portraits of the people being evicted, makes giant prints and then pastes those 'giant[phot]ographies' on the façades of the banks that are behind the forced evictions (Figure 18.3). This has two positive outcomes: on one hand, a process of organization and empowerment of those who are affected – the people being evicted; and, on the other, it is a way of achieving a strong media impact, publicly pointing out those who are responsible for so much misery: the banks.

Figure 18.3 Retratos fotográficos contra los desahucios de Calatunya Caixa/Portraits against the evictions by Caixa Catalunya, by *TAF!, Taller de Acción Fotográfica* / the photographic action workshop, in collaboration with PAH, the platform of people affected by the mortgage crisis, Barcelona, 2012
Photo: Oriana Eliçabe

The *TAF!* workshops are initiated by Oriana Eliçabe; she has lived and worked as a freelance photographer in Barcelona, since 1999, and was born in Buenos Aires. Eliçabe began her photographic career working in Chiapas, documenting over many years the struggles of the Zapatistas peasant movement in Mexico. She describes her work as a way of 'striving to provoke in others the desire for collaboration, in as much as solidarity, this is the intention of my work – to take part in social processes and collective practices'.[14] Her work focuses on photojournalistic projects and documentary photography that describe alternative stories of our times, exploring processes of social and political transformation, through narratives of everyday life, people and places. She is part of the artist collective *Enmedio*, that has taken part in several projects in the right to the city movement in Barcelona, *V de Vivienda*, the '*13M*' and the '*15M-Movement*', and worked with other artist collectives intervening in social processes. In a public interview the collective describes their mode of working as a way of 'interrupting the dominant narrative'. They explain:

> *Working with photographs and, in collaboration with PAH, we wanted to reverse the dehumanized and victim-like portrayals of people affected by foreclosure that the media puts out … These photographic interventions work in two ways. On the one hand, they empower the affected. They come to the workshop, they pose, see their photographs, then they are pasted up on the banks, and like this we break the wall of shame, they create a presence in public space. On the other hand, it's guerrilla imagery in the struggle between different depictions of the crisis, the day-to-day battle held on the walls of the cities, associating a face with the organization responsible for the foreclosure (foreclosures are often talked about in the media, but they never mention the names of the banks). The interruption of the dominant narrative to create our own is the sort of politics we're interested in.*[15]

---

14   Orianómada: www.7punt7.net (accessed 10 December 2012).

15   Interview by Amador Fernández-Savater with *Colectivo Enmedio*, 'The Interruption of the Dominant Narrative – an interview with Colectivo Enmedio', available at: http://guerrillatranslation. com/2013/06/23/the-interruption-of-the-dominant-narrative-an-interview-with-colectivo-enmedio/ Translated by Stacco Troncoso, edited by Jane Loes Lipton as 'Guerrilla Translation!', 23 June 2013 (accessed 27 March 2014).

The Mediterranean coastline and the straits of Gibraltar are a territory that mirrors global transformations taking place in the world today, showing the practice and results of globalization, migrations, border zones, informal settlements, illegal trafficking and technologies of surveillance and zones of low-intensity warfare. It forms a geographical area of transition, between Africa and Europe, the Mediterranean and the Atlantic. Today, this place plays a strategic role and performs the role of a physical and mental barrier, a fold line that splits our world into two parts, of legalities and illegalities.[16] Freedom of communication and distribution of knowledge have become the focus of various projects, meetings and initiatives, and these ideas have proven essential to recent protests and the development of new social movements.[17] One of the aims of establishing *IMC/Indymedia Estrecho* (referring to Estrecho de Gibraltar, the straits of Gibraltar)[18] was to use the technologies of connectivity in the production of this space and territory. It was also one of the catalysts in establishing a social movement, actions and projects around the border zone of the straits of Gibraltar. The aim was to construct a new territory, connecting both sides of the straits, known in Morocco as Madiaq.

Meetings and workshops were held by *Indymedia Estrecho* in Tangiers, Larache and Al Hoceima, to establish a platform that would facilitate communication between movements in solidarity with refugees and to spread information on human rights, asylum and border patrols, thus simplifying collaboration. The project *Fadaiat*,[19] organized by various art and activist collectives in collaboration with *IMC Estrecho*, was a series of open-air hacktivist (= hacker + activist) meetings and workshops on the themes of new media, cartographies and copyleft, i.e. allowing the right to freely distribute copies and

---

16   Since 1990, the Spanish Government has been part of the Schengen Agreement, which created the notion of a borderless European Area that operates as one state, with border controls for travel into and out of the area. As a consequence, the border area around the straits of Gibraltar and Tarifa has systematically been upgraded to become one of the most controlled borders in the world.

17   The free culture movement is an international social movement that defends the rights of freedom to produce, consume, share and modify digital and other cultural artefacts and knowledge. The use of social media in free cultural (art and media) activism takes on a range of online and offline forms, including: protests, alternative forums, seminars, workshops and social media such as Twitter, Facebook, YouTube, Vimeo, blogs and wikis.

18   Established in the midst of the global campaign against the Iraq War in March 2003, the media network, IMC Estrecho, was initiated in Seville to cover the geographical border zone of the straits of Gibraltar. Other cities and networks that are part of the project are Jerez, Malaga and Granada in Spain.

19   See https://leanbytes.co.uk/articles/fadaiat/ (accessed 20 April 2011).

modified versions of other people's work, but conditional on the same rights being preserved in later derivative works. The aim was to create a project that could transcend the physical boundaries of the straits and create a communicative space that could overcome language differences. The workshops were intended not only as a tool for alternative information (or counter-information), but also as an actual place of bio-political resistance and production. This proposed a new geography – a territory of networks, responses, actions and events, a mediated and constructed cartography that exists between geo-localities, and wider communication and media spaces.

TACTICAL MEDIA PRACTICES

These artistic projects, actions and networks may be defined as 'tactical practices' because they act as parallels to the use of the broader notion of tactical media in new social movements. These specific tactical practices are concerned with the process of creative production, relying as they do on interaction with, and subversion of, existing structures of control over the production and distribution of culture. Through such strategies, the use of new media not only offers opportunities for re-mixing and re-appropriating mainstream culture, but also for redistributing culture and developing new models of urban spatial action.

In an essay entitled 'The ABC of tactical media', David Garcia and Geert Lovink offer a theoretical distinction between tactical media and alternative media programmes from the 1960s and 1970s, suggesting that the former involves 'a class of producers' who seem uniquely aware of the value of these temporary reversals in the flow of power. And rather than resisting these rebellions, they do everything in their power to amplify them, and indeed make the creation of spaces, channels and platforms for these reversals central to their practice.[20]

Developing this notion further, Garcia and Lovink make reference to the analyses of Michel de Certeau in *The Practice of Everyday Life*, which define popular culture not as 'a domain of texts or artefacts but rather as a set of practices or operations performed

---

20   David Garcia and Geert Lovink, 'The ABC of tactical media', in the introduction to the event Next 5 Min, at the De Waag, Amsterdam, September 2003. A manifesto was written for the opening of the website of the Tactical Media Network, hosted by De Waag, the Society for Old and New Media. It was first distributed via Nettime in 1997. Available at: http://project.waag.org/tmn/main.html (accessed 20 April 2011).

on textual or text-like structures'.[21] A change therefore occurs here between what de Certeau calls 'the emphasis from representations in their own right to the "uses" of representations'.[22] In relation to this, Garcia and Lovink ask:

> How do we, as consumers, use the texts and artefacts that surround us? And the answer he [de Certeau] suggested was 'tactically,' or: in far more creative and rebellious ways than had previously been imagined. He described the process of consumption as a set of tactics by which the weak make use of the strong. He characterized the rebellious user (a term he preferred to consumer) as tactical and the presumptuous producer (in which he included authors, educators, curators and revolutionaries) as strategic.[23]

By establishing this dichotomy between the user and the consumer, de Certeau was able to develop a vast and comprehensive language of tactics, allowing him also to create a distinctive and recognizable aesthetic for such events. There are now many other definitions for tactical media, with, for example, Sandra Braman's contribution to *The Virtual Case Book Project* providing an in-depth overview that suggests

> [They] might be defined in both narrow and general terms: the narrow definition refers to the non-ideological, aesthetic, and humorous use of digital media as content. More generally, 'tactical media' may be used as an umbrella term to cover all four types of alternative media as they appear in the 21st century.[24]

Braman also points out the etymology of the word 'tactical' since, according to original military usage, tactics are short-term actions taken in pursuit of long-term strategies, which have been designed in accordance with doctrine or overarching principles.

Notwithstanding this wide range of definitions, and the diversity of those involved in producing them, the breadth of tactics and strate-

---

21   Quoting Michel de Certeau in *The Practice of Everyday Life*, in Garcia and Lovink (2003: 1).

22   Garcia and Lovink, (2003: 2).

23   Ibid.: 2.

24   Sandra Braman, 'Defining tactical media: an historical overview'.

gies that may be used in tactical media suggests a further relevance to practices using media and digital technology. My argument is that these tactics and strategies have been, and are being, deployed within artistic practices in a variety of fields. *The Handbook of the Communication Guerrilla,* as an example, has had as strong an impact on the development of tactical media as on tactical artistic practices.[25] As a strategic handbook, it describes the basic principles, methods, techniques, practices, groups and actions that can be used to intervene in social processes of communication. The range of examples in the book has broadened our understanding and definition of communication, not only by making reference to mass media, but also by the understanding of 'face-to-face communication' of everyday life.

AR/CTIVISM: NETWORKS OF TACTICAL PRACTICES

The redefinition of art activism practices as tactical practices, proposed here in relation to mass mobilizations and recent protests in new social movements, may be thought of as a shift in the creative process. The focus is not so much on the 'artwork', 'piece' or 'object', but on the tools, tactics and modes of working. Hence, the 'artwork' is understood to be *the social and cultural processes and social and political spaces generated, and the objects, or pieces of art produced, acquire meaning only when used or experienced.*

Here, creative processes and artworks are defined as part of networks, and these networks, by extension, as political subjects; indeed, the notion of the crowd, as seen in the writings of Hardt and Negri,[26] refers to a new political subject which is composed of multiple, independent and diverse agents, as a multitude of networks, interconnected by a net and able to produce creative convergences in specific circumstances. These artistic practices of activism, collaborative art projects and direct actions of civil disobedience also suggest a notable shift in the role of the artist. In this definition, the artist becomes a cultural producer – a political subject, a social and spatial instigator and a node within local and global social networks.

25   Blisset and Bruntzells (2000).

26   See Hardt and Negri (2000).

ACKNOWLEDGEMENTS

I would like to thank the members, from the various collectives mentioned, for their input and shared discussions. A special thank you for generously allowing me use their material: to photographer Oriana Eliçabe for her photographs, and to Pablo de Soto, Osfa/Jose Perez de Lama, Hackitectura and Fadaiat, for the maps/cartographic material, and to all the members of the Enmedio collective for their contributions. I am also grateful for input and ideas to Oriana Eliçabe, Leónidas Martín Saura, Mario Ortega and Anja Steidinger.

REFERENCES

Blisset, L. and Bruntzells. S. (2000) 'a.f.r.i.k.a.', in *Manual de Guerrilla de la Comunicación*, in the German edition, Berlin: Verlag Libertäre Assoziation (VLA), Verlag der Buchläden Schwärze Risse-Rote Strasse. Translated into Spanish, Barcelona: Virus Editorial Aurora, 2000.

Braman, Sandra (n.d.) 'Defining tactical media: an historical overview', in Barbara Abrash and Faye Ginsburg (eds) *The Virtual Case Book Project*. Available at: www.nyu.edu/fas/projects/vcb/definingTM_list.html (accessed 20 April 2011).

Garcia, David and Lovink, Geert (2003) 'The ABC of tactical media', in the introduction to the event, Next 5 Min, at the De Waag, Amsterdam, September.

Hailey, C. (2009) *Camps: A Guide to 21st-Century Space*, Cambridge, MA: MIT Press.

Hardt, M. and Negri, A. (2000) *Empire*, Cambridge, MA: Harvard University Press.

FURTHER READING

Betancour, A. (2006, 2008, 2012, 2013 and 2014) Various interviews with Oriana Eliçabe.
(2011) Interview with Ana Betancour, in M. Ericson and R. Mazé (eds) *DESIGN ACT, Socially and Politically Engaged Design Today: Critical Roles and Emerging Tactics*, Berlin: Sternberg Press.
(2012) 'Ar/ctivism', in C. Widenheim *et al.* (eds) *Work, Work, Work: A Reader on Art and Labour*, Berlin: Sternberg Press.

Blancop, P. *et al.* (eds) (2001) *Modos de Hacer, Arte crítico, esfera pública y acción directa*, Salamanca: Ediciones Universidad de Salamanca.

Boyd, A. and Mitchell, D.O. (eds) (2012) *Beautiful Trouble: A Toolbox for Revolution*, London: OR Books.

Caballero Roldán, T. (2009) 'Orianómada: Det fotoperiodismo and activism fotográfico global. La fotografía Oriana Eliçabe', in *Yuokali: Revista critica de las artes y el pensamiento*, 7, Estéticas de la Resistencia, Madrid: Tierradenadie ediciones.

Fernández-Savater, A. (2011) 'Estamos cansados de mirar, y hoy queremos vivir la imagen', interview with Leónidas Martín Saura, *Opiníon*, available at: www.Público.es (accessed 2 December 2011).

   (2013) 'Interrumpir el relato dominante y crear nuestro propio relato es la política que nos interesa', interview with the Enmedio collective, *Interferencias*, available at: www.El Diario.es. (accessed 6 July 2013).

Hamm, M. (2005) 'Ar/ctivismo en espasios físicos y virtuales', in D. Corbeira and M. Expósito (eds) *Brumaria no 5*, Madrid: Asociación cultural Bramania. Holmes, B. (2005) 'Estéticas de la igualdad', in D. Corbeira and M. Expósito (eds) *Brumaria no 5*, Madrid: Asociación cultural Bramania.

Monsell Prado, P. and De Soto Suárez, P. (2006) *Fadaiat: libertad de movimiento + libertad de conocimiento,* Barcelona: Fadaiat, Observatorio Tecnológico del Estrecho.

Pasquinelli, M. (2008) *Animal Spirits: A Bestiary of the Commons*, Rotterdam: NAi Publishers / Institute of Network Cultures.

Perez de Lama, J. and De Soto Suárez, P. (2005) 'Ar/ctivismo en espasios físicos y virtuales', in D. Corbeira and M. Expósito (eds) *Brumaria no 5*, Madrid: Asociación cultural Bramania. Ramírez Blanco, J. (2014)

Utopías artísticas de revuelta, Madrid: Cátedra.

Steidinger, A. (2013) 'Auto-representaciones del malestar', PhD thesis, Universitat de Barcelona, Barcelona.

Thompson, N. and Sholette, G. (eds) (2004) *The Interventionists: Users' Manual for the Creative Disruption of Everyday Life*, Cambridge, MA: MASS MoCA.

Yomango (2002) 'De las acciones a la Guerilla Manqueting', in D. Corbeira, and M. Expósito (eds) *Brumaria no 3*, Madrid: Asociación cultural Bramania.

19 – IN ACTION: SEARCHING FOR THE IN-BETWEEN CITY

Alex Axinte and Cristi Borcan (studioBASAR)

In a conference held at the University of Edinburgh, Bruno Latour gave a speech about 'progressive knowledge' that needs an 'accumulation of narratives'. He described it as 'loops' to run over, making you 'feel the consequences of your action before being able to represent yourself as having an action' (Latour, 2013). As this accumulation of loops adds up, the understanding of the place becomes more relevant.

From this perspective, studioBASAR's work in recent years could be perceived as looping around the topic of public space and its daily manifestations, in an action-based approach. This wasn't a process planned from the beginning, but it developed as a 'slow operation' (ibid.) that was driven by curiosity and naïvety, in a sort of stubbornness to understand and to adapt to the continuously changing Romanian public space.

The communist system in Romania increasingly exerted control over its inhabitants, a condition that became worse in the final years, before its brutal collapse in 1989. After decades of an atmosphere of fear and scarcity, society was reduced to a population who lived on a day-by-day basis. While communism seemed eternal, the everyday was the only space where people could breathe normally. After the fall of communism, in post-socialist Romania, to take action on your own felt liberating. Romanians rediscovered the appeal of action in public space, in politics and the civil society, in the economy, in the media or in culture. The city was recovering from the long period of standardization and top-down control. Still bleeding after the demolitions and restructuring which it endured in the 1980s, Bucharest burst into a revitalizing explosion of individuals' interventions in the built environment. Although such manifestations were present before and were almost subversive, after the fall of communism, everybody became an owner and was free to act in his or her own interests. It was not only individuals who had the chance to take these opportunities, but also private investors who took advantage of the lax areas in both the legislation and the city fabric. The city administration emphasized its role as the administrator of the public domain and started to transform the public space, often acting like a private entity (Figure 19.1). Amidst this turmoil, public space in Romanian cities

went from one extreme to another: from commercialization to deco-
ration and towards complete extinction under the sum of individual
users' actions.

Figure 19.1 The Palace of Parliament (formerly the House of the People) seen from Union Boulevard
(formerly the Victory of Socialism Boulevard), Bucharest, Romania, 2012
Photo: studioBASAR

Our interest in public space came from our own situation,
growing up professionally in the middle of the 'transformation' from
a communist, totalitarian society into a capitalist and supposedly
more democratic one. In these times public space, in its spatial and
social dimensions, has functioned as a kind of barometer, recording
Romanian society's turmoil in the past 25 years.

Before 1989, public space in Romania was said to be everyone's
and was owned by 'the people'. It was, in fact, state-controlled and,
as such, excluded any free, personal manifestations and took advantage of the users' own self-control to police their behaviour. Public
space was a politically and socially empty space, an impersonal
and representational territory, in which the power of the system was
exerted over the people in a concrete form. After the fall of communism, in contrast, public space became accessible to the people
as a common good, but it wasn't necessarily a good to share and

inhabit collectively, but was an open and free resource to be used by anyone in their own interest. Reflecting larger processes taking place in post-communist society, the public good that before the revolution was defined as top-down ceased to exist, and was dismantled by individuals' actions, such as the privatization of the public infrastructure or making certain areas exclusive.

Being 'in action on your own' became a practice enjoyed by everyone, including architects, who no longer worked for the (impersonal) state but for individual clients. After the era of 'grand gestures' that shaped the Romanian cities, towns and some villages was over, a time of 'small adaptations' followed. We were engaged in these processes, acting as architects and small-scale urban activators. By employing tactics, like the individual users' actions (defined by de Certeau as 'an art of the weak' (1997)), we could enter the current pattern of the transformation and occupation of public space through a series of micro-urbanism actions. Using minimum means and sometimes crossing the limits of legality, working in the 'space of the other' (ibid.: 3) and being opportunistic, subjective and basic, these 'calculated actions' (ibid.: 3), unlike the privatization drive followed by most of the individual users, *we were aiming to make places that are open and inclusive, flexible and reversible*. To achieve such a transformation, we used design components as a catalyst for change. We identified micro-problems that were highly representative of the whole city and constructed possible solutions to them on the spot. These were thus action-based design processes, which grew from the local condition that tested first, and theorized second.

This process involved a post-intervention 'zooming out', where lessons learned from the previous actions were progressively applied to the next ones. It was in these kinds of 'loops' that Latour spoke about, that we also discovered similar practices coming from different contexts, particularly Western Europe. These groups, who also practised forms of temporary urbanism, were both an inspiration for us in working with public space as 'a place for social interaction' (Lefebvre, 1991), but were also a constant reminder of the differences between historical or social, local contexts of such interventions. Being involved in projects that developed precisely in their contexts, such as 'Urban Spaces in Action'[1] was a step we took to develop a more 'participatory action research' approach to practising in Bucharest. In this project, the research phase precedes the action, seeking

---

1   A project coordinated by Komunitas Association, Bucharest, 2014–2015, see www.spatii-urbane.ro

to understand first the conditions – i.e. the community inhabiting the large socialist ensembles of blocks of flats – followed by actions that aim to involve some local agents in changing their environment.

Bucharest is a city in an almost continuous 'in-between' condition, born from a long history of never-ending transitions and intermediary moments that lasted long enough to leave their mark on its urban spaces and on the everyday habits of its people. The city works as a collection of superimposing contradictions and fractures that are negotiated in these intermediary zones, which criss-cross the city at every level: spatial, institutional and social. These boundaries and the interstices that structure Bucharest function as 'breathing spaces' for the city. These are rich territories where uncertainty reigns and where different uses and groups intersect and overlap. Such in-between spaces and their added uses are threatened by extinction, through privatization and exclusion executed not only by the city administration or by investors, but also by individual users' actions. Parking on the pavement, fencing the lawn in front of your flat, or extending your ground floor apartment are all expressions of the transformation of public space into a resource for personal use.

This is the context of our work, which engages Bucharest's in-between condition and manifests itself through self-formulated, elastic solutions. As so-called specialists in the built environment, fresh out of architecture school, we soon realized that we did not have adequate tools to understand what was going on in the city around us. The 'classical' professional tools that we were equipped with, such as the site analysis through historical plans, aerial views, street fronts or drawings and abstract models, namely, methods of objectifying urban phenomenon, were useless when one wanted to engage with people and the city's life.

We found that outside our discipline, in literature, cinema or contemporary art, for example, people were examining, documenting or directly recording the rhythms of the everyday. Urban anthropology and sociology too contributed new subjects and methods to understand the city. Given the nature of the studied object – the manifestations of everyday life – subjectivity is necessary as an examination and assessment tool. Without going so far as to develop a strategic approach to an urbanism of the everyday, we devised instead tactics of adaptation to the environment, and took Bucharest as both a laboratory and a playground.

While Bucharest does not have a unique profile among other cities, its current state makes it a good case study of what we can call the 'in-between' condition of public space: an intermediary state that

swings between regulated and contested, privatized or hacked, suffocated everywhere, yet re-produced spontaneously. This in-between
public space is paradoxically both defined by individuals' actions
and, at the same time, by the uncontrolled and entangled rules and
regulations of the public domain. This phenomenon takes place in the
middle of increasing commercialization, of both physical space and
people's behaviours. We started an 'action-based research' approach
to practice, documenting and formulating the city's operating
paradigm, followed by identifying and addressing the potential that
resulted from it. Walking the streets and looking at the city, observing
behaviours, engaging in ad-hoc conversations and participating in the
everyday city, we could identify patterns that arose from case studies
which we documented and archived in narratives, drawings, photos
and texts. We recorded the transformations generated by the actions
of micro-urbanism, and were able to both draw conclusions and
formulate projections about the relationship between users and their
public spaces. It was this praxis that for us turned Bucharest from an
object of study into a subject of work. From an observation tool, the
research became a means of concrete transformation of public space
through live actions.

   Our analyses of urban contexts consisted of introducing
emerging elements that were capable of provoking existing usages
and habits. These interventions were set up in different typologies of
spaces, from residual territories to non-conflict locations, and from
highly visible areas in the city, to more obscure or contested sites.
Their temporary and transitory existence, with a lifespan ranging from
a couple of hours to several years, was augmented by the impact of
these interventions, which varied from the symbolic presence of an
installation to the permanent transformation of the context in which
the intervention was located. Due to their capacity to produce not just
objects, but 'construct situations' (Debord, 1957: 8), these actions
and interventions were connected to Situationist thought and approaches. We became aware of this connection in the post-scriptum
stages of some of the more complex projects, when the developing
process could be read as a practice of applied Situationism. These
constructions were generating 'emotionally moving situations rather
than emotionally moving forms' (ibid.: 8), and were producing changes in the use of public spaces.

   The following case studies from our practice are important to us,
as they illustrate several typologies developed through our practice.
Having the 'in-between' condition of the city as a frame, each of them
has a different relationship with it. The *Letter Bench* deals with the

intermediary status of a place, an in-between location with unclear and flexible limits. The *Public Bath* works within the in-between time, in a street festival, that suspends the everyday rules of the city and creates an intermediary moment. The workshops programme aims to bridge the existing gap between formal education and experience, thus working in between pedagogy and practice. The final project presented here was developed in Sinaia, where we attempted to regenerate a community, a project that has placed us as architects in an in-between position in the middle of the inhabitants, the administration and the local organizations.

PUBLIC SPACE GENERATOR: THE PUBLIC BATH

In 2012, we contributed to the *Street Delivery* festival, an annual three-day event in the centre of Bucharest that, since it started in 2006, 'temporarily closes the street for cars and opens it for people'.[2] StudioBASAR's installation, the *Public Bath*, was an installation that acted like a possible utopia to evoke a one-to-one vision of the relationship between water and the city inhabitants in public (Figure 19.2). In Bucharest, bathing in the river and lakes is forbidden, and therefore water in the city has lost the capacity to generate interaction and public life. Distanced from its users, water is now only used for aesthetic reasons or, when it is used, it is accessible only when paid for in aqua parks, spas and wellness centres. At the same time, the current alternative uses of streets, such as the one where the festival takes place, are the usual 'pedestrian zone' options, offering the same globally consecrated consumers' urban packages: shopping, strolling, eating and drinking. During the hot summer days of the festival we installed an unexpected bathing place that popped up in the middle of the street. A small team of volunteers constructed a 6m x 12m rectangular structure made of stacked, rented wooden pallets, directly on the asphalt of the road. As the water container, we used a blue banner, similar to the commercial ones that cover the façades of the buildings, imprinted with the city map. Water was poured in from the hoses of nearby gardens, instantly transforming the street into a splatter place, a meeting and a resting point, a stage for concerts and projections. Set out as a temporary area that allowed free and instant access to the water for anyone, it generated surprising dynamics among the users, such as the ad-hoc negotiation or cohabitation

------

2   http://2014.streetdelivery.ro/

between people who are normally segregated in the contemporary social life of Bucharest. Although a temporary installation, it turned the street into a diorama of how public space could work in Bucharest, as an inclusive, tolerant and joyful place, where locals from the neighbourhood and inhabitants of the city can share and negotiate a place together. At the end of the festival, the water was drained off, the pallets returned, the blue map folded up and stored away for future workshops, and the street became the dull parking place it was before. But for the participants, the impossible had already happened, proving that small and short-lived structures can also make the city.

Figure 19.2 The Public Bath – temporary installation, Arthur Verona Street, Bucharest, 2012
Photo: studioBASAR

Over the years we have practised this type of public intervention in the local context of Bucharest and elsewhere. Designed as basic public space generators and having a high capacity to instantly transform the site, these fast action tools proved in some cases to be 'too ephemeral' for their given contexts. Such an event structure can activate, in the short term, a more generic, representative or even central public space in the framework of a festival, and can reveal the social structure of the city at that specific moment; however, it doesn't work as well in the public spaces of proximity – the physical and social space of a community, where a slower approach is required, with lasting effects and higher survival prospects. It is in these locations that we developed a different type of intervention, one that was more infrastructural and less 'connected to an event', which worked as public equipment.

PUBLIC EQUIPMENT: THE LETTER BENCH

In the same context of the *Street Delivery* festival in 2009, we proposed something that we hoped would function after the event finished, even if it were only to be just a bench. Built in front of Cărturesti bookshop, the linear bench was set as a reversible intervention, placed on the uncertain limit between an inaccessible green space and an alley used for car access and as an informal parking area. During the festival the structure was instantly used as a seating, meeting and chatting place. These may seem rather banal functions, but seen in the wider geography of the area, the bench provoked a shift in the use of public space. In this context public space practically is non-existent: the space between buildings is suffocated by traffic and cars parked everywhere. Due to the non-conflictual nature of its placing on a threshold, an uncertain legislative crack, belonging neither to the green area, nor to the alley, the authorities didn't notice it and the two irreconcilable parts, cars and pedestrians, coexisted peacefully for the next year. After 2010, the municipality refurbished the alley, leaving the bench untouched, probably again due to its placement on the limit of the jurisdiction.[3] Subsequent to this rehabilitation, the architect Şerban Sturdza placed a series of concrete seating benches, which made it difficult, if not impossible, for cars to park in the alley. Therefore, partly negotiated on site, a public space emerged as the result of a situation constructed in time, through consecutive actions of taming and accommodation. Thus, without being fully adopted by the local users in terms of caring, maintaining or repairing it, the bench was accepted as a familiar part of the context, harbouring a wide range of users, from everyday passers-by, bookshop visitors, local inhabitants, to street vendors and homeless people using it as a place to sleep.

We started to increase its chances of long-term survival, by protecting it with paper glued on and we even replaced some of the boards. This new layer of the bench encouraged spontaneous add-ons of stickers and posters, transforming it into a 'bench of letters', a live palimpsest with a changing skin, always new, but at the same

---

3   In Bucharest, streets and green spaces are managed by different municipal services, in some case even by different municipalities.

time also quite ragged, therefore well camouflaged in the everyday Bucharest landscape (Figure 19.3). The bench is still going, and is now in its sixth year of life.

Figure 19.3 The Letter Bench' – public furniture, Arthur Verona Street, Bucharest, 2009
Photo: studioBASAR

Alongside the more durable, transformative capacity of public equipment, this also provides an implicit potential for analysis and observation of the environment. In some situations, the inadequacy of the solutions to the specificity of the place resulted in failure. In 2012, we were invited to activate an underground pedestrian passage in Tbilisi, Georgia, and we wrote the proposal before arriving there to actually view it. The installation aimed to transform the passage's derelict access by inserting a support structure to be used as public equipment for different uses: to rest, to sit and chat, or even to exhibit. What wasn't obvious via email proved to be the most important ingredient: the place was also used as an informal public toilet, and the support structure inserted there didn't discourage the cycle of drinking and loitering. Although it offered shelter to homeless people and was used as a seat for a drink, one year later, the structure has slowly decayed and disappeared and the site has returned to the previous state.

EDUCATION: PUBLIC SPACE WORKSHOPS

Since 2012, we have been involved in a different type of intervention: public space workshops, initiated at the invitation of small local organizations, artistic or student associations. The workshops are in fact a continuation of a more general intervention process adapted each time to a different urban context. These workshops are specifically marked by their interest in education and professional training. The education process supposes, at least in Romania, knowledge accumulation and testing or experimenting in laboratory-like conditions, remote from the studied object. This workshop series, however, is conceived as a live education process that takes place in real time, in tangible urban settings. The participants cover, in a condensed loop of time, the distance from concept to finished design. The workshops begin with a mapping of the area on foot, which aims to anchor the group to the site's daily pace. From the beginning, the group becomes aware of the organization, resources and planning production, set as the starting point of the 'paper workshop' which works in a condensed space of discussions, ideas, proposals and presentations. This process of 'indoor' design is quickly transferred outside, where a hands-on approach takes place on the very perimeter of the future intervention (Figure 19.4). The production itself is a suspended time between the initial projections and their live testing, a collective working place where the details set on paper are often improved by the reality of the material, where ad-hoc design is made possible, where use comes before aesthetics and where the work is done with one's own means. The final stage of the workshop is set as a public event where the interventions are inaugurated, testing the initial intentions in real time, as well as the organizational skills of the group. Beyond these tangible outcomes, other qualities are also important, such as training one's observation skills, the cohesion of the group, the practice in real time, the empowerment of the host organization or the ability of the participants to generate future projects and initiatives.[4]

---

4   One of the last workshops we were part of was organized by a student participant in a previous one.

Figure 19.4 'Spaces of Representation' – student workshop, Timişoara, 2013
Photo: studioBASAR

All of the above typologies and examples have in common a low level of user's involvement in the initial process that takes place on site. The people rather are attending these interventions, sometimes accepting and practising the proposed usages, producing and maintaining the public space, but nevertheless, they rarely become part of the organizational structure. This has to do either with the framework of the event, or its spatial context, if these interventions are in public spaces, without local users. This situation is also influenced by cultural aspects, if the installations are set in places that are too meaningless for the activators, and are time-sensitive and without any follow-up to make them permanent.

MAKING COMMUNITY: SINAIA

In 2011, we were invited by the Romanian Order of Architects, within the framework of their annual event, to organize a series of events hosted inside a temporary pavilion set in a public park in the city of Sinaia. By organizing workshops, walks, drafting a city map and discussing with local residents, we established contacts with local organizations, NGOs, volunteer associations, schools and individuals that in time became part of an ongoing process. The partnerships initiated at the first event continued to grow and to produce

independent projects over the next couple of years. We contributed,
with local partners, to several educational activities, wood workshops
and temporary outdoor events, involving the young people from the
city. From a workshop with local school children, focusing on several
problematic places in the city, one site emerged as a potential subject
for a future temporary intervention, and in 2013 a double event took
place here. We opened a former heating plant that at that time was
used only as an election room. We hosted community activities there,
like workshops, projections, lectures, exhibitions and talks, and built
a temporary amphitheatre on the nearby chosen site, organizing a
concert and children's games (Figure 19.5). Because it's a common
outdoor area for drying laundry, the site is one of the last open areas
of public space between the blocks of flats in this neighbourhood. For
a couple of days, the former heating centre worked as a temporary
community centre, where the participants and local people together
shared a space for the first time. In 2014, we started a consultation
process on possible future actions in the neighbourhood, which was
followed by a one-day event, again held in the former heating plant.
We are now planning further actions in the neighbourhood, trying to
involve locals and the administration as partners into the transformation of a public space in their neighbourhood.

Figure 19.5 'My Place Behind the Blocks' – community action, Sinaia, 2013
Photo: studioBASAR

CONCLUSION

Through our projects, we have grown a spatial practice based on action-based research of and in public space. It advances in successive loops that are slowly erasing the difference between theory and practice, research and action, process and object. In this kind of practice we have constantly been 'in action', making and producing things, constructing situations and at the same time searching for the 'in-between' condition of the city. Working beyond architectural layouts and formal designs, and working without clear commissions and fixed schedules has proved to be a permanent struggle in coping with failure and irrelevancy, dotted from time to time with small victories. Microscopically small victories, if we speak of the *Letter Bench* that transformed an alley, or victories that lasted just a blink of the eye, as was the case with the three-day *Public Bath*, in the suspended time-space of the city without cars. Having no visible and immediate results, the public space workshops are also having uncertain effects on architecture students, who, after one or two weeks of engaging in public space, go back to 'education as usual'. The projects in the community also demand indefinite endurance and commitment, like the project in Sinaia, for example, which, after more than two years of working in the neighbourhood, still has no clear outcome in sight. Working in the everyday city for some time has taught us that change is possible and action is its engine. After a gradual accumulation of experiences, after learning and practising, after testing and developing tools and formats, we have arrived at a point where we wish to ground our loops in a more stable format, more focused on Bucharest's problems and potential, seeking partnerships with the citizens, administration and public institutions. Embedded in local contexts, this type of spatial practice can become an 'in-between' practice which is working at the same time with the structure and the dynamics of public space, dealing not only with its physical appearance, but also with social and collective uses, towards the reconstruction of community.

REFERENCES

Debord, Guy (1957) 'Report on the construction of situations and on the International Situationist tendency's conditions of organization and action', available at: www.cddc.vt.edu/sionline/si/report.html (accessed 21 August 2015).

De Certeau, Michel (1997) *The Practice of Everyday Life*, Berkeley, CA: University of California Press.

Latour, Bruno (2013) 'The Anthropocene and the destruction of the image of the globe', lecture given at the University of Edinburgh, 1 March. Available at: www.youtube.com/watch?v=4-l6FQN4P1c (accessed 21 August 2015).

Lefebvre, Henri (1991) *Critique of Everyday Life*, London: Verso.

FURTHER READING

Chase, John, Crawford, Margaret and Kaliski, John (eds) (2008) *Everyday Urbanism*, expanded edn, New York: The Monacelli Press.

Ghenciulescu, Stefan (2008) *Transparent City: On Limits and Dwelling in Bucharest*, Bucharest: Editura Universitar 'Ion Mincu'.

Jacobs, Jane (1992) *The Death and Life of Great American Cities*, New York: Vintage Books.

Petcou, Constantin, Petrescu, Doina and Marchand, Nolwenn (eds) (2007) *Urban Act*, Paris: atelier d'architecture autogérée, aaa–PREPAV.

20 – WAYS TO BE PUBLIC

Rory Hyde

> [W]e don't assemble because we agree, look alike, feel good,
> are socially compatible or wish to fuse together but because we
> are brought by divisive matters of concern into some neutral,
> isolated place in order to come to some sort of provisional
> makeshift (dis)agreement.
> (Latour, 2005: 13)

1. SINA'S CAFÉ

In Belfast's Skegoneill neighbourhood lies a broad field of rubble,
overgrown with green grass and ringed by a security fence. The site
was once occupied by row houses, but subjected to arson, violence
and destruction, these have since been torn down by the local
council. It is what's known as an 'interface', an intentionally vacant
buffer zone, designed to diffuse tension between adjacent Catholic
and Protestant areas facing off against each other.

Within this zone of barely suppressed hostility sit two pale grey
shipping containers. One container has been adapted to form a
café and shop, with one of the long sides removed and fitted with
full-height timber-framed glazing. Set back some metres, Sina's Café
faces towards the road, creating a small space in front with a few
chickens pecking around (Figure 20.1). It was created by William
Haire, who purchased the land from the council, cleaned up the site
and designed the structure himself. I visited the café in late 2012,
and briefly quizzed Haire on his motivations. He has no grand political
manifesto, but simply arrives at 7 a.m., cleans off any graffiti that's
accrued during the night, and remains open – selling coffee, milk,
eggs – until 7 p.m., seven days a week. The glass wall exhibits the
contents and function of the building for all to see, and, importantly,
it equally allows Haire and Lucinda, the café manager, to see out
and survey the intersection. This transparency is not metaphorical,
but literally allows 'eyes on the street', as Jane Jacobs would say, the
simple power of a human presence.

Figure 20.1 Sina's Café, Skegoneill, Belfast
Photo: Rory Hyde

Whether Haire would acknowledge it or not, he is – to refer to the title of this volume – engaged in the *social (re)production of space*. His modest shop has re-cast the social customs which govern this territory, from that of fear and threat, to that of passivity and respect. This most basic of architectural gestures opens up a zone of mild ambition and potential, for two opposing faiths to briefly drop their prejudices. A space of gentle publicness is produced where none existed before.

This is achieved through various factors, of which the design of the building is only one. The political ambiguity of the enterprise plays an important factor: Haire doesn't make his allegiances explicit, forging neutral ground. The container's function as a shop is equally disarming, as even across vast differences and histories people can still agree on coffee, milk and eggs. The design of the container itself plays its part, and although it may have become a cliché of 'informality' in architectural circles, the use of a shipping container in this instance is central to the message of the project. It speaks of transience, of provisionality, of adaptability, the opposite of the monolithic and entrenched ideologies that continue to plague this city. All of these factors are what make up the architecture of Sina's Café. It is a *way to be public*.

The project, in Haire's words, is beguilingly simple:

The example I always use is when you see young fellas standing about on the corner and you think, he's dodgy with his hood up. But as soon as he comes into the shop and stands beside me, I can see that he's human. An older person comes in, they can see the wee hoody is human. The kid can see that the older person is human. They can hear us talking about school, children or football or anything. It's all about these wee connections, that make a really big difference.[1]

This project, and the others explored in this chapter, each offer strategies for the creation of public space. They offer various examples of how infrastructure, urbanism, architecture, and strategic design can create new *ways to be public*. 'Public', in this instance, is understood to mean common ground, an open and shared zone of collective dignity. It is related to democracy, in that it is not dictatorial or pre-determined from above, but produced by the people who comprise it. These spaces are civic in that they allow the capacity for generosity which is greater than the individual. Difference is maintained, not flattened. As the example of Sina's Café illustrates, the physical aspects of these spaces shouldn't be overstated. The concrete manifestation sits at the intersection of complex social and cultural systems. It is architecture which allows these factors to be embodied in space, and to be reproduced over time.

2. SABARMATI WATERFRONT, AHMEDABAD

On a radically different scale to that of Sina's Café is the redevelopment of the Sabarmati Waterfront in Ahmedabad, in the north-west Indian state of Gujarat. Infrastructural in scope, and decades in the making, it forges a new civic space where one couldn't exist before. Ahmedabad has grown up along the banks of the Sabarmati River. Once the lifeblood of the city, serving irrigation and agriculture, this river is also a poison, listed as one of the most polluted rivers in India. The expansion of Ahmedabad to a population of more than 6 million today pressed the city's marginalised inhabitants to the fringes, in particular to the banks of the Sabarmati. The river became home to thousands of squatters living in informal structures in great precarity,

---

1   Paul Bower, 'Interview with William Haire', conducted as part of doctoral research in-progress, 'Beyond "post-conflict" architecture' (2014).

with seasonal flooding leading to the destruction of dwellings and loss of life. This linear slum also deprived the residents of greater Ahmedabad of access to the waterfront, an ostensibly public space at the heart of the city's self-conception.

Plans for the redevelopment of the waterfront were first proposed in 1961, followed by a second proposal in 1976, led by local professional Hasmukh Patel. Work began in earnest in 1997 with the formation of the Sabarmati River Development Corporation Limited, with construction following shortly after. An epic project, of a scale and ambition comparable only to London's Thames Embankment of the 1860s, the redevelopment of the waterfront stretches 10km on each bank, costing hundreds of millions of dollars, and taking decades to complete. Bimal Patel, lead architect on the project and son of Hasmukh, says: 'I've been working on this project for 30 years, and I expect I'll be working on it for another 30.'

The project is largely one of land reclamation. The overall width of the river has been substantially reduced, bounded by a new hard concrete edge (Figures 20.2 and 20.3). Of the land created between this new edge and the old city, 28 per cent is for road development, 26 per cent for public gardens, and 22 per cent will be sold for com- mercial development to finance the project. The remainder comprises the infrastructure of retaining walls, stormwater outfalls, ghats, jetties and sewage management and treatment facilities.

Figures 20.2 (opposite page) and 20.3 Sabarmati Waterfront, Ahmedabad, Gujarat
Photos: Rory Hyde

What does it mean for a city to gain access to the waterfront for the first time? It offers a civic dignity, a space reconnected to the river, with space to meet and relax, outside of the increasingly constrained urban centre. It shifts the culture of a place, creating a new typology of urban experience, opening up the potential for new forms of collectivity. Sitting here in London, where we take such public promenades for granted, it's easy to dismiss this as a simple 'beautification' project, as creating a space for the middle classes to enjoy an evening stroll. Indeed, like London's Embankment, executed by Bazalgette in the nineteenth century, which cleared out the mixture of docks and warehouses and created an homogeneous hard edge, the Sabarmati redevelopment is about erasure as well as addition. The relocation of slum dwellers is not uncontroversial, their social networks are disrupted, as are their opportunities for work. Patel views this as a fair trade-off, that the creation of a public space for the whole city justifies their removal.

The top-down nature of this development throws into question the notions of spatial justice that this volume is predicated upon. The 'right to the city', as proposed by Henri Lefebvre, and more recently championed by David Harvey, demands 'the exercise of a collective power to reshape the processes of urbanisation' (Harvey, 2008). Can the Sabarmati Waterfront project be included within this rubric, or is it simply further evidence of the forces of capital and gentrification imposing development upon a disempowered public? Must 'public' architecture be produced by the public themselves? What role, then, for the urban professionals?

So-called 'community architecture' purports to be an alternative to this authoritative mode of design, whereby the architect acts as a mere conduit for the desires of the constituents. It is the people who steer the pen, the professional merely holds it. But what is lost when we ignore the training and experience of the architect? On this point, Jeremy Till cites the philosopher Gillian Rose, who memorably states that, in community design, 'It is the architect who is demoted; the people do not accede to power.'[2]

A project on such a scale as the Sabarmati Waterfront undeniably requires expert skills and training. Patel claims to apply his skills in the service of the public interest. But the 'public' in this instance, is necessarily incomplete, and excludes those members of the public living on the site who have been relocated. The architect as paternalistic figure, deciding what's best, is hard to avoid here. London's Embankment may have destroyed the old jetties of Westminster, but its sewage system cured it of cholera, just as Ahmedabad's new waterfront fortifies the city against flooding.

Arguments for the greater good are inherently slippery, who gets to decide whose interests to promote? Despite this, Patel and his team have attempted to ensure this area of the city retains some of its diversity. The architects produced large-scale renderings of the proposal and exhibited them on the site. Care was taken to make the images believable, showing people in local dress, and including those normally excluded from the developer's imagery, such as hawkers and beggars. While the architectural rendering rarely corresponds with the built reality, it is useful in revealing its creators' aspirations. By depicting people from all levels of society, the aspiration here is for an inclusive public space.

In this instance, space is 'produced' not when the architect draws the retaining wall, but when the public inhabit the promenade. With the first section of the Waterfront recently launched, the public are now moving in, using and misusing it for their own purposes. The muscular forces of engineering and infrastructure are in this instance deployed to forge a backdrop for civic life. Architecture here creates a platform for the possibilities of a different kind of social production of space.

3. *KULTTUURISAUNA*, ONE OFFICE, HELSINKI

But what if providing the platform is not enough? What are the limits to architecture's capacity for social production? Can space alone generate specific social outcomes, or does it need coaxing along? Two architects in Helsinki have taken it upon themselves to ensure

---

2   Jeremy Till, *Architecture Depends* (2009: 165), citing Gillian Rose, 'Athens and Jerusalem: a tale of three cities', (1994: 337).

their architecture achieves its explicit social aims, not only by designing the building, but also by committing to operate it.

The *Kulttuurisauna*, or 'Culture Sauna', is a new public sauna in
the Kallio neighbourhood of Helsinki. Designed by Tuomas Toivonen
and Nene Tsuboi, partners of the practice *Now Office*, the *Kulttuurisauna* is more than a usual commission. The project was self-initiated
by the pair, as a public building which they plan to own and run for
the foreseeable future.

The building, which opened in 2013, contains a public sauna, a
classroom and a small office. Designed as a horseshoe in plan, the
building wraps around a small garden, accommodating an existing
tree, and opening out towards the Baltic Sea (Figure 20.4). Entry
is via a shallow colonnade, an explicit nod to the architecture of
'publicness'. It's a peculiar urban object, domestic in scale, and yet
public in purpose. It is uncompromisingly modern, its flat white walls
make few concessions to the rough-hewn tradition of Finnish saunas.
One corner of the building is capped with a squat pyramid, perhaps in
reference to a higher cosmic order.

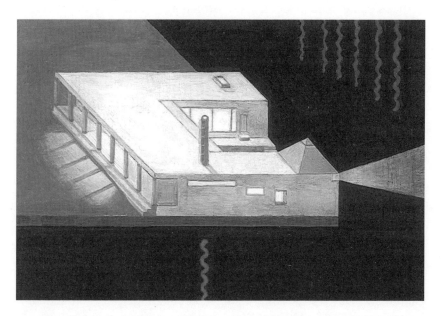

Figure 20.4 Painting by Now Office, architects of the *Kulttuurisauna*
Drawing: Now Office Architecture

Toivonen and Tsuboi are motivated as much by the lifestyle that
owning and running a bath house promises them individually, as they
are by the opportunity to operate as public citizens. As Toivonen

explains, 'We are contributing directly to the city through a building, not as designers, not as architects, but as citizens. Taking the role of making the city' (Seppänen, 2011).

With the rise of private saunas built into apartments, the social function of public bathing is being lost in Finnish urban culture. The revival of this tradition requires more than just the building to ac- commodate it, but also the particular personalities and commitment which Toivonen and Tsuboi bring. They describe the design process as encompassing both 'software' (the operations) and 'hardware' (the physical architecture). This is no different from any other design project in many ways, except being the ones to run the sauna allows them to push the design in a more extreme and personal direction. As Tsuboi explains, 'The software this time is extremely soft, because it's us' (ibid.).

Social space in the *Kulttuurisauna* is produced through personal manipulation, as if the mere presence of the architecture cannot be trusted to achieve it alone. As architects, ultimately we need to believe in the capacity of design to produce a social outcome, but perhaps sometimes it needs some extra help. As we face the crisis of public life, the *Kulttuurisauna* illustrates that what we need more than ever are not public *buildings*, but public *hosts*. People committed to producing social space in tandem with the capacity of architecture to create the platform for it.

4. FORENSIC ARCHITECTURE, ARCHITECTURAL TOOLS FOR JUSTICE

On 17 April 2009, Bassem Abu Rahma, a Palestinian farmer, was shot during a peaceful demonstration against the erection of a sepa- ration wall built on the lands of his village, Bil'In. The wall would sever access to an olive grove, and with it the livelihood of the village. Abu Rahma was hit in the chest by a tear gas canister fired by an Israeli soldier, causing massive internal bleeding which led to his death. The incident received widespread attention, and is documented in the Oscar-nominated 2011 film *5 Broken Cameras*, directed by Emad Burnat and Guy Davidi. Abu Rahma's parents engaged international human rights lawyer Michael Sfard and human rights organisation B'Tselem to bring a case against the Israeli Defence Force (IDF). The case hinged upon the ability to prove intentionality: whether the shot that killed Abu Rahma was aimed directly at him. This is a spatial question, a question of geometry, one which the tools of architecture could be used to uncover.

Sfard and B'Tselem invited Forensic Architecture, a research unit led by Eyal Weizman at Goldsmiths University of London, to investigate the case. Using the footage from *5 Broken Cameras*, plus two other films of the incident made by activists on the scene, Forensic Architecture, in collaboration with SITU Research, were able to use triangulation to create a virtual 3D model of the key actors involved and the geographic and architectural elements. This model was then used by the legal defence to contest the IDF's claim that the tear gas canister was deflected off a fence, rather than fired directly at Abu Rahma. Here, the tools of architecture are deployed in the pursuit of criminal justice. These illustrations and analyses are intensely social. They map the explicit relationships between individuals at a specific moment in time in an attempt to reveal their intentions, and therefore hold them to account.

The word 'forensis' is Latin for 'pertaining to the forum', meaning an object or debate to be had in public. It's an appropriate title for this project, which, like forensic science, takes secret or obscured information and creates documents that reveal and explain. What is radical about Forensic Architecture, and where it differs from forensics, is its subject. As Weizman explains in his Introduction to the book, *Forensis*, 'While police forensics is a disciplinary project that affirms the power of states, the direction of the forensic gaze could also be inverted, and used instead to detect and interrupt state violations' (Weizman, 2014).

If civics embodies the rights and duties of citizenship, this is civic architecture at its most fundamental. There are no monuments, colonnades, temple fronts or grandiose statements carved in sandstone, the symbolic language of public architecture, but merely documents to be used as evidence, in an attempt to advocate for the oppressed and under-represented. Social space is produced here indirectly, not through the creation of a public space per se, but through the creation of public rights where there are none. Like architecture, Forensic Architecture is about creating change, except, in this case, change is achieved in international courts of law, rather than on the building site.

The situation of Abu Rahma's death came about due to a devastating collapse of civics, a failure of generosity and consideration of the welfare of the other. In Bil'In, the positions of the Israeli military and the Palestinian villagers seem fundamentally segregated, and, yet, they are bound together by what Latour describes as 'divisive matters of concern': an explicit disagreement over the commons, and a legitimate right to terrain. Spatial justice is fractal, revealing its implications in self-similar formations, from the engagement between soldier and activist, to the conflict between two nations. The tactics of Forensic Architecture do not attempt to bridge this gulf, but to exacerbate it, by producing the tools to highlight injustices, and thereby enable resolution in international courts. Success will lead to the ultimate social production of space, a word that's almost unimaginable in this region today: peace.

CONCLUSION: IT'S WHAT YOU DO, TO MAKE DO

Each of the four examples presented here is imperfect. They are contingent and makeshift, making do under challenging circumstances. But this imperfection is a consequence of their reality. They sacrifice taut ethics and high-minded principles for the practical integrity of the real thing. *It's what you do, to make do.* And through this, they are each in their own way successful. They sketch out different, provisional means of creating publics. These ways to be public are at once contextually specific, and perhaps prototypical, able to be adapted to foreign circumstances. Here 'public' is used to mean assemblage, even 'common' would be too strong a word, a conglomerate that retains its difference.

But with such a flexible definition, what is really being *produced*? These projects each provide resistance to the overwhelming logic of capitalist realism, where the unchallenged value of producing space is production itself. These projects offer an alternative trajectory for architecture's production of the social. Their effects are not financial, but cultural. Their particular qualities and arrangements produce particular social forms which are at once radical and yet deceptively mundane: to buy eggs and milk, to walk along a riverfront, to chat in a sauna, and to tend to olive trees in peace.

REFERENCES

Bower, Paul (2014) 'Beyond "post-conflict" architecture', doctoral research, Queen's University Belfast (QUB). Supervised by Professor Ruth Morrow and Dr Agustina Martire.

Harvey, David (2008) 'The right to the city', *New Left Review* 53: 23–40.

Jacobs, Jane (1961) *The Death and Life of Great American Cities*, New York: Vintage Books.

Latour, Bruno (2005) 'From Realpolitik to dingpolitik', in Bruno Latour and Peter Weibel, *Making Things Public*, Cambridge, MA: MIT Press.

Lefebvre, Henri (1991) *The Production of Space*, Oxford: Blackwell.

Rose, Gillian (1994) 'Athens and Jerusalem: a tale of three cities', *Social & Legal Studies* 3(3): 333–348.

Seppänen, Antt (2011) 'NOW: Kulttuurisauna', online video, available at: http://vimeo.com/33106337 (accessed 2014).

Till, Jeremy (2009) *Architecture Depends*, Cambridge, MA: MIT Press.

Weizman, Eyal (ed.) (2014) *Forensis: The Architecture of Public Truth*, Berlin: Sternberg Press.

21 – CULTIVATING SPATIAL POSSIBILITIES IN PALESTINE: SEARCHING FOR SUB/URBAN BRIDGES IN BEIT IKSA, JERUSALEM

Nasser Golzari and Yara Sharif

This chapter reflects on a process of thinking and making that has been taking place while working in Palestine in recent years. In a fragmented landscape, with moving boundaries that suddenly appear and disappear to include some and exclude others, it is the Palestinians who are being pushed out. While Palestinians are forced to struggle for their livelihoods, their identity and the local narratives are slowly being erased. Within such a complex socio-political geography, where one cannot identify where the space starts or ends, it is crucial to rethink the role of architecture and question what architects can offer.

The historic village of Beit Iksa, located on the outskirts of Jerusalem, is one fragmented village (among 50 others) that we have been working on in collaboration with a local NGO in Palestine called *Riwaq: Centre for Architectural Conservation*.[1] Rethinking the

---

1 *Riwaq* is a non-for-profit organization based in Palestine. It was set up with the aim of protecting architectural heritage all over Palestine (www.Riwaq.org).

SURFACE

'I cannot get you into Nablus, but I can get you to Burin from where you can walk to the town just up the hill some thirty minutes or so.' 'Yes, yes, of course, we know, we have been on the road, or more accurately off the road, since eight in the morning. It is already three o'clock now. We started our trip by walking across the Birzeit checkpoint mound, and then Al Jawwal dirt mounds and Dora Al-Qare.'
(Amiry, 2002)

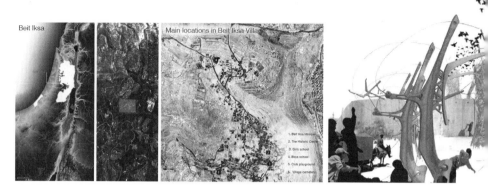

Figure 21.1 Surface, Air and Underground: cutting and breathing

historic villages and their relationship to the wider urban context has been a driving force for our design and activities as NG Architects as well as the Palestine Regeneration Team (PART).[2]

With the impermanent borderlines, checkpoints and other visible and invisible boundaries on the surface of the land, time and mobility have become key challenges in the dialogue of daily life. Today, Palestine is very much about memories of the past and the narratives of the present which mark time and space. Through our work, we have been reconstructing an alternative map born out of these narratives

---

2   The Palestine Regeneration Team (PART) was co-founded in 2009 by Yara Sharif, Nasser Golzari and Murray Fraser, and subsequently Miriam Ozanne became involved in various projects. Its aim has been to explore alternative forms of architectural practice in Palestine that can respond to the socio-political realities and help create conditions for change and empowerment from within. See www.palestineregenerationproject.com. See also ngarchitects.co.uk

Being conscious of one's surroundings is now related to how many checkpoints Palestinians have to go through daily, how many alternative routes one can create across the confused landscape, and indeed to the stories that one needs to make up in order to survive and get on with their life. As much as this troubles the mind, it is also loaded with potential and creativity, which then needs to be read in its spatial dimensions.

Since time and mobility have become key features in the dialogue of daily life in Palestine, the quest is for a counter-space which can carve out new urban and social realities. Perhaps the most outstanding outcome of such a reality is the everyday forms of spatial resistance already taking place. The emergence of small-scale networks and informal agencies in the West Bank, who are taking

and the different spatial patterns of resistance that Palestinians have built up. Our aim is to pursue a project that can heal, nourish and empower. These new layers, which are being created on the map and are what we call 'imagined moments of possibilities', should be seen as the matrixes and networks that can begin to stitch together the fragmented spaces of the Palestinian socio-political landscape. Some of these moments might be speculative in their nature, and at times they can even be seen as ironic. However, their ultimate aim is to provoke a critical form of architecture that engages with actual spatial and social realities.

control over their daily lives to survive, whether they are commuters, job seekers, farmers, porters, van drivers, etc.[1] are all in one way or another drawing new, if invisible, lines on the map.

1   Hammami, in her writings on Surda and Qlandia checkpoints, has referred to the role and importance of the Ford van drivers as a network, given the absence of other structures:

> In Palestine in the absence of mass organizations, networks of informal sector workers have stepped into the gap. Thus the unlikely symbols of the new steadfastness are not national institutions, but rather the sub-proletariat of Ford van drivers whose semi-criminal bravado is summed up by the ubiquitous Nike 'no fear' stickers emblazoned on their rear windshields … the same thuggishness has become a crucial force for everyday resistance and organizing at checkpoints – not just to deal with the crowds and traffic jams but also deal with the thuggishness of soldiers.
> (Hammami, 2004: 26–34)

CUTTING AND BREATHING: SURFACE, AIR AND IN-BETWEEN[3]

While looking at Beit Iksa in relation to the larger urban context of Palestine, different moments of possibilities were captured from within its fragmented map. These were taken by cutting through the occupied land in a process that was intended to re-read its potentials. The outcome has been a series of concepts that have emerged in response to the Surface, Air, and In-Between framework (Figure 21.1). These three spatial components have created the framework for restructuring our imagined spaces within Beit Iksa and beyond, and have hence informed our design propositions.

> *For those who pass it without entering, the city is one thing;*
> *it is another for those who are trapped by it and never leave.*
> *There is the city where you arrive for the first time; and there*
> *is another city which you leave never to return. Each deserves*
> *a different name.*
> (Calvino, 1978, iv)

In the critical location of Beit Iksa, sitting on the outskirts of Jerusalem, only 1,600 inhabitants are left to fight for their existence against the ongoing Israeli project of marginalization. The village is

---

3   This concept was developed in the PhD by Design thesis. 'Searching for Spaces of Possibility and Spaces of Imagination within the Palestinian-Israeli Conflict', by Yara Sharif. (2011).

Today, Palestine is very much about two aspects: memories of the past and the narratives of the present, which mark time and space with such brutal clarity. Informal travel routes have become embedded within Palestinian narratives. The sewage tunnel, the daily 'night hunters' crossing the border to seek work, Banksy's drawing of a hole on the wall, porters and vendors across no-drive zones, as well as many other attempts to capture moments of hope, all have started as individual initiatives and turned later into collective ones. Despite the ephemeral nature of such activities, and the fact that they appear and disappear with the emergence of conditions, what marks them out, however, is the way that so-called 'non-spaces' are being transformed by everyday life into real spaces:

today encircled by new Israeli settlements and two major pieces of infrastructure that separate its Palestinian residents from their nearby agricultural lands. One is the notorious 'separation wall' and the other is the proposed railway station. As in many other West Bank villages, the complex map on the ground, along with the scarcity of water and other essential natural resources, plus heavy surface pollution, has left this agrarian society with a level of unemployment that exceeds 75 per cent of adult males. Yet what might be treated today as marginal has been witness in the past to significant historic events, each of which has shaped its character and added to its built fabric. The most notable event was Napoleon Bonaparte's visit to Beit Iksa at the end of the eighteenth century, which duly gave the village its name, but also important historically was the strong ties between this village and the Ottoman Empire, when the village was one of the 24 so-called 'throne villages' used to govern the region.[4]

The 'invisible' village of Beit Iksa today retains underneath its quiet surface, beneath its skin, the will to resist and survive. The local residents through their informal practices to hunt for work and break the isolation, are carving out new spatial realities that need to be included within the matrix of spatial possibilities. These qualities and

---

4   In his attempt to capture Jerusalem at some point around 1799, it is believed that Napoleon Bonaparte took refuge in Beit Iksa in order to seek additional clothing for his army. Ever since, the village has had the name of the 'House of Clothing', which in Arabic is translated as Beit Iksa. Throne villages are located in the central highlands of Palestine known as the West Bank today. The villages acted as feudal centres and political power for their rural leaders known in Arabic as *Sheikhs*. Palestine is known for 24 throne villages stretching across its landscape, of which Beit Iksa is one.

I froze, listened and fearfully examined all that surrounded me: suddenly there were hundreds and hundreds of dark silhouettes. There were ghosts there, there were ghosts everywhere. Some appeared from behind ghostly olive trees, some were still winding along narrow paths ... some were fast in motion, some were slow, some hovered in large groups, some in small, some in pairs, some alone ... I stood there and wondered: was it a carnival of existence or a carnival for survival? Was it a dance for life or a masquerade of death? ... Once I got rid of my fears and the black spot in my heart, I figured out what it was: an innocent Saturday evening chase for a living.
(Amiry, 2010)

Figure 21.2 The concept of the Memory Belt as a tool to stitch the village to its surrounding context

the sheer scale of the challenge have put Beit Iksa on the list of the '50 Villages' project,[5] as a priority case, with a revitalization scheme now underway. Lying between dream and reality, this revitalization project of Beit Iksa might be one of the main historic villages where the play between the real and the speculative is best manifested. Through the aim to broaden the matrix of possibilities, a new dialogue between mapping, testing, making, imagining and constructing is currently being created.

---

5   The '50 Villages Project' is an initiative spearheaded by *Riwaq: Centre for Architectural Conservation*. It is aimed at protecting and regenerating 50 historic centres across Palestine, as it is estimated that 50 per cent of the surviving Palestinian historical built fabric will be preserved as a result. See also Golzari and Sharif (2011).

The formation of these collective moments in the West Bank, in their invisible and subversive manner, is managing to stretch social spaces far beyond the given. These creative daily practices are taking place within historic centres as well as on the margins and left-over spaces. They are leaving us with new readings to the map. By pulling together these micro-scale events, Palestine can no longer be read as merely being formed in the city or the village; it is also now the in-between, the left-over spaces, the moments in which people move, remember, wait and try to reconnect and heal. In summary, Palestine today is very much about the not-so-ordinary life (Sharif, 2011).

ZOOMING-OUT: A BIRD'S-EYE VIEW

In rethinking the conditions of the Surface, Air and In-Between framework, the scheme for Beit Iksa consciously seeks to question and redefine a counter-map in which the memories of the past and the narratives of the present are embedded in its many layers. Various components for the project are not only limited to thinking about the historic fabric of the village itself, but also to the farmlands and wider urban surroundings.

With this mapping in process, different elements are being developed to assist the strategy for re-stitching the fragmented village together. These include a 'Memory Belt' located on the surface to mark and celebrate the village's transition to the present (Figure 21.2). Another is to generate an 'Economic Corridor' that

AIR

It is a well-known fact that Palestine has one of the richest habitats for bird migration in the world, second only to Panama, and, as such, hosts about half a billion birds every season (Platt, 2008). However, what we found even more astonishing is another dimension that these birds hold, along with their beauty and poetic nature. Indeed, it is an ironic hidden layer that we came across while trying to understand the Israeli obsession with political and military control.

Apparently, this Israeli obsession with control has also so invaded the airspace above the West Bank that a new definition of aerial boundaries had to be invented just to deal with the Palestinian/ Israeli situation. Thus, according to the 1993 Oslo Peace Agreement,

can challenge the economic isolation of Beit Iksa and offer potential
job opportunities, while 'Moments of Whisper' have been carefully
located across the terrain to point out the forgotten spaces within and
around Jerusalem: the destroyed village of Lifta, the erased village of
Deir Yasin, and the underground water springs are all a stone's throw
away and yet are out of reach.

While offering a critique of the current strategies of Israeli
occupation, we also regard the *Air* as an added layer to the matrix.
By stepping back from the exhausted surface of the land, the flocks
of birds are seen as tools of spatial reclamation; they represent a
form of observing, reading and re-stitching, which cannot be reached
by humans on the ground. Taking hence the *Air* as our new medium
of intervention, we investigated how to reconnect the fragmented
landscape together in the sky. A series of design interventions in the
form of urban follies have emerged. Of course, all of this takes place
alongside the general, preventive conservation of the historic fabric,
which, as ever, *Riwaq* is spearheading.

'All aviation activity or usage of the airspace … shall require prior
approval of Israel.'[2] Consequently, it was proposed that the sovereign
'ceiling control for Palestinians should be significantly lowered,
leaving the upper layers of airspace in Israeli control' (Weizman,
2002). An invisible map of exhaustive surveillance and military action
has been created as a result, as described by Eyal Weizman (2002):

> The West Bank [and the Gaza Strip are the] most intensively
> observed and photographed terrain in the world … Every floor in
> every house, every car, every telephone call or radio transmis-

---

2   See the Oslo Interim Agreement, annex 1, article xiii.

ZOOMING-IN

Her space: the Eco Kitchen[6]

The Eco Kitchen is located on an intersection between the *Memory Belt* and the *Economic Corridor*, and is one of a range of interventions in single buildings that are now being implemented in Beit Iksa (Figures 21.3 and 21.4). We see in the process of its designing a conceptual shift embedded within a conscious approach to explore what could be done with limited resources, to cultivate possibilities for change from within the historic fabric itself.

The Eco Kitchen is intended as a prototype for exploring affordable methods of construction that will improve the quality of life for the residents. In aiming to empower the women of the village, it responds to their energy and celebrates their knowledge and skills, as well as their collective cultural traditions. This new kitchen is being designed for the Women's Association. It offers women a point of economic departure while also responding to the urgent environmental challenges that they face on a daily basis. Essential ingredients of the project therefore are testing out innovative building materials, exploring affordable methods to collect and filter water, and working with local community groups to develop low-cost passive forms of heating and cooling for the building.

---

6   The Eco Kitchen is part of the collaborative design project between *Riwaq*, NG Architects and the Palestine Regeneration Team (PART) in London.

---

sion, even the smallest event that occurs on the terrain, can thus be monitored, policed or destroyed from the air.

It is this same airspace, which in size is only 1/12th of the size of the UK, that enjoys more resident bird species than that found in the UK as a whole. Add to that the huge number of migrating visitors every spring from their wintering grounds in Africa en route to their breeding grounds in Europe, and the same number returning back in wintertime. During the peak period between 10 March and 20 April each year, the residents of Palestine wake up to the sound of wings of 500 million birds migrating over the Great Syrian-African Valley.

Figure 21.3 (above) Zooming into Her Space: moments from the Eco Kitchen and the children's Eco Play along with the bird folly

Figure 21.4 Construction in progress: working with the local team to develop the design and test out different technical and spatial ideas in and around the Eco Kitchen

'Take care … we share the air.'³ Ironically, the large numbers of soaring birds that migrate by day, so as to exploit the thermals rising from the land, in fact, seem to be the main political crisis in the airspace in terms of negotiations and signed agreements. The heavy dependence of Israel on its air force, with the high density of military airplanes and security measures, is disturbed by the possibility of mid-flight collisions with birds.⁴

---

3   A poster for a guidelines booklet, 'Take Care, We Share the Air' is produced by the Israeli Air Force to raise consciousness and regulate pilots while flying.

4   It is reported that Israel has lost more aircraft through collision with birds than through any war or action by so-called 'enemies'.

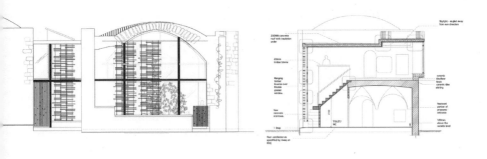

Photos: Nasser Golzari and Yara Sharif

For us, however, this magical reality bounding the airspace over Palestine is perhaps a key sign, both for a sense of roaming freedom and for a dream of return. Birds are the moments of dream and the representatives of possibility. We'd rather leave it to the birds to draw their own quiet map of possibility. Maybe they can remind us that there is still a level of weakness, somewhere on the other end, and a moment of power and hope that Palestinians can nourish on the surface of the land.

As a means to involve and empower women, and build upon their local knowledge and skills, a training programme has also been developed in partnership with another NGO, called MAAN. Through this programme, local women will be trained how to provide food for the local school in order to ensure a constant income for them. This process of network-building has also been expanded to include the whole neighbourhood. Indeed, as part of a private housing initiative, local residents are currently becoming involved in the revitalization process. Many have proposed some form of a 'swap scheme' whereby essential items will be exchanged in a barter system. For example, the blacksmith has agreed to produce all of the metalwork needed to restore Beit Iksa's historic fabric; in return, he will be provided with his own grey-water treatment system and a 'green roof' to enhance his own home. Once developed, the plan is to transfer these new techniques to the other 50 villages across Palestine.

His space: the bus stop

His space starts with a point of informal gathering along the *Memory Belt* that has already left its marks on the main road. The point is packed with men, children and work hunters, waiting for a change to happen. Women watch behind the scenes, involved in their gossip, in the hope that the one and only bus will be able to arrive and take them out of their trapped village.

In our scheme, a bus stop has thus been proposed to celebrate the informality of this meeting point. While defining the entrance to the village and the historic centre, the bus stop is also designed to

UNDERGROUND AND IN-BETWEEN

Travelling around the West Bank, one is struck by the amount of damage being caused to the environment and the cultural landscape of the region, especially near the big cities of Ramallah, Bethlehem, Hebron, Nablus and Tulkarem. In this case, we are not referring to the physical boundaries of concrete walls and checkpoints, or to the construction of high-rise building in historic centres, or to the illegal Israeli settlements occupying the top of the hills. What we are talking about are the sudden cuts one sees in the landscape of olive terraces whereby whole mountains and hills are being completely flattened to create formal and informal clusters of stone quarries operated both by Palestinians and Israelis (Sharif, 2011).

incorporate a shaded sitting area that is connected to the informal café, along with a kids zone made up of swings. The design explores the use of alternative building materials, such as rammed earth and gabion walls. Additionally, it tries to stretch its function to include some innovative environmental activities that can also be attractive to children (such as generating electricity through their energetic cycling).

Their space

The design proposals for Beit Iksa are not only centred on the buildings in the village. The initiative is also about the activities that adjoin the village, and hence an imaginative socio-economic programme has also been developed to ensure the project's future sustainability.

Following our exploration of the Air, a *bird folly* is designed to mark one of the key moments located on the Memory Belt. It aims to respond to the strategic location of the village in relation to Jerusalem and to the migratory movement of the birds in the air above. The folly offers a protected habitat for them to nest in, while also allowing a space for children to be able to feed and watch the birds. The strategic location of the folly overlooking the lost villages, is a starting point for creating a series of 'aerial bridges'. The strategy is to 'accumulate' this process over time by establishing bird stations/follies in different villages marking the birds' migration as a form of virtual stitching.

The Beit Iksa project incorporates a series of initiatives to further enhance the biodiversity of the area and to improve public provision generally. These new features include a public space with a *children's environmental play area*. Additionally, a series of vegetable gardens

Cutting underground, we are faced with a series of layers colliding with one another, no longer making sense of who owns what. Between the exploitation of natural resources, archaeology and the scarcity of water, and the exploitation of stone as a building material, more voids are being created underground and in the in-between level. These voids in return are shaping life on the surface, and, as such, they call for urgent action.

which spread across the village are proposed in the form of *green roofs*. These are also intended to celebrate the stepped terrain of the village, since it is hoped that the gardens will be fed by a grey-water filtration system sourced from the Eco Kitchen.

Furthermore, the 'green roof' technology was one of the first ideas to be developed along with the women of the village, in order to promote the use of recycled materials. Not only will this create a habitat for the different species, but it also helps to create an additional insulation layer for the roofs benefiting from its thermal mass.

The idea behind 'cultivating' these green roofs in Beit Iksa responds to what had accumulated on the Surface over the years; in our early process of gathering information about the village, it took us some time to realize that the historic fabric of Beit Iksa is absent from the aerial map as it had been covered by a green skin of overgrown vegetation following the deliberate destruction of the village by Israel in 1967. This invisible status of the historic fabric from an aerial view could have prompted a conscious strategy to occupy and erase; for us, however, it became all about a conscious strategy to empower Palestinian residents while still remaining invisible in the aerial photograph.

It is predicted that a serious shortage of raw building materials will occur within a decade in the West Bank, due to the rate of extraction, since three-quarters of what is quarried in the West Bank goes directly to Israel.
(Jeffay, 2009)[5]

With the different layers of peeling, erasing and inserting into the landscape, the need to question what happens Underground, and its mirror-reflection on the Surface, are things which are becoming ever more crucial. What will be left over on the surface and underground

---

5   For more on quarries, see also Sharif (2011).

SHIFTING SCALE AND SPECULATING

The revitalization of Beit Iksa marks a cumulative process. The changes might be regarded as too small, or even invisible at times, if seen
on their own. However, it needs to be read from a holistic perspective
that brings all the small elements together. Only then can one feel its
impact beyond the village scale.

The project rejects the mere creation of iconic buildings. Instead,
it adopts an architectural practice that is able to respond to, and
facilitate, the necessary transformations within the prevailing social,
political and cultural conditions. Therefore, capturing informal agencies, celebrating their daily practices, have very much informed the
work. This stems from the belief that engaging with the wider context,
one has to recognize what also happens at the micro-scale level, and
what happens on the edges and the in-between spaces, all of which
inform the map and the living patterns of the Palestinians.

Bringing in a speculative angle to the design has added another
dimension to the collaborative work. Combining the act of practice
with speculation and reality, with community aspirations, has helped
in drawing attention to layers, which might be invisible, yet are crucial
to push the boundaries further and break the isolation of Palestine,
not only in terms of physical space but also the space of imagination.
Indeed, we see it as a key tool to provoke a critical form of architectural thinking. As a result, being involved as academics, we tried to
bring forward a design-led approach where different ideas were

when illegal Israeli settlements are further 'decorated' with stone from
the West Bank, and with old-style windows and tiles 'stolen' from
traditional Palestinian villages? How will Palestine manage to get
back these dismantled layers in future years? Should they instead
stay and fight for control over the land, or the materiality of the land?
Will the day ever come when even potentially we will be arguing
about whether illegal Israeli settlements should also be protected as
part of our cultural heritage?

tested out with the involvement of students as well as the local community. By shifting scales, the *Air, Surface and In-between* were taken to their maximum limits.

INVISIBILITY AS CRITICAL PRACTICE

Of course, notwithstanding the sensitive issue of ethics, in live projects and when working in different contexts, one needs to be aware of the temptation to impose one's own personal agenda on the community. Therefore, the sustainability of any idea cannot be achieved without living up to the community's aspirations, respecting and engaging with their cultural practices and needs. However, these aspirations and needs cannot be seen in isolation from the socio-political conditions in Palestine and indeed the larger global context of capitalism.

Generating a lack of fair access to resources is one of the Israeli authorities' strategic methods to push Palestinian families out of their villages. As summed up by Erik Swyngedouw, a fair distribution of resources would be crucial to protecting the community's homes and above all their right to the city: 'The question of urban sustainability is not just about achieving sound, ecological and environmental conditions, but first and foremost about social struggle for access and control to the city itself' (2004).

Within such a context of political repression and extreme poverty in occupied Palestine, equitable and inclusive modes of environmental production require a responsive architecture (Swyngedouw *et al.*, 2006). Re-reading sustainability in this context should be seen more as a means to empower the marginalized, rather than create dependency. We could have looked, for example, into alternative high-tech solutions to address the challenging subject of water, heating and cooling. However, the design interventions were inspired by simple, affordable, daily creative practices that people already undertake, all of which became key components of the design.

The design interventions might not hold the answer to the Palestinian crisis, or indeed the global environmental crisis and its consequent socio/economic effects; however, it does suggest there is a need to start with small changes. Hopefully, by incorporating and stressing the significance of the tiny everyday details, this can help us to challenge and move away from the single-minded capitalist economy towards a fairer accessibility to resources.

The Beit Iksa project seeks to investigate, through design, the appropriateness of the 'ordinary' and the 'everyday' as a viable alternative to high-tech. Like most architects, we must admit that the ego-driven desire to create an 'iconic' building, which could become an architectural reference, was present at a certain moment of our career. However, the consequent unpacking of the process, the importance of a broader socio-economic and historical context in Palestine raised more urgent issues, which indeed reshaped our position. Focusing on the ordinary and the everyday is exactly about zooming in to explore people's daily narratives, with all their challenges. In contrast, stripping architecture away from its context, and limiting it only to its physical representations, only narrows its scope. The architect instead needs to become more of a facilitator, agent and curator. Above all, it is about creating the conditions for people to dream and build their aspirations. As such, the architect must remain 'invisible' within the process of making architecture.

Even though this may not be the conventional role of an architect in Western countries, or what our institutions might want to see, we do believe it is one way forward, at least until the socio-political map changes dramatically. Ironically, we were contacted by Al-Jazeera a few years ago to discuss a potential interview about what they called 'your Palestine projects'. Throughout the whole preliminary phone conversation, the journalist was clearly fascinated by our activities there. The conversation, however, came to an abrupt end when she realized that there was no iconic representation for them to use, or indeed any 'sexy' image to accompany her journalistic project. Although we are not waiting for any kind of these interviews to take place, we do, however, question how long the act of invisibility for an architect must last before this alternative form of architecture is recognized. Or should the 'invisible architect' remain the ideal feature of contemporary society?

In our view, this form of architectural practice, which might be invisible to some, needs to become more visible, recognized and embedded within the mainstream profession. Otherwise, it will risk being marginalized and limited to individual isolated initiatives that can slowly disappear at the time when this alternative approach is urgently needed.

This project won the Holcim Acknowledgment Award for sustainable construction in 2014.[7]

---

7   See 'Adaptive re-use: women's centre and playground'. Available at: www.holcimfoundation. org/Projects/adaptive-re-use (accessed 22 February 2015).

REFERENCES

Amiry, Suad (2002) 'Getting there', in Suad Amiry and Mouhannad Hadid (eds) *Earthquake in April*, Ramallah and Jerusalem: *Riwaq* and the Institute of Jerusalem Studies, pp. xii–xix.
(2010) *Nothing to Lose but Your Life*, Doha: Bloomsbury Qatar Foundation.

Calvino, Italo (1978) *Invisible Cities*, New York: Mariner Books.

Golzari, Nasser and Sharif, Yara (2011) 'Reclaiming space and identity: heritage-led regeneration in Palestine', *Journal of Architecture* 16(1): 121–144.

Hammami, Rema (2004) 'On the importance of thugs: the moral economy of a checkpoint', *MERIP Middle East Report* 34: 26–34.

Jeffay, Nathan (2009) Bibi's 'Economic Peace' faces key test at quarries', *The Jewish Daily Forward*, 24 April, available at: www.forward.com/articles/104861/ (accessed 2 February 2017).

Platt, Edward (2008) 'The migration', *Granta* 102, available at: http://granta.com/the-migration/ (accessed 2 February 2017).

Sharif, Yara (2011) 'Searching for spaces of possibility and spaces of imagination within the Palestinian-Israeli conflict: healing fractures through the dialogue of everyday behaviour', unpublished PhD thesis, University of Westminster, London.

Swyngedouw, Erik (2004) *Social Power and the Urbanization of Water: Flows of Power*, Oxford: Oxford University Press.

Swyngedouw, Erik, Heynen, Nikolas and Kaika, Maria (2006) *In the Nature of Cities*, London: Routledge.

Weizman, Eyal (2002) 'Control in the air', *Open Democracy*, 1 May, available at: www.opendemocracy.net/ecology-politicsverticality/article_810.jsp (accessed 2 February 2017).

22 – OLD NEWS FROM A CONTACT ZONE: ACTION ARCHIVE IN TENSTA

Meike Schalk

> *Reclaiming means recovering what we have been separated from, but not in the sense that we can just get it back. Recovering means recovering from the very separation itself, regenerating what this separation has poisoned.*
> (Stengers, 2012)

This chapter discusses reclaiming as a spatial practice, which engages in history-telling to recover 'diverse' histories of common space. It suggests that by changing perspective and 'reframing' architecture and urban history, repressed material can be regenerated that questions the hegemonic positions in urban development and that attempts to make openings for new spatial and political imaginaries.[1] The chapter explores the *unfinished situation* as a concept and the conflicting attitudes that arose from the research project *Action Archive in Tensta* as an opportunity to rethink the social (re)production of architecture.[2]

The expression 'social production and reproduction of architecture', as used here, follows Jane Rendell's concept of 'critical spatial practice'. Rendell draws a connection between Michel de Certeau's 'strategies' and Henri Lefebvre's 'representations of space', on the one hand, and de Certeau's 'tactics' and Lefebvre's 'spaces of representation', on the other, suggesting that the former operates to maintain and reinforce existing social and spatial orders, while the latter describes tactical practices to critique and question them (Rendell, 2011: 24).[3] Her 'critical spatial practice' then serves to describe both everyday activities and creative practices that resist the dominant social order of global corporate capitalism. In this sense, strategies reproduce normative practices and orders, while a critical spatial practice may produce tactical alternatives.

---

1   My use of the terms 'diverse' and 'reframing' are inspired by J.K. Gibson-Graham (2008).

2   Action Archive is an association founded in 2013 by Sara Brolund de Carvalho, Helena Mattsson and Meike Schalk. Many thanks to Helena and Sara for valuable comments on a draft of this article.

3   Rendell is referring here to de Certeau (1988) and Lefebvre (1991).

Action Archive is a not-for-profit association formed in 2013 on the occasion of the exhibition *Tensta Museum: Reports from New Sweden* at Tensta konsthall (Tensta Art Centre).[4] The project was situated in the Stockholm suburb of Tensta, a neighbourhood associated with what is called the Swedish Million Program. Through three participatory actions, Action Archive was concerned with collectively rewriting a critical urban history of a brief period of participatory housing renewal, 1987–1992, in Tensta, of which there were no records.

My point of departure in this chapter is the experience of crisis, which was inherent in our historical object of inquiry and arose again in our research process, making it necessary to find new terms and new ways of working. To grasp these conflictual moments of multiple voices with varied agendas, I borrow theoretical expressions from feminist and ethnographic studies, such as 'messy approaches' by Pattie Lather (1993) and 'messy moments' by Norman K. Denzin (1997).

In line with feminist critique, our research questions the central positions from which history is written, including its technologies, such as official archives. We considered it important to physically set up a mobile archive at Tensta konsthall as a medium for reaching out. Through a series of experimental practices, historical material was regenerated, and critical key terms were deployed and developed. The actions included a 'witness seminar' concerning the International Housing Renewal Conference 1989, a guided tour with the enactment of a dinner commemorating the inauguration of the Glömminge renewal project 1992, in Tensta, and a debate that mapped the recent production of common or civic spaces in Stockholm.

PLACE-BASED CONSTRUCTIONS OF THE PAST AND THE CONTACT ZONE

The *Million Program* areas were built in the 1960s and 1970s as a response to a severe housing crisis in Sweden.[5] The name Million Program is intimately linked with the image of suburbs in trouble. Tensta is home to a population primarily from North Africa and the

---

4   The show was curated and organized by Maria Lind, the director of Tensta konsthall, and her team, Emily Fahlén, Ulrika Flink, Asrin Haidari and Hedvig Wiezell, and took place from October 2013–May 2014. It included artists, architects, performers, sociologists, cultural geographers, philosophers and local associations. An accompanying programme was conducted in cooperation with numerous local associations, national organizations and institutions; many thanks to the Tensta konsthall team for support.

5   The *Million Program* was a Swedish governmental programme, in 1965–1975, to build one million flats in ten years.

Middle East.[6] The mainstream media tend to portray this neighbourhood in one-dimensional images, foregrounding the problems they
see rather than the place's diversity as a hopeful example of peaceful
togetherness. The Million Program areas are being reconsidered
for regeneration – and for their protection as cultural heritage sites
(Näslund, 2012). Given the cultural diversity of Tensta's population,
this raises important questions: which cultures and whose heritages
will be addressed, based on whose histories? Most crucially, what
spaces are hereby produced, by and for whom (Lind, 2014)?

According to the geographer Doreen Massey, places and
spaces are always shifting articulations of social relations that are
internal to that locale *and* linked elsewhere (the history of the global
construction of the locale) (Massey, 1994, 1995; Blokland, 2001).
'They are particular moments in such intersecting social relations,
nets of which have over time been constructed, laid down, interacted
with one another, decayed and renewed' (Massey, 1994: 120). Their
past is as open to a multiplicity of readings, as is the present. Massey
distinguishes between place-*bound* constructions and place-*based*
constructions of the past. While she sees place-bound relations as an
obstacle to inventing a place anew and likewise to the self-invention
of its inhabitants, place-*based* agency may become the basis for the
construction of radical politics and positive change.

Since the 1980s, in many places, social groups with histories and
ways of living different from the mainstream ones, have insisted on
these histories as part of their citizenship. In dialogue with dominant
institutions, many groups began asserting a rhetoric of belonging that
made demands beyond the representation and basic rights granted
from above. These shifts in demands call for different spatial and
political imaginaries. In contrast to the limiting idea of community that
underlies much of the thinking about language, communication and
culture, the ethnographer Mary Louise Pratt has developed the spatial
idea of the 'contact zone' (Pratt, 1991).[7] The *contact zone* describes
an open arena where cultural groups and languages co-exist and
where the phenomena of transculturalization, critique and collaboration can happen.

6   Around 85–90 per cent of the 19,000 residents of Tensta have first- or second-generation
immigrant backgrounds.

7   Thank you to Tom Avermaete for bringing the notion of the 'contact zone' to my attention.

The Tensta Museum exhibition departed from the assumption that a preoccupation with the past was fundamentally ambivalent. The right to memory can be emancipatory and can be employed to suppress others' memories and even to start a war (Lind, 2014). A link was drawn to the issue of rising nationalism, not only in Sweden but all over Europe,[8] and the right-wing employment of the notion of cultural heritage as an argument for who may be included in society and who may not. At the same time, the preoccupation with memory was seen both in relation to neoliberalism and to movements of 'domestic decolonization' and the emancipation of group identities with their particular memories (Nora, 2001; Buden, 2014). What is at issue are competing histories of the present, wielded as arguments of what should be the future: for Tensta, this could mean political demands for equal access to welfare and services for all or the provision of new space for urban development in favour of a more viable clientele.

REFRAMING HISTORY: THE ACTION ARCHIVE

Despite social media, archives continue to dominate professional national history writing and thus influence our understanding of places and events. Material that cannot be found in archives (or on the net) often ends up outside of established history in a mute space. *Action Archive* responds to questions of silence or ignorance with concrete interactions of participatory, historical reconstruction that bring together actors and publics around urban cultural, historical and political issues. The performance of the collective actions thus creates a public or civic space where forgotten material is made accessible and new archival sources are generated. The dynamic character of common historical research is seen as a possibility for the production of multiple meanings. Doing history in this way seeks continual re-examination and debate about what kinds of criteria form the basis for history writing. What material is collected for making history and what is omitted? And through this, what knowledge is (re)produced?

For the research process, besides the performance of three actions, we installed an archive as an ambulant research environment at Tensta konsthall between January and May 2014. The archive offered an actual place to meet and produce material on site and outside of official history writing. As an object, it had multiple identities: it was

8   Sweden, Hungary, Norway, Austria, France, the Netherlands, Denmark and Finland currently have a nationalist party as the third largest force in their governments. The Swiss People's Party is the strongest party in Switzerland. There are also strong nationalistic tendencies in the UK and in Germany.

a vehicle, a display case, a roundtable and a workstation with media such as films, newspaper clippings, letters, photos, maps, drawings and books (Figure 22.1).[9]

Figure 22.1 The mobile archive at the opening of the show, *Tensta Museum: Reports from New Sweden*, at Tensta konsthall (Tensta Art Centre)
Photo: Mattias Tydén

We specifically addressed the eventful years around 1989. The major geopolitical changes after the end of the Cold War[10] and national policies left their mark on Tensta. The population changed from being work migrants to become global refugees with other

---

9   The *mobile archive* contained a foldable table and stools, a library, a media archive and other archival materials. It was designed to precise dimensions in order to fit into the elevators of the metro system and be able to use public transport. During the exhibition, the archive vehicle was unfolded and served as a display case of exhibits and films. On the table top was an interactive timeline from 1965, when Tensta was planned until today, and a guestbook inviting visitors to leave information, comments, questions and their contact details. The time axis was structured into micro- and macro-political phases and events juxtaposing global and local issues, and colour-coded according to the three actions we conducted during the course of the exhibition. The archive vehicle was designed and built by Sara Brolund de Carvalho with the support of Gustav Vrang.

10   See the wars in the Persian Gulf region, Somalia and the former Yugoslavia and the formation of new states in Eastern Europe.

needs.[11] Between 1987 and 1992, the City of Stockholm supported
a series of participatory housing renewal projects inspired by a model
of community architecture with citizen involvement (typically from
the US or the UK). The projects were initiated by the Stockholm City
real-estate department and planned together with politicians, municipal housing company administrators and representatives of the police
department, the Stockholm housing service and the tenants' association. After considering all the housing areas built between 1965
and 1975, it was decided that Tensta, Rinkeby and Husby were the
districts most in need of improvement beyond the regular, ongoing
urban regeneration.[12] The aims were to improve the living conditions
of the inhabitants and to include them in the renewal. While earlier
renewal projects had focused primarily on physical improvements to
the buildings and public spaces, the agenda now was much broader
and included social, cultural and administrative change. One of the
objectives was decentralization, therefore, local project leaders were
appointed. It was expected 'the community' would ultimately take over
the process and continue to self-manage its regeneration.

In 1989, Stockholm's real-estate office organized a visionary
housing conference in Tensta, bringing international experts from
important renewal projects in England, Denmark, Finland, France, the
Netherlands, Turkey and the United States to meet local politicians,
administrators and inhabitants. The aim of the conference was to gain
inspiration and create guidelines for the new era of citizen participation and community spirit that would stop the negative spiral of
degradation in the suburbs. One of the renewal projects that emerged
from this was Glömmingegränd in Tensta. The conference led to a
publication and an exhibition that was displayed in the district council
building and travelled to the Nordic-Baltic Architecture Triennial
in Tallinn the following year. The short excursion into dialogical
approaches with tenants was abandoned abruptly in 1992 after an
election and regime shift. These experimental and individual projects,
which, in the case of Tensta, had involved hundreds of households,

11   Under the effects of Sweden's third-way politics and reorganization according to new,
public management principles, privatization was privileged over public financing. The previous
responsibilities of the state were reshuffled to other actors, and volunteer organizations started to
take care of arriving refugees, making it difficult for new citizens to distinguish between their rights
and the results of personal engagement or civil societal initiatives.

12   A criterion for selecting the suburbs in the greatest need of urban regeneration was the
percentage of foreign-born people living in an area. In the middle of the 1980s, only around 35 per
cent of the inhabitants in Tensta, Rinkeby and Husby came from abroad (Sven Lorentzi, the former
director of the real estate office, in his witness statement, 5 March 2014).

were never evaluated systematically.[13] Almost all the documentary
material from the conference was lost, probably in a reorganization
of the district council, perhaps also because of a lack of interest.[14]
Action Archive was especially interested in the meaning of the gap as
a phenomenon crucial to the understanding of the social reproduction
of Swedish architecture.

Gaps may also serve as beginnings. To conceptualize the experience of the brief era of participatory housing-renewal projects, we
considered them through the lens of an unfinished situation. The projects were cancelled after only a few years, and documentation was
removed without reflection on what had actually happened; yet the
situation seems not to have improved – quite the opposite was noted
in the witness seminar. Paul Goodman, social critic, poet and Gestalt
theorist, relates the term 'unfinished situations' to both personal
experience in individual development and communities, but also to
greater historical movements and 'unfinished revolutions' (Goodman,
[1960] 2012: 194–211). Goodman argues that governments have
failed to carry through a number of promising revolutions that the
modern world began and abandoned – among them, a democratic
revolution of individual participation in government (ibid.: 194–211).
In the case of the Million Program suburbs, the promise of greater
local self-determination in the renewal projects, which never became
real, can be seen in terms of an unfinished revolution. Furthermore,
Goodman argues that a forced or inauthentic settling of a conflict
would merely leave an unfinished situation for the next generation,
making the difficulties more complex in new conditions. But Goodman
also sees a therapeutic use of history, of reviving old causes by
renewing a conflict in new circumstances (1970: 206–207). In that
sense, the accumulation of unaccomplished or lost causes can be
turned into a programme for action. This happens when communities
and/or individuals assume ownership of past experiences, actively
remaking meanings and interpretations, discovering a new view of
an old situation, recognizing choices, learning how to influence one's
environment in dialogical relationships and bringing struggles to life
by enacting them in the present.

13   We found one report, which was not specifically about the projects in Tensta, Rinkeby and
Husby but includes a discussion of Glömminge, by Maud Alenmark, 'Att lyckas med förändring',
report no. 34, project no. 91-914 (Stockholm: SABO, 1992).

14   The International Housing Renewal Conference took place in Tensta, 10–19 June 1989. It
started with workshops, followed by a summing up and a public conference at Tenstaträff with 150
guests from all over Sweden and was concluded with a small gathering in the Stockholm archipelago
at the weekend.

In *Action Archive*, the three actions explored methods and practices, including a witness seminar, a guided tour and a memorial dinner, and a public time–space mapping of civic spaces. The actions foreground everyday activities such as walking, showing, telling and drawing in groups, as research by bringing them into a reflexive context. Equally, research becomes part of a real-life situation. We position ourselves thus as participating researchers and the approaches we apply can be called messy. *Messy* approaches identify their narrative apparatuses, they are sensitive to how reality is socially constructed and they are seen as 'framing reality' in a research process (Minh-ha, 1991), in which a journey of exploration and 'letting go and getting lost' is a precondition for creating new relations and knowing new things (Lather, 2008). We chose these approaches for their disruption of conventional divisions in, for example, public/ private, memory/presence, formal history/informal histories and production/reproduction. The idea was thus to explore the space between these oppositions. The actions created a common overall frame for participants, including us, to relate to and a way to relate to each other within it.

THE INTERNATIONAL HOUSING RENEWAL CONFERENCE 1989: A WITNESS SEMINAR

Action 1: 5 March 2014, 18.30–21.00
A *witness seminar* is a particular practice of oral history in contemporary history. Usually, several experts are invited who are associated with a particular event to meet and discuss their reminiscence together with an audience.[15] To the witness seminar at Tensta konsthall we invited former initiators, organizers and speakers from the International Housing Renewal Conference 1989 to witness (Figures 22.2 and 22.3). The witnesses were the deputy mayor and real-estate commissioner, the director of the real-estate office, the project leader of the Tensta project, a community architect from England and a planner from Turkey. The witnesses received questions beforehand to prepare a ten-minute statement about their roles in the housing conference and the ways in which they had been engaged in

---

15   Witness seminars have been performed at the Institute of Contemporary British History since 1986. In Stockholm, the Institute for Contemporary History at Södertörn University College has been developing its own model since 1998. Our witness seminar was supported by Tensta konsthall, the Department for Contemporary History at Södertörn University College in Stockholm and the Stockholm Architects Association.

the topics of housing renewal, community planning and participation in democratic planning processes. We asked the witnesses to position themselves and to speak about the most important issues the conference raised for them personally. After that, the discussion was opened to the public.

Figure 22.2 International Housing Renewal Conference in Tensta, 1989
Photo: Björn Erdahl

Figure 22.3 Witness seminar at Tensta konsthall
Photo: Tensta konsthall.

There were different memories of the conference and various views on how the situation had been in Tensta in 1989 and how it had changed. The politicians and administrators pointed out that since then, the housing companies had improved the management of the buildings, as the landscape department looked after the maintenance of the green areas and the public spaces. Stockholm's segregation was still seen as a major issue, and it was admitted that the aim of working towards more democratic structures and possibilities to influence decisions locally had not been achieved. The lack of continuity was mentioned as the major problem, with projects' lifespans depending on the central dominant political view: 'All the ambitions ... were shut down. That is a big problem. If you really want to change something you must do it one hundred per cent. We could not handle it the way we should have because of shifting majorities.'[16]

The international guests responded in emotional terms to what they believed they saw currently in contrast to their suggestions, which had been documented in 1989 and then omitted. They criticized the design of the renewal projects and the lack of colour, and they called the area a jail-like environment, sterile and anonymous. Houses, but not homes. They said that, looking at the faces of Tensta's citizens passing by that day, they noticed 'no happiness at all'. They found the reason in Sweden's centralized organization, which prevented any local democracy, and suggested solving the problem by handing over the housing blocks to the residents for them to take responsibility for their own environment.[17]

In the discussion with the audience, the idea of using experts, so central to the housing conference in 1989, was questioned:

> I noticed in the newspapers you showed in your presentation the headline 'Experter vet' [the experts know]. And it's a sort of paradox in conferences and seminars like this for the people who are here now. How shall we know, as you say, what one should do or not do in Tensta, or if the power should be given to the people? Is that another statement from an expert or what?

The paradox in the approach to segregation was pointed out:

> We talk about areas like this in a special way, about the lack of democracy, and so on. I live somewhere in the city, and the buildings, ... are they good? ... What is special about Tensta? Is it perhaps the socioeconomic structure? We have no programmes for [inner-city districts], but they are also part of the segregated city.[18]

Another paradox observed was the gap between the authorities' postulated aim of empowering people and the experience of hin-

---

16   Witness Monica Andersson, former Social-Democratic deputy mayor. Other witnesses on politics and administration were Anna Hesser, the project leader of the Tensta project, and Sven Lorentzi.

17   Witnesses Erol Sayin, planner from Turkey, and Rod Hackney, community architect from the UK.

18   Comment from the audience.

drance by state agencies when self-initiatives were actually taken.[19] A local resident gave examples of how discrimination and segregation were actually built into the physical structures with a planned road that would isolate Tensta from its surroundings even more, a tramline connection that was supposed to go through the adjacent district of Rinkeby but was moved to a more prosperous neighbourhood and a subway extension, which should have connected Tensta's line to an adjacent suburb but was shifted to another line. He witnessed:

> It was decided twenty years ago … and now it has been taken away. This happens all the time. And the citizens of Tensta, many of them don't even know about it, but maybe they feel how things are ruled, they are depressed.[20]

It was then suggested that we should move on from an idealistic view of participation as the solution to the challenges of participation, the power relations, conflicts, differences in opinions and interests. It was not enough to bring ideas from other parts of the world, because their success was not only about their method: 'Let's not repeat what happened in '89 of going elsewhere and trying to find examples and inspiration, but let's ask the people here and create the process based on the local conditions, based on the institutional context, based on the actors.'[21]

GLÖMMINGE: A GUIDED WALK AND MEMORIAL DINNER

Action 2: 27 April 2014, 14.00–19.00

One of the few collaborative housing projects inspired by the conference that was carried out was the renewal of Glömminge in Tensta.[22] The large complex contains approximately 240 flats in three wings.

---

19   Henrik Linton, architect, from the audience, reminded us that the roots of the Swedish public housing system are to be found in the cooperative movement, formed to empower people towards their landlords. Only at the second stage did municipal and state agencies take control of the housing market in order to provide decent housing for everybody.

20   Björn Erdal, citizen of Tensta, from the audience.

21   Camilo Calderon, architect and urban planner, from the audience.

22   The project was commissioned by the local government and included the communal housing company Familjebostäder, the tenants' organization and the architecture firm Loggia Architects, represented by Ylva Larsson. The tenants collaborated in the renewal of their buildings through a two-year-long dialogue, 1989–1991. Another unusual measure taken was that, during the following construction period, all tenants could stay in their homes. The project was completed with public artwork in the entrances of the buildings in 1995.

The redesign undertaken together with the tenants focused on rather small-scale interventions such as improving the entrances, creating a streetscape by simple means, renovating collective spaces such as the laundry rooms and adding a meeting and party room for the tenants. The architects turned part of the parking garage into small shops lining the street, and a bakery, a barbershop, a pizzeria and a news agency moved in. That created an identifiable small quarter with its own street life in a previously generic and mono-functional area. The entrances were expanded into glass pavilions, which invited people to sit and to play. The formerly dark inner corridors were opened to the garden for daylight, and the shared laundry rooms were given large windows to the corridors. Previously built-in balconies were added to the kitchens, thereby increasing the sitting area for families; balconies were instead added onto the façade for tenants who were ready to pay a higher rent for them. The renewal projects challenged a systemic approach. They created a contact zone, which required creativity, engagement and an attitude of caring in neighbourhoods where several languages were spoken; they were experimental and time-consuming.[23]

The architect of the project witnessed:

> We worked straight from what it said should be done [in the conference report] … I employed a student, and we worked day and night, and my eldest children grew up here during the evenings, because they had to follow me to the meetings. It was a project interacting with all the people; we connected in all the languages there were. You did not have to know Swedish, it was important to connect. There were 960 households. Glömminge is just a small part of it. We had to work within a normal budget, no extra money … We worked together on this renewal project for many years. And when it was really empowered, it was shut down. And nowadays, twenty years later, I think it was a political act, because the people here were empowered. They were in charge, and that wasn't really what was expected.[24]

---

23   The consultation process made workbooks available in several languages and distributed them to 960 households. In the workbooks, tenants could make suggestions in words and sketches as a basis for discussion in following meetings; after the meetings, the architects produced result books, which were published and handed back to the tenants in the languages most residents spoke in the respective quarters, such as Greek, Finnish and Arabic.

24   Architect Ylva Larsson from the audience at the witness seminar, 5 March 2014. We thank Ylva Larsson for her time, discussions and participation in Action Archive and the generous access she granted us to the private archive of her firm, Loggia Architects.

The second action included an architect-guided walk through Tensta for a group of twelve participants from Tensta and Stockholm (Figure 22.4). The walk led to places all over Tensta where small adaptations had been made and to places where interventions had been planned but were never completed. The walk ended in Glömminge at the former tenants' meeting and party room *Familjeboet* [family nest], with an enactment of a dinner in memory of the celebration of the opening of the space in 1992.[25] A short documentary film was shown about the collaborative work that had created this environment.[26]

Figure 22.4 Guided tour by architect Ylva Larsson of the participatory renewal project, Glömminge (1989–1995)
Photo: Helena Mattsson

Today, the generous room with an open kitchen is closed to the tenants because neighbours complained about the frequent use by noisy groups of youngsters. This decision points to two sympto-matic shifts that condition each other: the social disengagement of residents and the trend in Swedish housing production to regard collective spaces as obsolete. These days, the room is empty most of

25   There is only one elderly couple left in Glömminge who lived there in 1989. They were also involved in the renewal project.

26   *Tensta samverkan och förändring,*1989–1995 [Tensta collaboration and change, 1989–1995], documentary film produced by Levande Bilder/Bo-Erik Gyvberg with Familjebostäder, Loggia Architects, NCC and SABO.

the time and only open to members of the tenants association at their meetings.[27] Through the enactment, the room was made accessible for the evening.

THE DESIRE FOR COMMON SPACES: A DEBATE

Action 3: 8 May 2014, 18.00–20.00

In a concluding action we discussed the provision of civic space since the 1970s, together with activists of several generations and an audience at the Workers Education Association building (ABF-huset) in Stockholm.[28] We produced a map and a timeline together with the invited guests and the audience to capture the history of civic spaces in Stockholm. We started by recapitulating an era in which the state still provided access to space for citizens' political activities. Even large cultural institutions, such as the Museum of Modern Art, would give room to and support citizen movements. Under the current post-political conditions, generous institutional structures have disappeared, and a number of self-initiated and self-run places have emerged.

This action was also inspired by the observation, made at the exhibition, of the formation in Swedish suburbs of groups such Megafonen, Pantrarna, Streetgäris and Allt åt alla, who fight for a 'just society' and 'inclusive citizenship' with more influence on political decisions. In debates and demonstrations, they take up positions against structural racism and the recent wave of privatization of rental housing, and campaign for access to public services, such as health centres in the suburbs (Schierup et al., 2014). Above all, they fight for the power to make decisions over their own lives in relation to politics. A continuous demand throughout the debate was the need for physical civic space for social and political meetings.[29]

Action Archive strove to wake memories and forgotten histories by initiating conversation and storytelling through practices such as the witness seminar, the guided walk and the memorial dinner, and

---

27   To become a member of the tenants association requires a membership fee.

28   The guests were Eva Hernbäck, representing the Byalags movement, Alternativ Stad and the tenant association; Per Hasselberg, initiator of Konsthall C and member of the Hökarängen district council; Mathias Wåg of Allt åt alla; Elof Hellström of Cyklopen and Söderorts Institute for Different Visions (SIFAV).

29   This is what ethnographer Gary Alan Fine describes as interlocks, sites of communication that connect smaller communities of interest and experience to larger publics, often tied to places where groups can communicate in 'free space'. In Fine's view, they provide the basis of civil society, where politics are discussed and enacted (Fine, 2010).

the collective recording of the history of civic spaces. These messy approaches do not attempt to resolve the obvious conflicts but aim at reframing questions, recovering lost causes and producing different understandings of what is produced socially in architecture and how architecture (re)produces social connections and relationships.

The witness seminar revealed an engrained conflict, as well as frustration, resignation and cynicism about structures that seemingly could not be changed, all these were expressed. The messy approach, rather than the more conventional research method of gathering rational or objective evidence, opened the affective side of this complex, unfinished situation for all attendees and led to new ways of knowing. The brief era of participatory housing projects such as Glömminge ended before they could really take effect, and the few cases that were developed stayed only at the level of individual appearances and made a local difference. In the history of Swedish housing politics, however, they never gained much recognition. The projects were carried out due to an enormous investment of dedicated, emotional and idealistic engagement by numerous civic actors. They seem to have challenged Swedish organizational structures and probably also contested the cultural norms of its institutions.

Sweden has a reputation for centralized democratic and transparent decision-making processes in planning, as part of its welfare state structure. On the other hand, it seems strategies encouraging more local democracy were indeed desired and discussed in 1989 in answer to the growing diversity in society, expressed in translocal neighbourhoods, but they were never developed in political terms. Instead of political participation, the focus since the 1990s shifted to greater individual choice, selling rental flats to tenants and transferring public services to private actors. Recently, new place-based movements in contact zones, such as the Swedish suburbs, well connected to similar organizations all over Sweden, have emerged. They call, in Goodman's terms, on the unclaimed legacy of the unfinished modern revolution, which was promised but never carried through, as an opportunity for social transformation.

Cultural heritage processes do not necessarily have to reproduce an architecture of monolithic ideas along the lines of a Swedish culture. They could themselves work as a contact zone and encourage transcultural experiments. The architecture of the contact zone will produce new kinds of objects, communication and collaboration. These could include aspects of history, testimonies, but also mobile archives and new institutions.

REFERENCES

Blokland, Talja (2001) 'Bricks, mortar, memories: neighbourhood and networks in collective acts of remembering', *International Journal of Urban and Regional Research* 25(2): 268–283.

Buden, Boris (2014) *Cultural Heritage: The Context of an Obsession, available at:* www.tenstakonsthall.se/uploads/108-BorisBuden.pdf (accessed 8 January 2015).

de Certeau, Michel (1988) *The Practice of Everyday Life,* Berkeley, CA: University of California Press.

Denzin, Norman K. (1997) *Interpretative Ethnography: Ethnographic Practices for the 21st Century*, London: Sage.

Fine, Gary Alan (2010) 'The sociology of the local: action and its publics', *Sociology Theory* 28(4): 355–376.

Gibson-Graham, J.K. (2008) 'Diverse economies: performative practices for "other worlds"', *Progress in Human Geography* online: 1–20. doi: 10.1177/0309132508090821

Goodman, Paul ([1960] 2012) *Growing Up Absurd*, New York: New York Review of Books, pp. 194–211.
    (1970) *New Reformation*, New York: Vintage Books, pp. 206–207.

Lather, Pattie (1993) 'Fertile obsession: validity after poststructuralism', *Sociological Quarterly* 34(4): 673–693.
    (2008) '(Post) feminist methodology: getting lost or a scientificity we can bear to learn from', *International Review of Qualitative Research* 1: 155–164.

Lefebvre, Henri (1991) *The Production of Space*, Oxford: Blackwell.

Lind, Maria (2014) *Spring Department Tensta Museum: Reports from New Sweden, Tensta konsthall,* available at: www.tenstakonsthall.se/?s%C3%B6k (accessed 2 January 2015).

Massey, Doreen (1994) *Space, Place and Gender*, Minneapolis, MN: University of Minnesota Press.
    (1995) 'Places and their pasts', *History Workshop Journal* 39(Spring): 182–192.

Minh-ha, Trinh T. (1991) 'When the moon waxes red', in *Representations, Gender and Cultural Politics*, London: Routledge.

Näslund, Elisabet (2012) 'Programmet vi ärvde', *Arkitekten* 09(September): 22–30.

Nora, Pierre (2001) 'Reasons for the current upsurge in memory', *Transit* 22/2001, available at: www.eurozine.com/articles/2002-04-19-nora-en.html (accessed 2 January 2015).

Pratt, Mary Louise (1991) 'Arts of the contact zone', in *Profession,* New York: MLA, pp. 33–40.

Rendell, Jane (2011) 'Critical spatial practice: setting out a feminist approach to some modes and what matters in architecture', in Lori Brown (ed.) *Feminist Practices,* Farnham: Ashgate.

Schierup, Carl-Ulrik, Ålund, Aleksandra and Kings, Lisa (2014) 'Reading the Stockholm riots: a moment for social justice?' *Race & Class* 55(3): 1–21.

Stengers, Isabelle (2012) 'Reclaiming animism', *E-flux Journal* 36, 07/2012.

Tensta samverkan och förändring 1989–1995 [Tensta collaboration and change 1989–1995], documentary film produced by Levande Bilder/Bo-Erik Gyvberg with Familjebostäder, Loggia Architects, NCC and SABO.

23 – THE HUSTADT STORY – SO FAR

Apolonija Šušteršič

I'm back in Hustadt. This time I'm just a visitor. Matthias is very proudly showing me his café, 'HuKultur', which he is running now with volunteers and the Förderverein, Hustadt's oldest neighbourhood association. It's still in the colours as we designed it, together with Mari Rantanen, back in 2010. However, it's now furnished with new/old furniture that Meike Schalk and I donated to HuKultur just recently.[1]

Faruk is here as well, sitting in front of the café and really happy to see me. I'm equally delighted to see him. Faiza is in the kitchen screaming 'Hallo' – I enter to give her a hand. 'Long time no see!' I love the place. It smells of fresh baklawas – walnuts and honey. Professor Uhlig comes by and sits with us. He is a bit tired but obviously happy that his long-term project – the Förderverein – has started to 'fly again'. It seems that what we dreamt about so many years ago, when I moved to Hustadt to work on the project, is slowly becoming a reality. But it is not without its problems and not without struggle.

We are all sitting in front of the café looking at the Community Pavilion on the edge of the Brunnenplatz. There is canvas stretched over the front frame, facing the square. It has the printed title 'Ideen machten sich bezahlt!' (Ideas that pay!) … It seems the Pavilion was used as a site for another art project? But what a strange and enigmatic title, which sounds cynical or even slightly arrogant in this context. I got a bit worried.

The economic imperative forces itself on everything today, everything always seems to revolve around 'the money economy' and is NOT concerned with creating change for a better future. Even when we talk about ideas or new concepts, such ideas should apparently pay for themselves. They must be visible, they must not stay immaterial so that they can be measured and evaluated. They must produce some kind of material evidence and give a visual answer that justifies the investment. It seems to be extremely difficult to accept in the framework of capitalism we experience today, and difficult to imagine an alternative to the market economy. An alternative to a situation where the investment needs to produce a surplus value, and eventually produce bigger and bigger profits for those who invest. It

---

1   We made this furniture during the project KAFIČ for GfZK (Galerie für Zeitgenössische Kunst) in Leipzig. It needs some repair and it can be used again here in HuKultur café for some years. We are planning a new action in the near future!

looks like no-one is happy to invest in creating better futures, better relations, better communities, better places, without thinking that this will contribute to the production of increased rents and property value that only a few benefit from. Not only that, investment must turn around quickly – money has no time to wait! This 'economy of time' is a serious issue we face today, where everything must produce fast effects and fast profits. This is in contrast to the 'democracy project' as we know it, where decision-making processes take time; time which is 'lost' in discussions that aim to give everyone a voice and the right to speak. At the same time, the bureaucracy in place works according to global laws and isn't able to act in favour of local situations, the places where many initiatives originate. The questions that arise from such paradoxes are directed to the critique of capitalism and the market economy, and importantly, the opening up of other solutions and proposals. What would happen if we tried to ignore the time estimated that a specific investment needed to become profitable? What if we tried instead *to create a faithful process of democratic place-making, engaging the local population who are using the place daily?* What if we paid more attention to creating better relations between local populations and the place, rather then providing just another urban design, refurbished? The account that follows is a personal reflection of a project, which aimed to do just that.

THE CASE STUDY: THE HUSTADT PROJECT

The *Hustadt Project* emerged from an ordinary invitation from the city of Bochum in Germany. The commission was for a public art project in the central marketplace, Brunnenplatz, in the multicultural suburban neighbourhood called Hustadt. The art project was part of a larger urban regeneration programme in Hustadt, set up by the city. In this commission, a gap existed between the expectations of the commissioners and my own, participative approach to projects, an approach I bring to all my work. But this lack of knowledge and understanding of what the implications of a genuinely participative approach are, actually gave me the chance to work in Hustadt.

My reasons for accepting this invitation concern the challenges of the place itself, as well as a concern to provoke certain clichés within the art world[2] and to explore the hidden agendas behind this official invitation. The art world of today would view this invitation as very uninteresting, problematic or even wrong. It would be seen as the kind of invitation that could jeopardize an artist's integrity and lead to the instrumentalization of their work (and potentially, themselves). However, this is the very difficulty that makes me curious and it presents a real challenge. I had the idea of setting my own position as an artist working seriously in relation to a specific place. I decided I would *place my activity as a quotidian activity*, creating a new position, compared to other professionals dealing with the same questions. It was exciting to look into the process from the inside, as a *resident* and effect change on the way. However, the questions I asked myself from the beginning related to my own position within such a sensitive process of urban change. Would I be able to maintain a critical position, defend my own ideas (and not the ones of the public, or the politicians!) and yet still co-operate and discuss the process with both of them? I wanted to see how much 'space for resistance' an artist is allowed to use within the process of development. As an artist, I would be the only one who would represent an independent, and therefore possibly critical position. So I myself became part of an experiment!

The invitation from the city was clearly hoping that art would solve all those unnamed problems that the city itself, the social organization in place, or even the urban planners and architects were not able to resolve.

When I began to investigate the conditions of the area, and the conditions of invitation, I learnt of a number of interesting issues and formed the project around them. The biggest issues were those related to the inequitable distribution of socio-political work in public space.[3] Thus, the project circulates around questions of publicity and the public realm. It focuses on and discusses distributions of power in public space, the role of the artist (architect) within urban regeneration projects, the issue of 'spatial justice', and the appropriation of public space as understood by different actors. The project also

---

2   Here I'm referring to the position of the artist as an independent agent. Within art contexts and discussions there is a lot of speculation about the artist being instrumentalized by political, or other institutional, powers particularly when working within the domain of public art. I am interested in the mechanisms of instrumentalization and whether or not as an artist I could defend an autonomous position.

3   For example, who decides on the future of the place? There are politicians and planners who are not at all associated with or connected to the place, where the financial institutions who provide the funding are also distant. Within the process, there is no presence of the immediate public, who use this public space.

includes and examines several aspects of my own practice: action research; urban contexts as material to develop a project; process as product; and public participation as a vehicle to 'generate' community.

As an artist-researcher, I immersed myself in the life of the place. I shared the everyday situation with people living in Hustadt and, together with them, created a platform for a participatory process. In this case, I wasn't interested in a virtual interaction that is used as a strategy to provide or improve participation for direct democracy. Not only is the new technology not developed enough, it isn't widely available and access to it is usually limited to a specific social class. At the same time, I wanted to defend a direct relationship to space and to people; I wanted to confirm the importance of creating stimulating social situations within physical space.

CONTEXT: HUSTADT

Hustadt is a suburban neighbourhood on the south-eastern edge of the city of Bochum, Germany. It is surrounded by woods and fields on one side, with offshoots of the enormous campus of the Ruhr University Bochum, and on the other side, further housing areas. Hustadt was conceptualized in the frame of development of the Ruhr University area in South Bochum. The winning project by Professor Hanns Dustmann for this part of the city (Querenburg) proposed situating 6,500 housing units for about 25,000 people on 418 ha of land, of this, Hustadt would house 6,000 inhabitants.

The building process in Hustadt started in 1965, taking a few years to complete. The initial 500 apartments were finished by 1968 when the first young families moved in. This is also the time when the first Hustadt citizens' initiative – *Aktion bessere Hustadt*,[4] started to organize itself in order to deal with everyday life situations related to, for example, organized childcare and general communal living, which had only just begun.[5]

The place was meant to be what is called *Universitätsrahmenstadt* – a dwelling area to frame the university campus and the *Opel Werke, Bochum* – the Opel car factory situated on the other side of the Learholds Woods. It was intended to offer professors, students, academics, and public employees nearby living possibilities.

---

4   Aktion bessere Hustadt is the forerunner of the Förderverein that remains active today.

5   Haarmann, *Kleine Geschichte der Hustadt.*

Along the way Hustadt has met several changes as a result of different social, economic, and political developments related to today's changing global situation. Now the population has changed dramatically. The people living in Hustadt today come from all parts of the world, which makes Hustadt much more metropolitan than the main centre of Bochum itself. Today, there are approximately 56 different nationalities living in the neighbourhood. Many different cultures, lifestyles, and living habits are performed every day, in close proximity to one another, creating a microcosm of the world for good and for bad.

There is no need to say that outside of the neighbourhood itself, Hustadt has a reputation as a ghetto. It has acquired a very bad name, which has stigmatized the area for some time. High unemployment, lengthy integration processes and a constantly changing community limit the possibility for people to begin to relate to the place as their home. In Hustadt, 16 per cent of the population changes every year, with people constantly moving in and out. This means that it is not only difficult to build a relationship with the place as home, but it is also difficult to form a stable social environment and neighbourhood community. Consequently, the area is not able to create a sustainable community that manages itself and its everyday life to build a better place and a better reputation, where children are not ashamed to say that they come from Hustadt.[6]

PROCESS: AKTIONSTEAM

With the *Hustadt Project* I was aiming to produce change but I did not know what kind of change would be possible when I started. I was very aware of my own position as an artist, invited into a regeneration project in a place I did not know. It seemed all wrong, and so I decided to move to Hustadt to observe and learn from people living in the place and to learn from the situation as I experienced it. For the first few months I observed, listened, participated in public events in Hustadt, and discussed with the people I met in Hustadt in my everyday life there.

---

6   Namely, there was a case when the high schools in Bochum didn't want to accept students who had finished elementary school in Hustadt (Querenburg), acting on the rule of the school vicinity. Tom Thelen, 'Ablehnung von Grundschülern am NGB sorgt für Empörung in Bochum-Querenburg', *WAZ*, 2 March 2011, available at: www.derwesten.de/staedte/bochum/ablehnung-von-grundschuelern-am-ngb-sorgt-fuer-empoerung-in-bochum-querenburg-id4355167.html, Hustadt Episodaire, p. 2 (accessed 4 October 2011).

My commissioner, the city of Bochum, had expectations and projected them onto the work; however, my contract was open and my task was very much undefined, or non-prescribed. While they expected, or hoped, I would produce a sculpture (a replaceable, non-contextual object) and some neighbourhood kids would help me make it, I was pushing for more. I organized a local team of activists and people from the neighbourhood (which we called AKTION-STEAM) to work with me on conceptualizing the project and carry out the regeneration project directly. We worked together for a year on various spatial actions that were performed in the main square, the Brunnenplatz, where most of the neighbourhood would meet. Those actions became our tool for testing situations in space and time, and helped create arguments for public discussions with local politicians who were making decisions about the process and direction of the regeneration project.[7]

With our actions we performed everyday life activities in public space, which activated the public and the space. We danced, read in public, cooked, repaired bicycles, gardened, constructed a building, told stories, played music, and so on (Figure 23.1). We performed activities that would communicate with the public on several levels: bodily, culturally, and socially. The language of our actions was known to the public and therefore easy to adopt and participate in. Through the actions, we managed to activate the place and define it as a space; it became visible and present in the life of the neighbourhood. Following Michael de Certeau, who argues that, 'a space exists when one takes into consideration vectors of direction, velocities, and time variables' (1984: 117), we managed to place Brunnenplatz on the map of the city space. We managed to unfold a space that is composed of interactions of mobile elements, a space that is actuated by the ensemble of movements deployed within it, a space that occurs as the effect produced by the operations that orient it, situate it, temporalize it, and make it function in a polyvalent unity of conflictual programmes or contractual proximities. We managed to transform the space into a practised place (ibid.).

7   The whole process is described in my doctoral dissertation, completed in November 2013 at Lund University, Malmö Art Academy, www.lunduniversity.lu.se/lup/publication/4144448, pp. 27–80.

Figure 23.1 *Hustadt Project*, Actions, 2008–2011, Bochum, Germany
Photos: Apolonija Šušteršič

Those everyday life activities communicated our future project, the Community Pavilion – a meeting place in Brunnenplatz (Figure 23.2). Our actions had a direction. The actions that we performed, the everyday life activities were known to the public, yet were unusual at the same time as they were somehow 'out of place' or 'unexpected'. They just popped up without any extra official consent. We didn't ask the city for permission, except when it was really necessary. For example, when building the temporary pavilion (Figure 23.3), we just informed the city authorities via email about our action and we never received any official building permission for it. At one point in the process, things were developing so fast that we didn't have time to be engaged with bureaucracy. We just did it.

The spontaneity of our actions was beyond any official control, it was beyond expectations of how the project should develop and what could be expected at the end. It was an organic process that was built by reacting to previous events without much advance planning.

Figure 23.2 Brunnenplatz, *Hustadt Project*, Actions, 2008–2011, Bochum, Germany
Photo: Apolonija Šušteršič

PARTICIPATION: COMMUNITY PAVILION BRUNNENPLATZ 1

The *Community Pavilion* was not planned. It was never planned within the official budget of the 13 million euros that Hustadt had received for regeneration. While the budget did include finances for an art project, it did not include money to build the *Community Pavilion*; the budget was only to create an artwork![8]

The expectations of the commissioner towards the artist were different from how the project was actually developing. As an artist, I took freedom in experimenting and negotiating along the way.

It seems the process of regeneration, as imagined by the authorities and official politics, didn't include the unpredictability of an art project, where the main focus was a participatory process itself; a

---

8   However, the city built the basic structure of the pavilion with the money allocated to the art project from the outset. It was impossible to expect that the original financial plan for the regeneration process in Hustadt would extend (to 13 million euros) in favour of an art project. In order to finish the *Community Pavilion* as we imagined, I needed to do extensive fundraising. At the same time, nobody questioned the costs of the urban design project that was running in parallel and included a fountain that cost as much as the whole pavilion.

Figure 23.3 Temporary pavilion in progress, *Hustadt Project*, Actions, 2008–2011, Bochum, Germany
Photo: Apolonija Šušteršič

process where you work with people who are not professionals in the
field of art, architecture or urban development. They are just people
with different motivations, who came together to work on the *Hustadt
Project*. This creates a situation that is very difficult to predict and
control. However, control and predictability are of course at the core
of the conventional (urban) planning and in contrast to processes that
develop gradually and involve people's participation. With our project – the *Hustadt Project* – we ignored those aspects and reacted
according to the development of the art process.

Setting up a participatory process within an art project was
meant to test limits and question participation itself. When we
analyse such processes, we realize that there is a lot of unpredictability and improvisation involved. We need to be aware of the fact
that perhaps people who would participate in the process might
participate not only to agree but also to disagree and demand, to
have questions and want to get answers, and to even change the
proposed plan of the regeneration. The art project therefore became
a disturbance in the larger regeneration process, a kind of trouble
that it was necessary to deal with.

It became very clear that the participatory process, as a form of direct democracy, contradicts the general process of development within capitalist societies, which is directed to fast results and a predictable (planned) future. There is very little space for improvisation and uncertainty, which reveal the system itself to be inflexible and rigid, not corresponding to or even being able to correspond to human needs.

That's not news – democracy is in contradiction to capitalism! Capitalism and democracy have been locked in a contradictory yet interdependent relationship throughout their history. Despite popular conceptions, liberal democracy has emerged as a mechanism, which has in effect limited popular participation, and operated as a legitimating device to protect capitalism from more direct forms of democracy (Fisher, 1996). The *Hustadt Project* set up a platform for direct democracy and managed to create a situation that was not expected and beyond official control. Suddenly the Aktionsteam became the main negotiation partner with the city officials, regarding the regeneration process in Hustadt.

Our arguments for the *Community Pavilion* were very clear from the beginning: Hustadt has no place to house public meetings, it has no sheltered place to meet and discuss everyday life problems. There are spaces with religious designation, but these are not suitable to host the mixed public living in Hustadt.

The *Community Pavilion* was conceptualized to become a place for all the kinds of neighbourhood activities that were performed previously through our actions. It became a place for meetings, parties, a cinema, public readings and story telling, music and theatre performances, lectures, a place for children to play, to garden, draw and perform parts of the education programme. It is a simple structure with a roof, seating places, tables and benches, a small enclosed space, a poster board and a blackboard, a little herb garden, and anything more depends on the users' imaginations (Figure 23.4).

However, the *Community Pavilion* is not just a building, which resulted from an art project, it is much more: it has connected the loose strings of local activism that needed a platform for their activities; it has empowered those who wanted to be empowered in order to get on with their struggle, to keep the place alive in its everyday reality; discovering the potential that exists within its inhabitants at this moment, and through that, opposing the powers of gentrification.

Figure 23.4 Community Pavilion in progress, *Hustadt Project*, Actions, 2008–2011, Bochum, Germany
Photo: Apolonija Šušteršič

The process of the art project itself generated other self-organized projects and created other opportunities like the HuKultur café, the Hustadt Cinema Workshop, it activated existing NGOs such as UMQ (University meets Querenburg) and the Förderverein, who became keepers of the pavilion and who continue to work with strong links to the present local population.

The outcome of this participatory art project has resulted in numerous encounters, connections, and networks of relationships that enable people to understand what their own personal potential is, and how it would be possible to realize it. The art project made people believe in their own power. The inter-subjective situation created through the process of the *Hustadt Project* produced participants' awareness, which led to action. And this action is a continuous action that didn't stop when I left the project – it is still going on.

I started the project because of an official invitation by the city of Bochum as part of the institutionalized process, but ended up in a self-organized and independent formation. There has been a certain transformation within the process of developing the project that has by its actions produced a critique of the official system. I can confirm Chantal Mouffe's suggestion that it is possible to act politically within the existing system and affect its direction of change: as 'to believe that existing institutions cannot become the terrain of contestation is to ignore the tensions that always exist within a given configuration of forces and the possibility of acting in a way that subverts their form of articulation' (Mouffe, 2013: 100).

THE IMMATERIAL, THE RELATIONAL, AND THE PROCESSUAL

At the same time, I look at visual art and its relation to society today, particularly when it seems to be developing an interesting critique of capitalism but hasn't yet managed to distance itself from it. The 'dematerialization of the art object' (Lippard, 1997)[9] has turned itself into a 'production of value'[10] that feeds the art market continuously, even if the art object has disappeared. On the other hand, art that is produced 'outside' of the art institution (and art market) contributes to the production of space and potentially changes its value as well. In this case I believe that by acting ethically, we can stir the process against the accumulation of capital exclusively producing the social value of space. Working within the urban context (as an artist or architect), one needs to be aware of who will benefit from the change, in order to be able to shift the spatial development processes against gentrification and other socially negative processes.

Within the production of space, through experience and awareness, I focus on analysing the relationships, or the relational as Bourriaud (2002) put it. This approach creates an interaction with space that can lead to further participation and action. This finding is not a new one, but it connects loose strings and presents the subject in another light. The argument is a result of my long-term practice, and

9   Lucy R. Lippard's book, *Six Years: The Dematerialization of the Art Object from 1966 to 1972*, is a cross-referenced book of information on some aesthetic boundaries: consisting of a bibliography into which are inserted fragmented text, artworks, documents, interviews, and symposia, arranged chronologically and focused on what are called conceptual or information or idea art, with mentions of such vaguely designated areas as minimal, anti-form, systems, earth, or process art, occurring now in the Americas, Europe, England, Australia, and Asia (with occasional political overtones).

10   I'm referring here to the increasing value that is applied to art objects and art concepts produced for the art market, which transforms the value from the symbolic value of the artwork into the monetary value. Dematerialization, as a concept critical of material society and the greed of market capitalism, is an interesting idea. Yet as bodies we are still not dematerialized, even if the developments within technology nowadays suggest virtualization of the parts of our being (such as emotions or feelings), the physicality of our body remains. Therefore, we simply need physical space, and objects to relate to. The more urgent problem that I consider needs attention today is the production of value within the contemporary art context. That serves very well to feed the flow and supports the philosophy of the market-focused capitalist system.

therefore brings some new suggestions to the subject of participation, particularly on the inter-subjective relations in the process and the creation of informal situations for encounter. The key issue in creating participatory processes is participant motivation and desire. In my opinion, motivation and the desire[11] to participate are part of the sub-jective state of mind: experience and awareness. I unfold and analyse this statement within the specific context of the *Hustadt Project*.

In the *Hustadt Project*, as in my practice in general, I focus on a result that is not necessarily an object (that is, an architectural or art object that provides a physical presence within our living environment). Instead, I am interested in the process itself. Rather than a physical object, I'm interested in the process of communicative exchange. I'm interested in changing and affecting the established systems through their own production and development in order to provide a change.

However, it is important to understand the situation, the place where I work and who are the people living–making this space I'm engaged with. Therefore, I aim to embrace what Doreen Massey proposed to understand when working within space:

> *First, that we recognise the space as the product of interrela-tions; as constituted through interactions, from the immensity of the global to the intimately tiny. Second, that we understand space as the sphere of the possibility of the existence of multi-plicity in the sense of contemporaneous plurality; as the sphere in which distinct trajectories coexist; as the sphere therefore of coexisting heterogeneity. Without space no multiplicity; without multiplicity no space. If space is indeed the product of interrela-tions, then it must be predicated upon the existence of plurality. Multiplicity and space as co-constitutive. Third, that we recognise space as always under construction [as a process]. Precisely because space on this reading is a product of relations-between, relations, which are necessarily embedded material practices, which have to be carried out, it is always in the process of being made. It is never finished; never closed. Perhaps we could imagine space as the simultaneity of stories – so-far.*
> (Massey, 2005: 9)

---

11   I am following here Doina Petrescu's reading of desire and participation in Deleuzian terms (Petrescu, 2005).

REFERENCES

Bourriaud, Nicolas (2002)
Relational Aesthetics, Dijon: Les
presses du réel.

De Certeau, Michel (1984) *The
Practice of Everyday Life*, trans.
Stephen F. Rendall, Berkeley,
CA: University of California Press.

Fisher, Rebecca (ed.) (1996)
*Managing Democracy, Managing
Dissent*, London: Corporate
Watch.

Haarmann, Uhlig (2008) *Kleine
Geschichte der Hustadt*. Available at: https://lup.lub.lu.se/search/
ws/files/4001754/4145080.pdf
(accessed 11 May 2016).

Lippard, Lucy R. (1997) *Six
Years: The Dematerialization
of the Art Object from 1966 to
1972*, Berkeley, CA: University of
California Press.

Massey, Doreen (2005) *For
Space*, London: Sage.

Mouffe, Chantal (2013)
*Agonistics: Thinking the World
Politically*, London: Verso.

Petrescu, Doina (2005) 'Losing
control, keeping desire', in Peter
Blundell Jones, Doina Petrescu
and Jeremy Till (eds) *Architecture
and Participation*, London:
Spon Press.

24 – A BAKERY AS A SITE OF RESISTANCE

Jeanne van Heeswijk

PROLOGUE: ON THE PRODUCTION OF LIVED SPACE

In loving memory of Fred Brown
According to the French socialist and philosopher, Henri Lefebvre, space is socially and politically construed and manifests itself in three different ways. The first space is concrete and physical and it belongs to the material domain. The second is abstract space and it is a mental construction. The third is the so-called 'lived space'; this is where the physical and mental constructions of space meet. Space is construed here as a social product that alters through time. It is provided with symbols and significance by people who live and interact with each other in it (Lefebvre, 1991). In this way a bakery is only a bakery when people actually bake in it; and when they provide significance to that piece of the earth, they complete the whole. This text will follow *Homebaked*'s[1] becoming a living spatial entity, a lived space, from the project's outset in 2010 to the time of writing, at the end of 2014. In doing so, the chapter compiles some of the different ways the project has been viewed, described and evaluated in funding bids, reviews, poetry, personal letters, performance scripts, evaluation, planning reports, and in-depth writing by embedded researchers.[2]

One of the main characteristics of *Homebaked* is that it has constantly evolved. Creative improvised approaches to spotting and grabbing opportunities – like the potential of re-opening the bakery – have been more important than rigid systems or processes. At times, this has led to some confusion and tension; but the richness of learning how to take responsibility for the place together shaped the whole. Fred Brown, local artist and activist, would say:

---

1   *Homebaked* is an independent Community Land Trust and Co-operative Bakery, initiated by Jeanne van Heeswijk as part of the Liverpool Biennial.

2   This text is compiled from the introduction by Jeanne van Heeswijk and Britt Jurgensen to 'Homebaked: A Perfect Recipe', *Liverpool Biennial Journal* 2 (2014); an evaluation report by John P. Houghton, Principal Consultant of Shared Intelligence (2013); Yann Maury (ed.) *Les coopératives d'habitants, des outils pour l'abondance* [Inhabitants' co-operatives, tools for abundance], available at: http://chairecoop.hypotheses.org/4186; building and planning reports; Jeanne van Heeswijk, 'The right to live well: Urbanism's Core', *Harvard Magazine* 37 (2014); and personal letters from participants.

As in all baking, so it also should be with a developing idea.
Decide what it is you want to make, gather materials, including
people, do some frenzied work in preparation – then wait. Then
do some more frenzied activity – then wait again. Then apply the
required heat. Taking the time it needs is a recognised and vital
part of the baking process to produce the best results. In project
development it can be so frustrating as we wait on results. But it
needs to be done; the time needs to be taken. Give it the time,
give it the resources and try not to prescribe. We nurture each
other. As the dough rises, we rise.

Figure 24.1 As the dough rises, we rise by Fred Brown (Anfield Liverpool, 2011)
Photo: Jeanne van Heeswijk

WALKING DOWN ANFIELD

Walking around Anfield, a classic Northern English working-class
neighbourhood, famously the home of the Liverpool Football Club
(LFC), will leave you with disbelief as you encounter streets of
boarded-up houses with temporary grassed areas, where houses
have been demolished between pockets of newly built houses. The
high street consists mainly of closed fast food outlets, as they only
open to cater to match-day visitors. On the side of the Stadium where
LFC is planning to extend, residents are stranded in between the

'tinned up'[3] houses owned by the city or the club, leaving a fragmented and displaced community (Figure 24.2).

Figure 24.2 Housing market renewal, put on hold (Anfield, Liverpool, 2010)
Photo: Jeanne van Heeswijk

The current situation in Anfield is an example of the recent
history of unsuccessful large-scale regeneration programmes.[4] The
Housing Market Renewal Initiative (HMRI) was designed to reverse
the historic decline of low-demand areas in the North of England
and the Midlands and get money flowing through them. These
areas, identified by the government as 'market failures', were unlike
anywhere else in Britain; house prices had stagnated and HMRI was
tasked with demolishing surplus stock and replacing them with fewer
newer houses. The Anfield/Breckfield zone, considered to be one of
the most severely deprived parts of England,[5] was scheduled for the
largest clearance programme in the New Heartlands HMRI area, with
plans to demolish 1,800 residential and commercial properties.

---

3   Closed and secured with metal panels to prevent squatters.

4   Anfield is part of the 'Anfield/Breckfield' zone of the Merseyside 'New Heartlands' Housing
Market Renewal Pathfinder area, launched in 2003.

5   A report published by the Church Urban Fund identified Anfield as the third poorest part of
England, after only Toxteth East and Shaw Road in Oldham.

From the start, the programme was very unpopular with some residents who felt that it was pulling apart the community and unnecessarily demolishing pre-1919 terraces that could be more easily and quickly refurbished. Others welcomed the possibility of a 'newer house' and participated in scheme planning sessions. But, for those who owned their homes, it often turned out that they couldn't afford the new homes with the compensation given to them by the city. So they were either pushed into debt or had to start renting. Others lamented the stereotypically negative image of violence, drug abuse, copper theft and recurrent fires, which is how Anfield was portrayed in TV programmes, such as *The Secret Millionaire*,[6] which some people thought were actively enforced in order to roll out the red carpet for the 'Renewal' plan.

Jayne Lawless, a local resident and artist, stated in an interview about living in Granton Road:

> *The way I understand it, is that there was a big pot of gold at the European Union; in order to access this pot, the area had to tick many boxes in the magical world of deprivation. So, suddenly, we were told, at the time, that we were from this deprived area. I am not deprived; I don't feel deprived. We've all got food and clothes; both parents work. How am I deprived?*

The HMRI programme was slowed down by the housing crisis that followed the 2008 financial crash, as the developer pulled out and house building activity decreased. By 2010, only 72 new homes had been built in the area, which is significantly lower than planned, leaving Anfield in a state of limbo. That year, the Coalition government decided to withdraw funding from the entire Housing Market Renewal Programme and it was officially closed down in March 2011. The disappointment brought by the failure of another major regeneration scheme, coupled with years of lingering uncertainty about the future of Liverpool FC's ground,[7] on top of the wider societal picture of recession and spending cuts, left a legacy of frustration for many Anfield residents. Angela McKay, a local resident and social worker, stated:

---

6   *The Secret Millionaire*, Channel 4, episode 6, 2009.

7   A succession of plans to move or redevelop the football ground has been suggested for almost two decades, but none have been implemented. It was only in 2012 that the new owners of the club confirmed they intended to stay, but would increase the size of the ground.

*The local community has had their hopes repeatedly raised
and then dashed by promises of 'neighbourhood regeneration',
which has been slow to materialize. After 15 years of living
under these circumstances, many people have lost trust in any
government schemes. We are 'sick of waiting' for something to
be delivered. It's the numbers of times we've been made promises and been lied to. To me, HMRI means devastation, promises
broken, no consultation.*

STOP WAITING, START MAKING: THE PRODUCTION OF SOCIALITY[8]

A timeline of collective struggle/resistance (2010–2014)

At the beginning of 2010, a state of despair continued to haunt the
area. If anything could or should be done, it had to be something that
created change on the ground in a structural way. It had to change
local people's ability to influence the way their neighbourhood is
managed and developed and give them tools to take 'matters into
[their] own hands'. An often-heard critique of current planning and
development programmes in many parts of Europe is that they seek
to pre-determine and prescribe who the community should be, how
they should behave, and how they should interact with public spaces.
Communities, however, are not scripted. In Anfield, over-deterministic
planning, especially when it failed, led to a ten-year gridlock of the area.

In a review of Lukasz Stanek's book on Lefebvre's idea that space
is a social product, Christopher Knoll wrote:

*As Stanek stresses, Lefebvre's criticism aims at central plan-
ning's ensuing depoliticization, fragmentation and segregation
of 'possible communities', in other words, the very denial of
every citizen's right to the city as ongoing communal project of
co-habitation … Stanek thus stresses Lefebvre's search for an
urban architecture which would replace social isolationism and
antagonism by opening up to possible spaces of solidarity and
association. Stanek shows a Lefebvre whose take on 'spaces
as always unfinished œuvres in process', in which the individual
can come into discourse with the communal collective, and in
this way overcoming segregations of work-space and spaces*

---

8   Sociality is the degree to which individuals tend to associate in social groups and form cooperative societies.

of leisure, remained true to his own humanist Marxist version of
fighting for an equal right to the city for all its inhabitants.
(Knoll, 2012)

Tapping into the frustration, trying to turn it into a constructive
desire, and stimulating a community-based response to the regeneration of Anfield formed the start of the *Homebaked* project. In order
to create 'fields of interaction'[9] that could build the relationships and
trigger the debates that enable people to have a say and shape their
surroundings, a twofold timeline was developed. This marked the
steps that were needed, both in the social and building processes; it
spanned four years and tried to map the way in which the 'building of a
small-scale alternative' to the very apparent failure of the Housing Market Renewal Programme could be created for and with the community.
At the same time, *Homebaked* tried to create a meeting point for
different communities and stakeholders in the area, to become a place
where people gain a better understanding of the housing regeneration
process underway in their neighbourhood *together* and, importantly,
could acquire the skills and confidence to play an active part in
improving their surroundings. Slow learning and cumulative change
through an open and long-term process have been vital, but that has
been a difficult commitment to retain in the face of the urgency, even
desperation, which characterizes the needs of the local residents of
Anfield. This is especially so as regeneration strategies shift, change
and continue to threaten not only *Homebaked*, but their own homes.[10]
    Over the course of a year in 2010, a group of around twenty young
people took on the whole community as a client, tried to question the
existing master-plan and draw up a sustainable alternative. They worked
through a participatory design process led by local architect, Marianne
Heaslip (URBED architects), and put sustainable development, both
environmentally as well as socially, at the core of the work. They
attempted to create a small-scale, community-led alternative to the
large planning schemes and assist residents in confronting the issues
facing the otherwise stagnant development of their neighbourhood.
    Meeting after meeting, with the Housing Co-op, the City Council
and the development company, turned out to be, time and time again,

9   What is meant by this is a first attempt to create a temporary framework in which to start
working in the area. It is a frame of questions that circumscribe the particular problematics, tensions
and questions about publicness, social interaction and politics. It asks: 'How can places become
public again, that is platforms for meeting, discussion, and conflict?'

10   Derived from notes by independent researcher, Samantha Jones.

a dead end. Limited progress was made in identifying an appropriate residential property. Everyone was charmed by the idea but didn't want to give an inch of territory back to the community. Then, in January 2011, Mitchell's Bakery, an important landmark and meeting place in the community, closed down (Figure 24.3). For many residents, the closure of the bakery was clear confirmation of Anfield's decline. A lot of effort went into making the bakery and the adjoining houses the project's base camp and, by that, ground zero of the struggle.[11]

Figure 24.3 *Homebaked*, Brick by Brick, Loaf by Loaf we build ourselves, project block of houses and former Mitchells Bakery (Anfield, Liverpool, 2011)
Photo: Liverpool Biennial

A PROCESS OF SOCIALIZATION[12]

Since then, the bakery building became the site for public discussion and debate, as well as for weekly design workshops and planning sessions, focusing on the transformation of the building and the desire to re-open the bakery. The former bakery was turning into a site of resistance. As Don Mitchell wrote about this project:

---

11   A temporary lease on the building was negotiated with the Mitchell family.

12   Socialization is the process of structuring or restructuring an economy on a socialist basis, usually by establishing a system of production for use in place of the profit system, along with the end of the operation of the laws of capitalism.

There's a reason why it's so exciting when people take over spaces – disused buildings, abandoned lots and public sites – and either temporarily or permanently make them their own. The reason is that such occupation disrupts the logic of capital as it seeks to produce cities in its own image, a process, we are told over and over again, for which there is no alternative ... The taking of public spaces shows that there are alternatives; it disrupts, sometimes quite radically, the capitalist production of space.
(2014: 1)

Different organizational forms were discussed and, for all involved, a steep learning curve started as we tried to find out about alternative models of co-owning and managing land and houses. After many meetings and consultations, the model of Community Land Trusts (CLTs) was chosen.[13] CLTs are non-profit, democratically organized structures run by volunteers that enable people to take on the ownership and management of assets, develop housing, workspaces, community facilities or other assets that meet the needs of the area. The model ensured that the bakery and neighbouring houses would be owned by residents, controlled by the community, and be made available at permanently affordable levels. This model was also chosen because it presented the opportunity to use the potential of the *Localism Bill* for significant social benefit and impact, and not least because it allows genuine community ownership of the organization.

Homebaked became one of the first urban CLTs in the UK. As Gabriela Rendon has said:

Envisioning new housing paradigms amidst the current housing crisis may be overwhelming and sometimes disempowering for communities in large urban areas dominated by profit-driven development ... To reclaim the city, it is necessary to learn from successful experiences leading to housing justice and co-producing innovative processes achieving new housing paradigms. There is no perfect formula to embark on such an ambitious task.
(2014: 1)

---

13   The CLT model has its roots in the co-operative movement and Garden Cities of the nineteenth century, and has been extensively tested as an effective means for collective community ownership in deprived communities in the USA. More recently CLTs have been used by rural communities in the UK to provide much-needed affordable housing for local families.

Throughout this time, the bakery building and the adjacent block remained demarcated under a clearance order, meaning that it was officially still earmarked for demolition and could be handed a Compulsory Purchase Order at any time. There were constant negotiations with the City Council to get the order lifted and buy the building. However, the situation in Anfield remained frozen.

At the beginning of 2012, when thinking about re-opening the bakery, the idea had been to work with an existing local entrepreneur to re-open it, along with a café. But by then, a group was established within the slowly growing *Homebaked* community to re-open the bakery as a co-operative and social enterprise. For them, it was important that the bakery as a place of production should become a viable business, as this would also mean the community could generate its own resources, creating local jobs and skills. At this moment in time, the project started to advocate for wider social justice goals for Anfield, such as encouraging healthier lifestyles through good food and classes, as well as helping people get into work by offering apprenticeships and training to local people. With the support of the co-operative movement, a process of learning and planning was set up to develop the first business plan together. Finally, in June, the *Homebaked Co-operative Anfield Limited* was established (Figures 24.4 and 24.5).

Figure 24.4 Design workshop remodelling the bakery block (Anfield, Liverpool, 2012) Photo: Marianne Heaslip, URBED (urbanism, environment & design) Ltd

Figure 24.5 Baking workshops
(Anfield, Liverpool, 2014)
Photo: Mark Loudon

RAISING HOMEBAKED'S POLITICAL VOICE

The bakery had great symbolic importance. It was a local landmark which provided a literal and metaphorical shop-window and offered an accessible base. People regularly dropped in to ask for a loaf and/ or find out what the plans were. The bakery also resonated at a more universal level. Bricks and bread, providing sustenance and shelter, are the two most basic things a community needs. The sight of a community taking ownership of its buildings and creating their own bread is one of the reasons it started to attract attention.

With the *Anfield Home Tour*, a performative guided tour within the frame of the Liverpool Biennial Festival in the summer of 2012, *Homebaked* took a risk in going out to the world with their story of struggle when it was still being developed. Everybody thought it important to tell of the effect of the city's failed politics on the daily lives of people who were displaced or still stuck in decay. The *Anfield Home Tour* took visitors from the main exhibition venue in Liverpool city centre to Anfield through a historic landscape of clearance and displacement. Visitors met protagonists from *Homebaked*, both on the way and in their houses (Figure 24.6). The tour ended at the bakery, in order to sit down together and discuss the situation with other residents and possible partners and funders. The tour generated enormous attention and directed focus on the community's struggle. It gave people a voice and strength through owning the narrative. According to Tim Jeeves:

> The Anfield Home Tour gave voice to the people with, arguably, the most entitlement to the area: those whose identities are meshed with the bricks and mortar of the houses bought through the Housing Market Renewal Initiative. The significance

of this act of voicing narrative, (syn)aesthetically or otherwise,
can be used to intervene in assertions of ownership; change the
story that is told, and claims to ownership are also altered.
(2014: 4)

The story of the bakery as a place of resistance started spreading nationally and internationally, which encouraged *Homebaked* to start a crowd-funding campaign in November 2012, called 'An Oven at the Heart of Anfield', in order to buy the oven and kitchen appliances needed to supply the bakery. The campaign was successful in giving the bakery group a lot of momentum. Throughout this time, the bakery started opening on match days, with people bringing in baked goods to give out for donations. The Twitter following was growing. Following the initial fit-out of the bakery as a project space for test-driving the business and making the space suitable for welcoming the public, *Homebaked Co-operative Anfield* started a 'warm-up' phase of test trading, market research and product development at the bakery, along with organizing community and engagement events. Business plans were fine-tuned and the first talks on hiring bakers and café staff were held.

Every day more people stopped by and joined. But also, the first signs of fatigue were starting to appear, as well as the first ruptures in the group. Some of the people, who had been there from the beginning, were overwhelmed by the newcomers. People were becoming wary of the fact that telling the story over and over again, was sometimes taking away the focus from the real struggles still to be done on the ground. It was time to actually start baking bread now; would the project be able to live up to the moment? One of the strengths of *Homebaked* has been its evolutionary nature, the way it continued to develop and alter in the present and will continue to do so in future.

Figure 24.6 'Sue's House, Anfield Home Tour (Anfield, Liverpool, 2012)
Photo: Jeanne van Heeswijk

NEGOTIATING LOCAL POLITICS

In summer 2013, the Community Land Trust was awarded funding
from the Empty Homes Grant and Social Investment Bank (SIB) to
start the building process of the bakery and the flats above. The bakery was ready to open fully in October 2013 with a team of staff ready
to go. But in the background, the unresolved issue of the ownership
of the building and the clearance order pending on it still loomed.

While renting from the Mitchells, *Homebaked* started negotiating
buying the building from them and, at the same time, tried to get
the clearance order lifted by the City Council. The plans for a new
post-HMRI master-plan for Anfield, called 'The Anfield Project', were
made public, and *Homebaked* was not on the map! Along with the
rest of the high street, the block was to be demolished as planned,
with no design plan for the bakery's street or a possible builder/
investor (Figure 24.7). People from the community started going to the
planning offices and demanding answers and involvement. Frustrations
were building up as *Homebaked* was caught in a vicious circle again:
it couldn't spend the funding on refurbishing a building it didn't own;
and nobody wants to invest in a building threatened to be demolished.
Behind the bakery, the demolition began, Granton Road was going,
and the news of a pending Compulsory Purchase Order was delivered.

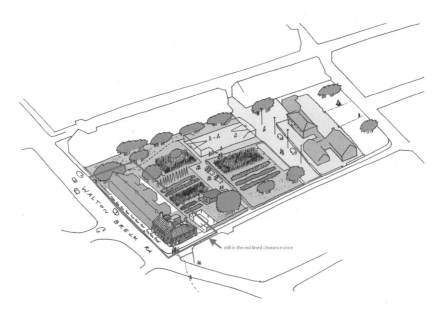

Figure 24.7 Homebaked still in the clearance zone (Anfield, Liverpool, 2013)
Drawing: Marcel van der Meijs

Over the following weeks, people went in groups to speak to different councillors and local MPs, to make sure the communal efforts were being noticed and ask for *Homebaked* to be included in the new master-plan for the area. While local people took over the political negotiations, the Board of the Community Land Trust was being reinforced with people with skills, expertise and connections to assist with the difficult negotiations. *Homebaked* made a firm decision to manifest physically by opening the bakery, working 6 days a week, in October 2013. In order to do the most necessary work on the building to bring it up to current standards, the shop-fit was done by lots of volunteers, partly using materials found in the building. The daily struggles were taking their toll on the core group of volunteers, but new people kept turning up and filling the gaps.

The potential initial capital development of *Homebaked CLT* was a movable feast for six months due to the changing politics. Originally, *Homebaked CLT* had been looking solely at the development of 193–199 Oakfield Road as a site for a social enterprise, which included the bakery and the associated sustainable affordable homes for 10–14 local people. In the negotiations with the council, *Home-baked* offered them a solution for the entire block, for which they had no plans. If they were absolutely set on demolishing, *Homebaked* offered to build new, as long as it could keep the bakery building and integrate it into the new-build mix-use scheme. That would include affordable housing, retail and the use of the 'old rec'[14] in the back for urban growing and recreation, under the stewardship of *Homebaked*.

Homebaked is a 'form of protest', a critique of mainstream house building and regeneration policies and practices, and an attempt to demonstrate that residents can do things for themselves. As the project evolved and the focus pointed to taking on ownership and management of the bakery and the properties, there was some concern that it would be seen as a more overtly political, oppositional campaign. This could be particularly problematic as the future of *Homebaked* depended on negotiations with the City Council over the demolition order and transfer of the properties and land to the Community Land Trust. So the question was, how could *Homebaked* stay a form of protest demanding an alternative to failed government schemes, and at the same time build a productive relationship with the City Council?

---

14   Behind the bakery there is a large empty lot which is partly used as a recreational area.

As of January 2014, discussions with the Liverpool City Council (LCC) have been regular and there is a draft 'Heads of Terms' agreement being finalized around the ambitions of *Homebaked CLT*. The agreement includes for LCC to purchase the bakery property from the current owners and then gift the property to the CLT to refurbish and develop it. Importantly, this agreement also allows the retention of the bakery property in some form, with an ambition to create a larger and more imaginative project. This is critical as it enables meeting the terms of the funding already secured through SIB and the Empty Homes agency. So, in July 2014, the bakery went through its third refurbishment, while the CLT is making definite plans for the development of housing in the rest of the block.

Finding ways of working as a collective, as well as giving individuals the space to do what they are good at, to learn and to be able to make mistakes, is maybe *Homebaked*'s biggest strength. It repeatedly dared to, in the midst of opacity, ground itself by manifesting its ideas in physical form. Those moments of manifestation were the ones when, as a group and a process, it was most vulnerable. The steps from being a protest, a projection and a dream to becoming a functioning Community-run Land Trust and bakery business were painful, but as a result it became self-sufficient as an organization that can offer training, and wants people to come together and address their situation publicly. It became a lived space where people teach each other what it means to be active citizens and where they take collective responsibility to produce change in order to make the processes work in a larger social political context. As such, it is important not only to offer a platform for good intentions, but also find ways to reset the public value of urbanism as a contributor to greater solidarity that co-produces an alternative together. For this, we have to go back again and again to create an understanding of lived space as a shared space, a space that everyone can contribute to and change. We all have the right to an environment that creates opportunities to work and live well.

REFERENCES

Jeeves, Tim (2014) 'Performance, participation and questions of ownership in the Anfield Home Tour', in *Homebaked: A Perfect Recipe, Liverpool Biennial Journal* 2, available at: www.biennial.com/journal/2/pdf/performance-participation-and-questions-of-ownership-in-the-anfield-home-tour (accessed November 2014).

Knoll, Christopher (2012) 'Book review: *Henri Lefebvre on Space: Architecture, Urban Research, and the Production of Theory*,' *Space and Culture*, 5 March, available at: www.spaceandculture.org/2012/03/05/book-review-henri-lefebvre-on-space---architecture-urban-research-and-the-production-of-theory/ (accessed November 2014, no longer available).

Lefebvre, Henri (1991) *The Production of Space*, Oxford: Blackwell.

Maury, Yann (ed.), *Les coopératives d'habitants, des outils pour l'abondance* [Inhabitants' co-operatives, tools for abundance], available at: http://chairecoop.hypotheses.org/4186 (accessed November 2014).

Mitchell, Don (2014) 'Taking space', in *Homebaked: A Perfect Recipe, Liverpool Biennial Journal* 2, available at: www.biennial.com/journal/2/ (accessed November 2014).

Rendon, Gabriella (2014) 'Envisioning public co-operative housing'. in *Homebaked: A Perfect Recipe, Liverpool Biennial Journal* 2, available at: www.biennial.com/journal/2/ (accessed November 2014).

Stanek, Lukasz (2011) *Henri Lefebvre on Space, Architecture, Urban Research, and the Production of Theory*, Minneapolis, MN: University of Minnesota Press.

van Heeswijk, Jeanne (2014) 'The right to live well: urbanism's core', *Harvard Magazine* 37.

van Heeswijk, Jeanne and Jurgensen, Britt (2014) 'Homebaked: a perfect recipe', in *Homebaked: A Perfect Recipe, Liverpool Biennial Journal* 2.

INDEX

activist, activism 5, 11, 52, 62, 63, 72, 81, 82, 93, 97, 103–5, 109n, 119, 122, 171, 199, 201, 203, 208, 219, 226, 262–3, 265, 272, 274, 275n, 278, 281, 307, 342, 352, 356, 361
Agamben, Giorgio 57, 104n, 264, 270
affect, affective 6, 77, 79, 82, 86–7, 89, 90, 91, 109, 132, 141, 268–9, 342
alliance, alliance building 9, 38, 93, 97n, 100–1, 103–5, 108–10, 170, 213, 223, 257
Appadurai, Arjun 35, 40, 43
appropriate, appropriation 4n, 10, 22–3, 26, 29, 30, 35, 37, 41–2, 62, 114–5, 119, 123, 125, 127, 137, 139, 194, 198, 202, 236, 242–3, 245, 246, 248, 249, 279, 349

Benjamin, Walter 268, 270
Bourriaud, Nicolas 66, 74, 189, 358, 360
Bookchin, Murray 193n, 209

camp 6, 12, 59, 61–2, 65, 80–4, 90, 228, 257, 260–7, 270, 273, 275, 283
campaign, campaigners 52, 59, 60, 62, 71, 98, 217, 228n, 261, 270, 273–5, 278n, 342, 371, 373
campus 82–4, 90, 91, 102–4, 106n, 107, 109, 350

care 1, 5n, 8, 9, 49, 63, 73, 99, 106, 119, 134, 147–8, 150, 155, 159–168, 171–2, 191, 192n, 193, 196, 202, 212, 241, 258, 265, 320, 334n, 350
Castells, Manuel 136, 137, 142, 267
citizen, citizenship 3, 4, 9, 13, 29, 30, 37, 38, 42, 52, 61, 62, 72, 78, 82, 103, 129, 155, 161, 192–4, 202, 205, 209, 211, 223, 225–6, 228, 230, 233, 235, 241, 260, 267, 297, 305, 306, 307, 331, 334, 338, 339, 342, 350, 365, 374
civic space 66, 68, 301, 330, 332, 336, 342–3
common, commons, commoning 2, 8, 9, 30, 42, 69, 71, 78, 80, 82–4, 87, 98, 125, 147, 159, 162–7, 171–2, 176, 180, 191–8, 200, 202–5, 207–10, 211, 223, 226, 232, 242, 251, 257, 259, 265, 273, 284, 286, 296, 301, 307, 308, 329, 330, 342
communicate, communication 31, 51, 64, 82, 129, 135, 136, 137, 139–41, 258, 266, 273, 275, 278, 279, 281, 331, 342n, 343, 352, 353, 359
Community Land Trust 2, 13, 123, 217, 219, 222, 361, 368, 372, 373
consumption 2, 148, 164n, 239, 245, 251, 280

conflict, post-conflict 1n, 6, 7,
    8, 32–3, 45–7, 54, 56, 61,
    65–8, 74, 78, 81, 90, 93,
    101, 110, 114, 272–3, 301n,
    308, 309, 314n, 328, 329,
    330, 335, 339, 343, 352,
    366n
(non-conflictual) 289, 292
contested, contested space 8,
    12, 45, 46, 53, 62n, 72, 74,
    206, 289, 258
co-operative (see housing,
co-operative)
co-produce, co-production 1, 7,
    8, 34, 41, 96, 120, 133, 156,
    223, 368, 374
counter-culture 192, 242

dalla Costa, Mariarosa 2, 14, 93,
    164, 165n, 173
de Angelis, Massimo 2n, 8, 14
de Certeau, Michel 239, 244–6,
    251, 252, 279, 280, 287,
    298, 329, 344, 352, 360
Debord, Guy 289, 298
decolonise, decolonising 5, 7,
    77–8, 81–6, 90, 91, 92,
    101, 106, 112, 332
democratic, democracy 1n, 5–7,
    10, 29n, 30, 38, 40, 41, 42,
    43, 44, 45, 56, 66–7, 91, 115,
    117, 119, 127, 129, 163,
    174, 181, 191, 193n, 194,
    205, 211, 230, 241, 242,
    261, 272, 275, 286, 301,
    328, 335, 337, 338, 343,
    348, 350, 356, 360, 368
dependence, dependency (see
also interdependence) 37,
    160–2, 171, 183, 229,
    232n, 244, 305n, 309, 320,
    326

disempower 123, 214, 257, 303
dissent 64, 213, 271, 272, 360

ecology, ecological 2, 4, 9, 12,
    21, 85, 144, 153, 161, 165,
    169, 173, 191n, 192, 193n,
    194–6, 199, 205, 207n,
    209, 240, 326, 328
economy, economies 1, 2n, 3, 4,
    8, 14, 21, 40, 54, 95, 102,
    104, 109, 116, 118, 120,
    126, 127, 147–57, 160,
    161, 163, 164, 174, 175,
    178, 180, 182–8, 191n,
    192, 208, 209, 212, 213,
    215, 217, 220, 242, 244,
    248, 251, 267, 285, 317,
    318, 319, 328, 347, 348
    alternative economies 125,
        163, 165
    capitalist economies 147,
        185, 235, 326
    community economies 147,
        148, 150–56
    diverse economies 8,
        147–53, 344
    neoliberal economies 97,
        122
    popular economies 239–41,
        247–8
    solidarity economies 156,
        231, 232
empower, empowerment 4, 11,
    29, 30, 34–6, 41n, 42, 43,
    85, 97, 118, 122, 123, 125,
    127, 206, 236, 269, 277,
    294, 312n, 313, 319, 323,
    324, 326, 338, 339n, 340,
    356
Engels, Friedrich 22–3, 25, 26, 27

ethics, ethical 3, 8, 14, 22n, 41, 52, 67, 77, 79, 103, 147, 150–1, 154–6, 157, 159n, 162, 174, 191n, 232n, 308, 326, 358

Federici, Silvia 2n, 14, 93, 111, 159, 162, 163, 169n, 173, 193, 209
feminist, feminism 2, 5, 7, 9, 15, 63, 93–7, 100–1, 104–6, 108–110, 111, 112, 148, 151n, 157, 159–60, 162–5, 171, 173, 174, 193, 209, 330, 344, 345
forensic 4, 6, 81, 91, 92, 306–8,
Foucault, Michel 46, 47, 57, 186, 263

gentrifying, gentrification 7, 95, 97, 99, 102–4, 107–9, 194n, 203, 205, 216, 272, 303, 356, 358,
Gibson-Graham, J.K. 2n, 8, 9, 14, 147–57, 171, 173, 181, 185, 188, 191, 209, 329n, 344
governance 25, 72, 114, 115, 117, 118, 127, 154, 155, 193, 239,
grassroots 2, 98, 115, 117, 215, 223, 271, 272, 273
Guattari, Felix 78, 91, 159n, 170, 173

Hardt, Michael 281, 283
Harvey, David 3, 4, 14, 30, 43, 45, 57, 114, 128, 193, 205, 209, 214, 223, 224, 265, 270, 303, 309
Haraway, Donna 5, 7, 14, 130–2, 142, 193, 195n, 199, 209

Hayden, Dolores 148, 157, 163–5, 173
housing 1, 3, 6, 10, 25, 31–4, 38, 43, 51, 54n, 99, 103, 108, 115, 119, 121–5, 148–50, 161n, 163–4, 166–7, 192–3, 194n, 203, 206, 211–223, 225–236, 237, 240, 249, 250, 261, 273–5, 299, 322, 330, 334–9, 341–3, 350, 362–4, 366, 368, 370, 374
    affordable housing 21, 29, 38, 41, 51, 120, 214, 217, 219, 225–236, 368n, 373
    cooperative housing 2, 9, 12, 211–13, 215–223, 231–236, 366, 368, 375
    public housing 192, 194n, 212, 214–5, 225n, 339n
hybrid, hybridity 9, 195n, 216, 217, 221, 223, 242, 243

immaterial 4, 14, 163, 171, 347, 358
injustice 3, 6, 7, 43, 45, 51–3, 100, 308
informal, informality 3, 10, 29, 32, 34, 40, 41n, 70, 116, 120, 150, 169, 225, 226, 239–40, 245, 246, 248, 249, 265, 278, 292, 293, 300, 301, 312, 313n, 314, 315, 322, 323, 325, 336, 359
instituting 78–80, 89, 90
institution, institutional 6, 36, 37, 46, 52, 72, 77, 78, 85, 90, 112–19, 122, 123, 125–7, 166, 170, 171, 235, 246, 262, 264, 274, 288, 297, 313n, 327, 330n, 331, 339,

342, 343, 349n, 357, 358
interdependence, interdependency
(see also dependence) 8–9, 35,
    39, 96, 104n, 147, 151–2,
    155, 160–2, 170, 172, 191n,
    193, 197, 199, 202, 356
invisible, invisibility 7, 13, 102,
    163, 174, 239, 245, 312,
    313, 315, 316, 318, 324–7,
    328

James, Selma 2n, 14, 173
Jacobs, Jane 298, 299, 309
justice 6, 7, 12, 14, 21, 45, 46,
    52, 57, 98–9, 100, 101,
    103, 108, 114, 117, 217,
    303, 306–7, 345, 349,
    368–9

labour 5n, 9, 15, 23, 80, 91,
    93–6, 100, 109, 148–9,
    151–2, 159, 160, 161n,
    162–3, 166, 172, 182, 186,
    187, 232, 283
Land Trusts (see Community
    Land Trusts)
Latour, Bruno 129, 142, 183,
    188, 285, 287, 298, 299,
    307, 309
Law, John 79, 91
Lazzarato, Maurizio 242, 252
Lefebvre, Henri 3, 4, 5n, 15,
    22–6, 27, 29, 30, 43, 45,
    111, 118, 125, 128, 189,
    193, 287, 298, 303, 309,
    329, 344, 361, 365, 375
Levinas, Emmanuel 79, 91
livelihood 41, 155, 163, 209,
    223, 248, 306, 311

map, mapping 31, 32, 47, 48,
    54, 57, 80, 94, 96, 97, 99,
    100–9, 111, 139–41, 156,
    207n, 272, 275, 282, 290,
    291, 294, 295, 307, 312–8,
    321, 324, 325, 327, 330,
    333, 336, 342, 352, 366,
    372
Marx, Karl 22, 211, 213
marxist 2, 5, 15, 22, 23, 80, 366
Massey, Doreen 160, 161, 174,
    189, 331, 344, 359, 360
method, methodologies 6, 26,
    38, 77–83, 86, 87, 89, 90,
    91, 96, 115, 117, 121, 125,
    126, 127, 130, 134, 135,
    139, 140, 141, 249, 281,
    288, 319, 326, 336, 339,
    343, 344
migrant 51, 52, 82, 331n, 333
mobile, mobility 63, 64, 67, 68,
    69n, 86, 106n, 136n, 139,
    152, 184, 207n, 246n, 260,
    263, 266, 275, 312, 330,
    333n, 343, 352
mobilise, mobilisations 11, 38,
    115, 116, 121, 122, 127,
    166, 169, 241, 269, 271,
    271, 281

movement (social, political)
(see also Occupy, Occupy
Movement) 7, 11, 38, 41n, 62,
    81, 93, 106, 115, 122, 123,
    134, 135, 136, 142, 154,
    164, 165, 167, 177, 189,
    192, 209, 211, 229, 235,
    241–44, 251, 257, 259,
    260–1, 264–7, 269, 271–9,
    281, 332, 335, 399n, 342,
    343, 368n, 369

Mohanty, Chandra Talpade 95, 100, 101, 104n, 105, 106, 110, 112

Mouffe, Chantal 5, 6, 15, 33, 43, 66, 357–8, 360

mutual, mutually 4, 6, 8, 30, 31, 33, 34, 37, 40, 42, 69, 90, 110, 123, 153, 159, 165–7, 169, 171, 172, 174, 182, 193, 215, 217, 219, 220, 221, 260

Negri, Antonio 281, 283

neoliberal, neoliberalism 1, 5, 6, 8, 11, 13, 21, 82, 89, 95, 97, 104, 108, 109,111,113, 114, 115, 116,117,118, 119, 120, 121, 122, 124, 125, 128, 154, 155, 157, 203n, 212, 223, 246, 272n, 332

network, networked 4, 5, 6, 12, 21, 29, 30, 31, 32, 33, 34, 35, 36, 38, 39, 40, 41, 42, 43, 68n, 99, 122, 128, 129, 132, 135, 136, 139, 140, 141, 142, 151n, 161, 162, 163, 165, 166, 169, 172, 175, 179, 183, 184, 201, 207n, 212, 259, 265, 267, 272, 273, 278n, 279, 280, 281, 284, 303, 312, 313n, 322, 344, 367

non-human, more-than-human 129, 131, 147, 156, 183, 191, 199

occupy, occupation 11, 12, 30, 45, 62, 86, 87, 91, 123, 127, 136, 137, 138, 222, 257, 258, 259, 261, 262, 264, 265, 266, 267, 268, 269, 270, 320, 322, 324

Occupy Movement 6, 12, 85, 102, 103, 119, 137, 257, 258, 259, 261, 263, 265, 264, 269, 268, 270, 275n, 287, 318, 332, 368, 336, 339, 340, 343, 350, 354, 355, 356, 357, 358, 359, 360, 375

participation, participatory 3, 5, 7, 9, 11, 12, 29, 30–44, 51, 67, 66, 74, 77, 83, 86, 90, 99, 115, 120, 121, 135, 202, 204, 217, 221, 241, 258, 272, 275, 287, 330, 332, 334, 335, 341, 343, 350, 354, 355, 356, 357, 359, 366

pedagogy 5, 77–9, 82–3, 85, 86, 87, 90, 91, 290

planning 3, 11, 13, 21, 31–3, 45, 54–5, 94, 102, 104n, 115–6, 118, 126, 150, 164, 185, 198, 203–4, 211–2, 220, 229, 343, 355, 365
  anti-planning 119
  community planning 31, 33, 337
  counter-planning 93

popular, popularisation (see popular economies) 4, 8, 10, 130n, 239, 240, 243–6, 248, 251, 356
  popular education 98
  popular architecture 240, 249, 251
  popular movements 241
  popular culture 240, 242–4, 247–8, 250, 279

political economy 3, 22, 115, 161n, 162

power 14, 21, 29, 30, 35–7, 43,
    46, 51, 57, 62, 68, 72, 86,
    98, 99, 136, 160, 173, 187,
    195, 205, 212, 223, 239,
    241, 244–6, 259–60, 272,
    279, 286, 299, 304, 328,
    349, 356–7
    collective power 30, 35–6,
        223, 259, 303
    hegemonic power 46, 106
    political power 36, 42, 216,
        223, 274n, 315n, 349n
    power relations, relationships
        7, 35, 46, 106, 136,
        246, 339
    powerful 9, 26, 29, 37, 40,
        45, 118, 121, 217
prison, prisoners 2, 5, 6, 45–57
processual 4, 358
property 127, 163, 211, 213–7,
    219n, 221m, 231, 257, 348,
    367, 374
    public property 23, 193
    private property 125, 166,
        211, 213, 231
    social property 211–6,
        222–3
protest, protesters 7, 11–3, 35,
    38, 52, 59–72, 98, 100,
    103, 106, 136, 198, 204,
    206, 237, 241–2, 250n,
    257–8, 260–7, 271, 273n,
    274, 278, 281, 373–4
provisional, provisionality 12,
    115, 299, 300, 308
public 8, 9, 41, 46–9, 57, 67, 71,
    104, 111, 126, 160, 162,
    175, 181, 184, 211, 219,
    264, 266, 299, 300–1, 304,
    307–9, 336, 344, 352
    public art 54, 86, 94n, 111,
        174n, 272, 348, 349n

public debate, discourse
    126, 152, 275
public good 23, 115, 203n,
    212, 287
public institution 46, 113,
    117–9, 297
public money 47, 54, 223
public participation 86, 350
public property, ownership
    23, 69, 193
public realm, sphere 125–6,
    175, 179, 180–1, 185,
    187, 246, 248, 265, 349
public sector 217, 222
public services 35, 241–3
public space 3, 5, 12, 21,
    47, 61, 66, 68, 82–4,
    115, 119, 167, 175,
    178, 181, 184, 186–7,
    191–2, 194–5, 198,
    200–1, 205–6, 208,
    241–2, 247, 248, 259,
    261, 266, 274, 277,
    285, 287–97, 301–4,
    307, 323, 334, 337,
    349, 352, 365, 368
public truth 6, 77, 81, 309
'public works' 68n, 169, 171n,
    178, 188

queer, queering, queerness
    134–5, 134–5, 137, 141–2,
    192
    queer technologies 7, 14,
        130, 134

Rancière, Jacques 45–7, 50, 57
refugee 6, 52, 78, 81–3, 90,
    206n, 260, 278, 333, 334n
relational 5, 66, 109, 132–4,
    269, 358, 360

relational art, aesthetics 62, 67, 74, 189
relational autonomy 39
relational practices 11, 183
resistance 13, 35, 52, 82, 86–7, 93, 97, 99, 100, 102, 108–10, 118, 123, 136, 180, 194n, 222, 242, 244–5, 258–62, 265, 270, 279, 308, 313, 349, 361, 365, 367, 371
right, rights 3, 38, 59–60, 62, 81, 98, 103, 111, 167, 181, 192, 205, 206n, 228n, 237, 306–7, 331, 332, 348, 361n, 374–5
    right to the city 3, 4, 14–5, 29, 30, 36, 43, 45, 48, 93, 96, 109, 118, 192–3, 223–4, 270, 277, 303, 309, 326, 365–6
    right to distribute 278–9
    right to housing 3, 108, 211, 225, 229n, 237, 273–5
    right to participate 4n, 30, 37, 258
    right to space/ spatial rights 3, 5, 6, 45

scale 2, 4, 5, 9, 12, 15, 26, 93, 95, 104n, 115, 126, 133n, 139, 151–3, 160, 163, 180, 185, 193, 197, 202, 207, 304–5, 316, 325–6
    large-scale 12, 38, 121, 125–7, 153, 192n, 200–1, 203–4, 363
    small-scale 24, 65, 79, 135, 181, 193, 240, 287, 312, 340, 366

school, schools 13, 40–1, 46–7, 54n, 68–71, 73, 84, 86, 88, 94, 97, 98, 102–3, 130, 140, 183–5, 212, 243, 267, 288, 295–6, 301, 322, 351n
    eco nomadic school 169–72, 176, 178–9, 181–2
self-organise 71, 97, 187, 229, 261, 357
self-manage, self-management 37, 118, 123–4, 147n, 215, 334
self-representation 275
Sennett, Richard 162, 174, 186, 188
Smith, Neil 123
software 7–8, 129–30, 132–5, 137–42, 306
solidarity (see also solidarity economy) 7, 93–102, 104–5, 108–10, 112, 151, 226, 261, 265, 277–8, 365, 374
species 191, 193, 195, 197, 199, 205, 207, 319, 324
    companion species 7, 14, 131–2, 137, 141, 142, 209
Spivak, Gayatri Chakravorty 77, 91
subjectivity 79, 170, 288

tactics, tactical 4, 6, 10, 12, 36, 147n, 216, 245–8, 251, 258–9, 275, 280, 287–8, 308, 330
    tactical media 272, 279, 280–1, 283
    tactical practices 271–2, 279, 281, 329
    tactical urbanism 113, 115–22, 126, 128

tents 199, 206, 259, 261–3
trade, trading 175, 177, 179–80,
    185
trans-local, trans-locality 9, 38,
    74–5, 78, 89–90, 153, 160,
    168–9, 171–3, 178–9, 182,
transversal, transversality 5–7,
    78–80, 85, 90, 95–6, 97n,
    100, 102, 105, 109–10,
    112, 153, 159, 168, 170–2,
    174,
tropicalism 243

uneven development, uneven
growth 29, 97, 104, 113–6,
    118–21, 125–8, 160, 174,
urban curating 94n, 96, 101,
    109, 111–2

war 1, 4, 6, 9, 62, 78, 80–1, 98,
    107, 114, 150, 192, 196,
    212, 271n, 278n, 320n,
    332–3,
witness, witnessing 11, 60n, 271,
    315, 330, 335–7, 338n,
    340, 342–3
Weisman, Leslie-Kanes 159,
    160n, 173–4
Weizman, Eyal 81, 92, 307, 309,
    318, 328

value, values 2, 3, 7–10, 12–4,
    24–6, 30, 34, 38, 41, 54, 68,
    71–2, 85, 100, 136, 149,
    151–2, 156, 159, 161, 172,
    186–8, 205, 221, 241–4,
    246, 279, 308, 347–8, 358,
    374

Young, Iris Marion 39